EARLY INTERVENTION IN PSYCHOS

The Wiley Series in

CLINICAL PSYCHOLOGY

Max Birchwood, *David Fowler* *and Chris Jackson* *(Editors)*	Early Intervention in Psychosis: A Guide to Concepts, Evidence and Interventions
Dominic H. Lam, *Steven H. Jones,* *Peter Hayward* *and Jenifer A. Bright*	Cognitive Therapy for Bipolar Disorder: A Therapist's Guide to Concepts, Methods and Practice

Titles published under the series editorship of:

J. Mark G. Williams   *School of Psychology, University of Wales, Bangor, UK*

Peter Salmon	Psychology of Medicine and Surgery: A Guide for Psychologists, Counsellors, Nurses and Doctors
William Yule *(Editor)*	Post-Traumatic Stress Disorders: Concepts and Therapy
Nicholas Tarrier, *Adrian Wells* *and Gillian Haddock* *(Editors)*	Treating Complex Cases: The Cognitive Behavioural Therapy Approach
Michael Bruch *and Frank W. Bond* *(Editors)*	Beyond Diagnosis: Case Formulation Approaches in CBT
Martin Herbert	Clinical Child Psychology (second edition)
Eric Emerson, *Chris Hatton,* *Jo Bromley* *and Amanda Caine* *(Editors)*	Clinical Psychology and People with Intellectual Disabilities
J. Mark G. Williams, *Fraser N. Watts,* *Colin MacLeod* *and Andrew Mathews*	Cognitive Psychology and Emotional Disorders (second edition)
Phil Mollon	Multiple Selves, Multiple Voices: Working with Trauma, Violation and Dissociation

A list of earlier titles in the series follows the index.

EARLY INTERVENTION IN PSYCHOSIS

A Guide to Concepts, Evidence and Interventions

Edited by

Max Birchwood
University of Birmingham, UK

David Fowler
University of East Anglia, UK

Chris Jackson
University of Birmingham, UK

JOHN WILEY & SONS, LTD
Chichester · New York · Weinheim · Brisbane · Singapore · Toronto

Other Wiley Editorial Offices

John Wiley & Sons Inc., 111 River Street, Hoboken, NJ 07030, USA

Jossey-Bass, 989 Market Street, San Francisco, CA 94103-1741, USA

Wiley-VCH Verlag GmbH, Boschstr. 12, D-69469 Weinheim, Germany

John Wiley & Sons Australia Ltd, 33 Park Road, Milton, Queensland 4064, Australia

John Wiley & Sons (Asia) Pte Ltd, 2 Clementi Loop #02-01, Jin Xing Distripark, Singapore 129809

John Wiley & Sons (Canada) Ltd, 22 Worcester Road, Etobicoke, Ontario M9W 1L1

British Library Cataloguing in Publication Data

A catalogue record for this book is available from the British Library

ISBN 0-471-97865-5 (cased)
ISBN 0-471-97866-3 (paper)

Typeset in 10/12pt Palatino by Saxon Graphics Limited, Derby
Printed and bound in Great Britain by Biddles Ltd, King's Lynn
This book is printed on acid-free paper responsibly manufactured from sustainable
forestry, in which at least two trees are planted for each one used for paper production.

CONTENTS

ABOUT THE EDITORS

Max Birchwood is Director of the Early Intervention Service in Birmingham, UK. The early intervention approach has been pioneered by Max Birchwood and colleagues from Birmingham and the Service is the first of its kind in the UK. He, together with colleagues, has developed a number of innovative approaches to the management and understanding of psychosis including relapse prevention methodologies, cognitive therapy for hallucinations and acute psychosis and for depression and suicidal thinking. He has published widely in these areas, including two jointly authored books published by Wiley: *Cognitive Therapy for Hallucinations, Delusions and Paranoia* and *Psychological Management of Schizophrenia*.

David Fowler is Senior Lecturer in Clinical Psychology at University of East Anglia and Consultant Clinical Psychologist in the Norfolk Mental Health Care Trust. He has had a longstanding interest in the development and evaluation of cognitive behaviour therapy for psychosis. His research interests concern the evaluation of psychological therapies for psychosis and the development of understanding, or formulation, of psychosis. Over the past four years his main clinical role has involved developing a service providing innovative psychological interventions for people with early psychosis in Norfolk. He is co-author of the book *Cognitive Behaviour Therapy for Psychosis* published by Wiley.

Chris Jackson is a Clinical Psychologist in the Early Intervention Service, Northern Birmingham Mental Health Trust and Honorary Senior Research Fellow at the University of Birmingham. He graduated from Aston University with an Honours Degree in Human Psychology, obtained a PhD from the Institute of Psychiatry, and a MSc in Clinical Psychology from Birmingham University. His clinical and research interests lie in early intervention approaches in the first episode of psychosis, particularly psychological aspects of recovery and adjustment.

LIST OF CONTRIBUTORS

Paul Bebbington

*Professor of Social and Community Psychiatry,
University College London Medical School,
Department of Psychiatry and Behavioural Sciences,
Archway Wing, 1st Floor, Whittington Hospital,
Highgate Hill, London N19 5NF, UK.*

Nick Bosanquet

*Professor of Health Policy, Department of Primary
Health Care & General Practice, Imperial College
School of Medicine, Norfolk Place, London W2 1PG,
UK.*

Max Birchwood

*Professor of Clinical Psychology and Director, Early
Intervention Service, Northern Birmingham Mental
Health Trust, Harry Watton House, 97 Church Lane,
Aston, Birmingham B6 5UG, UK.*

Val Drury

*Lecturer in Clinical Psychology, School of Psychology,
University of Birmingham, Edgbaston, Birmingham
B15 2TT, UK.*

Jane Edwards

*Assistant Director (Clinical), Early Psychosis
Prevention and Intervention Centre (EPPIC), Mental
Health Services for Kids and Youth—Youth Program,
North Western Health, 35 Poplar Road, Parkville, and
Associate of the Departments of Psychology and
Psychiatry, University of Melbourne, Australia, 3052.*

David Fowler

*Senior Lecturer in Clinical Psychology, School of
Health Policy & Practice Unit, University of East
Anglia, Norwich NR4 7TJ, UK.*

Lisa P. Henry

*Department of Psychiatry, University of Melbourne,
Early Psychosis Prevention and Intervention Service,
Parkville Centre, Parkville, 3052, Victoria, Australia.*

Marthe Horneland

Psychiatrist at Rogaland Psychiatric Hospital, PO Box 1163, Hillevag, Armauer Hansensv. 20, 4004 Stavanger, Norway.

Carol A. Hulbert

Spectrum: The Personality Disorder Service for Victoria, PO Box 135, Ringwood East, Victoria 3135, Australia.

Zaffer Iqbal

Research Psychologist, Department of Psychology, Institute of Psychiatry, De Crespigny Park, Denmark Hill, London SE5 8AF, UK.

Chris Jackson

Senior Research Fellow, University of Birmingham and Clinical Psychologist, Early Intervention Service, Harry Watton House, 97 Church Lane, Aston, Birmingham B6 5UG, UK.

Henry J. Jackson

Associate Professor, School of Behavioural Science, Department of Psychology, University of Melbourne, Parkville, Victoria, Australia 3052.

Jan Olav Johannessen

Chief Psychiatrist, Rogaland Psychiatric Hospital, Postboks 1163, Hillevag, Armauer Hansensv. 20, 4004 Stavanger, Norway.

Elizabeth Kuipers

Department of Psychology, Institute of Psychiatry, De Crespigny Park, Denmark Hill, London SE5 8AF, UK.

Tor K. Larsen

Coordinator in the TIPS -project, Rogaland Psychiatric Hospital, Postboks 1163, Hillevag, Armauer Hansensv. 20, 4004 Stavanger, Norway.

Don Linszen

Adolescentenkliniek, AMC/De Meren, Tafelbergweg 25, The Netherlands.

Fiona Macmillan

Medical Director, Walsall Mental Health Trust, Dorothy Patterson House, Alumwell Close, Walsall WS2 9XH, UK.

Sigurd Mardal

Chief Psychologist, Rogaland County Hospital in Haugesund, Department of Psychiatry, Karmsundsgt. 12, 5500 Haugesund, Norway.

Thomas McGlashan

Professor of Psychiatry, Yale Psychiatric Institute, PO Box 208038, 184 Liberty Street, New Haven, CT 06520—8038, USA.

Patrick D. McGorry — *Professor of Psychiatry and Director, Mental Health Services for Kids and Youth—Youth Program, North Western Health, 35 Poplar Road, Parkville, and Departments of Psychiatry, University of Melbourne, Australia, 3052.*

Eleanor Murray — *Assistant Psychologist, Early Intervention Service, Northern Birmingham Mental Health Trust, Harry Watton House, 97 Church Lane, Aston, Birmingham B6 5UG, UK.*

Kerryn Pennell — *Deputy Director, Education, Research and Development, Mental Health Services for Kids and Youth—Youth Program, North Western Health, 35 Poplar Road, Parkville, and Associate of the Department Psychiatry, University of Melbourne, Australia, 3052.*

James Plaistow — *Assistant Psychologist, Early Intervention Service, Northern Birmingham Mental Health Trust, Harry Watton House, 97 Church Lane, Aston, Birmingham B6 5UG, UK.*

David Raune — *Department of Psychology, Institute of Psychiatry, London SE5 8AF, UK.*

Alison Reeves — *Manager, Skallagrigg Crisis House, Harry Watton House, 97 Church Lane, Aston, Birmingham B6 5UG, UK.*

David Shiers — *GP and Primary Care Lead, West Midlands NHS Executive, Bartholomew House, Hagley Road, Birmingham B16 9PA, UK.*

Elizabeth Spencer — *Senior Clinical Medical Officer, Early Intervention Service, Northern Birmingham Mental Health Trust, Harry Watton House, 97 Church Lane, Aston, Birmingham B6 5UG, UK.*

Per Vaglum — *Professor at Department of Behavioural Scineces in Medicine, University of Oslo, Sognsvannsvn. 9, PO Box 1111, Blindern, 0317 Oslo, Norway.*

PREFACE

"If only we could have spotted the illness earlier ...". "My son needed the best treatment earlier, not when everything else failed". "If only I had this information and help at the beginning, all this pain and uncertainty could have been prevented".

These comments from people with psychosis and their relatives will be familiar to most mental health professionals. Indeed many mental health professionals would concur, but the classical teaching of psychiatry urges caution: "schizophrenia was coined on the assumption that these disorders are malignant and deteriorating in nature". This teaches us to "wait and see" which prognostic path the individual may follow, so overlooking major opportunity for secondary prevention.

There has been an unmistakable shift in these concepts in recent years. The heterogeneity of psychosis is well-documented and the influence of socio-cultural, psychological and biological factors on psychosis are now increasingly understood. Breakthrough research has shown that the early years of psychosis is a critical period whose outcome can be felt across the life span of the individual and provides a coherent theoretical backdrop for the concept of early intervention. These data are analysed in some detail by McGorry and Birchwood in Chapters 1 and 2.

From the perspective of clinicians working in busy mental health services, particularly in the inner city, the logic of early intervention has much face validity. The incidence of psychosis in the inner city is five times that normally observed: inner-city residence and social exclusion are major risk factors for psychosis. A large proportion of users will access services through circuitous and undesirable pathways, often after a long delay and under coercion. This kind of early experience of services is formative and provokes both treatment reluctance and service disengagement, particularly in the UK among Afro-Caribbean community.

Within two years many will have settled into a relapsing pattern, quickly consuming a large amount of health resources which most services deal with in a fire-fighting manner.

From the perspective of the service user and relatives (see Chapter 14), they often find that unless they are regarded as a 'risk' they can lose priority in the system and contact is lost, until the next crisis looms. In Chapter 14 Alison

Reeves describes how increasingly large, chaotic in-patient units can exacerbate stress, and exposure to drug side-effects itself is guaranteed to generate mistrust or services and, of course, of treatment.

This book arose out of a conference convened by the authors in 1997 in Stratford-upon-Avon, UK, which brought together an international group of academics, clinicians, users and carers committed to driving the early intervention concept forward. The meeting benefited considerably from the scholarly input of Professors McGlashan, Garety and Wyatt across a range of services. This book focused avowedly on the concept, practice and implementation of early intervention rather than first-episode psychosis per se.

In the first part of the book the rationale is considered in depth by McGorry and by Birchwood. There follows consideration of the individual's meaning (Fowler) and response to psychosis (Jackson). Elizabeth Kuipers and David Raune consider the nature of the family's response to illness and the factors that may lead to problem relationships.

The main section, Part II, focuses on the prodromal DUI implementation of interventions including: cognitive therapy (Drury, Chapter 8); help to promote personal adjustment to psychosis (C. Jackson, Chapter 3), family intervention in the context of the family developing adjustment to psychosis in their relatives (Linszen, Chapter 11).

Paul Bebbington (Chapter 7) considers the role of low-dose pharmacology and prophylaxis and Beth Spencer, Eleanor Murray and James Plaistow (Chapter 10) describe an approach to relapse prevention in the special context of first-episode psychosis where relapse is a risk and has yet to take place. The TIPS project in Norway (T. K. Larsen and colleagues, Chapter 6) is of profound importance to the early intervention field in terms of a community education approach to reducing untreated psychotic illness. The authors describe their innovative methods with great clarity and illustrate just what can be achieved if the will is there.

The "service implementation" is particularly important. Fiona Macmillan, David Shiers and the UK IRIS group describe their early intervention framework and illustrate the importance of an initial service audit procedure to ascertain what is actually happening on the ground, often very revealing. This should be read very closely with the chapter on "user perspectives" by Alison Reeves. Jane Edwards (Chapter 12) summarises and analyses the variety of service approaches and first-episode programmes around the world, and Nick Bosanquet rehearses some of the health economics implications of avoiding early intervention.

Editing this book has been a delight and we hope and believe this text will be of major benefit to clinicians, service communities and counsellors who are committed to improve our services to this young group of people.

Max Birchwood
David Fowler
Chris Jackson

Part I

THE CONCEPT OF EARLY INTERVENTION

Chapter 1

THE SCOPE FOR PREVENTIVE STRATEGIES IN EARLY PSYCHOSIS: LOGIC, EVIDENCE AND MOMENTUM

Patrick D. McGorry*

> *The best progressive ideas are those that include a strong enough dose of provocation to make its supporters feel proud of being original, but at the same time attract so many adherents that the risk of being an isolated exception is immediately averted by the noisy approval of a triumphant crowd.*
> MILAN KUNDERA (1996, p. 273)

INTRODUCTION

Why has preventive intervention become so popular?

In recent years there has been increasing confidence that preventive interventions in psychotic disorders might be a realistic proposition in clinical settings (Birchwood et al., 1997; McGorry, 1998a). This resurgence of interest has been long overdue, following many decades of pessimism. The origins of this pessimism have recently been discussed (McGorry, 1998a, b; Barrett, 1998a, b) and essentially relate to the conceptual framework of psychotic disorders and particularly schizophrenia, reinforced by other factors. The power of this mindset has been overwhelming until recently and is still strong in most parts of the world. Yet we are now witnessing something of a sea change in thinking along the lines referred to by

---

* University of Melbourne, Australia.

Early Intervention in Psychosis.
Edited by M. Birchwood, D. Fowler & C. Jackson.
© 2000 John Wiley & Sons Ltd.

Kundera. The early psychosis paradigm probably now meets Kundera's definition for a progressive idea. This was not the case when my colleagues and I began to develop our approach during the mid-1980s, when we were met by, at best, apathy and bewilderment, and, at worst, confidence-sapping resistance. What has brought about this transformation?

Firstly, the gradual dismantling and reform of the asylum model of care, developed for the previous century prior to the availability of any effective forms of treatment, has been a key factor (Thornicroft & Tansella, 1999). This has been especially important in Australia where this reform has been both more rapidly and responsibly implemented, at least until now (Rosen, 1999). In some places this process has been carried out in a less responsible manner, often with unfortunate consequences (Torrey et al., 1990). In Australia, these reforms have integrated mental health care of psychotic patients much better within the general community as well as within the health system, leading to greater visibility of such patients. They are no longer "out of sight, out of mind" to the same extent. However, the funding of this reform process remains inadequate and its ultimate success is still in the balance (Rosen, 1999). This is particularly so due to pressures generated from an increasing awareness of the level of unmet need in the high prevalence common mental disorders (Murray & Lopez, 1996).

Secondly, there has been a renaissance of interest in both the psychopharmacological and psychotherapeutic treatment of people with psychotic illnesses. The rediscovery of clozapine and the development of a new generation of antipsychotic medications with an improved side-effect profile has shown that symptomatic and neurocognitive outcomes, and quality of life, can be substantially improved. This has challenged the pervasive Kraepelinian archetype of inevitable disability. Disappointment regarding the partial ineffectiveness of the first generation of antipsychotics, the misuse of these agents, and the clinician's illusion (Cohen & Cohen, 1984) were additional background factors enhancing the impact of these new drug discoveries. Similarly, the application of cognitively oriented approaches to psychotherapy has begun to fill a serious gap in the management of people struggling to grapple with the impact of these disorders upon their lives. The tide of the cognitive revolution, originating within the realm of the less severe common mental disorders, is finally lapping on the shores of serious mental illness. The personal predicament of the person with a psychotic disorder is now being recognised and responded to—a trend reinforced by the belated rise of consumerism in mental health care.

Thirdly, a concentration for research reasons (Kirch, Keith & Mathews, 1992) on first-episode psychosis patients has enabled their special clinical needs to be more clearly perceived, and the preventive possibilities to be grasped. Fourthly, a clearer framework for guiding, designing and evaluating preventive interventions in mental disorders has been developed and will be outlined below. As a consequence a series of research projects and real-world service systems are being developed which will steadily add to the evidence base concerning the value of early intervention. Finally, several influential international figures and research groups have developed and cooperated in disseminating a more optimistic set of ideas concerning early intervention in psychosis (Wyatt, 1991; Birchwood & Macmillan, 1993; McGorry & Singh, 1995; McGlashan & Johannessen, 1996; Häfner et al., 1995). This has evolved into an international network (McGorry, Edwards & Pennell, 1999). This is a familiar pattern in scientific progress—namely, a number of groups or individuals coming to similar conclusions at around the same time—and ultimately it may be that the early psychosis focus comes to be seen as a Kuhnian paradigm shift. Those involved so far have generally been more than willing to support one another's work and thus foster the further development of ideas and, most importantly, an expanding evidence base. Evidence is critical if there is to be a real-world shift in attitudes and clinical practice and if we are to avoid a further false dawn in the history of this field. Furthermore, the psychiatric research community, although appropriately cautious, has generally been supportive of these developments and is interested to see how far the accumulating evidence supports their extension. For each element, we need to determine how much evidence is required before a change in practice is warranted. However, while evidence should be a *necessary* factor, it is never a *sufficient* factor for widespread adoption in standard clinical practice. There are countless examples confirming that, even when it is overwhelmingly amassed, other sociopolitical and educational forces need to be mobilised, and even then delays extend typically for over a decade or more. Data provide the key tools, as well as a safeguard and a guide, but tools need to be used effectively.

The alternative: too little too late

In assessing the potential value of the early psychosis paradigm, it is worth briefly considering the alternative scenario, that is, accepting that current standard approaches to psychotic disorders are satisfactory. Although this varies from culture to culture, in most countries it is not a very attractive option. In the resource-poor developing world, although some studies have shown a better outcome (for those who obtain treatment) (Jablensky et al., 1992; Padmavathi, Rajkumar & Srinivasan, 1998), it is common for a substantial proportion of people to never gain access to modern treatments for psychosis and to lead hidden lives characterised by suffering and disability (Padmavathi, Rajkumar & Srinivasan, 1998). In the developed world, the treated incidence and prevalence is higher, but treatment is typically delayed until the disorder is established, and in fact treatment is usually initiated in the context of a high-risk incident such as a suicide attempt or aggressive or disorganised behaviour. Furthermore, the settings are usually aversive and shabby, drug therapies are used crudely, and a person-centred approach is rare. Iatrogenesis is common, and treatment is generally focused on acute phases of illness with inadequate continuity and quality of care subsequently, particularly in the USA the wake of managed care. Rehabilitation tends to be confined to the most disabled group and later phases of illness, when it is much less likely to work, even though the need for it seems more obvious. It is all too little too late. No wonder the prospects for people with schizophrenia in the real world have not changed over the past century, despite advances in treatment (Hegarty et al., 1994).

I would argue that the burden of proof should be reversed in such a situation. Perhaps those requiring evidence to support improvements in the quality of care should be asked to justify the continuation of much of the traditional approach. The failure of what were correctly believed to be significant advances in treatment, such as lithium, neuroleptics and community-based psychiatry, to influence the course of psychotic illness in the real world (Hegarty et al., 1994) bears witness to the need for a paradigm shift. New treatments can help to drive this, but better implementation (which requires substantially more resources) of existing interventions, within a preventively oriented model is a commonsense path to follow. Complacency is very difficult to justify; however, funders will need to be convinced that more expensive systems of intervention clearly improve outcomes and cost-effectiveness. This will be a difficult task, since many models of funding will not respond to demonstrations of superior outcomes if higher costs are involved. This then becomes a sociopolitical issue (Murray & Lopez, 1996; Singh & McGorry, 1998).

Why is there still any resistance and scepticism?

Why then would there be any significant resistance to enhancing the intensity, quality and phase-appropriateness of treatment? Resistance to the seductive promise of the early intervention model varies according to the perspective of the observer.

Researchers have been increasingly keen to explore these issues; however, there is a sense among some that a high degree of certainty must be generated by research before increased funding is allocated or diverted to improving access, shortening delays and increasing the intensity of early treatment. How much evidence should be required? Would several multi-centre randomised controlled trials of each component of the preventive approach be enough? This is complex and perhaps unachievable in some respects. A standard needs to be agreed for each hypothesis and clinical focus. Interestingly, epidemiologists concerned with distal risk factors for psychiatric disorder may also grapple with the notion of early intervention, since it may not be based on a clear knowledge of risk factors causal to psychotic illness. Early intervention is essentially a preventive treatment strategy which is based pragmatically on more proximal risk factors and clinical interventions.

Perhaps because it is really closer to treatment than pure prevention, and because it has such strong face validity, there has been surprisingly little resistance among clinicians to the idea of early detection and treatment. The main concern that many clinicians have is that resources could be diverted from the treatment of more disabled patients with more established illnesses, thus worsening their plight, even before the benefits of early intervention can be demonstrated and flow into the growing incident cohort. The other barrier is the tenacious hold that the schizophrenia concept has on clinicians' minds with its connotation of failure to recover.

Policy-makers are largely concerned with the efficiency and acceptability of new models of care and tend to be rather enthusiastic in principle, though attempts to restructure services or change entrenched work practices frequently stimulate powerful resistance.

Funders are usually focused on costs alone, and although they often claim to be interested in improving cost-effectiveness, either they want demonstrated improvements in very short time frames, or they are looking for savings alone and, in truth, place little or no emphasis on the improvements in outcome. An approach that requires even short-term increases in funding, even it can demonstrate improved outcomes plus longer term net savings, will attract less support. Indeed, the current economic environment of service provision, immune so far to the implications arising from the report on the Global Burden of Disease (Murray & Lopez, 1996), actually constitutes the greatest source of resistance to change.

FRAMEWORK

One of the consequences of the alienation of people with psychosis and those involved in their care has been a relative isolation from mainstream ideas on health and disease, particularly in relation to prevention. The thinking of psychiatrists and other mental health professionals, the poor relations of the health care family, whether split off in their private practices or within detached psychiatric service systems, has remained almost impermeable to the logic of prevention and early intervention which is much better accepted across the landscape of health care in general.

This isolation and the conceptual stagnation embalmed preventive think-ing for nearly a century. Now that patients have emerged from such isola-tion and the treatment of psychosis is increasingly mainstreamed within general health care, it is possible to breathe life into a preventive approach for psychosis. For this we need a framework which is both logical and practical. Fortunately this is available and has been adapted from the orig-inal more general model of Gordon (1983) for use in mental health by Mrazek and Haggerty (1994). Before describing this framework, the need for a facilitating context for preventive intervention is worth considering.

The big picture: mental health promotion and preventive intervention

Health is not merely the absence of disease but is also a state of well-being, a state in which positive qualities can be experienced and detected. Health always coexists with disease, even in the individual patient. The promotion of these elements is a worthwhile goal in itself and may have the additional effect of reducing the risks for certain disorders. Health promotion also tends to create a positive morale and culture in which prevention and early intervention, and indeed good quality treatment and care, tend to flourish. This has only recently been appreciated in the mental health domain, and mental health promotion is a very new and vulnerable field of endeavour. If efforts to improve positive mental health can be integrated within the frontier of preventive interventions and early intervention in psychiatry, then dramatic changes in attitudes to mental disorders and in the culture of service provision may be within reach. All aspects need a balance between positive and negative emotions and expectations. In particular, service sys-tems and clinicians must strive to incorporate and nurture a positive dimension to their work, their culture and their attitudes. This is not easy to do and is often sadly lacking. Yet it is also tantalisingly achievable. One of the difficulties is that the health promotion and treatment perspectives are different, and bringing them together can get confusing.

For young people to use health and community services, they must not only be accessible but "youth friendly". This means eliminating stigma as completely as possible. This can be done by colocating them with other youth activities and venues where fun and leisure activities are taking place, forming "youth precincts". Within the mental health component of this model there also needs to be a recognition of the vital task of inculcat-ing positive themes and messages within the clinical environments, and within the therapeutic interventions themselves. For example, individual psychological interventions, which strive to empower as well as change, aim to introduce positive cognitions and emotions to balance negativity as a key strategy. This has been a key element of changing the clinician's attitude to the person with a first psychotic episode, which should be predominantly and unashamedly optimistic. The potential of the mental health promotion model has not been properly grasped yet within mental health services but it could transform what we do with clinical populations as well have a broader focus with the general population.

FOCI FOR PREVENTIVE INTERVENTION IN EARLY PSYCHOSIS

Realistic prevention in early psychosis can occur within three related foci: the pre-psychotic phase, early detection of fully fledged psychosis and intensive treatment of the first episode, and the subsequent recovery or "critical" period. To help orient a discussion of these foci, it may be useful to describe aspects of the Mrazek and Haggerty (1994) framework (Figure 1.1), in which interventions are classified into prevention, treatment and maintenance.

Within prevention, Mrazek and Haggerty subclassify interventions as universal, selective and indicated. *Universal* preventive interventions are targeted to the general public or a whole population group that has not been identified on the basis of individual risk, e.g. use of seat belts, immunisation, and prevention of smoking. *Selective* preventive measures are appropriate for subgroups of the population whose risk of becoming ill is above average. Examples include special immunisations

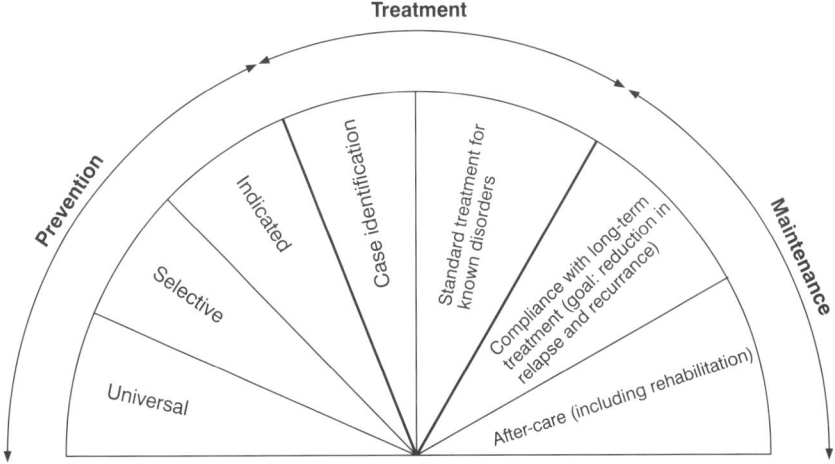

Figure 1.1 The mental health intervention spectrum for mental disorders.

such as for people travelling to areas where yellow fever is endemic and annual mammograms for women with a positive family history of breast cancer. The subjects are clearly asymptomatic. *Indicated* preventive measures apply to those individuals who, on examination, are found to manifest a risk factor that identifies them, individually, as being at high risk for the future development of a disease, and as such could be the focus of screening. Gordon's view was that such individuals should be asymptomatic and "not motivated by current suffering", yet have a clinically demonstrable abnormality. An example would be asymptomatic individuals with hypertension.

Mrazek and Haggerty (1994), made a critical change to Gordon's concept as follows:

> Indicated preventive interventions for mental disorders are targeted to high-risk individuals who are identified as having minimal but detectable signs or symptoms foreshadowing mental disorder, or biological markers indicating predisposition for mental disorder, but who do not meet DSM-III-R diagnostic levels at the current time.

This major definitional shift allows individuals with early and/or sub-threshold features (and hence a degree of suffering and disability) to be included within the focus of indicated prevention. Some clinicians would regard this as early intervention or an early form of treatment; however, the situation with these individuals is not so clear cut. While some of these cases will clearly have an early form of the disorder in question, others will not and hence represent false positives. However, they might have or develop other potentially serious disorders, and many individuals' sub-threshold for a potentially serious disorder like schizophrenia may have already crossed a clinical threshold where they either require or request treatment for another syndrome (e.g. major depression). Whether this is primary or secondary prevention, in the old terminology, is debatable, but the authors clearly believe the frontier for preventive efforts lies at this *cusp* just prior to the onset of psychosis.

> The best hope now for the prevention of schizophrenia lies with indicated preventive interventions targeted at individuals manifesting precursor signs and symptoms who have not yet met full criteria for diagnosis. The identification of individuals at this early stage, coupled with the introduction of pharmacological and psychosocial interventions, may prevent the development of the full-blown disorder. (Mrazek & Haggerty, 1994, p. 154)

This is both a radical position and a conservative one; radical in contrast to early intervention in first episode psychosis; conservative in relation to the ultimate dream of primary prevention. Pre-psychotic intervention will be considered further in a later section.

The next link in the preventive chain is more clearly secondary preven-tion, and involves early detection of those who have reached the full diagnostic threshold, that is, the *timing* of treatment. Reducing delays in treatment to the minimum has strong face validity and several lines of evidence supporting it as a preventive strategy. This can be called a "safety net" strategy which aims to limit the degree of secondary harm that may occur on either a biological or psychosocial level. Allied to this is the notion of intensive phase specific treatment of early psychosis, that is, the *quality* of treatment. The logic here is that the needs of patients and families in the first episode and the early years of illness are different from the needs of those with more established illness. Furthermore, if a more intensive effort is mounted at this stage of ill-ness, this will be cost-effective leading to long-term benefits. This might be due to a "damage control" effect whereby the intensive treatment acts as a further safety net limiting the extent of the disability flowing from the disorder. Alternatively, people at this phase may be more accessible and responsive to integrated biopsychosocial treatments, including atypical antipsychotic medications and psychotherapeutic interventions. In either case, this preventive approach is congruent with the notion of the "critical" or "sensitive" period, adapted from attach-ment theory by Birchwood (Birchwood & Macmillan, 1993)—see Chapter 2. Early detection and intensive phase specific treatment will be considered further below.

Focus 1: Pre-psychotic intervention: pipedream, panacea or Pandora's box?

Most, if not all, psychotic episodes are preceded by prodromal changes or changes in subjective experience and behaviour, yet only fleetingly has the prospect of intervening at this stage been contemplated during this cen-tury (Meares, 1959; Sullivan, 1927). For most clinicians and researchers, preoccupied with advanced phases of disorder, such an idea has remained a pipedream. However, what has hitherto seemed no more than a fantasy now seems potentially achievable.

The changes that occur during the prodromal phase have been broadly characterised by Häfner and colleagues (Häfner et al., 1995), though other more intensive studies are reviewed and summarised in Yung et al. (1996). These and other studies (Jones et al., 1993) showed that although diagnostic specificity and ultimately potentially effective treatment comes with the later onset of positive psychotic symptoms, most of the disabling consequences of the underlying disorder emerge and manifest well prior to this phase. In particular, deficits in social functioning occur predomi-nantly during the prodromal phase and prior to treatment. Häfner et al.

(1995) demonstrated clearly that the main factor determining social outcome two years after first admission for schizophrenia is acquired social status during the prodromal phase of the disorder. The importance of this phase was previously poorly appreciated because no conceptual distinction was made between premorbid and prodromal phases. The premorbid dysfunctions were thought to be fixed and longstanding, not dynamic and preventable. This conceptual failure is reflected in the limitations of instruments such as the Premorbid Assessment Scale (Cannon-Spoor, Potkin & Wyatt, 1982). It is now clear that the differences seen in epidemiological studies between cases of schizophrenia and controls are relatively slight and of no predictive value for subsequent adult disorder (Isohanni et al., 1999). They are also largely non-specific, overlapping with premorbid deviations seen in affective disorders (van Os et al., 1997). A decline in premorbid functioning from childhood to adolescence is of greater significance (Haas & Sweeney, 1992) and reflects the prodromal concept better, though it too may not be specific for any single psychiatric disorder. Häfner et al. (1995) found premorbid status prior to the prodromal phase to be fairly unimportant in predicting outcome two years post first admission. This increasing importance of clinical (or prodromal) changes in adolescence more closely accords with clinical experience, since most patients do not manifest deviations from normal prepubertally, at least as determined retrospectively. This implies a more dynamic vulnerability model with risk factors operating in conjunction with maturational processes (Rapoport et al., 1999) to produce expression of the clinical syndromes of psychotic disorder. Focusing on the period of risk for transition to the fully fledged syndrome in relation to proximal, rather than distal, risk factors has been termed the "close-in" strategy. If intervention at this point could be shown to stem the tide of transition to frank psychosis, then much of the disability and distress associated with psychosis would be potentially preventable.

However the latter is not that simple. The notion of the "at risk mental state" or the "precursor" state is more appropriate than "prodrome", which is by definition inevitably followed by the fully fledged syndrome, and hence can only be assigned retrospectively. The symptomatology during this period is generally a non-specific admixture of negative and depressive symptoms, features which may remit spontaneously or evolve into a range of psychiatric syndromes, not only psychoses. Substance abuse is an increasingly common concomitant which further complicates the predictive and diagnostic task. Problems therefore derive from the non-specificity and diversity of the features seen during all but the final part of the pre-psychotic phase (Häfner et al., 1995, McGorry et al., 1995). This means that false positive cases will be common on a population basis and still be problematic even in selected clinical samples (Yung et al., 1996).

This problem is less serious in the latter group since few are pure false positives, that is they will manifest *some* potentially serious axis 1 disorder (Leon et al., 1997). Specificity of ultimate syndrome is therefore the key, though it seems acceptable at this stage to treat individual syndromes as they present or emerge.

The boundaries of psychosis are a further unresolved issue. Although it is widely believed that most cases of psychotic disorder, particularly schizophrenia, do eventually receive treatment in mental health services, this is probably not true even for severe cases (Helgason, 1990; Padmavathi, Rajkumar & Srinivasan, 1998) and the border with normality is being more carefully explored with interesting results. The work of Kwapil, Chapman and Chapman (1999) Honig et al. (1998) and van Os, Ravelli and Nijl (1999) indicates that psychotic symptoms may commonly occur in more circumscribed and potentially non-progressive ways in the general community. Thus, they do not always connote either disability or need for treatment. Conversely, other work with help-seeking populations (GP studies and PACE) suggests that subthreshold symptoms can be associated with significant disability and distress and hence need for treatment. All this means that symptoms and need and desire for treatment are only partially correlated. When we add in the dimension of time and the predictive element, our goal is to detect those who show a tendency for certain symptoms to worsen or become associated with increasing and significant disability. These are the people upon whom we wish to focus our preventive endeavours.

How would we go about doing this? Ideally we would aim to offer early intervention for a relatively broad range of potentially serious mental disorders. We have found promoting awareness of specific criteria for high risk of transition to psychosis to be reasonably effective (Phillips et al., in press) however we know the majority of those eligible do not currently gain access. A better way might be to combine strategies for a high incidence disorder (such as depression), with low incidence disorders (such as psychosis).

Our research to date suggests that it is feasible to identify and engage in treatment a subset of those who ultimately develop a psychotic illness. We have data that suggest that it is possible to significantly reduce the risk of transition to psychosis, at least in the short term and at least while the treatment is being received (Phillips et al., 1999). The study of intervention at this indeterminate or subthreshold phase of disorder threatens to open a Pandora's box of issues. The downside is that at least some other cases who resemble these cases receive such treatment unnecessarily. However, this is a feature of all clinical trials and treatments, as reflected in the "number needed to treat" statistic (Cook & Sackett, 1995). It is implicit that in any such treatment situation that not all cases for whom a given treatment is indicated will actually require it to avoid the adverse event in question.

The cost–benefit ratio of treatment at this phase is similar to that of maintenance treatment following a first episode of psychosis, where relapse rates in the first year or two approach 40–50% as well. The other question spawned by the research is how long such treatment should be offered. Perhaps there are other forms of treatment which would be more effective at least for subgroups of cases. For example, some may be treatable with psychological treatments alone, some may be better helped by neuroprotective agents, and others may benefit more from different novel antipsychotics, mood stabilizers or antidepressants.

The recent study from Edinburgh (Hodges et al., 1999; Lawrie et al., 1999) and emerging work from our unit suggest that it may be possible to characterise the psychobiological changes that occur during the onset phase through a close-in research strategy. The Edinburgh group selected asymptomatic individuals prior to any possibility of onset, thus extending the period required for follow-up. It also relied solely on genetic risk for selection, resulting in a lower overall transition rate. The intent was similar to our own design which involves examining variables across several domains such as neuroimaging, neuropsychology, psychopathology, and neuroendocrinology at multiple time points over the onset phase. Such studies have two dimensions. One is the predictive dimension, the other is the better understanding of the neurobiology of the onset process. This could open another Pandora's box of aetiological theories, and help us to move beyond first-generation neurodevelopmental models. (See Figure 1.2.)

Focus 2: Early detection in first-episode psychosis: building confidence and evidence

Once someone has developed sustained psychotic symptoms and clearly meets the criteria for a DSM-IV or ICD-10 psychotic disorder, then we are on a firmer foundation for offering treatment. In most cases, perhaps nearly all, this would mean, along with psychosocial interventions, antipsychotic medication. However, not surprisingly, in the real world we discover that what we expect should happen—namely, that people should receive prompt assessment and treatment for a disorder as potentially serious as psychosis—does not commonly occur (Johnstone et al., 1986; Loebel et al., 1992). Indeed, for a substantial subgroup the delays are extreme, and a variable but probably significant number of people never receive treatment at all (Helgason, 1990; Padmavathi, Rajkumar & Srinivasan, 1998).

Does this really matter? Most clinicians, family members, and ultimately most patients themselves seem to think so. We have a set of disorders which confer an intense degree of distress and substantial disability, a

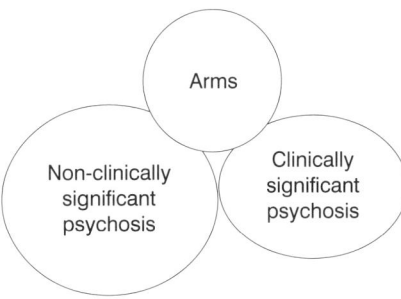

Figure 1.2   The relationship between psychotic symptoms and subthreshold or At Risk Mental States (ARMS).

range of treatments of proven and growing effectiveness, and examples of service models through which these treatments can be deployed very effectively in the real world. Many researchers have been galvanised by the new awareness of extensive delays in treatment to shift their research focus to the early psychosis field. However, from within the research field also comes a scepticism, based on the notion that the relationship between delay in treatment (or Duration of Untreated Psychosis—DUP) and outcome could be merely an association, confounded by latent clinical variables reflecting severity of illness. Let us consider this possibility.

There is a whole range of circumstantial evidence implicating delayed treatment with poorer outcome (e.g. Johnstone et al., 1986; Helgason, 1990; Loebel et al., 1992; Beiser et al., 1993). Although some studies tried to separate out potential confounders such as rate of onset and specific clinical features, the relationship remains an association and could be partially explained at least by other underlying variables connoting more severe disorder and worse prognosis rather than independent barriers to access (Verdoux et al., 1998a). The Northwick Park study of first-episode psychosis showed that delayed treatment was a very strong predictor of subsequently higher rates of relapse (Crow et al., 1986). This was surprisingly not confirmed in the recent follow-up of the Hillside first-episode sample (Robinson et al., 1999), perhaps due to the special nature and treatment experience of this sample, which was not an epidemiological sample and cannot have been representative of the full range of first-episode psychosis patients. The strongest evidence to date against the more deterministic view comes from a relatively old randomised-controlled trial carried out by May and colleagues (May, Tuma & Dixon, 1976). Wyatt (1991) recently revived the findings of this trial and marshalled other evidence to argue that early neuroleptic treatment does lead to improved outcome. The design of the May et al. study was good and it produced compelling data. While it will be difficult to carry out a similar study to replicate it, this may yet prove necessary. The study of Waddington, Youssef and Kinsella (1995) was also suggestive of an independent, and potentially reversible effect of DUP on outcome. This project contrasted the levels of functioning of patients treated with onsets of illness spread across the period before the introduction of neuroleptic drugs, and consequently varying degrees of delay in treatment, and found a significant relationship even after many years of illness. This suggested a formative influence of such treatment delay because a systematic bias influencing the timing of commencement of neuroleptic was probably absent, though a cohort effect cannot be ruled out.

McGlashan (1996) proposed an "early detection hypothesis" as follows:

> Reducing the duration of untreated psychosis by providing effective treatment with neuroleptic medication plus psychosocial management will result in an improvement in both short and longer term outcomes, compared to what would have otherwise occurred.

He went on to formulate a series of design alternatives which would test this hypothesis and, along with his collaborators, has put in place the most acceptable design short of a randomised controlled trial of delayed neuroleptic treatment in Norway and Denmark in a large scale study. This quasi-experimental study, which contrasts an experimental catchment area in which massive public education and enhanced service access is offered with two control sectors where "detection as usual" occurs, aims to determine firstly whether shortening the DUP can be achieved, and secondly if such a reduction translates into a corresponding improvement in outcome (see Chapter 6). While it is likely that the hypothesis can be tested with this design, it may be that interpretation of the data will be more complex than originally thought.

Our experience with a smaller scale attempt to implement the McGlashan design suggests to us that the effects of enhanced detection are two-fold. Firstly, the DUP is reduced; secondly, the treated incidence is increased. The second effect was not initially considered because most researchers have assumed that the treated incidence for an illness as apparently severe as schizophrenia is very close to the total incidence (Suvisaari et al., 1999). This is clearly not so in most settings (Padmavathi, Rajkumar & Srinivasan,1998; Helgason, 1990). The problem is more complex since it has to be psychosis not schizophrenia that we are seeking to detect, because of the flaws and circularity of our diagnostic system.

The effect of the public education and early detection program may be to shorten DUP for the "usual cases"—that is, the kind of patients that gain access to treatment when "detection as usual" is being offered. It will also increase the treated incidence for the sector, provided the actual incidence and prevalence of psychosis is higher than the treated incidence under standard conditions. In fact both these predicted effects—a marked reduction in DUP and an increase in the treated incidence of nearly 40%—have now been reported in the experimental (Stavanger) sector in Norway (Johannessen et al., 1999; Larsen & Foar, 1999; McGlashan, 1999). Thus the nature and composition of the samples in the experimental and control sectors will become different. If the additional cases treated in the experimental sector are numerous and also have a systematically different DUP level from the rest of the sample (either shorter or longer), then the data may be difficult to interpret in relation to the hypothesis. If the additional detected cases have a shorter DUP (known to possess a better outcome) then, unless they can be identified and excluded, at follow-up the study will spuriously appear to confirm the hypothesis that delay contributes to poor outcome. If the additional cases have a longer DUP then a different (most improbable) inference would be drawn that extra efforts to reduce delays in treatment actually result in a longer DUP. The effect on outcome here would be equally difficult to interpret. If the extra treated incidence were trivial or the effect on DUP dramatic, then these considerations may not matter. The treated annual incidence therefore needs to be carefully measured within this design to determine whether any changes in DUP between samples are due to changes in the sample or true changes. It may be possible to separate the two effects of the early detection strategy by focusing on those cases within each sample whose onset of frank psychotic symptoms occurred following the commencement of the enhanced detection strategy. Even this would only exclude any additional long DUP cases, while the potential penumbra of more transient short DUP cases could still enter the sample. As Figure 1.3 shows, further interpretation problems may result if there is differential recruitment form the samples of treated incidence into research samples in experimental and control sectors in the quasi-experimental model.

Finally, the boundaries of psychosis and the existence of a higher prevalence of people with psychotic features with minimal clinical significance in the community (van Os, Ravelli & Nijl, 1999; Honig et al., 1998; Verdoux et al., 1998b) is becoming increasingly appreciated. Verdoux et al. (1998b) also proposed that psychosis-proneness peaks during the adolescent-young adult period and that this not only influences the presentation of clinical syndromes in this age group, but also should suggest caution in screening for new cases of disorder. These complexities may mean that some ethically acceptable form of RCT (randomised controlled trial) or a closely related design, which eliminates sampling bias from the

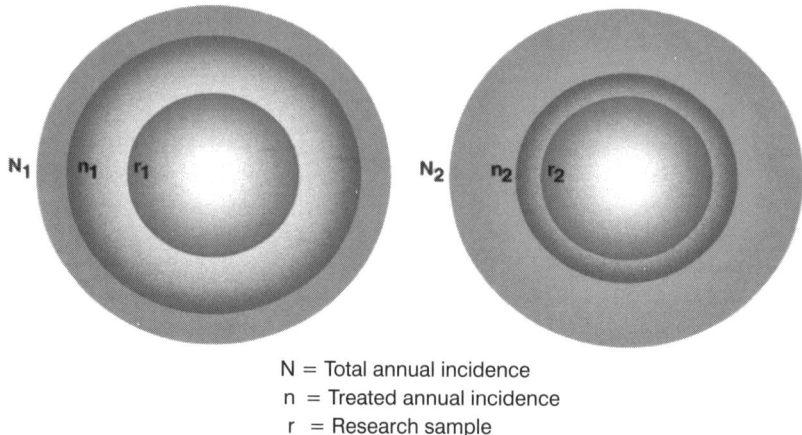

N = Total annual incidence
n = Treated annual incidence
r = Research sample

Figure 1.3   Sampling issues in early intervention.

experimental manipulation of the DUP variable, may ultimately be required to test the early detection hypothesis. To achieve a better resolution of the research issues, it may be necessary to consider designing an ethically sound means of carrying out a replication of the original RCT, at least for a stable subgroup of first-episode cases where, under certain conditions, neuroleptics can be safely delayed for a period while intensive non-neuroleptic therapy is provided. Alternatively, it might be useful to study over a short–medium time frame the staggered introduction of neuroleptic medication to parts of developing countries with no current access to such treatment. The latter design would be non-randomised at the level of the individual and ethical, and could be done within a framework of extending access to modern effective psychiatric treatments (not only drug therapies). A third strategy would be to more intensively study the effects of different intensities, durations and qualities of treatment within and beyond the first episode. This leads into the third focus considered briefly below.

Before such research efforts are made, however, perhaps we should stop and ask ourselves whether the highest levels of methodological purity really essential in answering this question? We seem to be caught in a double bind. On the one hand it is felt that to delay neuroleptic therapy once psychotic symptoms emerge may be unethical and anyway would be practically difficult for many patients with florid symptoms. Yet treatment is often not desired by patients and is often not available, at least in a timely fashion. Furthermore, there is the scepticism expressed by many regarding the causal relationship between earlier treatment and better outcome. Despite the growing world-wide enthusiasm for early intervention, the tension remains unresolved. Perhaps many believe that treatment works in the short term but does not really affect the longer term prognosis. We may need designs to separate out these two elements. What is a reasonable perspective to take in the meantime?

If we regard the variable DUP as an outcome in itself to which a range of variables could contribute as risk factors for delay, then it is quite possible that putatively intrinsic features such as poor premorbid social functioning, high negative symptoms or insidious onset could contribute to delays in recognition or awareness of illness and the need for treatment, while contributing independently to poor outcome. It is equally clear from clinical and research data that other independent factors influence the timing of treatment, such as the level of family support, the quality of primary care and the accessibility and quality of the specialist mental health services. It seems more useful as a working model to regard the process of entry to treatment as a dynamic one, rather than as somehow fixed or predetermined. Scepticism, while partially justified, essentially derives from an unreconstructed and obsolete Kraepelinian view of the illness which saw onset and course as following a variant of the dementia pattern, rather than the dynamic vulnerability clinicians see in real-world settings, and in other illnesses such as asthma and epilepsy. At best, the dementia model applies only to a small minority of patients, and it is this subgroup which still fuels attempts (e.g. Carpenter, Heinrichs & Wagman, 1988) to capture the "essence" of schizophrenia, a term which still lacks validity.

It is logical and clinically obvious that providing safe and effective antipsychotic treatment to a young man at 17, some weeks after he has become psychotic, will limit the damage in the short term to his sense of self, his peer group, his family and his vocational prospects, compared to delaying treatment for a further 12 months when he is clinically worse and forced into treatment following a high-risk incident. Whether there are long-term advantages or not will depend on how well he responds to the treatment, whether his illness vulnerability continues, and whether high-quality treatment can be continued for as long as is necessary.

Focus 3: Enhancing phase-specific treatment in first-episode psychosis and the critical period: getting a grip…hanging on

We have now seen how far we might push the envelope in early intervention in psychosis, even with existing levels of knowledge. These exciting preventive foci are coming rapidly within our reach. However, at the moment most professionals interested in this burgeoning field find themselves based in mainstream mental health services, and their most immediate possibility for preventively - oriented treatment focuses upon the first episode of psychosis and the critical period of the early months and years beyond this. How can the service model and clinical practice accommodate to the needs of these young people as they enter the specialist mental health system? What are their treatment needs? Improving the quality, effectiveness and acceptability of treatment in first-episode psychosis and beyond is a more immediately achievable reform, notwithstanding the promise and fascination of prepsychotic interventions and of early detection strategies. It is also one which is based on firmer evidence (National Early Psychosis Project, 1998). Surprisingly, it has not received as much emphasis within the early psychosis research network to date. There has also been a complacency that standard clinical care for psychotic disorders was already adequate for the first-episode patient. However, the care of the first-episode and recent onset patient can be enhanced firstly by eliminating the iatrogenic aspects of standard clinical care, secondly by developing a phase specific, developmentally sensitive and intensive recovery approach, and thirdly by ensuring continuity of care for as long as it is required.

The first target is the reduction of secondary morbidity due to crude and alienating treatment. The first experience of psychosis and the treatment system is all too often frightening, shameful and stigmatising (Lally, 1989; McGorry et al., 1991; Shaw, McFarlane & Bookless, 1997; Meyer et al., 1999). Add to this the impatient and crude use of drug therapies and the neglect of the psychotherapeutic and psychosocial aspects of treatment, and we have a cocktail designed to harm as much as help. Some of these effects flow from delayed intervention, available only *in extremis*, and some from a lack of empathy with the predicament of the person experiencing the emerging illness. Much of this iatrogenesis can be avoided or repaired if it is understood and appreciated. A low-dose neuroleptic strategy with sole use of atypical antipsychotics, and gentler modes of handling emergencies, such as benzodiazepines and skilled nursing and psychological interventions, is essential. There is ample empirical and neurobiological evidence to support this model (McEvoy, Hogarty & Steingard, 1991; Power et al., 1998; Remington, Kapur & Zipursky, 1998; Nyberg et al., 1999; Kapur, Ziputsky & Remington, 1999). Avoidance of aversive medication experiences and coercion at this stage lays a firmer foundation for continuing care and a therapeutic alliance (Power & McGorry, 1999; Edwards, Cocks & Bott, 1999). Home treatment in the first episode as an alternative to hospital admission is desirable wherever possible, but intensive support is required in many cases (Kulkarni & Power, 1999; Fitzgerald & Kulkarni, 1998). Streaming of young people with first-episode psychosis in units separate from older, more chronic patients is necessary if inpatient status is required (Merlo, 1999; McGorry et al., 1996; Resch, 1997).

The comprehensive care of young people and their families at this phase of illness involves addressing the full range of needs within an optimistic and integrated framework of care. A description of the key elements is now available (McGorry & Jackson, 1999) and a large number of centres across the globe are evolving new and more refined approaches (Edwards, McGorry & Pennell, in press). Integration of hospital and community care and of biological and psychosocial elements of treatment with sufficient skill and intensity are the hallmarks of a successful approach. The needs of subgroups, such as those with complicating substance abuse or personality disorders, need to be addressed and the skills required have not yet been developed or tested. Mindset and language are critical. For example, recovery rather than rehabilitation is the primary goal. Quality of life and health in a positive sense, not merely the abolition of symptoms in the shortest possible time, should be constantly focused upon. There is encouraging evidence that this approach is not only more effective but also more cost-effective than standard clinical care (McGorry et al., 1996; Power et al., 1998; Mihalopoulos, McGorry & Carter, 1999). Even non-streamed, predominantly biological, treatment with what is now recognised to be markedly excessive doses of neuroleptics, results in good remission rates within 6–12 months (Lieberman, Jody & Alvir, 1993). Modern approaches should be able to further enhance the short-term outcome at least. The emergence of the atypical neuroleptics have made a major contribution through improving tolerability, enhancing levels of remission to some extent, and creating a climate of optimism. On the other hand, more substantial and sustained improvements in outcome may come from sophisticated and intensive psychosocial interventions (Jackson et al., 1998; Kemp et al., 1996) and better service models (Thornicroft & Tansell, 1999).

The third element in enhancing outcome is the capacity to maintain the therapeutic grip with person during the critical period (Birchwood, McGorry & Jackson, 1997). The work of the Hillside group (Robinson et al., 1999) demonstrates the propensity for relapse seen in many earlier studies (Crow et al., 1986). For the majority, though not all, a reasonably intensive period of treatment to promote recovery and reintegration during the first or second year after onset of treatment is optimal. Beyond this, for a substantial minority at least, ongoing maintenance treatment is required. More research is required to determine who needs this and how to ensure that it is better accepted and also freely available at this intensity. The major threats to this are inadequate funding of mental health services, a reactive mindset within many services, and the natural treatment reluctance of many patients in the face of continuing illness—a stigmatised future life trajectory and a model of treatment which is difficult to accept. Each of these threats implies a different response. It is the failure of follow through with treatments of proved effectiveness which constitutes the greatest failure of modern psychiatry. This is responsible for the fact that the long-term course and outcome of major treatable disorders, such as schizophrenia (Hegarty et al., 1994) and bipolar disorder (Moncrieff, 1997) have failed to improve over the decades. Investment in new and better treatments must continue, but we must learn to deliver them effectively in real-world settings if we are to reduce the burden of mental disorders (Murray & Lopez, 1996). Particularly in the mental health field, this will involve a focus on health and quality of life as well as disease.

CONCLUSIONS

The scope and potential of preventive strategies in early psychosis is great, but there are many tasks to be accomplished. There is increasing momentum encouraging further progress and the paradigm has already reinvigorated a field which has been crying out for ways to improve the morale of clinicians and service settings. There have been many false dawns as psychiatry and those on its fringes have struggled to raise morale and exorcise the demons of psychosis and its potentially devastating effects. These have ranged from the chimera of insulin coma therapy to the extremes of psychosurgery and antipsychiatry. The current enthusiasm has firmer foundations, a logical and testable framework, and increasingly powerful tools at its disposal. Nevertheless, if it is to prosper and deliver a substantial benefit to millions of people across the globe, three things will need to happen. Firstly, the key strategies of early detection and intervention should be carefully researched in real-world settings. Secondly, the ethical issues flowing from the new paradigm need to be considered side by side with the level of proof required to justify a change in practice in each element of the early intervention framework. Thirdly, it will be essential to advocate effectively in the sociopolitical realm for the resources to deploy effective approaches in a comprehensive manner.

REFERENCES

Barrett, R.J. (1998a). Conceptual foundation of schizophrenia: I. Degeneration. *Australian and New Zealand Journal of Psychiatry*, **32**, 617–626.

Barrett, R.J. (1998b). Conceptual foundation of schizophrenia: II. Disintegration and division. *Australian and New Zealand Journal of Psychiatry*, **32**, 627–634.

Beiser, M., Erickson, D., Fleming, J.A.E. & Iacono, W.G. (1993). Establishing the onset of psychotic illness. *American Journal of Psychiatry*, **150**, 1349–1354.

Birchwood, M. & Macmillian, F. (1993). Early intervention in schizophrenia. *Australian and New Zealand Journal of Psychiatry*, **17**, 374–378.

Birchwood, M., McGorry, P. & Jackson, H. (1997). Early intervention in schizophrenia. *British Journal of Psychiatry*, **170**, 2–5.

Cannon-Spoor, H.E., Potkin, S.G. & Wyatt, R.J. (1982). Measurement of premorbid adjustment in chronic schizophrenia. *Schizophrenia Bulletin*, **8**, 470–484.

Carpenter, W.T., Heinrichs, D.W. & Wagman, A.M.I. (1988). Deficit and nondeficit forms of schizophrenia: the concept. *American Journal of Psychiatry*, **145**, 578–583.

Cohen, P. & Cohen, J. (1984). The clinician's illusion. *Archives of General Psychiatry*, **41**, 1178–1182.

Cook, R.J. & Sackett, D.L. (1995). The number needed to treat: a clinically useful measure of treatment effect. *British Medical Journal*, **310**, 452–454.

Crow, T.J., MacMillan, J.F., Johnson, A.L. & Johnstone, E.C. (1986). The Northwick Park study of first episodes of schizophrenia. II. A randomized controlled trial of prophylactic neuroleptic treatment. *British Journal of Psychiatry*, **148**, 120–127.

Edwards, J., McGorry, P.D. & Pennell, K. (in press). Models of early intervention in psychosis: an analysis of service approaches. In M. Birchwood, D. Fowler, B.C. Jackson (Eds), *Early Intervention in Psychosis: A Guide to Concepts, Evidence and Intervention*. Chichester: Wiley.

Edwards, J., Cocks, J. & Bott, J. (1999). Preventive case management in first-episode psychosis. In P.D. McGorry & H.J. Jackson (Eds), *Recognition and Management of Early Psychosis: A Preventive Approach.* (pp. 308–337). Cambridge: Cambridge University Press.

Fitzgerald, P. & Kulkarni, J. (1998). Home-oriented management program for people with early psychosis. *British Journal of Psychiatry*, **172** (Suppl. 33), 39–44.

Gordon, R. (1983). An operational classification of disease prevention. *Public Health Reports*, **98**, 107–109.

Haas, G.L. & Sweeney, J.A. (1992). Premorbid and onset features of first-episode schizophrenia. *Schizophrenia Bulletin*, **18**, 373–386.

Häfner, H., Nowotny, B., Löffler, W., van der Heiden, W. & Maurer, K. (1995). When and how does schizophrenia produce social deficits? *European Archives of Psychiatry and Clinical Neuroscience*, **246**, 17–28.

Hegarty, J.D., Baldessarini, R.J., Tohen, M., Waternaux, C. & Oepen, G. (1994). One hundred years of schizophrenia: a meta-analysis of the outcome literature. *American Journal of Psychiatry*, **151**, 1409–1416.

Helgason, L. (1990). Twenty years follow-up of first psychiatric presentation for schizophrenia: what could have been prevented? *Acta Psychiatrica Scandinavica*, **81**, 231- 235.

Hodges, A., Byrne, M., Grant, E. & Johnstone, E. (1999). People at risk of schizophrenia. Sample characteristics of the first 100 cases in the Edinburgh High-Risk Study. *British Journal of Psychiatry*, **174**, 547–553.

Honig, A., Romme, M.A., Ensink, B.J., Escher, S.D., Pennings, M.H. & deVries, M.W. (1998). Auditory hallucinations: a comparison between patients and nonpatients. *Journal of Nervous & Mental Disease*, **186**, 646–651.

Isohanni, M., Jones, P., Rantakallio, .P, Järvelin, M.-R., Mäkikyrö, T. & Isohanni, I. (1999) Childhood and adolescent predictors of schizophrenia. *Current Opinion in Psychiatry*, **12** (Suppl. 1), 252.

Jablensky, A., Sartorius, N., Ernberg, E., et al. (1992). *Schizophrenia: Manifestations, Incidence and Course in Different Cultures. A World Health Organization Ten-Country Study.* Psychological Medicine, Vol. Monograph Supplement 20. Cambridge: Cambridge University Press.

Jackson, H.J., McGorry, P.D., Edwards, J., Hulbert, C., Henry, L., Francey, S., Cocks, J., Power, P., Harrigan, S. & Dudgeon, P.. (1998). Cognitively oriented psychotherapy for early psychosis (COPE): preliminary results. *British Journal of Psychiatry*, **172** (Suppl. 33), 93–100.

Johannessen, J.O., Friis, S., Vaglum, P., Larsen, T.K., Mardal, S., Melle, I., Simonsen, E. & McGlashan, T. (1999). TIPS: a multi-center study of a comprehensive program for earlier detection and treatment of first-episode psychosis. *Current Opinion in Psychiatry*, **12** (Suppl. 1), 63.

Johnstone, E., Crow, T., Johnson, A. & MacMillan, J. (1986). The Northwick Park Study of first episodes of schizophrenia, I: Presentation of illness and problems relating to admission. *British Journal of Psychiatry*, **148**, 115–120.

Jones, P.B., Bebbington, P., Foerste, A., Lewis, S.W., Murray, R.M., Russell, A., Sham, P.C., Toone, B.K. & Wilkins, S. (1993). Premorbid social underachievement in schizophrenia: results from the Camberwell collaborative psychosis study. *British Journal of Psychiatry*, **162**, 65–71.

Kapur, S., Zipursky, R.B. & Remington, G. (1999). Clinical and theoretical implications of 5-HT$_2$ and D$_2$ receptor occupancy of clozapine, risperidone, and olanzapine in schizophrenia. *American Journal of Psychiatry*, **156**, 286–293.

Kemp, R., Hayward, P., Applewhaite, G., Everitt, B. & David, A. (1996). Compliance therapy in psychotic patients: randomised controlled trial. *British Medical Journal*, **312**, 345–349.

Kirch, D.G., Keith, S.J. & Matthews, S.M. (1992). Research on first episode psychosis: report on a National Institute of Mental Health Workshop. *Schizophrenia Bulletin*, **18**, 179–184.

Kulkarni, J. & Power, P. (1999). Initial management of first-episode psychosis. In P.D. McGorry & H.J. Jackson (Eds), *Recognition and Management of Early Psychosis: A Preventive Approach* (pp. 184–205). New York: Cambridge University Press.

Kundera, M. (1996). *The Book of Laughter and Forgetting* (p.273). London: Faber & Faber.

Kwapil, T.R., Chapman, L.J. & Chapman, J. (1999). Validity and usefulness of the Wisconsin Manual for assessing psychotic-like experiences. *Schizophrenia Bulletin*, **25**, 363–375.

Lally, S.J. (1989). Does being in here mean there is something wrong with me? *Schizophrenia Bulletin*, **15**, 253–265.

Larsen, T.K. & Foar, I. (1999). Identifying persons prodromal to first-episode schizophrenia: the TOPP-project. *Current Opinion in Psychiatry*, **12** (Suppl. 1), 207.

Lawrie, S.M., Whalley, H., Kestelman, J.N., Abukmeil, S.S., Byrne, M., Hodges, A., Rimmington, J.E., Best, J.J., Owens, D.G. & Johnstone, E.C. (1999). Magnetic resonance imaging of brain in people at high risk of developing schizophrenia. *Lancet*, **353** (9146), 30–33.

Leon, A.C., Portera, L., Olfson, M., Weissman, M.M., Kathol, R.G., Farber, L., Sheehan, D.V. & Pleil, A.M. (1997). False positive results: a challenge for psychiatric screening in primary care. *American Journal of Psychiatry*, **154**, 1462–1464.

Lieberman, J.A., Jody, D. & Alvir, J.M. (1993). Brain morphology, dopamine, and eye-tracking abnormalities in first-episode schizophrenia: prevalence and clinical correlates. *Archives of General Psychiatry*, **50**, 357–368.

Loebel, A., Lieberman, J.A., Alvir, J.M., Mayerhoff, D.I., Geisler, S.H. & Szymanski, S.R. (1992). Duration of psychosis and outcome in first-episode schizophrenia. *American Journal of Psychiatry*, **149**, 1183–1188.

May, P.R., Tuma, A.H. & Dixon, W.J. (1976) Schizophrenia—a follow-up study of results of treatment methods. *Archives of General Psychiatry*, **33**, 474–478.

McEvoy, J.P., Hogarty, G.E. & Steingard, S. (1991). Optimal dose of neuroleptic in acute schizophrenia: a controlled study of the neuroleptic threshold and higher haloperidol dose. *Archives of General Psychiatry*, **48**, 739–745.

McGlashan, T.H. & Johannessen, J.O. (1996). Early detection and intervention with schizophrenia: rationale. *Schizophrenia Bulletin*, **22**, 201–222.

McGlashan, T.H. (1996). Early detection and intervention in schizophrenia: research. *Schizophrenia Bulletin*, **22** (2), 327–345.

McGlashan, T.H. (1999). Treatment intervention in the New Haven PRIME Clinic prodromal sample. *Current Opinion in Psychiatry*, **12** (Suppl. 1), 64.

McGorry, P., Chanen, A., McCarthy, E., Van Riel, R., McKenzie, D. & Singh, B.S. (1991). Post-traumatic stress disorder following recent onset psychosis: an unrecognised post-psychotic syndrome. *Journal of Nervous Mental Disease*, **179**, 253–258

McGorry, P., McFarlane, C., Patton, G., Bell, R., Jackson, H., Hibbert, M. & Bower, G. (1995). The prevalence of prodromal symptoms of schizophrenia in adolescence: a preliminary survey. *Acta Psychiatrica Scandinavica*, **92**, 241–249.

McGorry, P. (1998a). Preventive strategies in early psychosis: verging on reality. *British Journal of Psychiatry*, **172** (Suppl. 33), 1–2.

McGorry, P.D. (1998b). Commentary on R.J. Barrett's "Conceptual Foundations of Schizophrenia". *Australian and New Zealand Journal of Psychiatry*, **32** (5), 635–636.

McGorry, P.D., Edwards, J., Mihalopoulos, C., Harrigan, S. & Jackson, H.J. (1996). The Early Psychosis Prevention and Intervention Centre (EPPIC): an evolving system of early detection and optimal management. *Schizophrenia Bulletin*, **22** (2), 305–326.

McGorry, P.D., Edwards, J. & Pennell, K. (1999) Sharpening the focus: early intervention in the real world. In P.D. McGorry & H. Jackson (Eds), *The Recognition and Management of Early Psychosis: A Preventive Approach* (pp. 441–470). Cambridge: Cambridge University Press.

McGorry, P.D. & Jackson, H. (Eds) (1999). *The Recognition and Management of Early Psychosis: A Preventive Approach*. Cambridge: Cambridge University Press.

McGorry, P.D. & Singh, B.S. (1995) Schizophrenia: Risk and Possibility. Chapter 27 in: B. Raphael & G.D. Burrows (Eds), *Handbook of Studies on Preventive Psychiatry* (pp. 491–514). Amsterdam: Elsevier.

Meares, A. (1959). The diagnosis of prepsychotic schizophrenia. *Lancet*, **I**, 55–59.

Merlo, M.C.G. (1999). The Bern First Episode Psychosis Program. Presented at *Early Psychosocial Intervention and Low Dose Medication in First Episode Psychosis: 10 Years of Bern First Episode Psychosis*, Symposium UPD–Ost Waldau, Bern, Switzerland.

Meyer, H., Taiminen, T., Vuori, T., Äijälä, A. & Helenius, H. (1999). Posttraumatic stress disorder symptoms related to psychosis and acute involuntary hospitalization in schizophrenic and delusional patients. *Journal of Nervous and Mental Disease*, **187**, 343–352.

Mihalopoulos, C., McGorry, P.D. & Carter, R.C. (1999). Is early intervention in first episode psychosis an economically viable method of improving outcome? *Acta Psychiatrica Scandinavica*, **54**, 1–9.

Moncrieff, J. (1997). Lithium: evidence reconsidered. *British Journal of Psychiatry*, **171**, 113–119.

Mrazek, P.J. & Haggerty, R.J. (Eds) (1994). *Reducing Risks for Mental Disorders: Frontiers for Preventive Intervention Research*. Washington, D.C.: National Academy Press.

Murray, C.J.L. & Lopez, A.D. (Eds) (1996). *The Global Burden of Disease*. Harvard University Press.

National Early Psychosis Project (1998). *Australian Clinical Guidelines for Early Psychosis*. Melbourne, Australia: EPPIC Statewide Services.

Nyberg, S., Eriksson, B., Oxenstierna, G., Halldin, C. & Farde, L. (1999). Suggested minimal effective dose of risperidon e based on PET-measured D2 and 5-HT2A receptor occupancy in schizophrenic patients. *American Journal of Psychiatry*, **156**, 869–875.

Padmavathi, R., Rajkumar, S. & Srinivasan, T.N. (1998). Schizophrenic patients who were never treated—a study in an Indian urban community. *Psychological Medicine*, **28**, 1113–1117.

Phillips, L.J., McGorry, P.D., Yung, A.R., Francey, S., Cosgrave, L., Germano, D., Bravin, J., MacDonald, A., Hallgren, M., Hearn, N., Adlard, S. & Patton, G. (1999). The development of preventive interventions for early psychosis: early findings and directions for the future. *Schizophrenia Research*, **36**, 331.

Phillips, L.J., Yung, A.R., Hearn, N., McFarlane, C., Hallgren, M. & McGorry, P.D. (in press). Preventive mental health: accessing the target population. *Australian and New Zealand Journal of Psychiatry*.

Power, P., Elkins, K., Adlard, S., Curry, C., McGorry, P. & Harrigan, S. (1998). Analysis of the initial treatment phase in first episode psychosis. *British Journal of Psychiatry*, **172** (Suppl. 33), 70–76.

Power, P. & McGorry, P.D. (1999). Initial assessment of first episode psychosis. In P.D. McGorry & H. Jackson (Eds), *The Recognition and Management of Early Psychosis: A Preventive Approach* (pp. 155–183). Cambridge: Cambridge University Press.

Rapoport, J.L., Giedd, J.N., Blumenthal, J., Hamburger, S., Jeffries, N., Fernandez, T., Nicolson, R., Bedwell, J., Lenane, M., Zijdenbos, A., Paus, T. & Evans, A. (1999). Progressive cortical change during adolescence in childhood-onset schizophrenia: a longitudinal magnetic resonance imaging study. *Archives of General Psychiatry*, **56**, 649–654.

Remington, G., Kapur, S. & Zipursky, R.B. (1998). Pharmacotherapy of first episode psychosis. *British Journal of Psychiatry*, **172** (Suppl. 33), 66–70.

Resch, F. (1997), Kooperationsmodelle zwischen Kinder- und Jugendpsychiatrie und Erwachsenenpsychiatrie. In G. Klosinski (Ed.), *Stationäre Behandlung psychischer Störungen im Kindes-und Jugendalter. Brennpunkte und Entwicklungen*. Bern: Verlag Hans Huber.

Robinson, D.G., Woerner, M.G., Alvir, J.M.A., Geisler, S., Koreen, A., Sheitman, B., Chakos, M., Mayerhoff, D., Bilder, R., Goldman, R. & Lieberman, J. (1999). Predictors of treatment response from a first episode of schizophrenia or schizoaffective disorder. *American Journal of Psychiatry*, **156**, 544–549.

Rosen, A. (1999). Australia: From colonial rivalries to a national mental health strategy. In: G. Thornicroft, B.M. Tansella (Eds), *The Mental Health Matrix. A Manual to Improve Services* (pp. 177–200). Cambridge: Cambridge University Press.

Shaw, K., McFarlane, A. & Bookless, C. (1997). The phenomenology of traumatic reactions to psychotic illness. *Journal of Nervous and Mental Disease*, **185**, 434–441.

Singh, B.S. & McGorry, P.D. (1998). The Second National Mental Health Plan—an opportunity to take stock and move forward. *Medical Journal of Australia*, **169**, 435–437.

Sullivan, H.S. (1927). The onset of schizophrenia. *American Journal of Psychiatry*, **151**, 135–139 (1994: reprinted).

Suvisaari, J.M,. Haukka, J.K., Tanskanen, A.J. & Lönnqvist J.K. (1999). Decline in the incidence of schizophrenia in Finnish cohorts born from 1954 to 1965. *Archives of General Psychiatry*, **56**, 733–740.

Thornicroft, G. & Tansella, M. (Eds) (1999). *The Mental Health Matrix. A Manual to Improve Services*. Cambridge: Cambridge University Press.

Torrey, E.F., Erdman, K., Wolfe, S.M. & Flynn, L.M. (1990). *Care of the Seriously Mentally Ill: A Rating of State Programs*. Washington, D.C.: Public Citizen Health Research Group and National Alliance of the Mentally ill.

van Os, J., Jones, P., Lewis, G., Wadsworth, M. & Murray, R. (1997). Developmental precursors of affective illness in a general population birth cohort. *Archives of General Psychiatry*, **54**, 625–630.

van Os, J. Ravelli, A. & Nijl, R.V. (1999). Evidence for a psychosis continuum in the general population. *Schizophrenia Research*, **36**, 57.

Verdoux, H., Bergey, C., Assens, F., Abalan, F., Gonzales, B., Pauillac, P., Fournet, O., Liraud, F., Beaussier, J.P., Gaussares, C., Etchegaray, B., Bourgeois. M. & van Os, J. (1998a). Prediction of duration of psychosis before first admission. *European Psychiatry*, **13**, 346–352.

Verdoux, H., Van Os, J., Maurice-Tison, S., Gay, B., Salamon, R. & Bourgeois, M. (1998b). Is early adulthood a critical development stage for psychosis proneness? A survey of delusional ideation in normal subjects. *Schizophrenia Research*, **29**, 247–254.

Waddington, J.L., Youssef, H.A. & Kinsella, A. (1995). Sequential cross-sectional and 10 year prospective study of severe negative symptoms in relation to duration of initially untreated psychosis in chronic schizophrenia. *Psychological Medicine*, **25**, 849–857.

Wyatt, R.J. (1991). Neuroleptics and the natural course of schizophrenia. *Schizophrenia Bulletin*, **17**, 325–351.

Yung, A.R., McGorry, P.D., McFarlane, C.A., Jackson, H.J., Patton, G.C. & Rakkar, A. (1996) Monitoring and care of young people at incipient risk of psychosis. *Schizophrenia Bulletin*, **22** (2), 283–303.

Chapter 2

THE CRITICAL PERIOD FOR EARLY INTERVENTION

*Max Birchwood**

INTRODUCTION

Interventions in psychosis, whether biological or psychosocial, have generally been blind to age of onset and phase of illness. Such neglect reflects the dominance of the two main paradigms of care. In the first paradigm, treatment is provided within the context of acute crisis care and further attempts to achieve prophylaxis. Rehabilitation is the second paradigm which sometimes arises from a failure of the first and involves focusing on the amelioration of disabilities, occasionally within a framework of relative asylum (Birchwood & Macmillan, 1993). Community outreach models frequently involve a blend of these two approaches. Both of these paradigms are rooted in the Kraepelinian nosological framework, and while long-term follow-up studies demonstrate the heterogeneity of outcomes in psychosis, they do appear, at first sight, to support the two paradigms. For instance, between one-third and one-half of patients have either single or multiple episodes with little or no residual symptoms; whereas the remainder have multiple episodes with varying and often increasing impairment (Hegarty et al., 1994). Thus, the early phase of psychosis may be viewed as a period during which it is possible to determine which path an individual is likely to follow and to direct resources appropriately. The early intervention paradigm turns this logic on its head and argues that the early phase of psychosis is a "critical period" influencing the long-term trajectory of psychosis and that the early course of disorder is particularly malleable to intervention, with major implications for secondary prevention. In this chapter, I will outline

*Northern Birmingham Mental Health Trust and University of Birmingham, UK

Early Intervention in Psychosis.
Edited by M. Birchwood, D. Fowler & C. Jackson.
© 2000 John Wiley & Sons Ltd.

the core elements of the concept, review evidence for this proposition and describe a prototype of intervention appropriate to the "critical period".

CRITICAL PERIOD

Prospective follow-up studies of first-episode psychosis

The bulk of follow-up studies of psychosis have reported on samples of convenience which are inevitably drawn from those maintaining contact with services: thus, a distorted picture, biased towards chronicity, may be evident. First-episode studies are not without their own problems: for example, determining their epidemiological representativeness is one issue that has been demonstrated only in the Determinants of Outcome in Severe Mental Disorder Study (DOSMD: Jablensky et al., 1992), and there are the perennial problems related to comparability of measures, sampling, and density of follow-up, and so forth, all of which constrain generalisation (Hegarty et al., 1994). On the other hand, it is also true that if findings from follow-up studies are so sensitive to methodology and context, then this itself brings into question whether general conclusions can be drawn. However, the follow-back studies and the prospective studies do permit key hypotheses to be tested and certain conclusions to be drawn. Since we are concerned with a supposed critical period of early psychosis, in this section I will focus only on first-episode prospective studies. Similar reviews have been undertaken by Ram et al. (1992), Warner (1994) and Hegarty et al. (1994), all of which will be referred to as appropriate. The studies are summarised in Table 2.1 and will be discussed below.

The pre-neuroleptic era

The studies of Stephens (1978), Bleuler (1978), and to a degree Wing (1966), bear on this important and intriguing area: was the outcome for schizophrenia one of remorseless chronicity before the neuroleptic era? The answer to this is undoubtedly in the negative. First-episode studies in the era of institutional care do not suffer from epidemiological bias: nearly all first-episode patients were admitted to hospital and were unlikely to be "camouflaged" within the community for appreciable periods (Ram et al., 1992). Twenty-three per cent of Bleuler's (1978) sample had recovered after 20 years and a further 20% showed long-term symptoms of mild severity: for the majority this was not a barrier to re-employment; 35% showed stable chronic symptoms and a further 30% continued to undulate between illness and well-being. After treatment, Stephens' (1978) patients were followed up from between 1948 and 1951 for 10 or more years. Twenty-four per cent had

Table 2.1 Prospective follow-up studies of first-episode psychosis

Study	Subjects	Inclusion criteria	Follow-up	Measures/criteria	Patterns of course/outcome
Biehl et al. (1986)	$n = 70$ (see Schubart et al., 1986)			Assessment schedule	Poor: 35%
Eaton et al. (1995)	$n = 90$ First episode: 1978–80	PSE; ICD-9 Repeated annually	10 years	–	See text
Helgason (1990)	$n = 107$ Iceland: 1966-67	ICD-9	21 years		Died: 23/107 No or minor symptoms (no treatment), 8%; minor symptoms, 22%; moderate symptoms, 50%; severe symptoms, 21%
DOSMD; Jablensky et al. (1992)	$n = 1379$ 12 centres 10 Countries	PSE/CATEGO	2 years	DAS	Mild (1 episode, no symptoms), 39%; Intermittent relapsing, 21%; Severe unremitting, 39%
Johnstone et al. (1996, 1990)	$n = 236$ First admissions in defined catchment area	CATEGO 'S' by PSE	2 years	Relapse/readmission	Relapse, 60%; no relapse, 40%

Mason et al. (1995)	$n = 67$ First episode 1978–80	ICD-9	13 years	DAS GAF	No or mild symptoms, 49%; no relapse in recent 2 years, 80%; good or fair social outcome, 55%; employed in last two years, 37%; independent community living, 97%; living alone, 28%; receiving treatment, 76%
Schubart et al. (1986)	$n = 70$	PSE/ICD-9	2 years	DAS	Good adjustment, 26%; intermediate, 39%
Scottish Schizophrenia Research Group (1988, 1992)	$n = 49$ 4 hospitals, first admissions	RDC	5 years	Readmission "Overall Outcome" Kraweicka scale	37% 'well'; 47% readmitted; 38% psychotic symptoms at follow-up; 23% employed
Shepherd et al. (1989)	$n = 49$ First admission over 18 months in semi-rural area	PSE/CATEGO	5 years	PSE, DAS	1 episode, no impairment; 22%

"recovered", whereas 30% were "improved"; overall, one-half were rated as having improved relative to their first discharge. John Wing's (1966) five-year follow-up of patients admitted to three British mental hospitals in 1956, showed that nearly one-half had an excellent prognosis requiring little attention from psychiatric aftercare or rehabilitation services. A further 38% were asymptomatic in the last six months of their follow-up. While we would not have known the employment status of those individuals without the interruption of psychosis, the Wing study paints a much more optimistic picture about the capabilities of those affected than is often the case. In fact, M. Bleuler's (1978) impression was that few of his patients completely recovered without some vestige of their illness remaining, but in spite of this, many were able to resume employment.

Without doubt, these studies used different diagnostic procedures, measures and follow-up periods; yet in spite of this, their results paint a similar picture and add strength to the conclusion that untreated schizophrenia is not a deteriorating and inevitably socially disabling disorder; in excess of one-third can recover symptomatically, and a further third can function quite independently without intensive community outreach.

Neuroleptics were not widely used until the late 1950s, in fact towards the end of the follow-up period in the Wing (1966) and Stephens' (1978) studies. The Bleuler (1978) sample was treated almost entirely within the pre-neuroleptic era and the sample was subject to minimal attrition. It is salutary to be reminded about the type of treatment provided by Bleuler's clinic in Canton, Switzerland, particularly as fully 60% of his patients recovered 20 years after their first episode—sufficient for them to be able to return to work and to support themselves. This figure is far in excess, for example, of that reported by Kraepelin (1896/1977) from his hospital in Munich—he labelled only 12% of his patients as "social recoveries". As Warner (1994) has explained, M. Bleuler's account of his treatment methods from the first decade of the twentieth century, reads like a model of those introduced half a century later as part of the social psychiatry revolution of post-war Europe. Bleuler de-emphasised institutional methods, advocating a high threshold for admission and rapid discharge. He championed active community rehabilitation, returning the patient to his own family, or, where this was not possible, to a substitute family: "Idleness facilitates the predomination of the complexes over the personality, whereas regulated work maintains the activity of normal thinking" (p. 11); thus return to an appropriate occupation was vital according to Bleuler to promote well-being, although faultless performance could not be expected. Minimising work stress, family troubles, or a sense of failure, were all part of Bleuler's philosophy of care. Warner (1994) argues that, "the modern pessimistic view of the untreated course of schizophrenia may have developed because the introduction of anti-psychotic drugs in the 1950s and their subsequent universal employment in the treatment of psychosis has masked what was previously known about the natural history of the illness" (p. 11). Warner also considers that excessive treatment with neuroleptics may have exacerbated disability consistent with recent findings (Schooler, 1994).

Nevertheless, the meta-analysis of follow-up studies by Hegarty et al. (1994) does point to an improvement in outcomes during the 1960s when neuroleptics were widely used: however, it should not be assumed that all the favourable outcomes we see today are solely attributable to neuroleptics—continuous care, support and community-based rehabilitation are potent influences on outcome. The WHO cross-cultural studies, for example, demonstrated favourable outcomes in cultures with extended family networks (Jablensky et al., 1992), in spite of the lesser use of neuroleptic drugs. In the classic review of the North American follow-up studies conducted in the neuroleptic era, McGlashan (1988) observed that "schizophrenia may be quite malleable to prolonged environmental/psychosocial perturbations...; these have negative potential when applied too intensively or ambitiously, but positive potential if applied steadily in a supportive rehabilitative mode in the context of stable and supportive community care" (p. 538). Studies from the pre-neuroleptic era caution against excessive pessimism about schizophrenia and excessive optimism about the efficacy of neuroleptic drugs.

These studies from the pre-neuroleptic must be set against recent work reviewed later in this chapter and elsewhere in this book suggesting that early neuroleptic treatment can prevent or minimise later symptoms, for example, arising from relapse. For example, Waddington, Youssef and Kinsella (1995) followed up 88 long-term residents in an Irish psychiatric hospital, many of whom had experienced decades of initially untreated psychosis (mean = 17 years) prior to the introduction of neuroleptics in Ireland. They found that the longer the duration of psychosis prior to the introduction of neuroleptics, the greater the poverty of speech at the "end state" (when the average age was 66 years), and the more continuous neuroleptic treatment had to be. The point to be made here, is that untreated psychosis is not inevitably "Kraepelinian", particularly where it is positively managed in a community context. Earlier and ongoing neuroleptic may enhance the outcome, but to assume that the illness course would otherwise be chronic and remorseless would seem to be erroneous.

Clinical and social outcomes

In their seminal paper, Strauss and Carpenter (1977) demonstrated that clinical recovery was not a prerequisite for social recovery; in fact, they reported substantial desynchrony between, for example, residual symptoms and social functioning, the correlations being no greater than 0.50. Normal processes as well as abnormal ones contribute to social functioning and social readjustment (Birchwood, Hallett & Preston, 1988) and the first episode studies follow the same general rule. The correlation between symptoms and functioning is of the same order (Shepherd et al., 1989), with social outcome in the early phase being better than might be expected in the light of clinical outcome alone. Thus, Shepherd et al. (1989) demonstrated that 30% of their patients showed moderate to severe social impairment, whereas 70% experienced multiple episodes and/or residual symptoms over the first five years. Mason et al. (1995) echo this point in the context of their long-term follow-up of first-episode psychosis in Nottingham, UK: "the status of symptoms may have little relevance to everyday social functioning" (p. 602). Schubart et al. (1986), and the linked study of Biehl et al. (1986), examined the course of social disability over the first five years using the WHO Disability Assessment Schedule (WHO-DAS; WHO, 1988). Neither baseline clinical symptoms, nor age or gender, predicted social outcome at five years; only WHODAS scores at six months predicted outcome at one, two, three and five years. Like Strauss and Carpenter, they found that the best predictor of social outcome was an earlier measure of social functioning. Similarly, the "Suffolk County" follow up study of Bromet et al. (1996) followed up 96 people with a first episode of DSM-III-R (1987) schizophrenia and found that the best predictor of functioning at six months was premorbid functioning, although functioning at six months was highly correlated with level of symptomatic remission by this time. Clearly, the onset of psychosis and the level of early remission can act like a "main effect" depressing social functioning, and it may be expected that improving early clinical outcome will enhance early social functioning; however, there are multiple influences on social functioning (e.g. social opportunities and individual psychological reaction to the onset of psychosis). Thus both "naturalistic" and "formal" psychosocial interventions will be essential to restore social functioning and improve quality of life.

The relationship between the "acute" and "treatment resistant" symptoms

What is the nature of the relationship between acute and residual positive symptoms? Only two of the prospective studies took sufficiently frequent and dense follow-up measures to address this question. The pattern of course from the five-year follow-up of Shepherd et al. (1989) in England is presented in Figure 2.1.

Thirty-five per cent of the patients in Shepherd et al.'s sample revealed a pattern of repeated relapse and an increasing incidence of persisting, drug-resistant psychotic symptoms between episodes; a further 35% also had several episodes but no residual symptoms. This finding is consistent with the view that repeated relapse can drive chronicity among a significant proportion of patients, but, of course, a general increase in illness severity may underlie both. The Madras study (Eaton et al., 1995; Thara et al., 1994) only reported whether patients experienced complete or incomplete remissions, although, as with the British study (Shepherd et al., 1989), the researchers found a clear differentiation between those with, and without, residual symptoms following a relapse. After 10 years, only 9% of the Madras sample were recorded as having positive symptoms and this compares, for example, with 40% of the 600 patients followed up after two years in the developed countries in the DOSMD study (Jablensky et al., 1992). This astonishingly low rate of residual symptoms is paralleled by the low rate of relapse; on average, patients experienced only two episodes over the 10-year follow-up period. A recent long-term follow-up study in Holland (Wiersma et al., 1998) finds that after each relapse one in six are left with residual symptoms they did not have before.

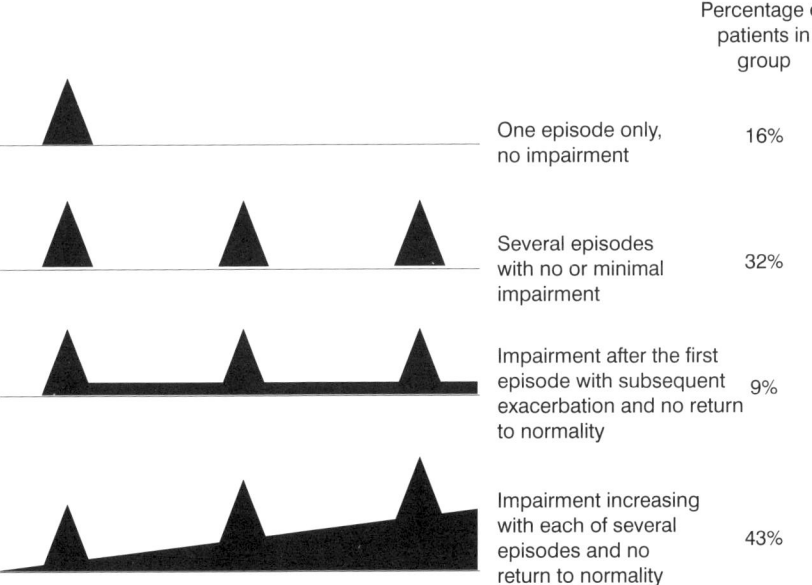

Figure 2.1 Five-year outcome following a first presentation of schizophrenia (adapted from Shepherd et al., 1989).

What can be said with certainty, is that "residual" or treatment-resistant symptoms arise as a result of the resistance of acute psychosis to treatment which may increase with each relapse. Therefore, in considering the management of residual symptoms (whether through pharmacological or cognitive means), I will argue for a focus on improving recovery from the acute episode and relapse prevention (see below).

The "plateau effect"

Bleuler's classic follow-up study (Bleuler, 1978) observed that patients reach a plateau of psychopathology and disability early in the course of illness, which, of course, is contrary to the Kraepelinian (1896/1997) notion of progressive psychopathology. This was neatly illustrated in the report from the Washington cohort of the International Pilot Study of Schizophrenia (Carpenter & Strauss, 1991) which followed up patients two, then 11 years, after the episode of inclusion. Table 2.2 summarises the results for all patients as well as for the subsample who were functioning initially at a lower level on the Level of Functioning Scale (Carpenter & Strauss, 1991). It is apparent that the early deterioration among many of the patients stabilised by two years and fully 75% of the patients showed no change in relapse, social contacts, occupational functioning and residual symptoms between two and 11 years. Indeed, amongst those patients struggling after two years, one-third showed improvement by 11 years, suggesting a relenting of the biosocial process—a notion taken up by Courtney Harding and her colleagues (Harding, Brooks & Ashikaga, 1987) in their Vermont study of chronic "backward" patients released into the community and followed up many years later.

Generally, the prospective first-episode studies have not addressed this "plateau" hypothesis: this requires a truly prospective design with multiple follow-up points. The one exception was the unique investigation conducted by Thara et al. (1994) and Eaton et al. (1995) in the city of Madras, which followed along a cohort of 90 first-episode schizophrenic patients monthly for 10 years; there was very little attrition. They discovered a steep decline in the prevalence of both the positive and negative syndromes during the first year of follow-up and the prevalence of subjects with either positive or negative symptoms stabilised to about 20% to 25% after two years; and as Thara et al. and Eaton et al. indicate, two years has been accepted as the standard threshold for chronicity prior to the era of community mental health care. Thara, Eaton and colleagues found no evidence for an increase in negative symptoms later in the course of the illness, and in fact, once two years had elapsed, the prevalence of negative symptoms was relatively low. There was, however, a small tendency for an increase in

Table 2.2   Two- vs eleven-year outcome in schizophrenia

Variable	Better (%)	Same (%)	Worse (%)
1. All patients			
Hospitalisation	11	89	0
Social Contacts	12	71	18
Employment	12	71	18
Symptoms	9	85	6
2. Patients functioning "poorly" at inclusion			
Hospitalisation	80	20	0
Social Contacts	36	46	18
Employment	36	55	9
Symptoms	21	79	0

the proportion of the cohort with both positive and negative symptoms from some time in the third year, through to the tenth year. There was no evidence for the "substitution" of positive for negative symptoms, and these two groups of symptoms were moderately independent, both cross-sectionally and prospectively, underlining the notion that we should be thinking in terms of groups of symptoms rather than "parcels" of schizophrenic disorder. Eaton et al. (1995) reported that relapses (as defined by hospitalisation) tend to cluster earlier rather than later in the course of illness and proposed a phenomenon of "progressive amelioration").

Harrison et al. (1996) present an analysis of the Nottingham Centre sample of the first-episode schizophrenic cohort which is part of the DOSMD Study (Jablensky et al., 1992; Mason et al., 1995) and bears upon the plateau hypothesis. They examined the relationship between short-term (two years) and long-term (13 years) trajectories of outcome when established predictors were controlled for. The established predictors were summarised in their baseline (onset) model which was developed to maximise prediction at year 2; this included (under ICD-10; WHO, 1992), male gender, less acute onsets, never married, and duration of untreated psychosis (DUP) greater than six months. The addition of information about the two-year course type to the baseline model, substantially increased prediction of outcome at 13 years in terms of social activity and psychopathology, but not hospitalisation or employment. The course type was a binary classification: complete or near complete remission at two years; versus the "continually psychotic", more than one relapse and/or residual personality change, with the latter predicting an unfavourable outcome.

These findings are supported by a flattening of the changes in symptoms and disability in terms of time spent in hospital with psychotic symptoms; and in the time to relapse. These imply that after the first year the proportion of time spent by the cohort in hospital or with symptoms is relatively stable over the follow-up period each year at 4 and 40% respectively. Data on the course of social adjustment are similar. The important finding here is the similarity in the profile of social adjustment between two and 13 years. Neither deterioration nor improvement was apparent: as Mason et al. note, "the course of schizophrenia is most stormy at onset and early in its manifest course, plateauing thereafter" (p. 585).

A similar study was recently reported by Wiersma et al. (1998) following up after 15 years an incidence cohort of 82 ICD-9 patients in a geographically circumscribed area of two provinces in Holland; 77% were recontacted (nine had committed suicide).They also found that where relapse did occur, it did so within five years of onset.

Like Shepherd et al (1989) they find that one in six do not remit fully following a relapse, revealing relapse to be one of the main "drivers" of persisting symptoms; however, they find that the risk of relapse *decreases* from 68% after the first episode to 47% after a fourth.

The Madras and Nottingham studies provide the strongest evidence yet for the concept of the plateauing of psychopathology and disability in the early course of psychosis. This conclusion is supported by less robust data from other Centres, for example, from the Agra Centre of the IPSS (Dube, Kumar & Dube, 1984) and from other follow-up studies (Achte et al., 1986; Huber, Cross & Schuttler, 1980). Collectively, these data support McGlashan's view (McGlashan, 1988) that deterioration, though variable, does occur in the pre-psychotic period and early in the course of psychosis (whether treated and untreated), but this will stabilise between two and five years and may even relent among those who initially deteriorate most.

Early relapse in schizophrenia

The definition of remission and relapse range across the studies. The Scottish Schizophrenia Research Group (1988) defined good outcome as the patient experiencing no readmissions and no positive symptoms or negative symptoms at follow-up. Sixty-one per cent of patients experienced a "good" outcome at one year, with this falling to 37% by two years accompanied by a 47 % rate of readmission. The Northwick Park Study (Johnstone et al., 1986) defined relapse as the development of psychotic features (as described by clinicians or relatives) leading to admission. At the end of two years, only 35% of patients were considered to be relapse free; however, this sample included many patients who had participated in a trial of maintenance neuroleptic medication. Shepherd et al. (1989) found that 22% of their first admission sample had not relapsed after five years (i.e. 78% relapse rate). A study conducted in inner-city Birmingham (Birchwood, Macmillan & Smith, 1992) found a one-year readmission rate of 35%, rising to 50% after the second year. The DOSMD study (Jablensky et al., 1992) reported that in developed countries, an average of 39% of patients experienced only one episode and only mild or no impairment after two years. A one-year follow-up of patients with DSM-III-R (APA, 1987) schizophrenia and other psychoses was conducted in Amsterdam, Holland, by Linszen, Dingemans and Lenior (1994). Using standard ratings and careful operational criteria for relapse, Linszen and colleagues found that in the region of 23% of patients suffered a relapse within one year, in spite of the high degree of medication compliance among the patients. Another study from Holland (Wiersma et al., 1998) found that 43% relapsed in the first year and a further 12% relapse in the second. The Nottingham study (Mason et al., 1995) reports that 63% can expect to relapse within two years.

There are so many predictors of early relapse that were not controlled for in these studies that it makes it difficult to draw a meaningful figure for the "true" one- and two-year relapse rates. At one extreme, we find the Madras study (Thara et al., 1994; Eaton et al., 1995) reporting an average of only two relapses over 10 years, whereas 60% of patients in the Northwick Park study (Johnstone et al., 1986)and Nottingham studies had relapsed within two years.

In view of the interplay of so many prognostic variables and the heterogeneity of the populations studied, it is best to summarise these data in terms of confidence intervals. Though limited, these studies do suggest a one-year relapse rate of between 15 and 35%, with a benchmark figure of 25%, and rising to between 30 and 60% over two years, with a benchmark figure of 45%, rising up to 80% within five years (Robinson et al., 1999). These results derived from the first-episode studies are broadly consistent with the findings of the meta-analysis of long-term follow-up studies of schizophrenia by Hegarty et al. (1994), which concluded that 40.2% of patients with schizophrenia had a favourable outcome. It is worth re-emphasising the point that clinical/symptomatic recovery is not an absolute prerequisite for social recovery; while it would be incorrect to assume orthogonality between these two dimensions, it may be helpful from a clinical point of view to distinguish between them since different kinds of interventions will be required to promote social recovery.

Long-term outcome

The study in Nottingham (Mason et al., 1995) found that, after 13 years, 49% of patients had no or mild symptoms, whilst 55% had good or fair social outcome as measured by the WHODAS (WHO, 1988). Nearly 40% of patients were employed in the two years prior to the 13-year follow-up; however, only 17% of the patients showed complete recovery (this being defined as patients exhibiting no symptoms, no disability and receiving no treatment). These data are consistent with follow-up studies conducted in the United Kingdom over shorter periods of time. The Scottish Schizophrenia Research Group (1988) reported that 46% of their patients had no active symptoms after five years; and Shepherd et al. (1989) reported that 57% of their first admission patients had no or minimal impairment after five years—this result being consistent once again with the plateau effect discussed earlier. Mason et al. (1995) also compared their results with Bleuler's (1978) very long-term outcome data conducted in the pre-neuroleptic era; using Bleuler's original criteria, they found remarkable similarities, with perhaps a marginally better outcome occurring over the shorter follow-up period of the Nottingham study. A 15-year follow-up of a Dutch cohort (Wiersma et al., 1998) reported that 44% had ongoing positive or negative symptoms; conversely 56% had one or more episode with complete remission or problems associated with anxiety/depression (quality of life was not assessed).

Although there are no truly very long-term prospective studies of first-episode psychosis, the available data do seem to support the conclusions of reviews of the outcome literature by Hegarty et al. (1994), McGlashan (1988) and Warner (1994); that is, while complete recovery is relatively rare, up to one-half achieve a favourable clinical and social outcome, with higher figures being reported in some cultures (Eaton et al., 1995). The meta-analysis of Hegarty et al. (1994) emphasises that these figures will differ according to the diagnostic criteria adopted. Thus, the DSM-III-R (APA, 1987) and DSM-IV (APA, 1994) definitions require a minimum of six months of illness (including prodromal or residual symptoms), i.e. they include a built-in chronicity requirement, and find that less than 30% will be substantially improved, whereas using broader criteria such as ICD-10 (WHO, 1992), which requires one month's duration of illness for a diagnosis of schizophrenia), the proportion showing substantial recovery rises to, on average, 46.5%. The circularity inherent in building in a chronicity criterion to a definition has been noted by many other authors (e.g. Warner, 1994) and reflects the influence of Kraepelinian doctrine. The problem from the perspective of this chapter is that with so many factors affecting prognosis, the pathways to chronicity will be many and varied; to define a subgroup within the psychotic spectrum as having a poor outcome and give them a diagnosis, rather assumes some kind of homogeneity of outcome, when in fact the reverse is likely to be the case. This is particularly unhelpful from the point of view of early intervention where the manipulation of prognostic variables early in the course of attention is our focus.

Suicide

Suicide is a tragic but common early outcome of people with schizophrenia but tends to be a neglected feature of outcome studies, often subsumed within attrition statistics (Caldwell & Gottesman, 1990). While exact figures are difficult to establish, the percentage of those with schizophrenia who commit suicide ranges between 8% to 15% (Caldwell & Gottesman, 1990), and risk factors, such as youth, male gender, higher IQ or educational attainment, have been identified (Drake et al., 1985).

Risk factors for suicide were investigated by Westermeyer, Harrow and Marengo (1991) in their study of 586 first-episode and early phase RDC-defined schizophrenic, "other" psychotic and non-psychotic disordered patients. Rates of suicide were 8.8% for schizophrenia, 7.2% for "other" psychosis, and 4% for depression. The predictors of suicide suggested two themes: failed expectations (with predictors including high IQ, good premorbid functioning, and high premorbid attainment), and fear of mental disintegration (with predictors including the presence of early relapse or disability). In view of the findings from the Madras and Nottingham studies that longer-term difficulties will be apparent by two years, it might be expected that by then patients will also have developed an awareness of the constraints and limitations upon their functioning. Thus, Westermeyer, Harrow and Marengo (1991) found that of those who committed suicide, two-thirds had done so by six years following the first episode, leading the authors to label it as a "critical period" of suicide risk. I shall argue later in this chapter, however, that patients' appraisals of the meaning of psychosis and the implications for the self, are active early in the course of psychosis and provide new meaning to the problems of comorbidity, including depression and suicidal thinking.

PREDICTORS OF OUTCOME

Social and family contacts

Low levels of non-family social contacts were associated with early relapse (Johnstone et al., 1990), general poor early outcome (Beiser et al., 1988; Beiser, Iacono & Erickson, 1989) and poor occupational functioning (Johnstone et al., 1992); however, social contact, social competence and features of the illness such as negative symptoms, are difficult to disentangle conceptually. The link between premorbid functioning and outcome suffers a similar problem. Nevertheless, higher educational attainment was linked to delayed relapse in the Northwick Park study

(Geddes et al., 1994). Birchwood et al. (1992) found isolation from family a major risk factor for early (12-month) relapse in an inner city sample in Birmingham, and the patients from Indian backgrounds who stayed with their families revealed a lower rate of relapse/readmission.

High expressed emotion (EE) in close relatives is a robust predictor of relapse (Bebbington & Kuipers, 1994) but its predictive efficacy with first episode patients is weaker (Linszen et al., 1996) or non-existent (Butzlaff & Hooley, 1998; Johnstone et al., 1986; Stirling et al., 1991). Studies of EE in first episode patients (Stirling et al., 1993) support previous assertions (Birchwood, 1992) that EE is not a family "trait", but a much more fluid characteristic. Stirling and colleagues reported a metamorphosis of the components of EE (emotional over-involvement to criticism) during the first 12 months after first treatment, and suggest there are processes at play in the family interior linked to relatives' emotional adaptation to the appearance of psychosis in their offspring.

These data are entirely consistent with these findings suggesting that expressed emotion is a weaker predictor of early relapse in first episode patients compared to those with multiple episodes, and underlines the notion that Expressed Emotion is a protean characteristic at this stage implying the presence of a developmental process. Linszen et al. (1998) found that expressed emotion changes over time in first episodes and that relapse was predicted by those families where expressed emotion *changed* over time, in whatever direction. Understanding the early development of family relationships holds the key to preventing their entrenchment (Birchwood, 1999).

Gender and age at onset

Like many follow-up studies, the first episode studies consistently find that males have a generally poorer outcome (Beiser et al., 1988; Eaton et al., 1995; Geddes et al., 1994; Scottish Schizophrenia Research Group, 1992), and that early age of onset is associated with more severe illness in many studies (e.g. Soni, Tench & Routledge, 1994), although there were some exceptions (Ram et al., 1992).

Depression

The presence of affective symptoms has long been held to be associated with favourable outcome (McGlashan, 1988); however, this finding has recently been challenged. Depression in the context of a non-affective psychosis is common (DeLisi, 1990) with point prevalence figures varying from 17.5% (Mason et al., 1995) to 30% (Harrow et al., 1995). Depression and suicidal thinking is often the cause of crisis and readmission (Shepherd et al., 1989) and has been shown to be predictive of later relapse (Johnson, 1981), and suicide (Roy, 1986). The Northwick Park Study (Johnstone et al., 1986) found that subjective feelings of depression and hopelessness at first admission predicted earlier first readmission; on the other hand, the presence of depressive delusions (i.e. suggestive of an affective psychosis) was associated with better early outcome. The presence of hopelessness has been shown to be a critical factor in suicide prediction (Drake et al., 1985) and it is precisely this variable which has been linked to early relapse in the Northwick Park Study (Johnstone et al., 1986).

Symptoms

The presence of early negative symptoms is predictive of poor early (Beiser et al., 1988; Beiser, Iacono & Erickson, 1989; Scottish Schizophrenia Research Group, 1988) and long-term (Eaton et al., 1995) outcome. For some patients, negative symptoms may represent a proxy variable for a different neurodevelopmental process linked to low genetic risk, soft neurological signs, and male gender (Johnstone et al., 1992; Pilowsky, Kerwin & Murray, 1993).

Depressive delusions were associated with a low rate of early relapse in the Northwick Park Study (Johnstone et al., 1986), whereas depression and hopelessness were linked to a higher rate of early relapse (see above). It might be argued that depressive delusions are indicative of affective psychosis which carries a more benign outcome; hopelessness on the other hand, is indicative of vulnerability to recurrent depression which has been linked to early relapse (Johnson, 1981).

Drug abuse

Potentially half of patients entering psychiatric treatment have significant drug and alcohol histories (Mueser et al., 1990) and the reason for this comorbidity has been the subject of recent concern. The relationships are numerous and complex (Ram et al., 1992); for example: To what extent are substances used to cope with psychotic symptoms?; To what extent does use or abuse precipitate onset in vulnerable individuals and bring forward in time the onset of psychosis?; In what circumstances does a history of abuse, or the quantity, frequency or variability of use, operate as a prognostic sign, whether positive or negative? Both in relation to the issue of onset and of relapse, disentangling cause and effect will be difficult to establish. In relation to the question of onset, the study by Hambrecht and Häfner (1996) reveals a complex picture which will require further clarification. Conversely, a recent study by Linszen, Dingemans and Lenior (1994) has gone some way to help clarify the relationship between relapse and cannabis use during the early course of recent-onset schizophrenia.

This study strongly suggests that use and abuse can significantly affect the timing, if not the probability, of relapse. Only intervention studies would be able to address this issue definitively, although the implications for treatment and care are clear.

Neuroleptic medication

Controlled trials of maintenance neuroleptic medication are rare in first episode psychosis: only three have been reported hitherto. Kane (1983) found that seven of eight patients in a placebo-treated group relapsed at a mean of 18 weeks. This compared to one of eight patients on active maintenance fluphenazine who relapsed at the 25th week. The Scottish Schizophrenia Research Group (1988) found an advantage for active treatment, and good initial response to neuroleptics was a predictor of lower relapse rate. The best controlled study is again the Northwick Park Study (Johnstone et al., 1986) in which 54 first-episode schizophrenic patients were assigned to drug treatment and 66 to placebo under double-blind conditions. The impact of this manipulation was significant, but marginal, compared to trials involving consecutive admissions: 60% of patients on placebo relapsed over two years versus 40% on active medication. The impact of medication was much less than, for example, another variable monitored in this study, the duration of untreated psychotic illness (DUP; see below). A subsequent analysis found that those with a short pre-treatment duration of untreated illness (less than one year) and who received active medication, had a poorer occupational outcome than those who received placebo, suggesting that early neuroleptic use (two years post-first episode) can exact a price in occupational terms. Given that 40% of patients functioned well on placebo over the two years, this finding emphasises the importance of predicting who is likely to relapse (and therefore likely to need medication). It also highlights the need for further research into the use of low-dose medication and complementary methods of relapse prevention. The discontinuation of medication in those with a short duration of illness should be considered together with the use of an "intermittent" or "targeted" medication paradigm in which treatment is provided at the earliest sign of relapse (Birchwood, 1995).

Untreated illness

In spite of the profound and distressing changes that accompany a first-episode of psychosis, it is surprising that the time to first presentation and treatment is highly variable. This issue is considered by Larsen and colleagues in Chapter 6. Considered collectively, a range of studies from North America, Europe and Australia show an average duration of untreated psychosis (DUP), or a treatment lag, of approximately one year in the case of schizophrenia and related psychoses. However, in all of these studies the standard deviation was generally greater than the mean, and where reported, the median was much less than the mean (e.g. mean of 74 weeks compared to a median of 20 weeks in the study by McGorry & Singh, 1995). This suggests a significant effect of outliers with very long durations and one should note that approximately a quarter of the Northwick Park sample had treatment lags in excess of one year. In this study, Johnstone et al. (1986) found that the longer time to presentation was associated with increasing complications of frank psychotic illness, including severe behavioural disturbance and family difficulties (often involving multiple failed attempts to access appropriate care), and life-threatening behaviour (Humphries et al., 1992). These findings underline the fact that individuals were in need of urgent treatment.

Two studies have demonstrated a close link between the DUP and the early course of schizophrenia. Johnstone et al. (1986) found that those patients taking longer than one year to access and exit services revealed a greatly increased (by a factor of 3) relapse rate over the following two years, when compared to those with a briefer DUP. The variable "DUP" emerged as the strongest predictor of relapse, greater than the impact of maintenance medication, which was also manipulated in this study (active versus placebo). Loebel et al. (1992) examined a first-episode sample using a standardised treatment and assessment protocol, and found that both the time to remission, as well as the degree of remission, were closely related to DUP when other prognostic variables were controlled (gender, age at onset, mode of onset, premorbid adjustment). Wyatt (1991) has suggested that delayed initiation of neuroleptics is associated with treatment resistance; thus less complete recovery from the first episode due to delayed presentation could be the result of biological change related to a putative toxic effect of the psychosis which might account for the raised risk of relapse in the Northwick Park Study (Johnstone et al., 1986) and the delayed and less complete remissions in the Loebel et al. study. Vulnerability models have been invoked to help to explain the problem of heterogeneity of outcome in schizophrenia (Zubin & Spring, 1977): I would propose that some of the variance in vulnerability may have its origins in events surrounding the first episode, in particular untreated psychosis. Also, during this period, significant psychosocial decline or stagnation can occur (Jones et al., 1993) and, at this crucial time of educational and vocational development, limits on long-term recovery may be set that some have argued can have long-term prognostic implications (McGlashan, 1988; Warner, 1994).

However, the relationship between DUP and early outcome remains circumstantial. Understanding the reasons for this variable but long duration of untreated illness is crucial in determining the direction of causality and the potential for reducing delay. The Loebel et al. (1992) study found no relationship between DUP and age at onset, mode of onset, premorbid adjustment, or severity of illness. Male gender, however, was associated with longer DUP and also earlier age at onset of illness. Loebel and colleagues comment that families may exhibit a greater tolerance for disturbed behaviour in male adolescents. Perhaps an even more likely explanation is that families have greater difficulty in recognising psychopathology in males and, accordingly, seeking help for them. Among males in particular, longer DUP is linked to a longer prodrome (Loebel et al., 1992). Thus, the transition from poor premorbid state to "at risk mental state", and onto frank psychosis, may be difficult to discern, and may lead to delay in recognition and acceptance of psychopathology. McGorry et al. (1996) found a significant correlation between duration of prodrome and untreated psychosis, thus supporting this possibility. A second factor concerns the pathways to care. A study in Birmingham (Birchwood et al., 1992) reported that longer DUP was documented among those living alone in the inner city (usually African-Carribeans and Whites), compared to those living in a family setting. Patients of South Asian origin were nearly always resident with their family and showed a correspondingly shorter period of untreated illness (14 weeks) than the sample as a whole (30 weeks). This study hypothesised that as the African-Caribbean group were living alone at onset and took a longer time to access services; this increased the likelihood of judicial agencies becoming engaged, compared to the South Asian group who were more likely to access care via GPs. Johnstone et al. (1986), in noting the relationship between long duration of untreated illness and multiple failed attempts to access care though GPs, suggest that one reason for delay may be due to the difficulty of, or lack of training among, GPs in recognizing psychosis. Other reasons might include a reluctance on the part of GPs to refer on in ambiguous cases, or point to "collusion" between the GP and family, driven in turn by the difficulty close relatives may experience in facing up to the possibility that their child is suffering from psychosis. In this respect, the fear and stigma associated with severe mental illness among patients and their supporters should not be underestimated (Perkins & Moodley, 1993).

THE CRITICAL PERIOD CONCEPT: SUMMARY AND EVALUATION

The heterogeneity of psychosis, the concept of stress vulnerability, and the introduction of effective interventions, have together provided the setting conditions for a more optimistic view of the treatment of psychosis. There are parallels here with changes which have occurred in oncology where early detection and intervention are seen as central to effective treatment. For similar changes to occur in psychosis, we require clarity about what we are preventing and how. We introduced the concept of the "critical period" (Birchwood & Macmillan, 1993; Birchwood, McGorry & Jackson, 1997) with this aim in mind. Here, we are proposing something different about this early phase of psychosis which we believe contains important implications for secondary prevention.

There are three propositions essential to the concept of the "critical period":

1. *The course of psychosis is most stormy at the onset and early in its manifest course, plateauing thereafter*

The prospective studies have shown that, for many, there is a rapid period of progression of psychosis prior to, and following, the first presentation. There is a well-documented prodromal period of untreated psychosis of varying duration linked to underachievement in psychosocial domains (Jones et al., 1993). The evidence for the risk of early progression is strong— the risk of relapse, for example, is high within two years, and nearly three-quarters of patients can expect to relapse within five years. Bleuler's early studies, taken together with the recent high-quality prospective studies from Madras and Nottingham, provide compelling evidence that the course type is predictable by year 3 (including on average, the 12 months of DUP), with a stabilisation of the absolute level of morbidity. This fact is probably not lost on those who are affected; suicide risk is particularly high during this early phase, especially following a relapse.

The therapeutic implications of this lies in its clarification of a time scale for early intervention. The first three years of (treated and untreated) illness offers a window of opportunity to prevent, or limit, this potential decline. Intervention efforts after the plateau of morbidity has been reached will face a greater challenge than that implemented at the first episode; however, the extent to which the damage is irreversible following the achievement of the plateau, is of crucial significance and is an interesting research question.

If the therapeutic implications of this are to be realised, then it must first be demonstrated that intervention can change the early course of psychosis, leading to a lower plateau of morbidity and changed course type than would otherwise have been the case. An interesting research question then arises: If the "grip" is then relaxed, will the individual deteriorate to another plateau, or, conversely, will the improvements require relatively little maintenance? This in part will turn on whether the interventions inhibit the development of "toxic" influences which, in their absence, will follow their natural course (e.g. neurobiological changes that are the consequence of relapse) or conversely introduce "healthy" influences which introduce a virtuous circle. There is likely to be a combination of these two processes and again this poses an interesting research question. One study bearing upon this issue is reported by Linszen et al. (1998) in which a family intervention programme was evaluated in first-episode psychosis with the aim of controlling early relapse. Family intervention was compared with an individual intervention which included in both groups neuroleptic treatment, case management and psychoeducation. Family intervention was offered therefore in the context of a high quality of care. The rate of relapse over 15 months was contained in both groups to 16%; however, when these patients left the trial (and the adolescent service programme) and followed up between 17 and 55 months later, the rate of relapse escalated to 64% in both groups. The median survival time (when 50% of the cohort had relapsed) was 19 months. Linszen et al. note that, after the study, all the people were referred to other services and the favourable impact of their intensive programme and the short duration of untreated illness (= five months) disappeared rapidly. The sample were very young (19.0 years) and male (70%) confirming that they are a particularly high-risk group. The "grip" was relaxed early in this group and relapse proliferated. The grip clearly needs to be maintained longer and, according to the authors, the only way to prevent poor outcome in schizophrenia seems to be continuation of medication and case management with the active ingredients of disease management, medication and stress management for a minimum period of five years, a period which approaches the "critical phase" (Birchwood & Macmillan, 1993, Linszen et al., 1998, p. 88).

This impressive study suggests that early outcome can be improved, but the issue of sustaining change is the major challege. The critical period concept argues that at least three years will be needed before even considering "relaxing the grip". McGlashan (1996) argues that interventions in schizophrenia are also effective as long as they are active; however we believe that if sufficient change can be achieved in all dimensions (clinical, social, occupational) then relaxing of the grip may, for some groups, be attempted. This is an important research question which needs to be addressed.

2. *The critical period witnesses the ontogeny of significant variables*

Here we argue that the biological, psychosocial and cognitive changes which are influential in the course of psychosis are not "given" but actively develop during this period. The possibility of a biological toxicity was first raised by Wyatt (1991) and supported by his re-analysis of the first episode study of May et al. (1976). Pre-treatment exposure to psychosis has been suggested by Wyatt as a key factor, but also the incidence of relapse, treatment resistance and episodes of untreated psychosis following the first treatment may also contribute to this theoretical toxicity. The prevention and the minimisation of relapse and the focus on early treatment resistance will be key therapeutic objectives here.

There is evidence that family relationships are also developing during this period. The metamorphosis of components of expressed emotion as we have seen occurs in one direction (EOI to criticism) and suggests the operation of a process consistent with recent concepts that EE should be viewed as a state, not a trait, characteristic. The results of the Amsterdam study (Linszen et al., 1996) failed to find any additional benefits of behavioural family intervention in the context of an individual case management approach. Therapeutically, the content of family intervention may need to change to reflect this flux of family relationships with a key therapeutic objective being the prevention of negative attitudes in the relationships. In this context it is perhaps not surprising that the Amsterdam First Episode Family Intervention study failed to find any additional benefits to standard family intervention when delivered in the context of needs-led case management. In fact, this study demonstrated negative reactions in some families, particularly families characterised as low EE, underlying the operation of a different process; for example, those involving early adjustment patterns centred around loss and mourning (Birchwood, 1999; Linszen et al., 1996).

Although a poorly researched area, there is a developing literature on the psychological adaptation to the onset of psychosis (see Jackson & Birchwood, 1996; Jackson et al., 1996; and Chapter 5 by Elizabeth Kuipers & David Raune discusses these issues at length). We believe that there are early developmental processes here which have implications for the prevention of long-term secondary difficulty, particularly depression and suicide.

There are two broad models of the individual response to psychosis: the trauma and the evaluative models. The trauma model focuses on the role of psychosis and the circumstances of its management as an event, posing threat to the physical and psychological well-being of the individual and its sequelae, e.g. post-traumatic stress (McGorry et al., 1991). Traumatic beliefs (e.g. "the world is not a safe place"; "people cannot be trusted") have been studied in other contexts but their relevance to psychosis has only began to be addressed (Jackson & Birchwood, 1996; Jackson et al., 1996; and Chapter 9 in this volume), although the potential link with social avoidance and withdrawal are apparent.

The evaluative model focuses directly on the beliefs or appraisals of the meaning of psychosis for the individual. One aspect focuses on the meaning of the diagnosis for the individual's identity and concept of self and social position. The second concerns the individual's model of the illness itself; for example, within a health belief framework (Budd, Hughes & Smith, 1996).

We have investigated early developmental changes within the evaluative framework that concern the perceived impact on the patient's social position and identity, and their relationship with depression and suicidal thinking (Birchwood & Iqbal, 1998; Rooke & Birchwood, 1998).Whereas cognitive theory argues that the lowering of self-regard has origins in early development, recent theories based on social ranking and power from ethology (e.g. Price et al., 1994) argue that life events alone may trigger depression if they impact on the individuals social status and role. Such situations are likely to be depressogenic where they are perceived to embody loss (e.g. acceptance of a forced and subordinate role); humiliation (events which undermine the person's rank, attractiveness or status); and entrapment in which the situation prevents the individual from moving forward and achieving desired goals or roles, and thus affirming an identity. Our recent work (Rooke & Birchwood, 1998) has established that depression was linked to evaluation of loss (e.g. "I am capable of little of value as a result of my illness"), humiliation (e.g. "I cannot talk to people about my illness") and entrapment (e.g. "I am powerless to influence or control my illness"). In a recent prospective study involving patients in early psychosis (Birchwood & Iqbal, 1998) it was found that changes, particularly in the appraisal of entrapment, anticipated changes in depressed mood and suicidal thinking in a sample of patients in the early phase of psychosis. The appraisal of entrapment itself changed over time, but was preceded in many instances by a compulsory admission which was seen by the individual to provide "hard evidence" for the perception that they were entrapped by a malignant illness and an omnipotent agency (e.g. psychiatric services). These appraisals were less plastic as time progressed suggesting that they were laid down in this early phase. The "sealing over" strategy (see Chapter 3) measured in the course of this prospective study was linked to both traumatic and evaluative beliefs, particularly the sense of entrapment in a relapsing psychotic illness and the internalisation of the negative social stereotypes of mental illness. Thus, patients attempt to "seal over", because the appraisal of psychosis embodies a challenge to the individuals identity and status which is painful and which patients attempt to suppress through the "sealing" process.

The therapeutic implication is that cognitive therapy should focus on these developing appraisals in the early phase of psychosis which address directly the problems of depression and suicidal thinking. These are discussed by Henry Jackson in Chapter 9, Val Drury in Chapter 8, and by Chris Jackson & Zaffer Iqbal in Chapter 5.

3. *The desynchrony between clinical and social functioning begins in early psychosis*

While symptoms and social functioning are clearly not orthogonal, the prospective studies, including those in early psychosis, emphasise their desynchrony on cross-sectional evaluation. The studies of Biehl et al. (1986) and Schubart et al. (1986) emphasise continuity within each domain, such that the best predictor of social functioning after 5 years is an earlier measure of the same characteristic. From a therapeutic point of view it should not be assumed that improvements in social and community functioning can be "bought" by a focus on symptoms alone. Early intervention may best be conceived as a process involving three domains: symptoms, psychosocial and psychological functioning, each requiring attention independent of the other. The domains of course clearly interact; for example, improvements in vocational functioning may enhance self-esteem and promote social engagement which may reduce vulnerability to relapse.

INTERVENTIONS IN THE CRITICAL PERIOD

The results of the DOSMD study (Jablensky et al., 1992) have confirmed earlier findings that sociocultural influences can affect early outcome for schizophrenia, and the recent follow-up study of first-episode schizophrenia in Madras (Eaton et al.,1995) suggests the apparent early advantage for developing countries is maintained after 10 years. This is consistent with the view that sustained early intervention can affect the long-term trajectory of psychosis. Changing the early course of psychosis will be no easy task as the variables at play are numerous; the critical period hypothesis suggests multi-modal intervention strategies will be essential and need to be sustained over at least two years. These strategies are considered below.

Reducing delay

It has been argued that in excess of one-third of first-episode psychotic patients experience a lengthy period of untreated illness that may have long-term consequences, much of which is, in principle at least, preventable (Birchwood & Macmillan, 1993; Helgason, 1990). Reducing these delays will require a clear understanding of the factors affecting delay; these are considered at length by Larsen and colleagues in Chapter 6.

Relapse prevention

Relapse is one factor that appears to underpin developing treatment resistance and early disability (Shepherd et al., 1989; Wiersma et al., 1998). As we have seen, some 40% are at risk of relapse within two years, rising to 80% within five years (Shepherd et al.,1989). Maintenance medication is of proven prophylactic efficacy (Robinson et al., 1999; Kane, 1989) but placebo-controlled follow-up studies of first episodes of schizophrenia are very rare; the Northwick Park Study (Johnstone et al., 1986) found that 60% of patients on placebo vs 40% on active medication relapsed within two years; thus 40% did not relapse even though they were not on active medication. Therefore, it is important to predict who will do well without, and who will fare badly in spite of maintenance medication. The apparently lower dose of neuroleptic required in the acute treatment study by McEvoy, Hogarty and Steingard (1991), for the subsample of first-episode cases compared to the multiple episode cases of schizophrenia, suggests that "lower" dose maintenance medication may be adequately prophylactic for this group (see Chapter 7, by Paul Bebbington).

This is important in view of the finding in the Northwick Park Study that among those with short pre-treatment psychotic illnesses, better outcome in occupational terms was associated with placebo prescription (Johnstone et al., 1990). Intermittent strategies offer no clear-cut advantage over conventional paradigms (Herz et al., 1991); however, there is evidence that low dose and targeted strategies combined can adequately control relapse, compared to low and standard doses alone (Marder et al., 1987; Marder, 1994). This may prove to be a helpful approach with a substantial proportion of first-episode (drug naive) patients and deserves careful study. Cannabis abuse has also been linked to early relapse in recent onset schizophrenia (Linszen et al., 1994) with clear therapeutic implications.

The early detection of impending relapse presents a further opportunity for relapse prevention since it is now understood that psychotic relapse describes a process with a modal period of 2–4 weeks in which changes in cognition, emotion and perception metamorphose into frank psychotic symptoms (Birchwood, 1995). These early symptoms have been characterised as "prodromal" (importing the biomedical concept) and have led to numerous studies attempting to establish the sensitivity and specificity of "early signs", with some considerable success (Birchwood & Drury, 1995; Jorgensen, 1998). The logical consequence of this model is that intervention informed by the presence of early signs is viewed as a means of "primary" prevention of relapse. Recent thinking has moved towards the view that prodromes are not a discrete stage but are continuous with relapse and best thought of as risk factors for relapse, and there may be several prodromal episodes prior to a full relapse; thus, early identification and intervention may be thought of as a form of secondary prevention (Birchwood, 1995).

We should be thinking, therefore, of reducing the duration and severity of relapse as well as its frequency. After all, as we have seen, the duration of psychotic symptoms is harmful. A second consequence of this model questions the assumption that prodromes are templates against which to compare each patient's mental state. Like relapse itself, the "prodromes" should show between-subject variability, but also within-subject temporal stability. It is for this reason that we introduced the concept of the "relapse signature"—a personalised set of early symptoms which may include core or common symptoms, together with symptoms unique to each patient. If a patient's early relapse signature can be identified, then it may be expected that the predictive power of "prodromal" symptoms may be increased, although it must be recognized that individuals may move into and out of early relapse, but also that the process might be "spontaneously" aborted for psychological, psychosocial or biological reasons (Birchwood, 1995).

With this in mind, the prevention of relapse using "early signs" methodology should be considered as a form of secondary prevention, reducing the severity and frequency of symptoms. The early detection and management of early relapse is considered in Chapter 10 by Elizabeth Spencer, Eleanor Murray and James Plaistow. A recent study by Marder (1994) reports the outcome of a similar strategy in which patients maintained on low doses (5–10 mg every two weeks) of fluphenazine decanoate received active or placebo supplementation depending on the onset of prodromes. A reduction of relapse in the second year was reported, although the specificity of a prodrome for relapse was not high; however, the occurrence of a prodrome was a good marker of a patient at high risk of ultimate exacerbation, this being consistent with the concept of the prodrome as an "at risk mental state" (Yung et al., 1996).

Family intervention is a further option for relapse prevention (Kavanagh, 1992), although the predictive efficacy of high expressed emotion among first episode patients is somewhat weaker (Birchwood, 1999) possibly because harmful, stressful relationships may take some time to evolve (Stirling et al., 1991) and may account for a failure of family intervention to control early relapse (Linszen et al., 1996). The development of a strategy to prevent the development of harmful criticism and hostility is indicated—one which will require a clear understanding of the genesis and early development of expressed emotion (Birchwood, 1999). The issues are considered in more detail in Chapters 5 and 11.

Cognitive therapy in the early psychological adjustment to psychotic illness

As we have seen, the psychological well-being of individuals following the first diagnosis of schizophrenia is not a well-researched topic, yet there is considerable evidence that the problems of early adjustment can have serious consequences. Suicide is one such consequence, and is by no means usually a direct consequence of psychotic thinking (Caldwell & Gottesman, 1990). Risk factors such as awareness of the deteriorative effects of illness in the context of good premorbid adjustment (Cotton, Drake & Gates, 1985), and fear of mental deterioration (Drake et al., 1985), are well established. Chronic depression arising out of the acute episode (Johnson, 1981) has similar correlates, including hopelessness, perceived loss of control over illness, and the absorption of the negative stereotypes of mental illness (Birchwood et al., 1993). Short-term traumatic reactions to acute, particularly first-psychotic episodes, have been documented during the recovery phase, including depression (McGlashan & Carpenter, 1976) and post-traumatic stress disorder (McGorry et al., 1991); both of which have links to the experience of illness and the circumstances of its management (see Chapters 3 and 9 in this volume). Poor premorbid psychological and social adjustment are well documented in schizophrenia, and the developing concept of self and identity are likely early casualties. Adjusting to the onset of psychosis will require cognisance of personal developmental stage in addition to specific issues of adjustment to psychosis (e.g. trauma, loss, fear of relapse, etc.).

Denial of illness is a frequently used defensive manoeuvre that has its own costs (e.g. drug non-adherence); acceptance of illness, on the other hand, can lead to pessimism and loss of self-efficacy (Birchwood et al., 1993; Warner et al., 1989). What kind of adjustment should be the aim? We have argued that a central feature should be the blame-free acceptance of illness, together with the encouragement of a sense of mastery over illness through education and inculcating strategies of control (see Birchwood & Tarrier, 1994). Facing up to the reality of the disorder, yet at the same time avoiding "engulfment" in the chronic patient role, will require more than the provision of information and skills; an ongoing supportive therapeutic relationship will be needed to assist the client's passage into psychological well-being (Frank & Gunderson, 1990).

These are some very specific implications for cognitive therapy arising from the evaluative model discussed earlier in the prevention and management of depression, hopelessness and suicidal thinking. In summary, empirical and theoretical work has confirmed the relationship between the symptoms of depression/hopelessness/suicidal ideation, and the cognitive appraisals of self and psychosis (loss, humiliation and entrapment), self and symptoms (e.g. the power and malevolence of voices), and the implications for self-evaluation (failure, worthlessness). Cognitive therapy is ideally suited to focus on these appraisals (Chadwick, Birchwood & Trower, 1996); for example, interventions have been developed which enhance control over psychotic relapse (Birchwood, 1995); change the appraisals of the power and authority of voices (Birchwood & Chadwick, 1997); and change patients' beliefs about the self and psychosis in the course of recovery from acute psychosis (Drury et al., 1996)—all of which impact on depression. Our experience of implementing cognitive therapy in acute psychosis has suggested that appraisals of self and psychosis are more accessible during the acute crisis (Birchwood & Drury, 1995) and should start during this period.

The theme of the cognitive therapy should therefore, embrace a focus on key appraisals of self and psychosis, aiming to challenge and put them to the empirical test. These appraisals include: entrapment in psychotic illness (beliefs about psychosis as a malignant and uncontrollable illness, and beliefs about the power and malevolence of auditory hallucinations), loss and humiliation (belief that the individual has lost all valued goals and roles, and is capable of little of value and is devalued by others), causal attribution (a belief that psychosis arises as a result of a defect of the self or personality), and self-evaluative beliefs, particularly regarding worthlessness and failure. The entrapment belief may be addressed in two ways. First, by working with individuals to improve methods of detecting and controlling early signs of relapse (Birchwood, 1995) in the context of psychoeducation about psychosis as an external stressor that can be brought under an individual's control, individuals are debriefed about the events leading up to the onset of psychosis, and helped to identify possible triggers (see Chapter 00). Second, key beliefs about the power of voices should be challenged and tested (Chadwick & Birchwood, 1994), including related persecutory beliefs. Negative self-evaluation can be addressed in two ways. First, individual sessions can be conducted using cognitive therapy to challenge negative self-evaluations together with goal setting in valued interpersonal and achievement domains. Second, a group intervention can be conducted such as the one employed in a trial of cognitive therapy for acute psychotic symptoms (Drury et al., 1996). This included those elements unique to the individual to rebut any challenge to the individual's social status (see Chapter 8).

Early social recovery

Prior to the first treatment, prodromal changes can impact heavily on interpersonal and vocational relationships (Jones et al., 1993) and cause damage to, and shrinkage of, the social network for many young people (Hirschenberg, 1985). Social isolation is a known prognostic factor in psychosis (Jablensky et al., 1992) and "tracks" long-term outcome (McGlashan, 1988). While there are few guidelines for developing interventions in this area (Jackson & Edwards, 1992), community-oriented care involving assertive outreach, can improve the quality and quantity of the social network (Thornicroft & Breakey, 1991). Returning to, or establishing a work pattern, can become increasingly difficult with the passage of time without work; and the diagnosis of schizophrenia makes such a prospect doubly difficult (Warner, 1994). Normal pathways to employment can be frightening and overwhelming for people with psychosis and may require specific cooperation between health, social services and employment agencies, in order to facilitate the pathway and to guard against relapse.

Managing early treatment resistance

After five years, up to 50% of patients will experience residual, treatment-resistant symptoms (Shepherd et al., 1989; Wiersma, 1998). These have long-term prognostic implications; for example, a recent long-term follow-up study by Harrow et al. (1995) found that where "delusions are found in a schizophrenic patient after the acute phase they are likely to recur or persist over the next 2 to 8 years" (p. 102).

The long-term first-episode follow-up studies reviewed earlier, show that long-term treatment resistance has its origins in the critical period; thus efforts to focus directly early treatment resistance will be repaid over the long term. Clozapine is used increasingly with treatment-resistant symptoms of a more protracted nature and may find useful application earlier than is usually considered. Cognitive therapy is another option.

Cognitive therapy, which has been widely employed in the treatment of neurotic disorders, has found recent application and early success with psychotic symptoms (Chadwick, Birchwood & Trower, 1996; Garety, Kuipers & Fouler, 1994; Kingdon & Turkington, 1994). The approach involves the direct engagement of the delusional beliefs (including delusions about voices), and examining the inferences and evaluations patients make about situations (e.g. voice activity) that are linked to delusional thinking by, using challenging evidence for beliefs and empirical tests (see Chapters 4 and 8).

For reasons outlined above, our approach to treatment resistance has focused on the acute psychotic episode as the origin of residual symptoms or treatment resistance. We believe that this is the most appropriate setting to implement CT and hypothesise that delusional thinking is encapsulated by a need to reject otherwise stigmatising labels and eth-nosemantic constructs of madness which, because of fragile self-esteem, individuals are unable to resist (Birchwood & Drury, 1995). Furthermore, in the acute phase we believe that the individual is psychologically more accessible and defences more permeable.

CONCLUSION: WHY EARLY INTERVENTION?

The early phase of psychosis as a critical period embodies both ethical and practical implications for the management of psychosis. The follow-up studies show that "the course of schizophrenia is more stormy at the onset and early in its manifest course, plateauing thereafter" (Mason et al., 1995, p. 585); this challenges the conventional view that first-episode psychosis is benign and relatively uneventful and deserves more not less attention. The dictum that says "lets wait and see" how the individual fares must surely now be abandoned. This group of young people have not received the attention and resources they so patently deserve. The *practical* implica-tions of the critical period hypothesis are the opportunities it presents for secondary prevention to limit or prevent difficulty and distress: relapse, the cycle of coercive management, suicide, unemployment and social exclusion are key targets.

Interventions that can alter the trajectory of psychosis are at hand, and in my view improving early outcome should not be too difficult. *Sustaining* change however is the main challenge. Relaxing the grip too early, as Don Linszen suggested in the Amsterdam study, may lead to a proliferation of relapse; the critical period concept suggests that three years is the minimum period necessary to sustain change before the grip, can, if at all, be relaxed. Many of the chapters in this book present in detail the interventions and service structures that are essential to promote and maintain a better outlook.

REFERENCES

Achte, K., Lonnqvist, J., Juusi, K. Piirtola, O. & Niskanen, P. (1986). Outcome stud-ies on schizophrenic psychoses in Helsinki. *Psychopathology*, **19**, 60–67.

APA (1987). *Diagnostic and Statistical Manual*, 3rd edn, revised. Washington, D.C.: American Psychiatric Association.

APA (1994). *Diagnostic and Statistical Manual*, 4th edn. Washington, D.C.: American Psychiatric Association.

Bebbington, P. & Kuipers, L. (1994). The predictive utility of expressed emotion in schizophrenia: An aggregate analysis. *Psychological Medicine*, **24**, 707–718.

Beiser, M., Erickson, D., Fleming, J.A.E. & Iacono, W.G. (1993). Establishing the onset of psychotic illness. *American Journal of Psychiatry*, **150**, 1349–1354.

Beiser, M., Fleming, J.A.E., Iacono, W.G. & Lin, T. (1988). Refining the diagnosis of schizophreniform disorder. *American Journal of Psychiatry*, **145**, 695–700.

Beiser, M., Iacono, W.G. & Erickson, D. (1989). Temporal stability in major mental disorders. In L.N. Robins & J.E. Barrett (Eds), *The Validity of Psychiatric Diagnosis*, (pp. 77–98). New York: Raven Press.

Biehl, H., Maurer, K., Schubart, C., Krumm, B. & Jung, E. (1986). Prediction of outcome and utilisation of medical services in a prospective study of first onset schizophrenics: Results of a prospective five-year follow-up study. *European Archives of Psychiatry and Neurological Sciences*, **236**, 139–147.

Birchwood, M. (1992). Family factors in psychiatry. *Current Opinion in Psychiatry*, 5, 295–299.

Birchwood, M. (1995). Early intervention in psychotic relapse: cognitive approaches to detection and management. *Behaviour Change*, **12**, 2–19.

Birchwood, M. (1999) Psychological and social treatments: course and outcome. *Current Opinion in Psychiatry*, **12**, 61–66.

Birchwood, M., Hallett, S. & Preston, M. (1988). *Schizophrenia: An Integrated Approach to Research and Treatment*. Harlow: Longman.

Birchwood, M., Cochrane, R., Macmillan, F., Kucharska, J. & Cariss, M. (1992). The influence of ethnicity and family structure on relapse in first episode schizophrenia: a comparison of Asian, Caribbean and White patients. *British Journal of Psychiatry*, **161**, 783–790.

Birchwood, M., Macmillan, F. & Smith, J. (1992). Early intervention. In M. Birchwood & N. Tarrier (Eds), *Innovations in the Psychological Management of Schizophrenia* (pp. 115–146). Chichester: Wiley.

Birchwood, M. & Macmillan, F. (1993). Early intervention in schizophrenia. *Australian and New Zealand Journal of Psychiatry*, **27**, 374–378.

Birchwood, M., Mason, R., Macmillan, F. & Healy, J. (1993). Depression, demoralisation and control over psychotic illness. *Psychological Medicine*, **23**, 387–395.

Birchwood, M. & Tarrier, N. (1994). *The Psychological Management of Schizophrenia*. Chichester: Wiley.

Birchwood, M. & Drury, V. (1995). Using the crisis. In M. Phelan, G. Strathdee & G. Thornicroft (Eds), *Emergency Mental Health Services in the Community*, (pp. 116–148). Cambridge: Cambridge University Press.

Birchwood, M. & Chadwick, P. (1997) The omnipotence of voices: testing the validity of a cognitive model. *Psychological Medicine*, **27**, 1345–1353.

Birchwood, M. & Iqbal, Z. (1998). Depression and suicidal thinking in psychosis: a cognitive approach in outcome and innovation. In T. Wykes, N. Tarrier & S. Lewis (Eds), psychological treatment of schizophrenia. Chichester: Wiley.

Birchwood, M., McGorry, P. & Jackson, H. (1997). Early intervention in schizophrenia (Editorial). *British Journal of Psychiatry*, **170**, 2–5.

Bleuler, M. (1978). *The Schizophrenic Disorders: Long Term Patient and Family Studies* (S. Clements, translator). New Haven: Yale University Press.

Bromet, E.J., Jandorf, L., Fennig, S., Lavelle, J., Kovasznay, B., Ram, R., Tanenberg-Karant, M. & Craig, T. (1996). The Suffolk County Mental Health Project: demographic, premorbid and clinical correlates of 6-month outcome. *Psychological Medicine*, **26**, 953–962.

Budd, R.J., Hughes, I.C.T. & Smith, J.A. (1996). Health beliefs and compliance with antipsychotic medication. *British Journal of Clinical Psychology*, **35**, 393–397.

Butzlaff, R. & Hooley, J. (1998). Expressed emotion and psychiatric relapse: a meta analysis. *Archives General Psychiatry*, **55**, 547–552.

Caldwell, J. & Gottesman, I. (1990). Schizophrenics kill themselves too. *Schizophrenia Bulletin*, **16**, 571–590.

Carpenter, W. & Strauss, J. (1991). The prediction of outcome in schizophrenia. V: Eleven year follow-up of the IPSS cohort. *Journal of Nervous and Mental Disease*, **179**, 517–525.

Chadwick, P. & Birchwood, M. (1994). Challenging the omnipotence of voices: a cognitive approach to auditory hallucinations. *British Journal of Psychiatry*, **164**, 190–201.

Chadwick, P. & Birchwood, M. (1995). A cognitive approach to auditory hallucinations. In G. Haddock & P. Slade, (Eds), *Cognitive-Behavioural Interventions in Psychosis*, (pp. 71–85). London: Routledge.

Chadwick, P., Birchwood, M. & Trower, P. (1996). *Cognitive Therapy for Hallucinations, Delusions and Paranoia*. Chichester: Wiley.

Cotton, P., Drake, R. & Gates, C. (1985). Critical treatment issues in schizophrenics. *Hospital and Community Psychiatry*, **36**, 534–536.

DeLisi, L. (1990). *Depression in Schizophrenia*. Washington, D.C.: American Psychiatric Press.

Drake, R., Gates, C., Cotton, P. & Whittaker, A. (1985). Suicide among schizophrenics: Who is at risk? *Journal of Nervous and Mental Disease*, **172**, 613–617.

Drury, V. (1994). Recovery from acute psychosis. In M. Birchwood & N. Tarrier (Eds), *Psychological Management of Schizophrenia*, (pp. 23–51). Chichester: Wiley.

Drury, V., Birchwood, M., Cochrane, R. & Macmillan, F. (1996). Cognitive therapy and recovery from acute psychosis: a controlled trial. *British Journal of Psychiatry*, **169**, 593–601.

Dube, K., Kumar, N. & Dube, S. (1984). Long-term course and outcome of the Agra cases in the International Pilot Study of Schizophrenia. *Acta Psychiatrica Scandinavica*, **170**, 170–179.

Eaton, W., Thara, R., Federman, B., Melton, B. & Liang, K.-Y. (1995).Structure and course of positive and negative symptoms in schizophrenia. *Archives of General Psychiatry*, **52**, 127–134.

Frank, A. & Gunderson, J. (1990). The role of the therapeutic alliance in the treatment of schizophrenia: relationship to course and outcome. *Archives of General Psychiatry*, **47**, 228–236.

Garety, P., Kuipers, L. & Fowler, D. (1994). Cognitive behavioural therapy for drug-resistant psychosis. *British Journal of Medical Psychology*, **67**, 259–271.

Geddes, J.R., Black, R.J., Whalley, L.J. & Eagles, J.M. (1994). Persistence of the decline in the diagnosis among first admissions to Scottish Hospitals from 1969–1988. *British Journal of Psychiatry*, **163**, 620–626.

Hambrecht, M. & Häfner, H. (1996). Substance abuse and the onset of schizophrenia. *Biological Psychiatry*, **40**, 1155–1163.

Harding, C.M., Brooks, G.W. & Ashikaga, T. (1987). The Vermont longitudinal study of persons with severe mental illness. II: Long-term outcome of subjects who retrospectively met DSM-III criteria for schizophrenia. *American Journal of Psychiatry*, **144**, 727–735.

Harrison, G., Croudace, T., Mason, P., Glazebrook, C. & Medley, I. (1996). Predicting the long-term outcome of schizophrenia. *Psychological Medicine*, **26**, 697–705.

Harrow, M., MacDonald, A.W., Sands, J.R. & Silverstein, M.L. (1995). Vulnerability to delusions over time in schizophrenia and affective disorders. *Schizophrenia Bulletin*, **21**, 95–109.

Hegarty, J.D., Baldessarini, R.J., Tohen, M., Waternaux, C. & Oepen, G.(1994). One hundred years of schizophrenia: a meta-analysis of the outcome literature. *American Journal of Psychiatry*, **15**, 1409–1416.

Helgason, L. (1990). Twenty years follow-up of first psychiatric prevention for schizophrenia: What could have been prevented? *Acta Psychiatrica Scandinavica*, **81**, 231–235.

Herz, M., Glazer, W., Mostert, M., Sheard, M., Szymanski, H., Hafez, H., Mirza, M. & Vana, J. (1991). Intermittent vs maintenance medication in schizophrenia. *Archives of General Psychiatry*, **48**, 333–337.

Hirschenberg, W. (1985). Social isolation among schizophrenic out-patients. *Social Psychiatry*, **20**, 171–178.

Huber, G., Cross, G. & Schuttler, R. (1980). Longitudinal studies of schizophrenic patients. *Schizophrenia Bulletin*, **6**, 592–595.

Humphries, M., Johnstone, E., Macmillan, J. & Taylor, P. (1992). Dangerous behaviour preceding first admissions for schizophrenia. *British Journal of Psychiatry*, **161**, 501–505.

Jablensky, A., Sartorious, N., Emberg, G., Anker, M., Korten, A., Cooper, J. & Bertelson, A. (1992). Schizophrenia: manifestations, incidence and course in different cultures. A World Health Organisation Ten Country Study. *Psychological Medicine*, Monograph Supplement 20.

Jackson, C. & Birchwood, M. (1996) Early intervention in psychosis: Opportunities for secondary prevention. *British Journal of Clinical Psychology*, **35**, 487–502.

Jackson, H.J. & Edwards, J. (1992). Social networks and social support in schizophrenia. In D. Kavanagh (Ed.), *Schizophrenia: An Overview and Practical Handbook*, (pp. 275–292). London: Chapman & Hall.

Jackson, H.J., McGorry, P. D., Edwards, J. & Hulbert, C. (1996). Cognitively oriented psychotherapy for early psychosis (COPE). In P. Cotton & H. Jackson (Eds), *Early Intervention and Prevention in Mental Health*, (pp.131–154). Melbourne: Australian Psychological Society.

Johnson, D. (1981). Studies of depressive symptoms in schizophrenia. *British Journal of Psychiatry*, **139**, 89–101.

Johnstone, E.C., Crow, T.J., Johnson, A.L. & Macmillan, J.F. (1986). The Northwick Park Study of first episode schizophrenia: I. Presentation of the illness and problems relating to admission. *British Journal of Psychiatry*, **148**, 115–120.

Johnstone, E.C., Macmillan, J.F., Frith, C.D., Benn, D.K. & Crow, T.J. (1990). Further investigation of the predictors of outcome following first schizophrenic episodes. British *Journal of Psychiatry*, **157**, 182–189.

Johnstone, E., Frith, C., Crow, T., Owen, D., Done, D., Baldwin, E. & Charlette, A. (1992). The Northwick Park Functional Psychosis Study: diagnosis and outcome. *Psychological Medicine*, 22, 331–346.

Jones, P.B., Bebbington, P., Foerster, A., Lewis, S.W., Murray, R.M., Russell, A., Sham, P.C., Tone, B.K. & Wilkins, S. (1993). Premorbid social underachievement in schizophrenia: results from the Camberwell Collaborative Psychosis Study. *British Journal of Psychiatry*, **162**, 65–71.

Jorgensen, P (1998). Early signs of psychotic relapse in schizophrenia. *British Journal of Psychiatry*, **172**: 327–330.

Kane, J.M. (1983). Low dosage medication strategies in the maintenance treatment of schizophrenia. *Schizophrenia Bulletin*, **9**, 528–531.

Kane, J.M. (1989). The current status of neuroleptics. *Journal of Clinical Psychiatry*, **50**, 322–328.

Kavanagh, D. (1992). Recent developments in expressed emotion and schizophrenia. *British Journal of Psychiatry*, **160**, 601–620.

Kingdon, D.G. & Turkington, D. (1994). *Cognitive-Behavioural Therapy of Schizophrenia*. Brighton: Erlbaum.

Kraepelin, E. (1896/1997). Dementia Praecox. In J. Cutting & M. Shepherd (Eds), *The Clinical Roots of the Schizophrenia Concept* (pp. 13–24). Cambridge: Cambridge University Press.

Linszen, D., Dingemans, P., Van der Does, J., Nugter, A., Scholte, P., Lenior, R. & Goldstein, M.J. (1996). Treatment, expressed emotion and relapse in recent onset schizophrenia. *Psychological Medicine*, **26**, 333–342.

Linszen, D., Dingemans, P. & Lenior, M. (1994). Cannabis abuse and the course of schizophrenic disorders. *Archives of General Psychiatry*, **51**, 73–79.

Linszen, D., Lenior, M., De Haan, L., Dingemans, P. & Gersons, B. (1998) Early intervention, untreated psychosis and the course of early schizophrenia. *British Journal of Psychiatry*, **172** (supp.), 84–89.

Loebel, A.D., Lieberman, J.A., Alvir, J.M.J., Mayerhoff, D.I., Geisler, S.H. & Szymanski, S.R. (1992). Duration of psychosis and outcome in first episode schizophrenia. *American Journal of Psychiatry*, **149**, 1183–1188.

Marder, S., Van Putten, T., Mintz, J., McKenzie, J., Labell, M., Faltico, G. & May, R. (1987). Low and conventional dose maintenance therapy with fluphenazine decanoate. *Archives of General Psychiatry*, **44**, 518–521.

Marder, S.R. (1994). Fluphenazine vs placebo supplementation for prodromal signs of relapse in schizophrenia. *Archives of General Psychiatry*, **51**, 280–287.

Mason, P., Harrison, G., Glazebrook, C., Medley, I., Dalkin, T. & Croudace, T. (1995). Characteristics of outcome in schizophrenia at 13 years. *British Journal of Psychiatry*, **167**, 596–603.

May, P.R., Tuma, A.H. & Dixon, W.J. (1976). Schizophrenia: A follow-up study of results of treatment methods. *Archives General Psychiatry*, **33**, 474–478.

McEvoy, J.P., Hogarty, G.E. & Steingard, S. (1991). Optimal dose of neuroleptic in acute schizophrenia. *Archives of General Psychiatry*, **48**, 739–745.

McGlashan, T. (1988). A selective review of North American long-term followup studies of schizophrenia. *Schizophrenia Bulletin*, **14**, 515–542.

McGlashan, T.H. (1996). Early detection and intervention in schizophrenia: Editors introduction. *Schizophrenia Bulletin*, **22**, 197–199.

McGlashan, T. & Carpenter, W. (1976). Post-psychotic depression in schizophrenia. *Archives of General Psychiatry*, **33**, 231–239.

McGorry, P.D. (1992). The concept of recovery and seondary prevention in psychotic disorders. *Australia and New Zealand Journal of Psychiatry*, **26**, 3–18.

McGorry, P.D., Chanen, A., McCarthy, E., Van Riel, R., McKenzie, D. & Singh, B. (1991). Post-traumatic stress disorder following recent onset psychosis. An unrecognised postpsychotic syndrome. *Journal of Nervous and Mental Disease*, **179**, 253–258.

McGorry, P. Edwards, J., Mihalopoulos, C., Harrigan, S.M. & Jackson, H.J. (1996). EPPIC: An evolving system of early detection and optimal management. *Schizophrenia Bulletin*, **22**, 305–326.

McGorry, P. & Singh, B. (1995). Schizophrenia: risk and possiblility. In B. Raphael & G.D. Burrows (Eds), *Handbook of Studies on Preventative Psychiatry*, (pp. 491–514). Amsterdam, The Netherlands: Elsevier Science.

Mueser, K.T., Bellack, A.S., Morrison, R.L. & Wade, J.H. (1990). Gender, social competence, and symptomatology in schizophrenia: a longitudinal analysis. *Journal of Abnormal Psychology*, **9**, 138–147.

Perkins, R.E. & Moodley, P. (1993). The arrogance of insight. *Bulletin of the Royal College of Psychiatrists*, **17**, 233–234.

Pilowsky, L.S., Kerwin, R.W. & Murray, R.M. (1993). Schizophrenia: a neurodevelopmental perspective. *Neuropsychopharmacology*, **9**, 83–91.

Price, J., Sloman, L., Gardner, R., Gilbert, P. & Rohde, P. (1994). The social competition hypothesis of depression. *British Journal of Psychiatry*, **164**, 309–315.

Ram, R., Bromet, E.J., Eaton, W.W., Pato, C. & Schwartz, J.E. (1992). The natural course of schizophrenia: a review of first-admission studies. *Schizophrenia Bulletin*, **18**, 185–207.

Robinson, D., Noerner, M., Alvir, J., Bilder, R. et al. (1999). Predictors of relapse following response from a first episode of schizophrenia. *Archives of General Psychiatry*, **56**, 241–247.

Rooke, O. & Birchwood, M. (1998). Loss, humiliation and entrapment as appraisals schizophrenic illness: a prospective study of depressed and non-depressed patients. *British Journal of Clinical Psychology*, **37**, 259–268.

Roy, A. (1986). Suicide in schizophrenia. In A. Roy (Ed.), *Suicide*, (pp. 128–147). Baltimore: Williams & Wilkins.

Schooler, N.R. (1994). Deficit symptoms in schizophrenia: negative symptoms versus neuroleptic-induced deficits. *Acta Psychiatrica Scandinavica*, **380** (Suppl.), 21–26.

Schubart, C., Krumm, B., Biehl, H. & Schwartz, R. (1986). Measure of social disability in a schizophrenic patient group: definition, assessment and outcome over 2 years in schizophrenic patients of recent onset. *Social Psychiatry*, **21**, 1–9.

Scottish Schizophrenia Research Group. (1988). The Scottish First Episode Schizophrenia Study. V: One year follow-up. *British Journal of Psychiatry*, **152**, 470–476.

Scottish Schizophrenia Research Group. (1992). The Scottish First Episode Schizophrenia Study: VIII: Five year follow-up: Clinical and psychosocial findings. *British Journal of Psychiatry*, **161**, 496–500.

Shepherd, M., Watt, D., Falloon, I. & Smeeton, N. (1989). The natural history of schizophrenia: a five-year follow-up in a representative sample of schizophrenics. *Psychological Medicine*, Monograph Supplement 15.

Soni, S.D., Tench, D. & Routledge, R.C. (1994). Serum abnormalities in neuroleptic-induced akathisia. *British Journal of Psychiatry*, **165**, 669–672.

Stephens, J.H. (1978). Long-term prognosis and follow-up in schizophrenia. *Schizophrenia Bulletin*, **4**, 25–47.

Stirling, J., Tantum, D., Thonks, P., Newby, D. & Montague, L. (1991). Expressed emotion and early onset schizophrenia. *Psychological Medicine*, **21**, 675–685.

Stirling, J., Tantam, D., Newby, D., Montague, L., Ring, N. & Rowe, S. (1993). Expressed emotion and schizophrenia: The ontogeny of EE during an 18 month follow-up. *Psychological Medicine*, **23**, 771–778.

Strauss, J. & Carpenter, W.T. (1977). Prediction of outcome in schizophrenia. III: Five year outcome and its predictors. *Archives of General Psychiatry*, **34**, 159–163.

Thara, R., Henrietta, M., Joseph, A., Rajkumar, S. & Eaton, W. (1994). Ten-year course of schizophrenia—the Madras longitudinal study. *Acta Psychiatrica Scandinavica*, **90**, 329–336.

Thornicroft, G. & Breakey, W. (1991). The COSTAR Programme. 1: Improving social networks of the long-term mentally ill. *British Journal of Psychiatry*, **159**, 245–259.

Tien, A.Y. & Eaton, W.W. (1992). Psychopathological precursors and sociodemographic risk factors for the schizophrenic syndrome. *Archives of General Psychiatry*, **49**, 37–46.

Waddington, J.L., Youssef, H.A. & Kinsella, A. (1995). Sequential cross-sectional and 10-year prospective study of severe negative symptoms in relation to duration of intitially untreated psychosis in chronic schizophrenia. *Psychological Medicine*, **25**, 849–857.

Warner, R., Taylor, D., Powers, M. & Hyman, J. (1989). Acceptance of the mental illness label by psychotic patients: effects on functioning. *American Journal of Orthopsychiatry*, **59**, 398–409.

Warner, R. (1994). *Recovery from Schizophrenia: Psychiatric and Political Economy* (second edition). London: Routledge.

Westermeyer, J.F., Harrow, M. & Marengo, J.T. (1991). Risk for suicide in schizophrenia and other psychotic and non-psychotic disorders. *Journal of Nervous and Mental Disease*, 179, 259–266.

WHO (1988). *Psychiatric Disability Assessment Schedule*. Geneva: World Health Organisation.

WHO (1992). *Manual of the International Classification of Diseases, Injuries and Causes of Death*, 10th Revision. Geneva: World Health Organisation.

Wiersma, D., Nienhaus, F.J., Sloof, C. & Giel, R. (1998). Natural course of schizophrenic disorders: A 15 year follow-up of a Dutch incidence Cohort. *Schizophrenia Bulletin*, 24, 78–85.

Wing, J.K. (1966). Five year outcome in early schizophrenia. *Proceedings of the Royal Society of Medicine*, 59, 17–18.

Wyatt, R.J. (1991). Neuroleptics and the natural course of schizophrenia. *Schizophrenia Bulletin*, 17, 325–351.

Yung, A., McGorry, P., McFarlane, C.A., Jackson, H.J., Patton, G.C. & Rakkar, A. (1996). The prodromal phase of first episode psychosis: past and current conceptualisations. *Schizophrenia Bulletin*, 22, 283–303.

Zubin, J. & Spring, B. (1977). Vulnerability: A new view of schizophrenia. *Journal of Abnormal Psychology*, 86, 103–126.

Chapter 3

PSYCHOLOGICAL ADJUSTMENT TO EARLY PSYCHOSIS

Chris Jackson* and Zaffer Iqbal†

The end of the beginning of the individual's journey through psychotic illness occurs during the period of time following a first episode which is now known to be critical and formative (Birchwood, Todd & Jackson, 1998). The individual's psychological adjustment and adaptation during the early years of psychosis appears to be important but remains poorly understood (Jackson & Birchwood, 1996) and has attracted relatively little interest from clinicians and researchers.

Psychological adaptation and adjustment to the first episode may have implications beyond the active phase of psychosis. For instance, adherence with medical and psychosocial treatments, which can be viewed as a form of coping behaviour in its own right (Leventhal, Meyer & Nerenz, 1980) may have a powerful influence upon outcome (Bebbington, 1995). Such adherence and engagement are likely to be influenced by a wide variety of clinical and psychological factors (Buchanan, 1996a) tied up with the adjustment process.

Although we understand little about early adaptation to psychosis, we do know that it can be a very difficult and painful period (Jackson & Farmer, 1998): trauma (McGorry et al., 1991), depression (Koreen et al., 1993) and suicide (Caldwell & Gottesman, 1990) are very common in the early period of recovery. Social withdrawal and isolation may begin and significantly worsen during the first two years as social networks shrink (Erickson, Beiser & Iacono, 1999) and are not replaced (Jackson & Edwards, 1992). Drug and alcohol abuse may also have their origins in this early phase (Kovaszany et al., 1997). In this chapter we examine the

*University of Birmingham, UK. †Institute of Psychiatry, London, UK.

Early Intervention in Psychosis.
Edited by M. Birchwood, D. Fowler & C. Jackson.
© 2000 John Wiley & Sons Ltd.

process of adjustment to psychosis, drawing upon a number of theoretical models which may help to explain why such adaptation "succeeds" or "fails". These are illustrated by a number of case descriptions to illustrate and illuminate the adaptation process and we provide a summary of our recovery protocol.

COPING WITH EARLY PSYCHOSIS: THEORETICAL MODELS

Theoretical approaches explaining and predicting adaptation to early psychosis need to be broad enough to understand the myriad of psychosocial reactions witnessed during this phase but specific enough to be clinically useful. Unfortunately most theories of early adpation are "borrowed" or "imported" from other areas of psychology and psychiatry and for the most part remain untested. For such reasons they provide only frameworks or hypotheses for further exploration.

It is possible to divide these theories into four areas: (1) health belief models, (2) coping models, (3) trauma and (4) evaluative models (beliefs about psychosis).

Health belief models

Theories of health and illness beliefs derived from physical medicine, describe health and illness cognitions and their relationships to health and illness behaviours. The two theories attracting most attention within this domain, and those with perhaps the most relevance for early psychosis, are the Health Belief Model (Rosenstock, 1966) and the Self-Regulatory Model (Leventhal, Meyer & Nerenz, 1980). Over the years the Health Belief Model (Rosenstock, 1966; Becker & Rosenstock, 1984) has been used to predict preventative health behaviours and behavioural responses to treatment in acutely and chronically ill patients with both physical and mental illness (Ogden, 1996). In psychosis, it has been utilised mostly as a model to predict compliance with antipsychotic medication (Budd, Hughes & Smith, 1996; Pan & Tantam, 1989; Kelly, Marion & Scott, 1987).

The Health Belief Model assumes that people's health-related behaviours are the result of rational information processing which involves the weighing up of the potential costs and benefits of that behaviour (Ogden, 1996). There are five components which are thought to predict the likelihood of that behaviour: (a) susceptibility to illness (e.g. "my chances of my psychotic symptoms returning are high"; (b) the severity of the illness (e.g. "psychosis is very unpleasant"); (c) the costs of a health related behaviour (e.g. "if I talk to someone about my first episode of psychotic symptoms it will make me upset"); (d) the benefits of the behaviour (e.g. "if I do talk to someone about my symptoms or take antipsychotic medication, it might make me better"); (e) cues to action which may be internal (e.g. early signs of relapse) or external (e.g. psychoeducation).

Unfortunately, the Health Belief Model has attracted little interest from researchers studying adjustment and adaptation to early psychosis (Clifford & Jackson, in prep.) and results from studies exploring the efficacy of the model in medication compliance with more chronic psychosis samples provide, at best, only equivocal support (Budd, Hughes & Smith, 1996).

One of the reasons for this may be the underlying assumption of the Heath Belief Model that people behave on the basis of rational decision-making. There is now a wealth of evidence from social and cognitive psychology (Power & Dalgleish, 1997) and more specifically from studies of people recovering from psychosis (McGlashan, 1987) that this view may not be entirely appropriate. Emotional factors such as fear and denial of illness remain crucial to understanding the process of adjustment to early psychosis (Drayton, Birchwood & Trower, 1998; H. Jackson et al., 1998; Jackson and Farmer, 1997). Others have argued that health is not necessarily the absence of illness (Lau, 1997) and, as a result, theories exploring illness cognitions which also take into account emotional reactions may be more relevant to exploring psychological adjustment to psychosis (Clifford & Jackson, in prep.).

Leventhal's Self-Regulatory Model of illness behaviour (Leventhal, Meyer & Nerenz, 1980) which has been succinctly reviewed by Ogden (1996), suggests that people deal with psychosis in much the same way as they would deal with any other problem. When people first perceive they are 'ill' (psychotic), have psychotic symptoms or through social messages (family, friends) feel they deviate from the norm, they will be motivated to return to a state of premorbid normality (hence, the term "self-regulatory"). It is suggested that people will seek to achieve such a return to "normality" in three stages. Firstly, they will try to *interpret* or make sense of the problem. It is known, for instance, that 70% of people experiencing early psychotic symptoms will themselves approach their GP at some point in their pathway (Cole et al., 1995). Alternatively, their first awareness of psychotic symptoms may be through the messages of others (i.e. professional, friend or family). Appraisals of psychosis would then be constructed along the following dimensions: identity (symptoms); cause (why the illness happened); time line (how long the illness will last); control/cure (beliefs about controllability of the illness) and perceptions of the consequences of the illness if no treatment were taken.

At this point the individual will select the most appropriate *coping* strategy. However, such selection will also depend upon his emotional reaction to the event.

Although such coping may take many different forms it can usually be reliably classified as either approach coping (adherence to treatment) or avoidance coping (denial). Thus, when faced with early psychosis the patient will adopt coping strategies, which he believes, will return him to a state of premorbid mental health. Over time these coping strategies will be appraised by the individual and will be changed if they are not helping him to achieve such a goal or will be continued if they are.

Although there is some partial support for the model as a predictor of compliance with antipsychotic medication (Clifford & Jackson, in prep.) it is unlikely that this applies to the early phase of psychosis in view of the strong emotional responses to psychosis at this time.

Despite this, the self-regulatory theory provides a good rationale for the much-observed phenomena in early psychosis of "sealing over" or denial of the psychotic experiences. That is, there is a need to preserve a state of healthy normality by denying either the relevance of the psychosis or its likelihood of recurrence.

Coping Theories

Strauss (1989) has claimed that the behavioural patterns adopted by people with psychosis are akin to the "wood shedding" activities of jazz musicians who take time out to enhance their creativity. Deliberate and strategic social withdrawal is confirmed by researchers (Wing, 1975, Carin & Lauren, 1982) as one of the most important strategies open to a person with schizophrenia. Such studies paint a picture of a person with psychosis oscillating between social withdrawal and engagement in order to achieve equilibrium in the course of managing a fluctuating disorder (Drayton, Birchwood & Trower, 1998).

McGlashan and colleagues (1987, 1984, 1976, 1975) have argued that people recovering from psychosis will adopt one of two recovery or coping styles: "sealing over" or "integration".

People who "seal over" during recovery are thought to isolate their psychotic experiences. They view it as alienating and incompatible with their life goals and consequently seek to encapsulate it. The individual is disinclined to any investigation of his symptoms. Once free from psychosis they maintain an awareness of its negative aspects and fail to become emotionally invested with others in an exploration of their experiences.

"Integrators", on the other hand, are characterised by an awareness of the continuity of their mental activity and personality before, during and after the psychotic experience. "Integrators" are thought to take responsibility for their psychotic predictions and have an awareness of both the pleasure and pain involved in the psychotic experience. During "integration" the psychotic experience is used as a source of information (McGlashan, Levy & Carpenter, 1975; Drayton, Birchwood & Trower, 1998).

Little is still known about how denial, sealing over and strategic withdrawal is used in the early stages of the recovery process. H. Jackson el al. (1998), in their evaluation of COPE (Cognitively Oriented Psychotherapy for Early Psychosis), reported significant changes from a "sealing style" to an "integrating" style in a sample of first-episode patients receiving the COPE psychological intervention. Those refusing the intervention or not receiving any form of case management did not demonstrate such changes and were less likely to be aware of or accept their psychiatric disorder (see Chapter 9). It is unclear at this stage whether there are any disadvantages to early "integration", e.g. in terms of increased anxiety, depression and possible relapse. The early COPE data suggest that this is not the case. It should be noted, however, that those who refused the COPE psychological intervention, and arguably were denying or avoiding discussions and reminders of their illness, demonstrated a significantly greater reduction in depressive symptoms (as measured by the BDI) than the psychotherapy group. Although further research is needed, these findings are suggestive of the possibility that refusing to talk about or discuss their own psychotic illness, at least in the short term, may act as a useful strategy to reduce adverse emotional states and maintain a psychological equilibrium during the early recovery phase. Later in this chapter we review research which shows that "insight" into psychosis is often accompanied by higher depressive symptoms. Useful parallels can be drawn between such "sealing over/integration" theories and trauma models (McGorry et al., 1998; C. Jackson et al., 1998).

TRAUMA AND PSYCHOSIS

Case Study

Damion is a 23-year-old man who was initially referred to the Early Intervention Service from the acute admission ward of the local psychiatric hospital. At time of the referral, he was living with his parents. Damion initially presented with a number of psychotic symptoms, including auditory hallucinations, ideas of reference, depressed mood with suicidal ideation and paranoia.

Nine months prior to this Damion was living in another city where he began to experiment with a variety of illicit drugs including cannabis, amphetamines and LSD. At the time he was a singer in a rock band. He found this very stressful because of the constant arguments and fighting between group members. He was also unable to find permanent accommodation and chose to squat instead. He recalled feeling lonely and isolated at the time, made worse by the fact that his girlfriend was living 300 miles away. He became increasingly angry and agitated with his urban environment and what he saw as people's "disrespect for their surroundings". On one occasion he attempted to stop cars and challenge people who were dropping litter in the street. He then started to hear voices, initially as a whisper but after a while as loud commentaries. He also believed he could read people's minds and "transmit pain between one brain and another using telepathy". Emotionally, at the time, Damion described himself as "lost, depressed, and suicidal".

Damion initially sought counselling for these problems. However he was unsuccessful in seeking this help and decided instead after moving in with his parents, to contact his general practitioner. His GP then referred him to a psychiatrist who admitted him to hospital on a voluntary basis. Later this was changed to a Section (3) under the UK Mental Health Act. Damion's admission lasted approximately five months, in which time he made two serious attempts to kill himself.

Approximately one year after this admission Damion was still experiencing intrusive thoughts and memories related to his time on the psychiatric hospital ward. Up to that point he had found it difficult to talk about events surrounding his first episode of psychosis. Re-experiencing his sense of isolation, incarceration and lack of control during his admission was very distressing for him and was often triggered by periods when he was alone in his flat.

> "You get some image or feeling of what happened there, you're often distracted by and go quiet in the middle of a conversation … it draws you in like the voices did, wanting you to listen harder or closer."

Upon questioning, he also cited how the experience had impacted upon some of his beliefs about himself and his relationship to the world.

> "It made me think about my role, my dreams, making them more realistic, plausible and attainable; at the time I thought I didn't exist - now I constantly ask the question who am I? Where am I? I know the answers will constantly change throughout my life"

He also admitted that he found it difficult to concede that he could lose control of his thinking processes and his mind could be invaded by voices and other psychotic phenomena. As a result of his admission and acute episode Damion claimed to have lost "all self-worth". In order to recover "I had to forgive myself and all those around me, begin to like myself again".

Shaner and Eth (1989) argue that psychotic symptoms themselves (persecutory delusions, malevolent voices, etc.) may give rise to PTSD-type symptoms as they cannot be distinguished from tangible threats. For example, the first author recently saw a client who, on the first anniversary of her admission to hospital, experienced intrusive thoughts and memories of the paranoid and persecutory delusions she had during her first episode of psychosis; coupled with avoidance of triggers (i.e. the hospital ward, her daughter's school) which reminded her of her delusions, the client experienced recurrent and distressing recollections of her acute episode to such an extent that she believed she was relapsing.

People may also be traumatised by the events surrounding admission to hospital such as compulsory detention, involvement of the police or the stressfulness of temporary residence on an acute psychiatric ward. McGorry et al. (1991), using a conventional definition of PTSD, found that 35% of their sample displayed symptoms consistent with the diagnosis 11 months after their first episode, and that many people cited their experience in hospital as a major cause of their traumatic reactions.

Conversely, Meyer et al. (1999), in an older sample of people diagnosed with schizophrenia and delusional disorder, noted that in general "schizophrenic and delusional symptoms were more traumatic than the coercive measures used to control them" (p. 343). While this may simply point to the differences between the experiences (and the impact of those experiences) of first and multiple episode patients, it also gives credence to the notion of individualised determinants of traumatic reactions.

Defining PTSD and trauma

In DSM-IV (APA, 1994), one of the defining characteristics of PTSD is the exposure of people to a traumatic event in which they "experienced, witnessed or were confronted with an event or events that involved actual or threatened death or serious injury or a threat to the physical integrity of self or others".

While the aetiological events that lead to PTSD reactions are important, it is the *impact* of the event or events and how they influence a person's view of himself, the world and others which appears crucial (Power & Dalgliesh, 1997). While some patients experiencing psychosis for the first time may be overwhelmed by malevolent and "powerful" symptoms which threaten to harm them both physically and psychologically, for others it may be less obvious factors such as being contained on an acute ward with others who are disturbed (McGorry, 1991).

There are three symptom groups which characterise PTSD and traumatic reactions:

1. Persistent re-experiencing of the event or aspects of the event, including intrusive memories and thoughts, images, nightmares and dreams.
2. Avoidance of reminders of trauma and a general numbing of a person's responses. This may take the form of behavioural and/or cognitive avoidance i.e. reluctance to talk about an event and the use of distraction techniques.
3. Symptoms indicating increased arousal such as irritability, difficulty concentrating, falling asleep and hyper-vigilance.

PTSD and trauma reactions may also give rise to emotional disorders such as depression and anxiety, and in schizophrenia and psychosis may be associated with negative symptoms (Stampfer, 1991; McGorry et al., 1991).

It is still unclear at this stage whether PTSD as a diagnostic label is a valid and useful concept for people recovering from a first episode of psychosis. Studies claiming that it is, are either anecdotal (Shaner & Eth, 1989; Lundy, 1992; Jeffries, 1977) or employ measures such as the Impact of Events Scale (IES) (Horowitz, 1979) and the Clinician Administered PTSD Scale (Blake et al, 1990). These authors argue that the presence of PTSD symptoms complying with diagnostic criteria such as DSM-IV implies PTSD (McGorry et al., 1991; Meyer et al., 1999; Shaw, McFarlane & Bookless, 1997); yet people experiencing psychosis for the first time are likely to have numerous psychological reactions to these events including terror, anguish, anger, ambivalence (Shaw, McFarlane & Bookless, 1997), intense anxiety (Frosch, 1983), helplessness (James, 1993) and depression (Birchwood & Iqbal, 1998). There is likely to be significant phenomenological overlap and so it is not always easy to differentiate between these reactions on the basis of aetiology alone (i.e. whether due to the traumatic impact of psychosis or to the secondary consequence of psychiatric impairment such as loss of job and decline in interpersonal relationships). Only long-term follow-up studies could truly tease these factors out.

Distinguishing between PTSD and normal but transient reactions to a first episode of psychosis appears to hinge on the distinction between abnormal and normal reactions to traumatic events. Could PTSD type responses to psychosis as described in McGorry et al. (1991), Shaw, McFarlane and Bookless (1997) and Meyer et al. (1999) be correlates of a normal adaption process?

Attempts to understand and explain normal and abnormal responses to traumatic events have, over the years, produced a variety of theories, models and paradigms but none of these has emerged as the definitive framework to describe and explain the complex array of symptoms and responses.

Emotional processing

One of the most influential theories to have emerged in the last 20 years that provides a way of understanding some of the symptoms witnessed in PTSD (particularly intrusive symptoms such as nightmares) has been Rachman's (1980) theory of emotional processing. Although not a theory specifically about traumatic responses, Rachman has managed to provide a missing link between a number of clinical phenomena such as nightmares, obsessions and abnormal grief. "Emotional processing" is a general theory of normal and abnormal emotions but one which is highly relevant to explaining some of the coping responses and reactions of people recovering from a first episode of psychosis.

In essence, Rachman argues, much like Freud (1958) before him, that people adapt to and recover from stressful events through a process in which absorption of disturbing cognitive material passes through a staged process, beginning with awareness of emotional disturbance, decline in the strength of such disturbance and finally a return to premorbid routine behaviour. As with bereavement (Horowitz & Reidbord, 1992), the important point is that there is a "working through" which is often preceded by (or in some cases blocked by) a denial or "sealing over" stage.

Rachman (1980, 1990) outlines when such "absorption" or "working through" has been successfully completed.

> Broadly, successful processing can be gauged from the person's ability to talk about, see, listen to or be reminded of the emotional events without experiencing distress or disruptions. (Rachman, 1980, p. 52)

Factors that may promote satisfactory emotional processing may be satisfactory engagement, a sense of control and relevant conversation. Factors impeding emotional processing might be avoidance of disturbing situations or reminders of it (i.e. hospital ward), a refusal or inability to talk about the psychosis and an absence of perceived control.

Undoubtedly theories of emotional processing provide a useful framework to explain many aspects of personal and psychological recovery after a first episode of psychosis. For instance, many first-episode patients do not always find talking about their psychotic experience either helpful or desirable (H. Jackson et al., 1998). This may lead to problems with engagement, inadequate treatment and poor outcome (Frank & Gunderson, 1990), if not addressed appropriately in the early stages. Emotional processing or working through the emotional aspects of early psychosis (i.e. loss, fear, bewilderment, etc.) may need to be considered before moving on to potentially more difficult topics such as psychoeducation, relapse prevention and cognitive therapy for symptoms.

Horowitz's two-factor model

Compatible with Rachman's theory, but placing less emphasis upon emotional arousal and more on information processing, Horowitz's theory describes a motivational process of assimilation and integration of information (thoughts, ideas, images) related to the traumatic event. Horowitz proposes that personal schemata related to the world and themselves are used to interpret incoming data. That is, new information is incorporated into existing cognitive models in a process that Horowitz terms the "completion principle".

Traumatic events present information that is incongruous with existing schema or models and therefore initiates a process which describes a typical traumatic response (i.e. a stress response requiring reappraisal and revision of the model). A set of interrelated processes consisting of repetition in active memory leading to emotional distress are attenuated by counter processes of inhibition which allow the patients to "emotionally dose" themselves. Two sets of competing responses can be observed in the initial response and subsequent recovery: denial and intrusion. This is akin to the avoidant and re-experiencing symptom groupings defined in DSM-IV. It is proposed by Horowitz (1986), and by Rachman (1980), that PTSD is an indication of incomplete processing. Thus intrusive thoughts, nightmares and flashbacks are, according to the theory, indications of a breakdown in the inhibitory control mechanism. If such cognitive inhibition is overly powerful, overt and covert avoidance may occur. Denial and numbing—an unconscious process according to Lazarus (1991)—may be an extreme extension of such avoidance.

In practice, the person recovering from a major traumatic event such as a first episode of psychosis is likely to oscillate between avoidant and intrusive symptoms. This, however, may depend on other factors such as recovery style (i.e. McGlashan, 1984; C. Jackson et al., 1998).

Janoff-Bulman's "Shattered Assumptions Theory"

Unlike the previous theories, Janoff-Bulman's theory of "shattered assumptions" (1992) places more emphasis on individuals' pre-trauma appraisals and assumptions about the self and the world. It is argued that these can become shattered by the impact of a traumatic event such as psychosis.

The theory is based on Lerner's "just world hypothesis" (Lerner, 1980) which claims that individuals hold the belief that "people get what they deserve and deserve what they get". Janoff-Bulman (1992) argues that an individual holds three types of pre-existing assumptions: the assumption of personal invulnerability; the perception of the world as meaningful or comprehensible; and the view of the self as worthy and good. The shattering of such assumptions about the world and the self are seen as the basis of a PTSD/trauma response as the individual attempts to rebuild his personal models of the world and himself. Symptoms such as intrusions and avoidance, anxiety and depression are seen as by-products of this rebuilding process (Janoff-Bulman, 1992).

Conclusion

Viewing adjustment to first-episode psychosis within a trauma framework is appealing. The impact of a life event such as a first episode of psychosis upon the individual's model of the self and world would intuitively be seen as central to any conceptualisation of adjustment and adaptation to early psychosis.

Whether adjustment to early psychosis is viewed within an emotional or information processing framework or through its influence upon pre-traumatic assumptions (Janoff-Bulman & Frantz, 1997) is perhaps at this stage unimportant. Absorption of new material which is integrated, assimilated or "worked through" in the recovery process allows new models and representations of the self and the world (incorporating personal perceptions of a psychotic illness) to emerge. Denial and avoidance of illness according to such theories of trauma, although initially useful, would only inhibit this rebuilding process with adverse consequences for adaptation in the long term. Conversely, such theories would also predict that some degree of intrusive thinking and re-experiencing of the events surrounding the psychosis would aid integration and psychological recovery as long as this was not too extreme (i.e. nightmares, flashbacks; C. Jackson et al., 1998). Helping individuals to keep such intrusive phenomena within acceptable limits (i.e. by timing interventions such as relapse prevention which may increase the patients' recall of their psychosis) should be individualised and staged within an early intervention recovery protocol.

Some trauma theories, such as that of Janoff-Bulman (1992), fail to take account of observations which suggest that early adversity (Kilpatrick et al., 1985) is more likely to lead to more severe outcomes following a traumatic event. Rather than "shattering" assumptions, events such as a first episode of psychosis may *confirm* premorbid models of personal vulnerability and negative evaluations (Power & Dalgleish, 1997). In line with this, Drayton, Birchwood and Trower, (1998) reported that people with psychosis who were "sealing" or denying significant aspects of their illness were more likely, according to the PBI (Parental Bonding Scale; Parker, Tupling & Brown, 1979) to view their parents as being less caring than those "integrating" their psychotic illness. The sealers were a highly vulnerable group.

Making sense of psychosis and rebuilding new models of the self and the world may ultimately be dictated by early life experiences and the views of the self and world held prior to early manifestations of psychotic illness (Jackson & Farmer, 1998). Adapting or changing old assumptions and schemata into new more adaptive models appears to hold the key to successful adjustment.

DEPRESSION AND SUICIDE IN EARLY PSYCHOSIS: COGNITIVE APPRAISALS OF PSYCHOSIS AND IMPLICATIONS FOR THE SELF

Depression is now regarded as an integral part of the course of psychotic illness (Siris, 1991), and a precursor to suicide when associated with hopelessness (Drake & Cotton, 1986). However, relatively few studies have measured the prevalence of depression occurring after a first episode. Estimates of the number of people with early psychosis who go on to develop depression vary depending on how it is measured and assessed. Addington, Addington and Patten (1998), for instance, studied the longitudinal course of depression following a first episode of psychosis using the Calgary Depression Scale. After three months median depression scores were significantly higher than those experiencing a relapse of their acute psychotic symptoms (i.e. multiple episode patients). Some studies have focused on more specific depressive symptoms such as hopelessness, during and after the first admission. Aguilar et al. (1997) reported that mean scores on the Hopelessness Scale (Beck et al. 1974) of 7.6 were significantly higher than would be expected in a normal population (4.45) (i.e. 396 randomly selected adults; Greene, 1981) and more akin to the average score of 9.00 for suicide attempters reported in the original study by Beck et al. (1974).

The prevalence of depression in first-episode schizophrenia falls into a range between 22% (House, Bostock & Cooper, 1987) and 80% (Bustamante et al., 1994). Koreen et al. (1993) followed up 70 first-episode cases over a period of five years using both the Hamilton Rating Scale and a syndromal definition of depression based on the Research Diagnostic Criteria. They found that the level of depression (75% on both criteria) was greatest at the time of the acute first episode but improved over time. At the lowest point only 22% of all patients were considered depressed on both criteria. From this the authors concluded that depressive symptoms may represent a core part of the acute illness or that depression is seen as intrinsic to psychosis. This may be a premature conclusion, however.

Depression as intrinsic to psychosis

The term "intrinsic" suggests that the depression is an integral part of the psychotic syndrome. As such, depressive symptoms should be discernible at one or more stages during the course of an acute psychotic episode. Powerful evidence is available from the literature in support of this notion. A relationship between positive symptoms and depression is upheld by studies where depression has been observed prior to (Hirsch & Jolley, 1989), during (Knight & Hirsch, 1981) and following (i.e. "postpsychotic depression"; McGlashan & Carpenter, 1976) the onset of acute psychosis.

Leff, Tress and Edwards (1990) argue that the hierarchical schema of symptoms developed by Foulds and Bedford (1975) implies that, as part of the psychosis, an individual should also display "symptoms of affective psychoses", e.g. grandiose delusions, "symptoms of neurotic disorder", e.g. phobic anxiety, and "non-specific psychological symptoms", e.g. irritability (see Figure 3.1). Thus, a schizophrenic patient at level 4 should also display "symptoms of affective psychoses", "symptoms of neurotic disorder" and "non-specific psychological symptoms", i.e. levels 3, 2 and 1 respectively. Green et al. (1990) investigated the relationship between psychotic symptoms and depression in first-episode patients at two-weekly periods over the course of one year. These findings suggest that recovery from acute psychosis is not the sole factor determining the onset of depression. Finally, Johnson (1981) argues that depression emergent following psychosis may be a distinct entity from that surrounding

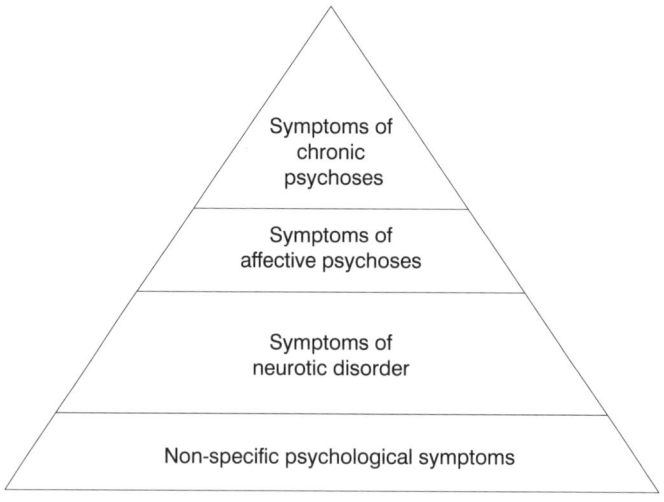

Figure 3.1 The hierarchical schema of symptoms (Foulds & Bedford, 1975).

the acute stage of the illness. This is particularly relevant as depressive symptoms do emerge in long-term maintained patients without prevailing acute psychosis.

Depression as a dysphoric response to neuroleptics

Various suggestions have been put forward concerning the role of neuroleptic medication in the development of depression in psychosis. The drug-induced syndrome of akinesia, described as the *"behavioural state of diminished spontaneity characterised by few gestures, unspontaneous speech, apathy and difficulty with initiating usual activities"* (Rifkin, Quitkin & Klein, 1975), has a high association with depressive type symptoms. Van Putten and May (1978) suggested that "akinetic" depression may provide a means of distinguishing depression following psychosis from other affective disorders, and reported that antiparkinsonian medication improved the depression. Other parkinsonian side-effects such as anhedonia, where the individual is unable to feel pleasure, akathisia and motor symptoms may also lead to the development of depressive symptoms. However, a 10-year follow-up study by Berrios and Bulbena (1987) refutes the claim that neuroleptic drugs are a causal factor in the onset of depression in psychosis, suggesting that more reasonable factors were excessive relapse, extent of auditory hallucinations and duration of illness.

Siris (1995) suggests that as neuroleptics block dopamine receptors, and as dopamine is associated with feelings of pleasure, it is arguable that an anhedonia-type state results. There is acknowledgement that in individual cases such a "pharmacogenic" depression may develop. However, these theories are unlikely to have wide application: Leff, Tress and Edwards (1990), among others, provide data showing that subjects' depressive symptoms *decreased* as acute psychotic pathology was combated by the administration of neuroleptic drugs. Furthermore, analyses which differentiate patients on the basis of whether they are/are not depressed do not, in the main, find that neuroleptic therapy is a discriminating variable (Hirsch & Jolley, 1989).

Finally, it has been contended that the pharmacogenic effect may be associated with particular neuroleptics, such as Haloperidol (Kumari Hemsley et al., 1998), rather than the newer atypical drugs. This theory would concur with the most recent findings that refute the link between drug side-effects and depression (Birchwood et al., in press; Harrow & Sands, 1999). The question remains as to whether this effect is due to better clinical management of the side-effects (a function, perhaps, of the trend towards a more individual approach to treatment than an ever-increasing choice of drugs) or due to the less "intrusive" nature of the newer neuroleptics.

Depression as a case of "mistaken identity"

Another hypothesis argues that depression in psychosis is an erroneous concept which is only observed as the many diagnostic systems employed fail to provide a clear picture of the different disorders: depression then should be subsumed under a 'better' diagnostic system. Munro (1987) highlights the diagnostic problem by outlining three "grey areas" where errors occur in the differentiation between affective disorders and schizophrenia: "mistaken identity", as affective and psychotic symptoms can be observed in separate disorders; "interbreeds", as some patients have a long-standing mixture of psychotic and affective disorders; and "distinct syndromes" which resemble schizophrenia or affective disorder, e.g. delusional disorder and brief reactive psychosis. Although this argument may provide an answer to the different stated incident rates for depression in psychosis, it is unlikely that every study would have employed consistently poor diagnostic classification.

Such diagnostic issues also extend to the negative symptoms of schizophrenia. Although symptom overlap is a possible hazard, it is suggested that individuals with depression show a distinct "low mood" while those with negative symptoms exhibit blunted affect (Barnes et al., 1989). Recent work suggests that the experienced clinician should have little difficulty in separating the two. Newcomer et al. (1990) report that depression and negative pathology can be successfully distinguished through careful assessment, e.g. using subscales of the Brief Psychiatric Rating Scale (Overall & Gorham, 1962). Siris (1995) suggests that the clinical feature of "blue mood" is the most likely aspect to allow the diagnostic separation of negative symptoms and depression, as it is generally present in the latter. Recently, Haskins, Shutty and Kellogg (1995) report the development of a reliable tool for the assessment of processing deficits (namely, spontaneous prosody, prosodic repetition and comprehension, and recognition of facial affect), which can only aid the clinician's assessment of negative affect.

Depression as a reaction to psychosis

Although our understanding of unipolar depression has benefited greatly from the application of cognitive and psychosocial frameworks (Beck et al., 1979; Brown & Harris, 1989), such an approach has not been adopted for the study of depression in psychosis. It has been argued that depression following a psychotic illness may be a reaction to the changes associated with the psychosis itself. Individuals experience a radical change in their personal lifestyles and commonly express feelings of alienation and loss of self-esteem. Roy, Thompson and Kennedy (1983) suggest that patients with negative symptoms are at greater risk as these can cause dif-ficulties for the patient in commencing his or her lifestyle, and may also lead to further undesirable life events. Barnes, Curson Liddle and Patel (1989) observed that subjective experiences of deficits in chronic schizo-phrenia, in areas such as thinking, feeling and perception, were associated with vulnerability to depression. The development of a depressive illness following an acute psychotic phase can be regarded as a sign of "accept-ance" of the psychosis, and is regarded in some quarters as a favourable prognostic sign (Roth, 1970). Comparisons of schizophrenics who had or had not developed depression suggest that the experience of psychosis is a major factor in the onset of depression (Chintalapudi, Kulhara & Avasthi, 1993). Depressed subjects were found to have had a significantly longer duration of the acute psychotic phase, better premorbid adjustment, i.e. good social and sexual adjustment prior to the onset of psychosis, and an excess of stressful life events. Similarly, results from Birchwood et al. (1993) show that depression following acute psychosis may be viewed as a psy-chological response (demoralisation) to an apparently uncontrollable life event (the psychosis) and all its attendant disabilities. Moreover, there is now emerging evidence to suggest that it is adjustment to the first episode of psychosis that produces the greatest levels of post-psychotic depression (Addington, Addington & Patten, 1998; Johnson, 1981). For example, Johnson (1981) found a statistically significant difference in the numbers of people satisfying a criteria for depression (according to a combination of scores on the Beck Depression Inventory and Hamilton Rating Scale) between a group of people with first episode psychosis (48%) and those relapsing (34%). Recent longitudinal studies (Birchwood et al., in press; Addington, Addington & Patten, 1998) support this view and point to the particularly depressogenic impact of a first episode of psychosis.

SUICIDE IN PSYCHOSIS

Prevalence

Suicide is regarded as one of the most intractable problems in the mental health field at the present time and one which particularly affects young people developing psychosis for the first time (Drake et al, 1985; Young et al., 1998). Westermeyer, Harrow and Marengo (1991) report a follow-up study of 586 first episode and people with early phase schizophrenia treated over a mean period of 13 years. They found a suicide rate of 9% over this period with the highest period of suicide risks being the first six years, by which time 6% of the 586 people had killed themselves. The risk of suicide during the prodrome and the period of untreated psychosis may add further to this figure (Jackson & Birchwood, 1996). Parasuicidal risk in psychosis averages 20–30% (Birchwood & Preston, 1991; Roy, 1986), On the other hand, in one year alone in the USA, 3,800 schizophrenia sufferers committed suicide (Jones et al., 1994) and suicidal thinking in one long-term follow-up study was as high as 40% (McGlashan, 1984).

Predicting suicide

The difficulty of combating this serious problem is acknowledged by clinicians and researchers alike (Jenkins, Griffiths & Wylie, 1994), and is matched by the difficulty of establishing predictively valid precursors and a convincing and testable theory. In schizophrenia, as in unipolar depression, suicide attempts, age and gender are indicators of future suicide. In the Westermeyer, Harrow and Marengo (1991) study results clearly indicated a significantly higher proportion of subjects with psychotic illness committed suicide than non-psychotics. In addition, there is a higher risk during the early stages of psychosis in people with schizophrenia who are young and male. Other factors which increased suicidal potential further when coupled with these variables included high intelligence and never having married. The researchers suggest that psychotic patients who are severely unhappy with their lives due to the chronic nature of their illness and inability to cope with its debilitating effects, will develop feelings of hopelessness and a vulnerability to suicidal behaviour.

The predictive efficacy of these variables is not, however, high. For example, the most promising precursor is normally considered to be parasuicide, but the relationship between parasuicide and suicide in schizophrenia is not straightforward, and there is no consensus between the studies (Allebeck et al., 1987; Drake et al., 1985). Since the prevalence of suicide is so high among people with schizophrenia who share other risk factors (youth, male gender, etc.) it may be considered that parasuicide *raises the risk* of future suicide. Nevertheless, the ability to predict who in the long term will kill themselves using known risk factors such as history of deliberate self-harm, age, gender, parasuicide, high education level, etc., is little better than chance (Pokorny, 1993).

PRECURSORS OF SUICIDE FOLLOWING EARLY PSYCHOSIS

Recent research has isolated three factors, which may provide a better understanding of the dynamics between psychotic illness and suicide: depression, hopelessness and suicidal ideation. Levels of hopelessness following a first episode are common and at a level comparable with chronic psychosis (Aguilar et al., 1997) and it is in chronic psychosis that the link between hopelessness, depression and suicide have been most readily explored. Jones et al (1994) investigated whether depression and positive or negative symptoms of schizophrenia differentiated multiple episode patients with and without a history of suicide. Their findings indicated that depression during the acute phase of the illness was a significant factor in deciphering between the suicidal and non-suicidal histories of subjects, although negative symptoms were not a distinguishing factor. Depression during the most recent admission prior to suicide was reported by Addington and Addington (1992) when their sample was followed up over the course of the following 12 months. However, the work of Drake and Cotton (1986) concluded that it was depressed mood and the psychological aspects of depression (warmlessness, guilt, hopelessness) and not the vegetative symptoms which were important; for example, depression in the absence of hopelessness was not predictive of later suicide.

The importance of hopelessness is entirely consistent with the theme of factors known to distinguish suicide non-attempters from attempters and completers (Drake et al., 1985), which include fear of mental disintegration in the context of high personal expectations (as indexed by high IQ, educational achievement and poor current work functioning). Depressed mood peaks during acute psychosis (Leff, Tress & Edwards, 1988) and in the immediate post-psychotic phase (Siris, Morgan & Fagerstrom, 1987), which probably accounts for the high risk of suicide during this period (Goldacre, Seagrott & Hawton, 1993; King, 1994). Even among outpatient suicides reported by Drake et al. (1985), 70% had killed themselves within six months of discharge.

In conclusion, depression, hopelessness and suicidal ideation during and immediately following an episode of acute psychosis are necessary but not sufficient conditions for parasuicide, and demonstrate that suicide is not always a rational decision but often occurs in the context of a distressed mental state. Although evidence is sparse it is predicted that this will also be the case for early psychosis. The presence of *psychological* vulnerabilities we believe supports a cognitive framework for depression and suicide in psychosis. In a recent study (Birchwood et al., in press) of 105 schizophrenic patients followed up for 12 months subsequent to an acute episode of psychosis (of whom 17% were first episodes), a sound rationale for pursuing this stratagem is suggested (see Table 3.1, which shows percentage prevalence for depression, hopelessness and suicidal thinking). The need for treatment is further underlined by a 20% increase in depression scores at 4, 8 or 12 months compared to the point of discharge from hospital (recovery). The targeting of these aforementioned precursors would be essential. To develop an effective intervention we also need a theoretical model of depression and suicide to understand the role of these

Table 3.1. Twelve-month prevalence of depression, hopelessness and suicidal thinking

Assessment points	At least moderately depressed	At least moderately and moderately hopeless	At least moderately depressed or suicidal thinking/ plans
Recovery, 4,8,12 months	68.3%	36.6%	44.9%

Using the Calgary Depression Scale (for schizophrenia): Addington, Addington and Matricka-Tyndall (1993).

risk variables. Here we argue that patients' appraisals of the meaning of their psychosis and its symptoms provides such a backdrop. We consider the appraisal of symptoms, illness and their implications for self-evaluation during the early phases of psychosis.

COGNITIVE APPRAISAL OF SELF, SYMPTOMS AND ILLNESS

Although there has been little systematic investigation of the relationship between symptoms of the psychosis and depression in first-episode schizophrenia, depression has been linked to the presence of auditory hallucinations during the acute stage (Hafner et al., 1994) in about 40% of patients ($N = 276$). An interesting development was recently reported by McGorry et al. (1998) when they examined the dimensional structure of each subject's psychosis, in a group of 509 first-onset cases using a broad sweeping multi-diagnostic instrument assessing 92 core symptoms. Their results clearly reveal a four-factor solution: negative symptoms, positive symptoms (of which auditory hallucinations were the strongest loadings), mania and depression. These results, in the context of the sample sizes employed by these authors, clearly implicate voices as a primary feature of early psychosis, which should be targeted for psychological investigation and intervention. Jackson et al. (1996) report that about 10% of first-episode patients do not obtain full relief from their psychotic symptoms, and in the context of the four-factor solution outlined above, this finding means that a notable number of cases will have residual positive symptoms. The need to clarify the link between depression and voices is therefore a priority for any early intervention resource, as outlined below in the context of recent research.

In a recent study it was noted that some two-thirds of a sample of multiple episode patients exhibited residual voices alongside at least moderate levels of depression (Birchwood & Chadwick, 1997). The depression pathology observed in this group, although linked to the presence of auditory hallucinations, can be clearly defined in terms of key beliefs held by the individual about the power and purpose or intent of their voices (Chadwick & Birchwood, 1994, 1995), as opposed to voice topography or content. As with Milgram's (1974) famous experiment which highlighted the power of the experimenter and the compliance of subjects administering what they believe to be lethal electrical shocks to other subjects, results of these early studies confirmed a similar foundation for auditory hallucinations. Subjects in these studies who reported voices were imbued with power and authority; *malevolent* or persecutory voices resisted and aroused feelings of hostility, fear, anger and depression. Conversely, *benevolent* voices were regarded as reassuring and even amusing in some cases. Although this theory is as yet untested in an early psychosis sample, there is nothing to suggest that these appraisals of psychotic symptoms are any less relevant or predictive of distress (including depression). Indeed, changes in psychotic pathology associated over the longer term or multiple-episode course of schizophrenia, are argued to only emerge at a significant level in individuals after about a 10-year or longer duration of illness (Tsunashima et al., 1999). It is also likely that such appraisals extend to persecutory beliefs, which are also linked to depression. In first-episode patients with residual symptoms, a sense of powerlessness over these symptoms might be a trigger/risk for depression.

Loss, humiliation and entrapment as appraisals of psychotic illness

Research into the role of life events in triggering the onset of unipolar depression in a sample of community based female subjects (Brown, Harris & Hepworth, 1995) provides a framework which helps to understand how patients might appraise the emergence of a psychotic illness and its social implications. Although lowering of self-esteem has been linked to depression (Beck et al., 1979), theories based upon "social mentalities" suggest that the implications of the power and rank of certain life experiences involving loss are of significance in the emergence of depressive symptoms (Gilbert, 1992). Depression in such instances is believed to result in: the lowering of self-esteem as a result of acceptance of a subordinate role ("loss"); events which threaten the individual's position or status ("humiliation"), and the perception of containment in a punishing cycle of events which result in the disbelief to reaffirm an identity or sense of belonging ("entrapment"). Brown, Harris and Hepworth (1995) concluded that such experiences, which triggered feelings of humiliation and entrapment, were more important in provoking depression than the perception of loss alone. These concepts have clear application to the way patients construct their psychotic illness and a process that no doubt begins soon after the first episode.

As suggested by Birchwood et al. (1993), the experience of psychosis can, as a result of the stigma attached to such disorders, result in feelings of humiliation. The experience and expectation of recurring symptoms following a first episode and/or the presence of residual voices may lead to feelings of entrapment and defeat. This hypothesis has been tested in a cohort of multiple episode patients, who were followed up over 2.5 years later in order to determine the stability of such appraisals and whether *changes* in depression over this period were linked to changes in appraisal of illness (Rooke & Birchwood, 1998). Stability was apparent in the appraisals of entrapment, loss of social role and attribution of causality (self vs illness), but not for perceived loss of social status and humiliation.

Once again, replicating earlier findings, comparisons between depressed and non-depressed patients revealed that depressed patients perceived themselves as more entrapped in their illness and also to have lost more in terms of their social role. Also, depressed subjects experienced more compulsory admissions, a greater drop in employment and more residual auditory hallucinations. Results from the Birchwood et al. study clearly suggest that depression at the acute stage remitted in line with the psychosis, and that 36% of cases developed PPD approximately eight months following recovery from psychosis. Prior to developing PPD these patients experienced greater loss, were likely to attribute the cause of their illness to self, had lower self-esteem and were more self critical than those who did not become post-psychotically depressed, or those who relapsed. Furthermore, upon becoming depressed, participants had greater insight, lower self-esteem and held more negative appraisals of illness in terms of loss, humiliation, entrapment, shame and self blame, in comparison to both non-depressed and relapsing patients. Finally, traditional cognitive vulnerability factors for unipolar depression did not differentiate subjects who developed PPD from either the non-depressed or relapsing group, suggesting that a different mechanism mediates the onset of PPD.

Although further replication of these findings in other settings is necessary, the helplessness of the individual in overcoming the implications of a stressful life event, clearly lends itself to the future investigation of PPD from within a similar framework. This is felt to provide perhaps a more lucid and testable alternative to the cognitive model of depression. The utility of such a methodology in this instance is the argument that depression can occur in *anyone* given the "right" circumstances, without necessary recourse to cognitive vulnerability. Psychotic illness is clearly a stressful life event and the findings of this study suggest that participants who develop PPD perceive themselves as suffering from a significant loss of greater autonomy, being socially humiliated, and losing control over their illness (entrapment). Hence, these results provide support for a model of PPD entrenched in the *realities* of psychosis and the patient's reaction to the conflict and social implications generated by its onset.

In summary we suggest that it is the events that punctuate a long-term difficulty such as psychosis (for example, compulsory admissions, persistent voices, loss of job) that may be appraised as signifying loss and entrapment and confirm the absence of a way forward in respect of core roles, relationships and autonomy. Such events are likely to be ego-involving since autonomy and success in roles and relationships (Oatley & Bolton, 1985) are endemic in western culture. Also such events can confirm a disbelief in the individual's ability to reaffirm a sense of identity and belonging (Price et al., 1994), and encourage engulfment and internalisation of the schizophrenic identity as a defensive manoeuvre (Birchwood et al., 1993). It is likely, although once again untested, that such an evaluative process begins soon after the first episode of psychosis (Jackson & Farmer, 1997).

Case Study

Shakur was a 26-year-old engineering post-graduate who lived at home with his parents and two brothers. He was referred to the Early Intervention Service from the local Home Treatment Team following an admission to hospital for a first episode of psychosis. Acute symptoms included paranoid and grandiose delusions, thought broadcast, second-person auditory hallucinations, delusions of reference, "mind reading" and disturbed sleep. Three years prior to his admission, following the disappointment of an unsuccessful attempt to start a relationship with a woman he liked, and the failure to secure employment as an engineer (despite possessing relevant post graduate qualifications), Shakur started to feel dysphoric and "deflated". He had "high hopes of getting a job" after his course. As a reaction to his disappointment and upset, Shakur started travelling long distances all over the country. Soon after, he gradually started to experience telepathic type delusions where he indulged in two-way conversations with the woman who had turned him down in order to "get her back". Over the following year, 18 months prior to his first admission, his delusions of telepathy generalised to other women as he also became more grandiose and paranoid and started to hear "voices". Soon after, he began to withdraw to his bedroom and cut himself off from his family. Approximately 12 months later his father contacted the family GP. Stelazine was prescribed and Shakur was admitted to hospital informally. This was later changed to a Section (2) after Shakur did not agree to stay in hospital. His admission lasted approximately three months after which he was referred to the Early Intervention Service.

Six months later Shakur was referred to the first author by his Keyworker who was concerned that he was considerably depressed, hopeless and suicidal despite the remission of his psychotic symptoms. Upon assessment it became apparent that the reality of what had happened had begun to "hit" Shakur. He held strong beliefs about being "entrapped" and helpless within a unrelenting psychotic illness and that he would never succeed in a career he valued (i.e. engineering) and that his future was "dark and uncertain". These views were endorsed by items on the PBIQ (Birchwood et al., 1993) and the Beck Hopelessness Scale. At the time he admitted that he felt "suicidal" about his position although he had not made any attempts on his own life. He felt powerless to prevent further relapses ("there is nothing I can do about it, it will just happen") or control any aspects of his illness. He also entertained strong beliefs about himself as a failure because of his lack of achievement (i.e.: humiliation) within his valued roles and goals (i.e. engineer, boyfriend/husband). In line with Champion and Power (1995) there was some evidence to suggest that because of the possible cultural, familial and personality factors these roles and goals were somewhat "over valued" premorbidly and so made him more vulnerable to post-psychotic depression.

The formulation was then discussed with Shakur and an intervention planned. Interventions were based on the recovery protocol discussed later but in essence consisted of group and individual cognitive therapy to explore appraisals of entrapment, humiliation (running parallel with vocational and pre-vocational training), relapse prevention, personalised psychoeducation to increase beliefs of control over relapse and psychosis as well as normalising his emotional reactions. After two months Shakur's sense of hopelessness and depressed mood began to abate (despite being unable to secure any employment or find a girlfriend). An increased sense of control and knowledge about his psychotic illness reduced his appraisals of entrapment and humiliation (according to the PBIQ). He still held strong views about work, at first not considering anything but a top engineering position as suitable. After a while, however, he became more flexible and accepted a position as a clerk in an engineering firm; he also took up squash, swimming and other sports to give his life a "wider focus" than had been suggested previously.

IMPLICATIONS FOR INTERVENTION

It is argued that a person experiencing the trauma and distress of a first or an early episode of psychosis needs to undergo a number of psychological adjustments and adaptations. It is important to view such a process, not as a unitary transition period but one of multiple psychological transitions, which fall under the "umbrella" of integration.

A number of models imported from other areas of the psychosocial literature (PTSD, coping, health and illness beliefs, depression) may help explain such an "integration" process, but only partially. The integration of aspects of a psychotic illness requires both assimilation and accommodation of new information with existing schema of the self and world (i.e. new models; Williams, Stiles & Shapiro, 1999). It may also require "emotional processing" to occur; that is, the absorption of emotional material related to the psychosis (i.e. loss, traumatic memories, etc.; Lutgendorf & Auroni, 1999).

Both the coping and PTSD literature point to the use of flexible cognitive and emotional strategies to maintain a state of emotional and psychological equilibrium, so that covert and overt avoidance (through non-engagement, distraction, etc.) may provide a control lever or "emotional brake" for such emotional processing and "integration" of the illness experiences. We believe that encouraging flexible coping, and timing treatments such as psychoeducation, cognitive therapy and relapse prevention so that people can appropriately and emotionally "dose" themselves, should all be indicted in an early intervention protocol.

Depression, hopelessness and suicide, as an index of a failure to adjust and adapt to early psychosis, remain considerable problems. Recent results from randomised-controlled trials (Tarrier et al., 1998; Garety et al., 1997) indicate that current cognitive therapy-based treatments for psychosis have little impact on PPD and may reflect the inadequacies of current models of depression imported from elsewhere (i.e. Beck et al., 1979). New models, theories and treatments for PPD need to be developed which take into account appraisals of entrapment and humiliation which so often accompany the onset and course of a psychotic disorder (Birchwood & Iqbal, 1998; Rooke & Birchwood, 1998; Birchwood et al., in press).

Teasdale's (1988) argument that maintenance and severity of depression are fuelled by negative schema, rather than activating the depression itself, provides a possible explanation of the high severity of depression reported in first-onset cases (Birchwood et al., in press; Addington, Addington & Patten, 1998). This argument has recently been explained by Parker et al. (1998) who advocate a "lock and key" hypothesis of depression where early adverse memories and linked schema (locks) are activated by present-day experiences (keys). In other words, it is possible that this population is perhaps *more* likely than others to have experienced early trauma that may be "unlocked" by the experience of particular life events, including psychosis. The prodromal period itself, which is frequently characterised by social isolation and interpersonal difficulty (Birchwood, 1992), is likely to lead to the development of abnormal, interpersonal schema that may be reactivated following the onset/diagnosis. These vulnerabilities could affect the flexibility with which individuals respond to threats to major roles/goals, for example a psychosis (Champion & Power, 1995). As noted previously, Drayton Birchwood and Trower (1998) found such an interaction, where cognitive vulnerabilities emerging from early negative experiences of family relationships were associated with the "sealing" strategy of coping with psychosis.

It is argued that PPD is a response to a potentially shattering life event (the onset of acute psychosis) which carries a greater psychological implication, and hence higher risk in first-onset cases, in contrast to patients who have experienced multiple relapses over a number of years—the latter being more resilient through a greater opportunity to adapt to the psychosis and to the mechanisms argued to modulate the onset of PPD (Birchwood et al., in press). This argument would provide one explanation for the lower prevalence of depression in multiple-admission subjects (see Siris, 1995, for a review) in contrast to first-onset cases, and opens an interesting avenue for research investigating factors such as the role of coping, integration and acceptance of illness.

Reducing the sense of entrapment by increasing control during the critical period appears paramount. For instance, treating the client as an "active agent in their own recovery" (Brier & Strauss, 1983; McGorry, 1992) is a key aim. Of course, in reality, appraisals of entrapment will fluctuate in line with specific and general aspects of the psychotic illness, such as relapse, thwarted roles and goals (unemployment, relationship difficulties, etc.) and other life events. However, according to Rooke and Birchwood (1998), one particular aspect of treatment appears to have the greatest impact on appraisals of entrapment (or perceived loss of control of psychotic illness): compulsory admission. Reducing involuntary admission, especially during the early course of psychosis, remains a top priority for Early Intervention. (McGorry et al., 1991; Jackson & Birchwood, 1996).

A FRAMEWORK FOR PSYCHOLOGICAL INTERVENTION IN EARLY PSYCHOSIS

Drawing upon these models and existing protocols (e.g. COPE: H. Jackson et al., 1998) we propose here a framework for interventions which are devised to encourage adaptation and adjustment to a first episode of psychosis. This protocol is implemented routinely in the Birmingham Early Intervention Service.

Engagement and assessment, which are pivotal of any psychological intervention, have been described in detail elsewhere in the book (see Chapters 4 and 8). Where clients initially decline an offer of psychological therapy, it is important to try to maintain contact until an appropriate assessment can proceed (even if this is for very short periods, i.e. 10 minutes per week over a few months).

Formulation

The formulation should describe specific problem areas related to adjustment (i.e. depression, trauma). Facts related to the onset and maintenance of these difficulties, and how the different problems may be interacting with one another, are then translated into working hypotheses which can be shared with the client (i.e. depressed mood being maintained by appraisals of entrapment and thwarted roles and goals, etc.). Specific interventions can then be tailored to these hypotheses in order to bring about therapeutic change and promote recovery following a first episode. In addition, factors increasing vulnerability to relapse (social isolation, illicit drug use) should be identified and used as a basis for a relapse prevention strategy (see Chapter 10).

Intervention

It is intended that interventions should directly reflect individual formulations which can be translated into an "individual recovery plan". Although, in theory, no one individual recovery plan will be the same, in practice it is likely that there are common features. Plans will incorporate interventions, which might be applied as a discrete piece of work over a five- or six- week period. After a short break of a few weeks, this can be repeated for another piece of work or "therapeutic module" over the first two or three years following a first episode. A series of interventions are given below.

1. Personalised psychoeducation

The rationale behind this is to provide a framework for patients to understand their experiences, symptoms, emotional reactions and treatment (McGorry, 1995; Fowler et al, 1995). Although this may draw on traditional psychoeducation approaches, it is likely that information will be best delivered as part of an individualised approach, taking into account the client's experiences, beliefs and recovery style (i.e. sealing over vs integration).

Stress-vulnerability models (Zubin & Spring, 1977) can provide a conceptual framework for such personalised psychoeducation and be compared against individual models. To encourage normalisation, analogies with medical conditions (asthma, diabetes) can be made. It should be borne in mind, however, that many first-episode clients may not make sense of their initial experiences and symptoms in this way.

Finally, the use of diagnoses such as schizophrenia and manic depression are initially avoided and not discussed openly with clients unless otherwise indicated (i.e. they have already been given a diagnosis). Such diagnoses are avoided because: (a) they are believed to be unreliable and unstable at the first episode (McGorry, 1991); (b) they encourage negative stereotyping; (c) they set up low expectations for clinicians, families, clients and others; and (d) they are unlikely to contribute to outcome and recovery (McGorry, 1992). The less contentious term "psychosis" is used instead.

2. Reducing the impact of trauma

As noted previously, it is unclear at the early stage whether the "traumatic" reactions observed in first-episode patients (intrusive re-experiencing, avoidance, etc.) are simply the result of a normal adjustment process or of "abnormal" processes akin to PTSD (C. Jackson et al., 1998). In practice such symptoms are likely to fall on a continuum where extreme adjustment reactions to the first episode of psychosis in the absence of appropriate coping meet the criteria for a diagnosis of PTSD (McGorry et al., 1991; Shaw, McFarlane & Bookless, 1997; Meyer et al., 1999). In parallel with this there is now a substantial body of literature on the treatment of psychological reactions to non-psychotic trauma (Joseph et al., 1995). Although it is still unknown at this stage whether one can apply intervention approaches developed for non-psychotic trauma to psychotic trauma, useful frameworks have been suggested. For example, Hodgkinson and Stewart (1991) claim that there are four main strands to the treatment for PTSD:

(a) *Exploring memories of the traumatic event.* This may be done in conjunction with personal psychoeducation or personal model-building as mentioned previously. Alternatively, if more appropriate, this may take place at a later stage as part of a relapse prevention approach. Debriefing, whenever this occurs, should incorporate "empathic listening" allowing for expression of anxieties and normalising reactions (Manton & Talbot, 1991).

(b) *Cognitive appraisal and the challenging of dysfunctional beliefs.* Given that it is the impact of a first episode on the individual model of the self and world which is central to psychological recovery, challenging unhelpful appraisals and beliefs (i.e. "the world is unsafe", "bad things like psychosis happen to bad people", "anything can happen to my mind") is indicated. However, tried and tested cognitive therapy techniques such as Socratic dialogue, guided discovery, etc., may have to be especially tailored for an early psychosis population (see Chapter 9). The over-glorification of the premorbid self (McGorry et al., 1998) and overly positive beliefs about invulnerability prior to trauma (Janoff-Bulman, 1992) may also need to be explored and gently challenged.

(c) *Disturbed feelings—over-arousal.* Careful assessment is required to distinguish these from prodromal signs of psychotic relapse. However, once this is done these may respond to relaxation, systematic desensitisation or additional medication.

(d) *Avoidance and intrusive re-experiencing.* Exposure therapy, which allows people to return to the situation in which some aspects of the trauma occurred (i.e. acute admission ward, police station, university, etc.), may be useful. The first author has successfully used this with three clients. Because many of the traumatic aspects of the psychosis may be related to the psychotic symptoms (Meyer et al., 1999) imaginal techniques may be considered. However, these should be used with extreme caution as they remain untested for people with psychosis. Instead, distraction and/or gentle exploration should be considered.

3. Cognitive therapy for delusions, voices and paranoia

Although the vast majority of first-episode patients make full symptomatic recoveries within six months of starting antipsychotic medication (Lieberman et al., 1993; Edwards et al., 1998), a significant minority will continue to experience residual symptoms. Drawing heavily on the work of Chadwick, Birchwood and Trower (1996) and Fowler et al. (1995), misinterpretations of evidence (from social situations and altered states) and beliefs about psychotic processes (i.e. voices) are addressed if they contribute significantly to distress or poor functioning. Cognitive behavioural strategies may also need to be suggested in order to promote self-regulation of psychotic symptoms (Tarrier, 1992). Cognitive (e.g. attention switching) behavioural (e.g. increasing and decreasing activity levels), modifying sensory input (e.g. listening to music) and physiological (e.g. relaxation) techniques address beliefs about control and power and as such, should address appraisals of entrapment (again, see Chapter 4).

*4. Cognitive therapy addressing appraisals of psychosis and the
implications for the self*

Cognitions of "entrapment" (i.e. "I am capable of very little as a result of
my illness"; Birchwood et al., 1993; Brown, Harris & Hepworth, 1995)
and shame (Gilbert, 1992) are damaging to the psychological recovery
process. Perceived entrapment as a result of psychosis often involves
beliefs related to opportunities, and a person's ability to use these opportunities to fulfil particular roles and goals (Power & Dalgleish, 1997;
Gilbert, 1992; Birchwood & Iqbal, 1998). Assessing the nature of the
entrapment in relation to the individual's valued roles and goals is
imperative. For instance, many young people with psychosis value work,
social autonomy and youth culture. Providing opportunities to engage
in such roles will often need to be addressed. However, the authors also
find group problem-solving techniques an appropriate vehicle to
address themes of helplessness and entrapment. Getting clients in small
groups to generate their own ideas of overcoming their "blocks to recovery" can be extremely productive. Likewise, shame and stigma may also
be addressed at a group level (Drury et al., 1996). However, because
shame about psychosis often leads to concealment, avoidance and poor
engagement (Pennebaker, 1988), long-term individual work is often indicated. It is important in the early stages not to focus on shame as this may
encourage non-engagement.

A psychological intervention should also seek to separate mental illness
as a label from their identity as a person (Taylor & Perkins, 1991). In line
with theories of trauma and adaptation reviewed previously, integration is encouraged but sealing over is recognised as a necessary stage in
the recovery process. Based on the critical distinction between integrators and those sealing over, the following themes in the intervention
should be addressed: clients are encouraged to consider their first
episode of psychosis in the following ways: (a) that it has had an important effect on their lives; (b) that psychosis is a meaningful personal
event which is related to other life experiences; (c) that it contains both
negative and positive (i.e. allowing clients to address issues) aspects; (d)
that it is something that is potentially controllable and for which the
client must take some responsibly (i.e. relapse prevention); (e) that psychosis has added to their life experience and will be a source of future
personal information about themselves, as opposed to trying to forget
about it; and (f) that information-seeking about psychosis should be
encouraged (i.e. reading relevant books, etc.). Where "sealing over" pre-
dominates, the patient is not forced into an "integrating" coping style;
instead, alternative strategies should be explored. These may include
more activity and social-based interventions (sport, cinema, music),
non-directive counselling and skills training which do not focus on the

meaning of psychosis but minimise the distress related to it (Drayton, Birchwood & Trower, 1998).

Relapse prevention

Applying established techniques of relapse prevention will impart a sense of control and collaborative involvement with their own care and lead to improved appraisals of entrapment, and hopelessness. Relapse prevention in early psychosis is described in more detail in Chapter 10.

CONCLUSION

When implementing psychological interventions aimed at personal recovery it is important to be focused but flexible. Psychological therapy with first-episode clients needs to be conducted at a pace which allows "emotional dosing" to critical events and the future to be optimised. Cognitive Oriented Psychotherapy for Early Psychosis (COPE), described by H. Jackson and colleagues in Chapter 9, provides further guidance as to how such a balance can be achieved when working with young people experiencing psychosis for the first time.

REFERENCES

Addington, D.E. & Addington, J.M. (1992). Attempted suicide and depression in schizophrenia. *Acta Psychiatrica Scandanavica*, **85**, 288–291.

Addington, D., Addington, J. & Maticka-Tyndale, E. (1993). Assessing depression in schizophrenia: The Calgary Depression Scale. *British Journal of Psychiatry*, **163** (suppl. 22), 39–44.

Addington, D., Addington, J. & Patten, S. (1998). Depression in people with first-episode schizophrenia. *British Journal of Psychiatry*, **172**, (Suppl. 33), 90–92.

Aguilar, E.J., Haas,G., Manzanera, F.J., Hernandez, J., Gracia, R., Radado, M.J. & Keshavan, M.S. (1997). Hopelessness and first-episode psychosis: a longitudinal study. *Acta Psychiatrica Scandinavica*, **96**, 25–30.

Allebeck, P., Varla, A., Kristjansson, E. & Wistedt, B. (1987). Risk factors for suicide among patients with schizophrenia. *Acta Psychiatrica Scandinavica*, **76**, 414–419.

APA (1994) Diagnostic and Statistical manual of Mental Disorders (4th edition). Washington, DC: American Psychiatric Association.

Barnes, T.R., Curson, D.A., Liddle, P.F. and Patel, M. (1989). The nature and prevalence of depression in chronic schizophrenic in-patients. *British Journal of Psychiatry*, **154**, 486–491.

Bebbington, P.E. (1995). The content and context of compliance. *International Clinical Psychopharmacology*, **9**, 41–50.

Becker, M.H. & Rosenstock, I.M. (1984) Compliance with medical advice. In A. Steptoe and A. Mathews (Eds), *Health Care and Human Behaviour*. London: Academic Press.

Beck, A.T. & Greenbert, R. L. (1974) Coping with depression (a booklet). New York: Institute for Rational Living.

Beck, A.T., Weissman, A., Lester, D. & Trexler, L. (1974). The measurement of pessimism: The Hopelessness Scale. *Journal of Consulting and Clinical Psychology*, **42**, 861–865.

Beck, A.T., Rush, A.J., Shaw, B.F. & Emery, G. (1979). *Cognitive Therapy of Depression*. New York: Guilford.

Bermanzohn, P.D. & Siris, S.G. (1994). Non-compliance with antiparkinsonian medications in neuroleptic-treated schizophrenic patients: three cases of an unreported phenomenon. *Journal of Clinical Psychiatry*, **55** (11), 488–491.

Berrios, G.E. & Bulbena, A. (1987). Post psychotic depression: The Foulburn cohort. *Acta Psychiatrica Scandinavica*, **76**, 89–93.

Birchwood, M. & Chadwick, P. (1997) The omnipotence of voices III: Testing the validity of the cognitive model. *Psychological Medicine*, **27**, 1345–1353.

Birchwood, M., Iqbal, Z., Chadwick, P. & Trower, P. (in press). A cognitive approach to depression and suicidal thinking in psychosis. I: the ontogeny of post-psychotic depression. *British Journal of Psychiatry*.

Birchwood, M., Todd, P. & Jackson, C.(1998) Early intervention in psychosis: the critical period hypothesis. *International Clinical Psychopharmacology*, **13**, (suppl. 1), 31–40.

Birchwood, M. & Iqbal, Z. (1998). Depression and suicidal thinking in psychosis: a cognitive approach. In T. Wykes, N. Tarrier & S. Lewis (Eds), *Outcome and Innovation in Psychological Treatment of Schizophrenia*. Chichester: Wiley.

Birchwood, M.J., Mason, R., Macmillan, F. & Healy, J. (1993). Depression, demoralisation and control over psychotic illness: a comparison of depressed and non-depressed patients with a chronic psychosis. *Psychological Medicine*, **23**, 387–395.

Birchwood, M.J. & Preston, M. (1991). Schizophrenia. In W. Dryden & R. Rentoul (Eds), *Adult Clinical Problems*. London: Routledge.

Blake, D., Weathers, F., Nagy, L., Kaloupek, D., Klauminzer, G., Charhey, D. and Keane, T. (1990). *Clinician-Administered PTSD Scale (CAPS)*. National Center for Post Traumatic Stress Disorder, Behavioural Science Division, Boston.

Brier, A. & Strauss, J.S. (1983). Self control in psychotic disorders. *American Journal of Psychiatry*, **40**, 1141–1145.

Brown, G.W., Harris, T.O. & Hepworth, C. (1995). Loss, humiliation and entrapment among women developing depression: a patient and non-patient comparison. *Psychological Medicine*, **25**, 7–21.

Brown, G.W. & Harris, T.O. (1989). *Life Events and Illness*. New York: Guilford Press.

Buchanan, A. (1996a). *Compliance with Treatment in Schizophrenia*. Maudsley Monographs. Hove: Psychology Press Ltd.

Buchanan, J.A. (1996b). Social support and schizophrenia: a review of literature. *Archives of Psychiatric Nursing*, April 9 (2), 68–76.

Budd, R.J., Hughes, I.C.T. & Smith, J.A. (1996). Health beliefs and compliance with antipsychotic medication. *British Journal of Clinical Psychology*, **35**, 393–397.

Bustamante, S., Maurer, K., Loffler, W. et al. (1994). Depression in the early course of schizophrenia. *Fortschrittle der Neurologie-Psychiatrie*, **62**, 317–329.

Caldwell, J. & Gottesman, I. (1990). Schizophrenics kill themselves too. *Schizophrenia Bulletin*, **16**, 571–590.

Corin, E. & Lauzon, G. (1992). Reconstruction of experience amongst schizophrenics. *Psychiatry*, **55**, 266–278.

Chadwick, P. & Birchwood, M. (1994). Challenging the omnipotence of voices: a cognitive approach to auditory hallucinations. *British Journal of Psychiatry*, **164**, 190–201.

Chadwick, P. & Birchwood, M. (1995). A cogntitive approach to auditory hallucinations. In G. Haddock & P. Slade (Eds), *Cognitive-behavioural Interventions in Psychosis* (pp. 71–85). Routledge: London.

Chadwick, P., Birchwood, M. & Trower, P. (1996). *Cognitive Therapy for Delusions, Voices and Paranoia.* Chichester: Wiley.

Chadwick, P. & Birchwood, M. (1997). The omnipotence of voices: testing the validity of a cognitive model. *Psychological Medicine, 27*, 1345–1353.

Champion, L. & Power, M. 1995. Cognitive approaches to depression: A theoretical critique. *British Journal of Clinical Psychology, 25*, 201–212.

Chintalapudi, M., Kulhara, P. & Avasthi, A. (1993). Post-psychotic depression in schizophrenia. *European Archives of Psychiatry Clinical Neuroscience, 243* (2), 103–108.

Clifford, C. & Jackson, C. (in preparation). Compliance with medication in psychiatric patients: a test of the self-regulatory and health beliefs model.

Cole, E., Leavey, G., King, MB., Johnson-Sabine, E. & Hoare, A. (1995). Pathways to care for patients with a first episode of psychosis: a comparison of ethnic groups. *British Journal of Psychiatry, 167*, 770–776.

Corin, E. & Lauzon, G. (1992). Reconstruction of experience amongst schizophrenics. *Psychiatry, 55*, 266–278.

Davidson, L. & Strauss, J.S. (1992). Sense of self in recovery from severe mental illness. *British Journal of Medical Psychology, 65*, 131–145.

Drake, T. & Cotton, T. (1986). Relationship of psychosis and suicide amongst schizophrenics: a comparison of attempted and completed suicides. *British Journal of Psychiatry, 149*, 784–787.

Drake, R., Gates, C., Cotton, P. & Whittaker, A. (1985). Suicide among schizophrenics: who is at risk? *Journal of Nervous and Mental Disease, 172*,s 613–617.

Drayton, M., Birchwood, M. & Trower, P. (1998). Early attachment experience and recovery from psychosis. *British Journal of Clinical Psychology, 37*, 269–284.

Drury, V., Birchwood, M., Cochrane, R. & Macmillan, F. (1996). Cognitive Therapy and recovery from acute psychosis: a controlled trial. *British Journal of Psychiatry, 169*, 593–601.

Edwards, J., Maude, D., McGorry, P.D., Harrigan, S.M. & Locks, J.T. (1998). Prolonged recovery in first-episode psychosis. *British Journal of Psychiatry, 172* (Suppl. 33), 107–116.

Erickson, D.H., Beiser, M. & Iacono, W.G. (1999). Social support predicts 5-year outcome in first-episode schizophrenia. *Journal of Abnormal Psychology, 107*(4); 681–685.

Foulds, G.A. & Bedford, A. (1975). Hierarchy of classes of personal illness. *Psychological Medicine, 5*, 181–192.

Fowler, D., Garety, P. & Kuipers, L. (1995). *Cognitive Behaviour Therapy for Psychosis.* Chichester: Wiley.

Frank, A.F. & Gunderson, J.G. (1990). The role of the therapeutic alliance in the treatment of schizophrenia: relationship to course and outcome. *Archives of General Psychiatry, 47*, 228–236.

Franz, M., Lemke, M.R., Meyer, T., Ulferts, J., Puhl, P. & Snaith, R.P. (1999). German version of the Snaith-Hamilton-Pleasure Scale (SHAPS-D), Anhedonia in schizophrenic and depressive patients. *Fortschr. Neurol. Psychiatry, 9*, 407–413.

Freud, S. (1958). Remembering, repeating and working through. In J. Strachey (Ed.), *The Standard Edition* (Vol. 12). London: Hogarth.

Frosch, J. (1983). *The Psychotic Process.* New York. International Universities Press.

Garety, P.A., Fowler, D., Kuipers, E., Freeman, D., Dunn, G., Bebbington, P.E., Hadley, C. & Jones, S. (1997). The London–East Anglia randomised controlled trial of cognitive behaviour therapy for psychosis. II: Predictors of outcome. *British Journal of Psychiatry*, **171**, 420–426.

Gilbert, P. (1992). *Depression: The Evolution of Powerlessness*. Hove, Sussex: Erlbaum.

Goldacre, M., Seagrott, V. & Hawton, K. (1993). Suicide after discharge from psychiatric in-patient care. *Lancet*, **342**, 283–286.

Greene, S. (1981) Levels of measured hopelessness in the general population. *British Journal of Clinical Psychology*, **20**, 11–14.

Green, M.F., Nuechterlein, K.H.,Ventura, J. & Mintz, J. (1990). The temporal relationship between depressive and psychotic symptoms in recent-onset schizophrenia. *American Journal of Psychiatry*, **147**, 179–182.

Haftner, H., Reichler-Rossler, A., Maurer, K., Fatken Heuer, B. & Loffler, W. (1994). First onset and early symptomatology of schizophrenia. *European Archives of Psychiatry and Clinical Neuroscience*, **242**, 109–118.

Haskins, B., Shutty, M.S. & Kellogg, E. (1995). Affect processing in chronically psychotic patients: development of a reliable assessment tool! *Schizophrenia Research*, **15**, 291–297.

Hirsch, S.R. & Jolley, A.G. (1989). The dysphoric syndrome in schizophrenia and its implications for relapse. *British Journal of Psychiatry*, Suppl. 5, 46–50.

Hodgkinson, P.E. & Stewart, M. (1991). *Coping with Catastrophe: A Handbook of Disaster Management*. London: Routledge.

Horowitz, M.J. (1986). *Stress Response Syndromes* (2nd edn). Northvale, NJ: Jason Aronson.

House, A., Bostock, J. & Cooper, J.E. (1987). Depressive syndromes in the year following onset of a first schizophrenic illness. *British Journal of Psychiatry*, **151**, 773–779.

Horowitz, M.J. & Reidbord, S.P. (1992). Memory, emotion and response to trauma. In S.A. Christianson (Ed.), *The Handbook of Emotion and Memory: Research and Theory*. Hillsdale, NJ: Erlbaum.

Horowitz, M.J. (1979). Psychological response to serious life events. In V. Hamilton & D.M. Warburton (Eds), *Human Stress and Cognition: An Information Processing Approach*. New York: Wiley.

Jackson, C. & Birchwood, M. (1996). Early intervention in psychosis: opportunities for secondary prevention. *British Journal of Clinical Psychology*, **35**, 487–502.

Jackson, C. & Farmer, A. (1998). Early intervention in psychosis. *Journal of Mental Health*, **7**, (2), 157–164.

Jackson, C. & Knott, C., Skeate, A. & Birchwood, M. (1998) The impact of a first episode of psychosis: cognitive processing of an adverse experience and its implication for recovery. Paper presented at the World Congress of Behavioural and Cognitive Therapies, Acapulco, Mexico, 21–26 July.

Jackson, H.J. & Edwards, J. (1992). Social networks and social support. In D.J. Kavanagh (Ed.), *Schizophrenia: An Overview and Practical Handbook*. London: Chapman & Hall.

Jackson, H.J., McGorry, P., Edwards, J. & Hulbert, C. (1996). Cognitively-oriented psychotherapy for early psychosis (COPE). In P. Cotton & H.J. Jackson (Eds), *Early Intervention and Prevention in Mental Health*. Australian Psychological Society: Melbourne.

Jackson, H., McGorry, P., Edwards, J., Hulbert, C., Henry, C., Francey, S., Maude, D., Locks, J., Power, P., Harrington, S. & Dudgeon, P. (1998). Cognitively-oriented psychotherapy for early psychosis (COPE). *The British Journal of Psychiatry*, **172**, (Suppl. 33), 93–100.

James, N.M. (1993) On the perception of madness. *Australian and New Zealand Journal of Psychiatry*, **27**, 192–199.

Janoff-Bullman, R. (1992). *Shattered Assumptions: Towards a New Psychology of Trauma*. New York: Free Press.

Janoff-Bullman, R. & Frantz, C.M. (1997). The impact of trauma on meaning: from meaningless world to meaningful life. In M. Power & C. Brewin (Eds), *The Transformation of Meaning in Psychological Therapies*. Chichester: Wiley.

Jefferies, J.J. (1977). The trauma of being psychotic: a neglected element in the management of chronic schizophrenia. *Canadian Psychiatric Association Journal*, **22**, 199–205.

Jenkins, R., Griffiths, S. & Wylie, I. (1994). *The Prevention of Suicide*. London: HMSO.

Johnson, D. (1981). Studies of depressive symptoms in schizophrenia. *British Journal of Psychiatry*, **139**, 89–101.

Jones, J.S., Stein, D.J., Stanley, B., Guido, J.R., Winchel, R. & Stanley, R. (1994). Negative and depressive symptoms in suicidal schizophrenics. *Acta Psychiatrica Scandinavica*, **89** (2), 81–87.

Joseph, S., Williams, R. & Yule, W. (1995). *Understanding Post-Traumatic Stress: A Psychological Perspective on PTSD and Treatment*. Chichester: Wiley.

Kelly, G.R., Marion, J.A. & Scott, J.E. (1987). Utility of the health belief model in examining medication compliance among psychiatric outpatients. *Social Science and Medicine*, **25**, 1205–1211.

Kilpatrick, D.G., Veronen, L.J. & Best, C.L. (1985). Factors predicting psychological distress among rape victims. In C.R. Figley (Ed.), *Trauma and its Wake*. New York: Brunner/Mazel.

King, E. (1994). An epidemiological sample and implications for clinicians. *British Journal of Psychiatry*, **165**, 658–663.

Knight, A. & Hirsch, S.R. (1981). Revealed depression and drug treatment of schizophrenia. *Archives of General Psychiatry*, **40**, 893–896.

Kovaszany, B., Fleischer, J., Tenenberg-Karant, M., Jandorf, L., Miller, A.D. & Bromet, E. (1997). Substance user disorder and the early course of illness in schizophrenia and affective psychosis. *Schizophrenia Bulletin*, **23**, 195–201.

Koreen, A.R., Siris, S.G., Chakos, M.H., Alvir, J.M.J., Mayerhoff, D.I. & Lieberman, J.A. (1993). Depression in first-episode psychosis. *American Journal of Psychiatry*, **150**, 1643–1648.

Kuipers, E., Garety P.A., Fowler, D., et al. (1997). The London–East Anglia Trial of Cognitive Behaviour Therapy for Psychosis I: Effects of the treatment phase. *British Journal of Psychiatry*, **171**, 319–327.

Kumari, V., Hemsley, D.R., Cotter, P.A., Checkley, S.A. and Gray, J.A. (1998) Haloperidol—induced mood and retrieval of happy and unhappy memories. *Cognition and emotion*, **12**, 497–508.

Lau, R.R. (1997). Cognitive representations of health and illness. In D. Gochman (Ed.), *Handbook of Health Behaviour Research*, Vol. I.

Lazarus, R.S. (1991). *Emotion and Adaption*. New York: Oxford University Press.

Leff, J., Tress, K. & Edwards, B. (1990) Depressive symptoms in the course of schizophrenia. In L. Delisi (Ed.), *Depression in Schizophrenia*. Washington (USA): American Psychiatric Press.

Leff, J., Tress, K. & Edwards, B. (1988). The clinical course of depressive symptoms in schizophrenia. *Schizophrenia Research*, **1**, 25–30.

Lerner, M.J. (1980) *The Belief in a Just World*. New York: Plenum Press.

Leventhal, H., Meyer, D. & Nerenz, D. (1980). The common sense representation of illness danger. In S. Rachman (Ed.), *Medical Psychology* (Vol. 2; pp. 7–30). New York: Pergamon.

Lieberman, J., Jody, D., Geisler, S., Loebel, A., Szymanski, S., Woerner, M. & Bornstein, M. (1993). Time course and biological correlates of treatment response in first episode psychosis. *Archives of General Psychiatry*, **50**, 369–376.

Lundy, M.S. (1992). Psychosis-induced post traumatic stress disorder. *American Journal of Psychotherapy*, XLVI, 485–491.

Lutgendorf, S.K. & Auroni, M.H. (1999). Emotional and cognitive processing in a trauma dislcosure program. *Cognitive Therapy and Research*, **23**, 423–440.

Manton, M. & Talbot, A. (1991). Crisis intervention after an armed hold-up: guidelines for counsellors. *Journal of Traumatic Stress*, **3**, 507–522.

McGlashan, T.H. (1987). Recovery style from mental illness and long term outcome. *Journal of Nervous and Mental Disease*, **175**, 681–685.

McGlashan, T.H. & Carpenter, W.T. Jnr (1976). Postpsychotic depression in schizophrenia. *Archives of General Psychiatry*, **33**, 231–239.

McGlashan, T.H. (1984). The Chestnut Lodge follow-up study II: Long term outcome of schizophrenia and affective disorders. *Archives of General Psychiatry*, **41**, 586–601.

McGlashan, T.H., Levy, S.T. & Carpenter, W.T. (1975). Integration and sealing over: Clinically distinct recovery styles. *Archives of General Psychiatry*, **32**, 1269–1272.

McGorry, P. (1991). Negative symptoms and PTSD. *Australian and New Zealand Journal of Psychiatry*, **25** (1), 9–13.

McGorry, P., Henry, L., Maude, D. & Phillips, L. (1998) Preventively-orientated psychological interventions in early psychosis. N.C. Perris & P. McGorry (Eds), *Cognitive Psychotherapy of Psychotic and Personality Disorders*. Chichester: Wiley.

McGorry, P., Chanen, A., McCarthy, E., Van Riel, R., McKenzie, D. & Singh, B. (1991). Post-traumatic stress disorder following recent onset psychosis: an unrecognised postpsychotic syndrome. *Journal of Nervous and Mental Disease*, **179**, 253–258.

McGorry, P.D. (1992). The concept of recovery and secondary prevention in psychotic disorders. *Australia and New Zealand Journal of Psychiatry*, **26**, 3–18.

Meyer, H., Taiminen, T., Vuori, T., Aijala, A. & Helenius, H. (1999). Post-traumatic stress disorder symptoms related to psychosis and acute involuntary hospitalisation in schizophrenic and delusional patients. *Journal of Nervous and Mental Disease*, **187**, 343–352.

Munro, A. (1987). Neither lions nor tigers: disorders which lie between schizophrenia and affective disorder. *Canadian Journal of Psychiatry*, **32**, 296–297.

Newcomer, J.W., Faustman, W.O., Yeh, W. & Csernansky, J.G. (1990). Distinguishing depression and negative symptoms in unmedicated patients with schizophrenia. *Psychiatry Research*, **31**, 243–250.

Oatley, K. & Bolton, W. (1985) A social theory of depression in reaction to life events. *Psychological Review*, **92**, 372–388.

Ogden, J. (1996) *Health Psychology: A Textbook*. Buckingham: Open University Press.

Overall, J.E. & Gorham, D.R. (1962). The Brief Psychiatric Rating Scale. *Psychological Reports*, **10**, 799–812.

Pan, P.C. and Tantam, D. (1989). Clinical characteristics, health beliefs and compliance with maintenance treatment: a comparison between regular and irregular attenders at a depot clinic. *Acta Psychiatrica Scandinavica*, **79**, 564–570.

Parker, G., Tupling, H. & Brown, L.B. (1979). A parental bonding instrument. *British Journal of Medical Psychology*, **52**, 1–10.

Parker, G., Gladstone, G., Roussos, J. Wilhelm, K., Mitchell, P., Hadzi-Parlovic, D., Austin, M.P. & Hickie, I. (1998). Qualitative and quantitative analyses of a key thesis of depression. *Psychological Medicine*, **28**, 1263–1273.

Pennebaker, J.W. (1988). Confiding traumatic experiences and health. In S. Fisher and J. Reason (Eds), *Handbook of Life Stress, Cognition and Health*. Chichester: Wiley.

Pennebaker, J.W., Kiecolt-Glaser, J., and Glaser, R. (1988). Disclosure of traumas and immune function: health implications for psychotherapy. *Journal of Counselling and Clinical Psychology*, **56**, 239–245.

Pokorny, A. (1993). Predictors of suicide in psychiatric patients. *Archives of General Psychiatry*, **40**, 249–253.

Power, M. & Dalgleish, T. (1997). *Cognition and Emotion: From Order to Disorder*. Hove: Psychology Press.

Price, J., Sloman, L., Garner, R., Gilbert, P. & Rohde, P. (1994). The social competition hypothesis of depression. *British Journal of Psychiatry*, **164**, 309–315.

Rachman, S. (1980). Emotional processing. *Behaviour Research and Therapy*, **18**, 51–60.

Rachman, S.J. (1990). *Fear and Courage* (2nd edn). New York: W.H. Freeman.

Rifkin, A., Quitkin, F. & Klein, D.F. (1975). Akinesian: a poorly recognised drug induced extrapyramidal behavioural disorder. *Archives of General Psychiatry*, **321**: 672–674.

Rooke, O. & Birchwood, M. (1998). Loss, humiliation and entrapment as appraisals of schizophrenic illness: a prospective study of depressed and non-depressed patients. *British Journal of Clinical Psychology*, **37**, 259–268.

Rosenstock, I.M. (1966). Why people use health services. *Millbank Memorial Fund Quarterly*, **44**, 94–124.

Roth, S. (1970). The seemingly ubiquitous depression following acute schizophrenic episodes: a neglected area of clinical discussion. *American Journal of Psychiatry*, **27**, 51–58.

Roy, A. (1986). Suicide in schizophrenia. In A. Roy (Ed.), *Suicide* (pp. 128–147). Baltimore: Williams & Wilkins.

Roy, A., Thompson, R. & Kennedy, S. (1983). Depression in chronic schizophrenia. *British Journal of Psychiatry*, **142**, 465–470.

Shaw, K., McFarlane, A. & Bookless, C. (1997). The phenomenology of traumatic reactions to psychotic illness. *The Journal of Nervous and Mental Disease*, **185**, 434–441.

Siris, S.G. (1991). Diagnosis of secondary depression in schizophrenia: implications for DSM-IV. *Schizophrenia Bulletin*, **17**, 75–98.

Siris, S.G. (1995). Schizophrenia. In S.R. Hirsch and D.R. Weinberger (Eds), *Schizophrenia*. Oxford: Blackwell Science.

Siris, S.G., Morgan, V. & Fagerstrom, R. (1987). Adjunctive imipramine in the treatment of post-psychotic depression. *Archives of General Psychiatry*, **44**, 533–539.

Stampfer, H.G. (1990). "Negative Symptoms": a cumulative trauma stress disorder? *Australian and New Zealand Journal of Psychiatry*, **24**, 516–528.

Strauss, J.S. (1989). Subjective experiences of schizophrenia: towards a new dynamic, II. *Schizophrenia Bulletin*, **15**, 179–188.

Tarrier, N., Usupoff, L., Kinney, C., McCarthy, E., Gledhill, A., Haddock, G. & Morris, J. (1998). Randomised controlled trial of intensive cognitive behavioural therapy for patients with chronic schizophrenia. *British Medical Journal*, **317**, 303–307.

Tarrier, N. (1992). Management and modification of residual psychotic symptoms. In M. Birchwood & N. Tarrier (Eds), *Innovations in the Psychological Management of Schizophrenia*. Chichester: Wiley.

Taylor, K.E. & Perkins, R.E. (1991). Identity and coping with mental illness in long stay rehabilitation. *British Journal of Clinical Psychology*, **30**, 73–85.

Teasdale, J. (1998). Cognitive vulnerability to persistent depression. *Cognition and Emotion*, **2**, 247–274.

Tsunashima, H.A., Watanabe, K., Ishiara, I., Terada, T. & Uno, M. (1999) Symptom classification of schizophrenia changes with duration of illness. *Acta Psychiatrica Scandinavica*, **99**, 447–452.

Van Puten, T. & May, P.R.A. (1978). "Akinetic depression" in schizophrenia. *Archives of General Psychiatry*, **35**, 1101–1107.

Westermeyer, J.F., Harrow, M. & Marengo, J.T. (1991). Risk for suicide in schizophrenia and other psychotic and non-psychotic disorders. *Journal of Nervous and Mental Disease*, **179**, 259–266.

Williams, J.M.G., Stiles, W.B. & Shapiro, D.A. (1999). Cognitive mechanisms in the avoidance of painful and dangerous thoughts: elaborating the assimilation model. *Cognitive Therapy and Research*, **23**, 285–306.

Wing, J.K. (1975). Social influences on the course of schizophrenia. In R.D. Wirt, G. Winokur & G. Roffs (Eds), *Life History Research and Psychopathology*, Vol. 4. Minneapolis, MN: University of Minnesota Press.

Zubin, J. and Spring, B. (1977). Vulnerability: A new view of schizophrenia. *Journal of Abnormal Psychology*, **86**, 103–126.

Chapter 4

PSYCHOLOGICAL FORMULATION OF EARLY EPISODES OF PSYCHOSIS: A COGNITIVE MODEL

*David Fowler**

INTRODUCTION

First psychotic episodes are distressing and debilitating events, both to those who experience them and to those around them. Such episodes can also mark the onset of what become chronic mental health problems characterised by the development of treatment-resistant delusions and voices, problems in social functioning, vulnerability to further episodes of psychotic relapse, emotional disturbance and risk of suicide. This chapter is concerned with making sense of the psychosocial factors associated with the onset of early episodes of acute psychosis and the psychological factors which lead to the maintenance of delusions and hallucinations. Understanding the factors associated with the onset and maintenance of the symptoms of acute psychosis is of critical importance. Such symptoms are often profoundly distressing and disruptive (Garety & Hemsley, 1994) and it is the presence of persecutory delusions and hallucinations that is most likely to lead to hospital admission at first psychiatric contact (Castle et al., 1994). While longitudinal studies suggest that symptomatic recovery does not necessarily imply social recovery (Strauss & Carpenter, 1977) the presence of continuing psychotic symptoms is closely associated with severe problems in social functioning (Harrow, Rattenburg & Stoll, 1988). Furthermore two sets of findings in particular suggest that factors associated with the problems in recovery from acute psychosis may be critical in influencing vulnerability to a long term course. Firstly, the time spent in acute psychosis (duration of untreated psychosis) appears to be associated

*University of East Anglia, Norwich, UK.

Early Intervention in Psychosis.
Edited by M. Birchwood, D. Fowler & C. Jackson.
© 2000 John Wiley & Sons Ltd.

with poorer long-term outcome (Johnstone et al., 1986; Loebel et al., 1992); secondly, the proportion of people who suffer from residual psychotic symptoms increases after each acute relapse (Shepherd et al., 1989; Wiersma et al., 1998). Psychological formulation is concerned with identifying the factors which underpin the content and characteristics of psychotic symptoms and the maintenance of residual delusions and hallucinations. Attempts to make sense of the such factors is of direct clinical relevance. Such individualised formulation provides the basis for cognitive behavioural therapy for psychosis (see Drury, Chapter 8 in this volume). Psychological approaches to understanding psychotic problems can also assist mental health professionals towards interventions and services which are collaborative with, rather than at odds with, the views of users (see Reeves, Chapter 14 in this volume)

TOWARDS A PSYCHOLOGICAL FORMULATION OF EARLY PSYCHOSIS

The clinical problems of acute psychosis present a considerable challenge to clinicians attempting to make sense of their difficulties. Initial encounters with people in acute psychosis tend to be confusing. The problems presented are always very severe, frequently multidimensional and one case can differ markedly from another. Most commonly people with psychosis present with syndromes of mixed symptomatology. Any variety and combination of symptoms may be presented and such symptom patterns may change over time. Some cases may illustrate the point.

Case Studies

Robbie came into contact with mental health services via the court. He had been violent and aggressive to strangers in the street. On first meeting he was actively suspicious and guarded. He said there was a group out to get him. This included the police but also several other people who were following him and keeping an eye on him. He expected to be attacked at any moment. He had been hearing voices for several months which told him about the threat. Most of the time he tried to stay at home which was better, although he was still preoccupied with the threat and the voices often said when he would be attacked. When he went out he felt terrible, really frightened because lots of people were looking at him and he could trust no one.

Ben came into contact with mental health services because his mother was worried about him. He had recently left home to live in a bedsit. He had become increasingly disorganised. His flat walls were covered in paintings and he was preoccupied with drawing, not sleeping and not eating or looking after himself.

He talked in a bizarre way about God, good and evil and about how his task was to save the world. He said that painting helped him to make sense of things. He was clearly listening to voices. He said these were God and the Devil talking to him. He said he didn't need any help.

Sarah was brought by her mother. She had dropped out of university after a bad experience taking ecstasy. She had become paranoid and felt that others could read and see into her mind her mind. This was still occurring episodically most days of the week, especially when she went out. When it happened she was sure that she was connected to a malevolent group of strangers in some way. She felt ashamed that these people could see her as she really was. Unworthy and morally weak. Most of the time when she was away from social situations she could recognise that these thoughts were not real. However, she was very frightened of going mad. She had become very withdrawn had given up her studies, had not seen her friends for months and tried not to go out unless it was absolutely necessary.

UNDERSTANDING THE BIOPSYCHOSOCIAL CONTEXT IN WHICH PSYCHOSIS OCCURS: FROM VULNERABILITY-STRESS MODELS TO PSYCHOLOGICAL FORMULATION

Problems such as those above can be described as psychoses or schizophrenia spectrum disorders. Most theorists assume that these are heterogeneous and multi-factorial disorders, best understood within a biopsychosocial framework as is consistent with the widely accepted vulnerability stress models (Zubin & Spring, 1977; Strauss & Carpenter, 1981). Such models are consistent with research suggesting that psychosis occurs in a context of a vulnerable predisposition (of biopsychosocial origin), that onset is triggered by events (life events, adverse social circumstances, drugs) and that this leads to a disruption in cognitive processes of attention, perception or judgement often accompanied by emotional changes (Fowler, Garety & Kuipers, 1995). Such models provide a useful first step to developing a psychological formulation. A key insight is that there may be different types of vulnerabilities, triggers and stresses for different cases. In some cases history-taking may reveal drug abuse as a precipitant of psychosis (as was particularly the case of Robbie who had injected amphetamines and other drugs, and Sarah whose problems were triggered by taking ecstasy and smoking cannabis). In others a history of traumatic or abusive interpersonal relationships may be present (as was the case for Robbie who had had a very adverse and aversive upbringing with abusive and neglectful parents). In others strong family histories of severe mental disorder may be present (in Sarah's case several members of her close family had problems with mental illness, Robbie's uncle had schizophrenia). In yet other cases, such as Ben's, there had been long-term social difficulties which dated back to childhood, possibly suggestive of a neuro-developmental problem. There are also differences in social context in which psychosis can arise. In Robbie's case, the crisis had developed from falling out with a set of criminal contacts and at the same time coming to the attention of the police. In Bill's case, he had heard voices and had some odd and eccentric ideas and behaviours for some years, but he had been doing well at home with his mother providing a lot of support. Only when he moved to living alone in a bedsit did problems occur. His problems in managing this move had been compounded by being mugged and taunted by local youths. In Sarah's case, she had been a student (with relatively normal concerns of young adults about getting on with others, about her sex life, etc.) until her experiment with ecstasy. This triggered a range of paranoid experiences and she had felt others could read her mind and see her thoughts. These continuing experiences appeared to have exacerbated her fears and concerns about herself.

Assessment of the background to psychosis with reference to the idiosyncratic vulnerabilities and stresses starts to place an individual's psychotic episode within a specific biological, psychological and social context. This is a useful and necessary first step to a person-based or individualised formulation. However, a set of critical questions relating to how psychosis emerges from these factors remain unanswered. In particular:

- How do these different factors converge to form the symptoms of psychosis ?
- What drives and maintains the strange experiences, paranoid or deluded thinking, and voices ?
- How are such problems maintained ?

In the following we aim to trace the emergence of acute psychosis from early schizotypal experiences through to recovery or the formation of delusions and voices. We aim to review research on the range of factors which underpin the occurrence of individual psychotic symptoms such as delusions and voices and highlight critical factors associated with the individual's search for meaning. We illustrate this throughout with case material.

From schizotypy to acute psychosis

It is being increasingly recognised that the severe anomalies of thought, behaviour and affect which characterise psychosis can be viewed as continuous with anomalies of normal experience (Claridge, 1985). Surveys reveal that the presence of anomalies in experience belief and thinking, which have previously been regarded as prodromal features of schizo-phrenia, are in fact relatively common in the normal population. In one survey of 657 adolescents, 10–15% reported they often experienced magi-cal ideas and unusual perceptual experiences and 50% reported that they occasionally had such experiences (McGorry et al., 1995). However, only a relatively small proportion of those who can be identified as having high levels of schizotypal experiences and mild psychosis go on to develop a mental health problem (Chapman & Chapman, 1988). Furthermore, rela-tively large subgroups of people in the normal population hear voices and believe strange things which could be regarded as delusional without recourse to psychiatric services (Romme & Escher, 1989; Tien, 1991). Delusions are traditionally defined in part by their content. But even beliefs with similar content to delusions can be found in the normal popu-lation (Peters, Joseph & Garety, 1999). What, then, differentiates delusional beliefs and psychotic symptoms from normal beliefs and anomalies of experience? It can be useful to think of psychosis as, to some degree, on a continuum with normal beliefs and anomalies, although people with delusions tend to present with much higher levels of preoccupation, con-viction and distress concerning their beliefs than people with odd beliefs in the normal population (Peters, Joseph & Garety, 1999). While many non-psychotic people may acknowledge the occurrence of abnormal beliefs they tend to be able to distance themselves from these beliefs and largely disregard them so that they can lead a normal life. By contrast, clin-ical problems with people in acute psychosis occur when people become committed, highly convinced and emotionally preoccupied and distressed by their beliefs. Such beliefs may also become associated with behavioural disturbance. Similarly, the anomalous experiences associated with psy-chotic disorder (e.g. voices, perceptual disturbances, thought disorder) may be recognisably of similar form to schizotypal experiences. They become clinical problems when people become disabled as a result of their higher frequency and longer duration and when the distressing content cannot be disregarded.

From prodrome to psychosis

Most isolated psychotic experiences or symptoms can be identified as having similarities to schizotypal experiences. However, the experience of acute psychosis is no longer of fleeting isolated anomalies but of beliefs and experiences which completely take over consciousness and which lead to what has been described as people becoming lost in a wak-ing dream or nightmare of psychosis (Jung, 1907). What are the factors associated with the shift from having anomalous experiences and even frank voices and bizarre beliefs to an acute episode of psychosis? In a seminal study of symptoms in early psychosis Chapman (1966) carried out retrospective interviews with 40 patients in early stages of psychosis. This study highlighted the presence of what would now be regarded as schizotypal experiences (e.g. visual, cognitive and perceptual abnormalities) preceding frank psychotic symptoms. Chapman (1966) suggested that a build up of these experiences was associated with reports of increasing inability to control one's thoughts and emotional disturbance, which progressed to further feelings of loss of control, dysphoria and disinhibition to the onset of frank symptoms of psychosis. Recently, several careful prospective studies have confirmed that the build up to psychotic relapse is often preceded by increases in anxiety, dysphoria, interpersonal sensitivity/withdrawal and mild psychotic symptoms such as suspiciousness and experiential anomalies (see Spencer, Murray & Plaistow, Chapter 10 in this volume and Birchwood, Macmillan & Smith, 1994, for a general review of this topic). Symptoms of both emotional disorder and disruptions of conscious experience (perceptual/cognitive abnormalities) co-occur in the build up to psychotic relapse. However, there is no evidence of a linear development in stages, instead there is widespread individual variability in relapse profiles. This pattern is illustrated in the cases described above; in each case there is a highly individual and different pattern of symptoms and reaction to it. In many cases specific anxieties and threats precede the presence of perceptual/cognitive abnormalities (as in case of Robbie) but the reaction or compensation to ongoing social threat in his case appeared to become intertwined with his appraisals of anomalies of experience. In others anomalous experiences are the trigger (as was the case of Sarah taking street drugs). However, in her case the attempt to make sense of anomalies of experience became associated with pre-existing personal concerns. Ciompi (1981) has described how, as the build up to psychosis progresses, disorders of both feeling and thinking emerge and appear to exacerbate one another.

Birchwood (1996) provides a cognitive model which emphasises a person's emotional reaction to the increasing experience of anomalies and thought disorder in the build up to relapse. Following Maher (1988), he suggests that the link may be a search for meaning triggered by the presence of anomalous experiences associated with psychosis. At first the person may be perplexed, but later may appraise psychotic experience as a threat which may lead to increasing panic and feelings of loss of control and thus a vicious cycle leading to relapse. In the following we develop a model which similarly focuses on individual search for meaning in psychosis. However, we also discuss how an individual's appraisal of anomalous psychotic experience as a threat may often be closely related to pre-existing personal concerns and beliefs about self and others. An important basis for psychological formulation may be a view of acute psychosis as a product of both cognitive disorder and emotional disorder.

WHAT IS HAPPENING IN THE ACUTE PSYCHOTIC STATE?

Most people with psychotic disorder have periods in which they have anomalous conscious experiences (e.g. thoughts being experienced as voices, alterations in the experience of thoughts; disordered or heightened sensory perception; unconnected events appearing connected, etc.). Robbie saw changes in people's facial expressions; he heard voices saying that specific individuals were out to get him; he saw threatening looks, signals, and gestures everywhere. Bill saw visions, heard voices and at times felt that thoughts were being placed in his mind by a higher being. Sarah felt that people could see right into to her mind and hear her innermost secret thoughts. As we described above, these unusual experiences also tend to build up in the prodrome to acute psychosis. What, then, is the nature of the disorder which may underpin such experiences ?

Perspectives on the basic cognitive disorder in psychosis

The disorder which underpins acute psychosis has been described variously as a confusion between dreams, fantasies, fears and reality (Jung, 1907); as a breakdown in reality testing (Freud, 1924/1961) as a loss of ego boundaries (Federn, 1953). and as a disruption, decompensation or fragmentation in the sense of self (Bleuler, 1950; Cutting, 1989; Hemsley, 1998). Central to these ideas are hypotheses about cognitive disorders which may lead to confusion between inner events (memories and expectation) and outer event (ongoing current perceptions and sensations). Hallucinations may be described as occurring when individuals incorrectly attribute internally generated experiences (thoughts, memories) to be external events (Bentall, 1990; Frith, 1992). Delusions of reference may be described as occurring when there is a confusion between non-significant events and feelings of personal significance (Hemsley, 1993). In contrast to theories which suggest that either a single cognitive deficit or emotional problems may underpin such disorder. Our proposal is that that the inner–outer confusion (Figure 4.1) which characterises psychosis may arise from a catastrophic interaction between a basic neurocognitive disorder in cognitive processes underpinning perception, and beliefs, appraisals and emotional biases.

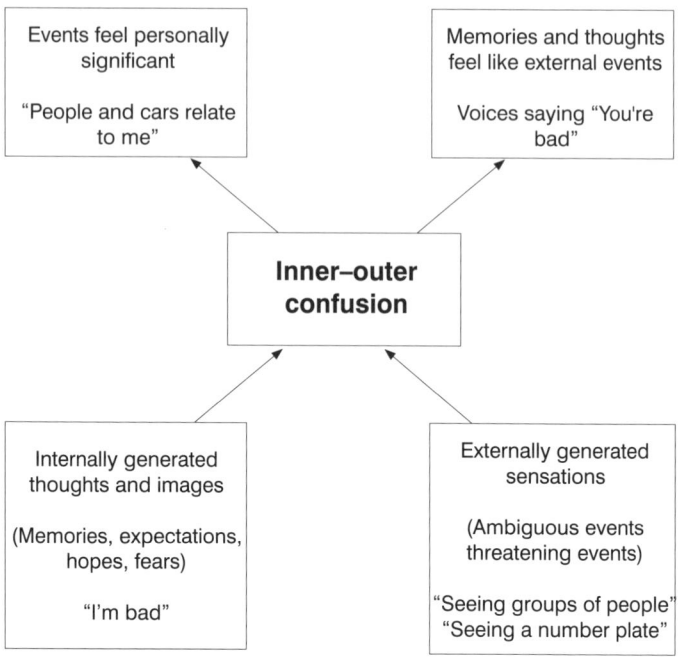

Figure 4.1   Experiential consequences of inner–outer confusion.

A basic abnormality in perception

An influential group of theorists have focused on perceptual/cognitive
abnormalities as probably representing basic symptoms which may be
closely related to the neural basis of psychotic disorder (Hemsley, 1993,
1998). We noted the occurrence of such abnormalities in the build up to
early psychotic episodes above. Such theorists assume that in a predis-
posed individual a triggering event may give rise to a disruption of cognitive processes, thereby leading to a breakdown in Gestalt (Cutting, 1989) or
perceptual fragmentation (Arieti, 1966) and thus a range of anomalies of
experience. Such disruptions are assumed to arise as a result of a changed
or altered brain state becoming manifest as disordered cognitive processes.
Currently a leading hypothesis suggests that a breakdown in some of the
basic automatic cognitive processes which bring together and monitor the
current state of a person's perceptual world with predicted states may
underpin such anomalies of experience (Gray, 1998). Disturbances in the
moment to moment integration of stored regularities with current sensory
input (Hemsley, 1993) may be associated with disruptions in self-monitoring of intentions and actions (Frith, 1992) and thus may lead to abnormalities in perception, experience and action and the experience of disorder in

the sense of self in psychosis (Hemsley, 1998). Theories of this type can provide a useful basis for understanding those aspects of the clinical phenomena of psychosis relating to the presence of anomalies of experience (see Chapter 5 and Fowler, Garety & Kuipers, 1995). They are consistent with current theorising about the way the brain works and provide a stimulating and useful basis for thinking about how biological vulnerability or predisposition may become manifest under certain conditions as cognitive disorder and give rise to psychotic experience. However, they do not provide a complete explanation of psychosis. In particular they fail to take account of the peculiar personal or emotional significance which characterises psychotic experience.

The need to take account of the personal and emotional significance of psychosis

In all the cases described above, the experiences of psychosis consists not only of anomalous experience, but also of meaningful and, in many cases, emotionally charged experience. For Robbie, psychotic experience was consistent with the feeling that people were against him and about to attack him. For Ben, psychotic experiences were consistent with a struggle between good and evil and his attempt to manage this. For Sarah, the experience was odd and to some degree she recognised it as anomalous; however, at the time she experienced it, it felt related to deep concerns about her sexual and moral identity. We have already noted that the histories of such cases are in varying degrees consistent with the hypothesis of a biological vulnerability which becomes manifest as disorder, triggered by factors such as taking street drugs, stress, etc. The final common pathway of such a disorder may be usefully characterised as a cognitive deficit in automatic processes underpinning conscious experience (Hemsley, 1998). However, it is also clear that psychosis is an emotionally laden experience and that, to some degree, emotion drives psychosis. Several psychotherapists from different traditions—both psychoanalytic Garfield (1995) and cognitive (Bannister, 1983)—have noted that the content of psychotic symptoms can be meaningfully related to personal issues and current concerns. As noted by Garfield (1995), to some degree Shakespeare's maxim that "though there be madness there be method in it" may be applicable to understanding the content of psychotic symptoms. Understanding psychotic symptoms as a problem which derives from both biological predisposition and personal adaptation (appraisal, meaning and emotion) is the basis of psychological formulation. In the following we review research findings which indicate that both affective and non-affective cognitive biases are associated with delusions and hallucinations.

PSYCHOLOGICAL REACTIONS AND THE FORMATION AND MAINTENANCE OF DELUSIONS

Reasoning biases

There are now a firmly established set of replicated findings which show that people with delusions often have biases in reasoning (see Garety & Freeman, 1999, for detailed review). People with delusions often make decisions on the basis of less information than others, they literally "jump to conclusions" (Garety, Hemsely & Wessely, 1991), a tendency which may be exaggerated with material with emotive or self-referent content (Dudley et al., 1997). It is likely that such biases are greater under conditions of stress (Garety & Hemsley, 1994). Such bias may lead to early acceptance of incorrect or implausible ideas and also a tendency to rapidly change views or reject hypotheses. As suggested by Chapman and Chapman (1988), on the basis of a careful prospective study of the initial formation of delusions, problems of this type may underpin clinical observations of people forming delusions apparently "out of the blue" in the context of implausible explanations of everyday events. This tendency to form delusional ideas out of the blue or on the basis of very little evidence was readily apparent in the cases described above. Ben, for example, interpreted his seeing a number plate beginning with HEX (a common number plate in Norfolk) as firm evidence that the Devil was after him. Robbie interpreted almost any social interaction, including minor glances and looks, as evidence of a conspiracy. One way in which cognitive therapy works in psychosis may be to help people become more flexible about their interpretations and the evidence on which it is based and thereby compensate for delusional thinking which is based on such reasoning biases (Garety et al., 1997).

Evidence for emotional biases

There is consistent evidence from a series of studies that people with persecutory delusions show biases in the processing of emotionally salient material. People with paranoia have a tendency to make external personal attributions for threat; they are vigilant for emotional threatening words and have biased recall of threatening adjectives (see Bentall, Kinderman & Kaney, 1994; Garety & Freeman, 1999, for reviews). There is also evidence that people with psychosis have negative views about self and others (e.g. Perris et al., 1998). Schematic ideas about the self (beliefs that self is vulnerable or weak, that one is unworthy, that one is bad or needs to be good) or about others (that others are bad, not to be trusted) and related processing biases clearly occur amongst people with psychosis. However, the

degree to which such emotion processing biases are associated with delusion formation and maintenance is a critical issue.

Are persecutory delusions defensive, or consistent with, ongoing threats to self-esteem ?

An influential contemporary hypothesis suggests that persecutory delusions are maintained as an aspect of a psychological defence which functions to protect the individual from the consequences of low self-esteem
(Bentall, Kinderman & Kaney, 1994). Chadwick, Birchwood and Trower
(1996; see also Chapter 7) suggest there may be two forms: "good me" and
"bad me" paranoia. Only in "good me" paranoia are delusions suggested to
be compensatory. In "bad me" paranoia they are said to be consistent with
not defensive, of low self-esteem. The evidence on self-esteem and persecutory delusions is somewhat equivocal. An important recent study indicated that people with persecutory delusions tend to have low self-esteem
and that persecutory delusions can recover independently of self-esteem
(Freeman et al., 1998). There is also no evidence that loss of persecutory
delusions as a result of treatment with cognitive therapy leads to worsening of self-esteem or depression (Chadwick & Lowe, 1994; Kuipers et al.,
1998; Garety et al., 1994). These findings are at odds with a defensive
account of persecutory delusions. They are more consistent with the idea
that persecutory delusions are correspond to ongoing beliefs about self and
others (which are often negative amongst people with psychosis). In such
cases persecutory beliefs may reflect pre-existing negative beliefs about self
and others and social learning in the context of adaptation to difficult interpersonal circumstances. Such a view is often consistent with detailed
assessment of clinical phenomena. For Robbie his paranoia clearly related
to a sense of interpersonal threat from others that appeared to derive from
negative beliefs about others and lack of trust deriving from long term
interpersonal problems. Histories of including problems in attachment
(Drayton, Birchwood & Trower, 1998) and trauma (Mueser et al., 1998) are
relatively common precursors to frank psychotic disorder. These types of
factors in individual personal histories—and potentially also ongoing iatrogenic threats and experiences of humiliation associated with the social
predicament of psychotic disorder (Rooke and Birchwood, 1998) and
trauma associated with hospitalisation (McGorry et al., 1991)—may serve
to reinforce negative beliefs about self and others and pre-existing
expectancies of threat from other people. Possibly, expectancies of threat
from others (which may be consistent with the experience of ongoing or
past threats in the world) might influence the preoccupation with threat
and evil that characterises paranoid thinking. However, cases in which
delusions are associated with high or normal self-esteem have also been

described and in such cases loss of delusions as a consequence of drug treatment and hospitalisation can appear to result in increased depression (Roberts, 1991). Many of these cases in this study had delusions which contained grandiose as well as paranoid elements.

The need for a multi-factorial account of delusions

In most cases a complex combination of factors is involved in the formation and maintenance of delusions. Garety and Freeman (1999) conclude their review of experimental studies of delusions by suggesting that there is support for a multi-factorial model in which "delusions, seen as a person's attempt to explain experiences or events, develop in the context of a person's existing personality and beliefs and in the context of some combination of disturbances/biases in perception, affect or judgement". As we noted above, a characteristic of psychosis is heterogeneity. There is a need to be aware of complex and multiple factors which may underpin and maintain delusions. Both cognitive biases, such as jumping to conclusions, and emotional biases are involved in delusional thinking. We have noted previously how delusions can reflect a search for meaning associated with making sense of anomalies of experience, as suggested by Maher (1988). The way that sense is made is biased by faulty judgement and by emotional concerns which may often reflect previous experience and areas of affective concern. The negative expectancies of threat from others associated with persecutory delusions may frequently be consistent with longstanding pre-existing beliefs about others and self in relation to others. However, in many cases, especially in the more chronic, delusions may also serve a function to give a meaning and purpose in life (Roberts, 1991) and secondary gain or defensive processes may be involved in their maintenance. Detailed analysis of Ben's case suggested that his preoccupation with good and evil related to pre-existing religious ideas and a need to build an identity for himself in the context of threatening events and failures to achieve a secure basis of relationships, work and independent living. It should also be noted that many delusions are complex and incorporate both grandiose and persecutory elements. In Ben's case longitudinal assessments revealed transitions from feelings of strong personal significance in beliefs (e.g. belief in being close to god) alternating with feelings of threat (e.g. starting to be threatened by the devil). Ben was vigilant for, and actively seeking, a psychotic experience which was attributed by him to be personally significant; however, his beliefs also incorporated paranoid elements which were highly distressing. Currently such phenomena are poorly understood. There is a need for further research to tease out the processes which influence changes in such complex beliefs.

PSYCHOLOGICAL REACTIONS TO VOICES

What is the problem with hearing voices ?

Theories which suggest that auditory hallucinations arise from misinterpretations of inner speech, and problems in self-monitoring are supported by experimental evidence, although there is debate about whether this arises from a single cognitive deficit or biases and expectations (see Bentall, 1990; Morrison, 1999, for review). However, from a clinical perspective it is important to recognise that hearing voices per se does not necessarily constitute a clinical problem. For example, Ben had heard benevolent voices for many years before these became part of his acute psychosis. What appears to be associated with voices becoming clinical problems is changes in voice content and in the meaning attached to voices. These differences may reflect different relationships people have with their voices (Benjamin, 1989) and the beliefs they have about them (Chadwick & Birchwood, 1994). Romme et al. (1992) surveyed a large sample of hallucinators who were both in contact and not in contact with psychiatric services. This study showed that those who were not coping with their voices were more likely to rate themselves as less strong than the voice and to experience more negative voices and commanding voices. There were also differences in the behavioural reaction to the voice. Those who were coping with their voices tended to listen selectively to the voice and set limits on it. More recently, Lauder et al. (1998) undertook a detailed comparison of the voice content of 14 people with schizophrenia who heard voices and 14 students who heard voices. This study showed that in many aspects the voices were similar in the two groups. The voices in both groups evaluated and judged the voice hearers and tended to relate to ongoing activities and influenced voices hearers decisions on how to act. But voice hearers with clinical problems considered less often the worth of what the voices were saying. People with schizophrenia heard more critical and abusive voices which more often instigated violence.

Does the meaning of voices influence distress and behavioural reactions ?

There appear to be consistent links between experience of a voice, the individual meaning attributed to it and the subsequent affective response and behaviour. Voices appraised to be malevolent (e.g. critical, evil, threatening) tend to be resisted and provoke negative emotional reactions whereas people tend to engage with, and are not threatened by, voices believed to be benevolent (Chadwick & Birchwood, 1994, 1995; Birchwood & Chadwick, 1997). Close and Garety (1998) observed that malevolent voices were more common (and almost universal) in their clinical sample. These researchers also carefully assessed negative self-evaluations associated with voices and described consistent relationships between voice content, negative self-evaluations and behavioural and emotional reactions. These findings are consistent with observations that depression tends to be associated with negative and critical voice content (Chadwick & Birchwood; 1995; Birchwood & Chadwick, 1997). Possibly it may be most useful to regard the links between mood, self-evaluation and voice content and appraisal of the voice as reciprocally interactive or mutually augmenting.

In a recent study carried out at UEA, Newman-Taylor (1998) found that the reaction to hearing a voice was not just dependent on the attribution of malevolence but also the degree to which the person felt a sense of control and ability to resist in such a context. Malevolent voices were more likely to be resisted by people who showed themselves as having a greater tendency to be an agent in respect to the voice. Potentially, sense of agency in reaction to perceived threat by voices may also relate in a wider way to people's general style of reacting to interpersonal and other threats e.g. whether they have a general sense of agency and whether they adopt a "submissive" or "dominant" position to other people as represented by voices. We are currently exploring the association with relationships with voices and with other interpersonal relationships in more depth.

As well as influencing affective and behavioural reactions to them, beliefs about voices via expectation may have some role in maintaining voices. Recent studies have found associations between positive beliefs about psychosis and negative metacognitive beliefs and predisposition to hallucinations (see Morrison, 1999). These and other findings are consistent with the hypothesis that beliefs about voices, via influences on vigilance and avoidance, could potentially serve to maintain and reinforce confusion about the origins of one's thoughts and emotions and thus represent a set of cognitive biases which may potentially be maintaining the occurrence of voices in the absence of any underlying deficit in cognitive processes (Bentall, 1990).

The relation of voice content to past interpersonal experience

In a careful analysis of people with chronic "treatment-resistant" voices and delusions who were treated in the London–East Anglia trial of cognitive therapy, we observed that in around 50% of these cases it was possible for therapists to make sense of the content of problematic voices in terms of their relationship to key figures associated with trauma in individuals lives (sometimes this related to problematic relationships with attachment figures, but, as frequently, with bullies or abusers) (Fowler et al., in preparation). Other cognitive therapists have described similar types of cases (Kingdon & Turkington, 1994; Chadwick, Birchwood & Trower, 1996) and we have found similar phenomena in our ongoing analysis of early psychosis cases. Vince, for example, heard the voice of his drill sergeant who had severely bullied him while in the army and Janice heard the voices of a group of men who had raped her when she was an adolescent. What is striking in cases of this type is that voice hearers may not be aware of such relationships, even when a relatively clear relationships between voice content and previous relationship or traumatic experience can be detected. Instead they more often view their voices as reflecting an ongoing threat rather than a reflection or sequellae of past experience. For example, Vince felt the drill sergeant was still getting at him even though he had left the army two years previously; Janice was terrified of being raped by the men who she thought were still taunting her every night. In such cases helping voice hearers to become aware of the relationship between their voice content and past experience (and to label voices as reflecting memories not ongoing events) can be an important aspect of cognitive therapy. Why people may lose their awareness of what may be internal reasons for the generation of their voice experiences is as yet unclear. (In some cases who have experienced severe trauma, one reason may be active dissociation in the face of a traumatic experience which gave rise to voice experiences as suggested by Mollon (1996); however, this does not seem to be true of all cases.) It is of interest that the Lauder et al. (1998) study suggests that voice hearers without clinical problems are more aware of the determinants of their voices than people with chronic mental illness. Furthermore, Nayani and David (1996) have shown that chronic voices are more closely associated with delusional beliefs about voices than those of cases of early psychosis. Helping people to understand the origins of voice content and the nature of the relationships they have with their voices may be an important ingredient of cognitive therapy for voices. Possibly, the earlier such work is started the better its results may be.

Interactions between emotion and cognitive disorder in psychosis

Research reveals that a variety of biases may be associated with the maintenance of both delusions and voices. Non-affective reasoning biases and disruptions or deficits in automatic cognitive processes may be involved. However, emotional processing biases which may reflect ongoing and possibly pre-existing beliefs about self and others also seem to be involved. Emotional processes may be particularly associated with the content of critical and abusive voices and threatening persecutory delusions. Understanding how emotional processes and disruptions in automatic cognitive processes could potentially interact in a catastrophic manner might be useful in understanding how deluded or paranoid thinking or threatening reactions to voices are maintained and how people might become stuck in psychosis. What may be important is the interaction between emotion and cognitive disorder.

Becoming stuck in psychosis

Before the onset of psychosis Robbie had felt threatened and interpreted events negatively, but in the psychotic state he started to "see" and "hear" evidence of such threats in the world. Before his psychosis Ben had sought religion as way of making sense of his personal problems and identity crisis. In the context of psychosis he started to "see" and "hear" positive experiences associated with religious fulfilment (e.g. have what feels like direct experience of God). He also saw threats in the world and heard the devil talking to him. In the psychotic state anomalies (which may arise as a result of cognitive disorder) appear to the person experiencing it as "evidence" in the world to confirm their fears, hopes. concerns, etc. Psychotic experience has an emotional tone which is often consistent with ongoing mood and the accessing of relevant meanings and associated thoughts and images. The pre-existing emotional and personal concerns of these people appear to provide a context for the colour and flavour and content of psychotic experience. Furthermore, expectations associated with beliefs about self and others may then drive what is "heard" or "seen" in psychosis.

From the perspective of emotion regulation these phenomena can present a severe problem. Contemporary cognitive theories of depression suggest that emotional processing may become "gridlocked" into "vicious cycles" which maintains the production of depressive or anxious thoughts and images (e.g. Teasdale & Barnard, 1993). These gridlocks will continue until external stimuli intrude, or an alternative model, is accessed. In the context of psychosis we might predict that it would become even more difficult to escape from such gridlocks. Indeed, what should provide independent external feedback from sensations or events in the world can only, in the context of disorder in automatic cognitive processes leading to inner–outer confusion, present a mirror of the fears that lead to generation of such problems in the first place. Indeed, the cycle of expectation and test which characterises emotional processing may lead to feedback from the environment repeatedly confirming one's worst fears. Voices and delusional thoughts come to represent an additional feedback loop in psychosis which may exacerbate any pre-existing negative evaluation of self or others.

Because people with critical and abusive voices tend to regard these experiences as a set of independent external events, voices may serve as "evidence" to compound negative beliefs about self in the absence of any current real external events. Likewise the experience of a nightmare paranoid world may be interpreted in the context of reinforcing any pre-existing lack of trust or negative beliefs about others.

This clearly occurred in the case of Robbie. While there was a real fear of police and criminals this became exaggerated. He saw potential threat everywhere and listened only to his voices. He withdrew from all others and for a period of months he lived alone in a nightmarish world in which everyone was against him. Similarly with Bill. He started to seek God. He looked for visions. He sought to become closer to God by painting. He experienced the bullying and taunting as acts of the Devil, who also talked to him through the voices. He became lost in a nightmarish dreamworld alternatively ecstatic and terrifying from which there was no escape. In both these cases, despite there being very serious problems, it was very difficult to engage them into services. Neither was aware he had a mental health problem. For a long time Robbie thought mental health professionals were part of the conspiracy. Bill thought he was in touch with God. He said he didn't need any help. These problems presented a considerable barrier to treatment and in the end, both had to be compulsorily admitted to hospital.

The critical importance of the appraisal of psychotic experience

Whether someone recognises, or becomes aware of, the nature of his or her problems may be crucial in determining whether anomalous experiences become full-blown psychotic symptoms. Sarah, while distressed by her paranoid experiences, could not be described as deluded. Sarah started to recognise her paranoid fears as anomalous herself and sought help first from her mother then from mental health professionals. Her ability to recognise that her problems arise from personal vulnerability was crucial in seeking help and in gaining consensus information on the paranoia. When paranoid thoughts occurred she learnt to make what was probably a crucial attribution that "it feels like they can read my mind but I know it is probably me". By contrast Robbie and Ben had no rationale to seek help and indeed, for the mental health professionals involved, the first problem was how to work with someone who had no rationale for help. Furthermore, by repeatedly synthesising the idea that "everyone is against me" in Robbie's case and "this is the way to get in touch with God" in Ben's drove them into cycles of cognitive processing and behaviour which maintained their problems. For these and many other patients this lack of awareness or insight into their difficulties was a critical problem.

If one accepts that the basic disorder underpinning psychosis occurs in cognitive processes which are usually automatic, then to some degree lack of awareness of disorder in psychosis is unsurprising. We are only usually aware of products of cognitive processes not the processes themselves (Nisbett & Wilson, 1977). There is no reason why people should necessarily have conscious awareness of the confusion which lead to the change in their experiences. People with psychosis only experience the consequences of such disorder as perceptual and cognitive abnormalities and anomalous experience. However, such psychotic experience "feels" like a change in the world and people are driven to seek explanations for such experiences (see Maher, 1988). They are likely to attribute the change in their experience to a change in the world rather than a change in themselves. Even for Sarah, when it was happening it felt real, only later was she able to tell herself that it was not real. What may be critical is the duration of periods of severe cognitive disorder. If these are time limited and fleeting and interspersed with periods of normal functioning (as in Sarah's case) the person can become "unstuck" from psychosis and make sense of the world in another way. However, in cases where cognitive disorder is longer lasting and anomalies continue (particularly when these occur in the context of altered feelings) there can become an increasing association between beliefs about self and beliefs about psychosis. As meaningful links are created between interpretations of the experiential consequences of inner-outer confusion and beliefs about self and others, this can potentially become the basis of more enduring delusional ideas and hallucinations.

Reactions to the trauma of psychosis

The personal and emotional significance of psychosis can remain long after the psychotic state has passed. Even in cases where psychotic experiences are time limited, such as Sarah's, the threat of such experience can be very powerful. Psychotic experience can remain in memory as very powerful and direct experiences of persecution or of personal criticism and can continue to provide a threat to self-esteem. Even after her psychosis recovered Sarah was still very concerned about sexual and personal issues which had been associated with the content of her paranoia, but which had not been salient issues before her episode. Sarah still needs help in coming to terms with her problems and in returning to her studies. She also needs help in finding a way to label her problem which is less personally threatening. Although Sarah has awareness of her problems she became terrified that she was going mad. While feeling that people could read her mind and were part of a strange occult group following her was threatening, so was thinking that she was going crazy. There is a dilemma in coming to an awareness of personal vulnerability to psychosis. Lack of awareness can lead to delusions, but awareness can lead to worries and anxieties about going crazy and associated stigmatisation. Birchwood (1996) notes that one of the reasons why people with psychosis seek external attributions for their experiences and avoid illness explanations may be defensive because of avoidance of the potential threats to self-esteem which may arise from an internal attribution of believing oneself to be mentally ill. There are various reactions to the trauma of psychosis while some attempt to integrate their experiences into their lives, other seal over. These issues are discussed more fully by Jackson and Iqbal in Chapter 3 in this volume.

TOWARDS A PSYCHOLOGICAL FORMULATION OF PSYCHOSIS: AN OVERVIEW AND SUMMARY

To the person experiencing it, psychotic experience often "feels" as if it is externally generated. However, we have suggested that it is possible to make sense of the form of such experience in the context of knowledge about cognitive processes and biases, and to make sense of the content of such experiences in the context of knowledge about people's backgrounds, their relationships with others, their longstanding beliefs about self and others, and their expectations and hopes. The model implies vulnerability of two types. A biological predisposition (which may be characterised as a proneness to disorder in automatic cognitive processes underpinning conscious experience) and an emotional vulnerability (which may be characterised by negative beliefs about self and others and biases in emotional processing). Psychosis can be assumed to arise within a definable biopsychosocial context and may become elaborated over time. This is represented in Figure 4.2. Factors associated with the maintenance of psychosis (or getting stuck in psychosis) are represented in Figure 4.3. What is represented in Figure 4.3 is how certain types of appraisals may drive cycles of processing which characterise preoccupation with delusions and voices. It is proposed that it is continuing to appraise psychotic experience as a personally significant external event which may drive a search for meaning and thus maintain psychosis. Common appraisals of this type include those which appraise psychotic experience as an external interpersonal threat (e.g. "these experiences mean everyone is against me" for Robbie) but also appraisals which suggest that psychotic experience is an existentially meaningful event (e.g. "I am in touch with god" in the case of Ben). In the context of persecutory ideas the search for meaning may

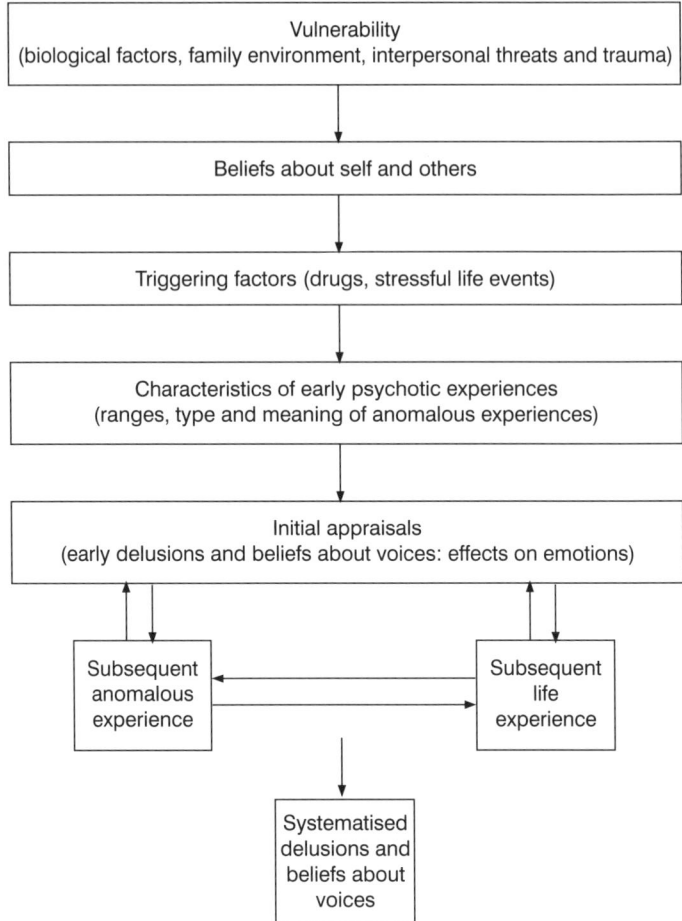

Figure 4.2   Development history of delusions and beliefs about voices.

drive further processing by processes of worry, vigilance to threat and suspiciousness. This may lead to distress and defensive behavioural reactions,
a focus on delusional meanings and possibly the maintenance of persecutory ideas via biased recall of delusion-related material or delusional interpretations of day-to-day experiences. Appraisals of voices as personally
significant (e.g. "It is the controller talking to me") and expectations of
hearing voices of a certain content (e.g. "I must listen to the controller and
do what he says") may also potentially assist the maintenance of the experience of auditory hallucinations. It is the continuing attribution of psychotic experience as a personally significant external event which is
assumed to be critical in maintaining the cycle. Appraisals of psychosis as

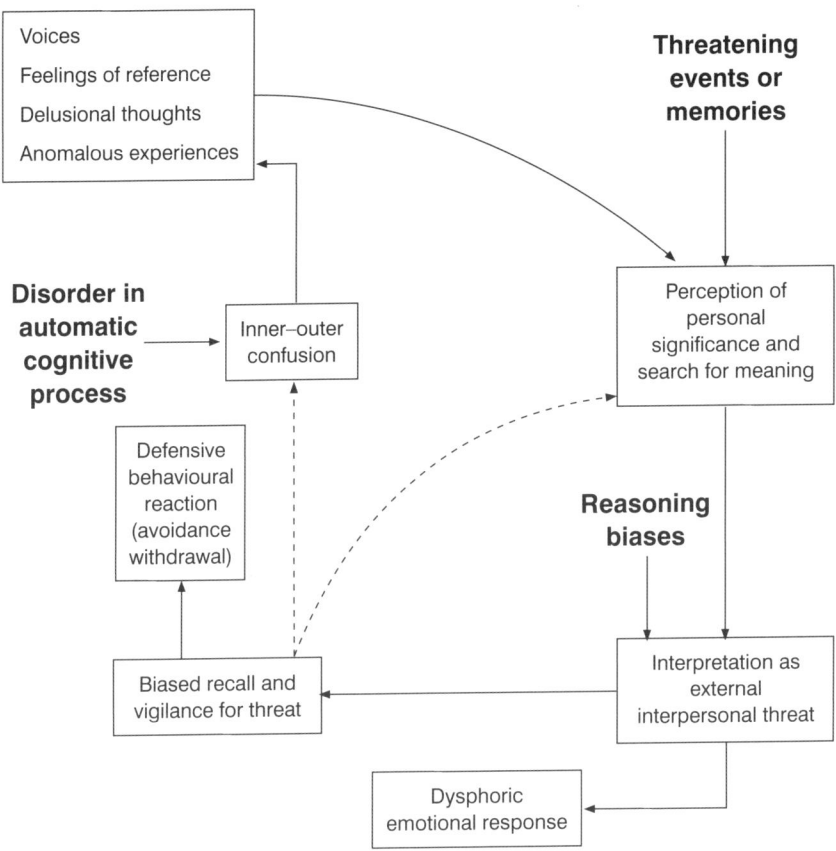

Figure 4.3   Maintenance of threatening reactions to psychosis.

personally meaningful external events may also lead to a search for meaning and cycles of processing characterising "seeking psychosis".

Conversely, appraisals of psychosis as reflecting experience which derives internally (as an aspect of one's own cognitive processes) and as reflecting an aspect of personal vulnerability may be protective. In the case of Sarah the initial feeling of personal significance which accompanied her experiences of mind reading were quickly compensated by an appraisal that "there is something wrong with me; am I going mad ?". This appraisal cut off a further search for meaning and led her to disregard what initially felt personally significant. It possibly averted the sequences of deluded thinking which could have potentially exacerbated her paranoia. The model represented in Figure 4.3 is consistent with that proposed by other theorists who have suggested that the experience of incipient psychosis (Birchwood, 1996) and voices (Morrison, 1999) may constitute triggers for a psychological reaction in a similar manner to which bodily experience may constitute a trigger for panic (Clark, 1988). Further research is needed into this cognitive model, but many of the research findings discussed above can be regarded are consistent with a framework of this type.

The model provides a basis for understanding how periods of acute psychosis can lead to a risk of developing residual psychotic symptomatology. Essentially, chronic delusions and voices may be assumed to be maintained by a similar pattern to that represented in Figure 4.3. Over time the search for meaning which starts with appraisal of anomalous experience in early psychosis may generalise into a systematised delusional system. This may occur when specific attributions for anomalous psychotic experience become associated with ongoing appraisals of day-to-day threats and interpretations of past and current experience. A delusion may come to reflect the accessing of a higher order meaning structure which may come to be accessed by day-to-day events and threatening memories as well as emotional and anomalous experience. Chronic delusions can also come to be associated with high levels of feelings of meaning and purpose in life (Roberts, 1991). Once such beliefs acquire such functions, which may not be available in the person's real life, giving up delusional beliefs may be difficult. The risk for Ben of seeking relief in delusions if he cannot find a satisfactory work and social life is clear. Robbie may well maintain his persecutory ideas if a way cannot be found of helping him out of the threatening lifestyle he currently leads.

Implications for intervention in early psychosis

The first reaction of a mental health professional encountering a person in an acute psychotic state is that the problems are confusing and do not make sense. It is necessary to tolerate this confusion, and the severe emotions that may accompany it, then patiently and calmly to assess the background and history to the problem and work with the individual to assess the psychotic experience and the biases associated with their search for meaning. The nature of triggering events often provide clues as to emotional problems involved. Assisting people with early psychosis to develop a wider understanding of

(a) the internal or personal basis for their experiences (in relationship of ongoing experiences and feelings, their personal history, pre-existing beliefs, etc.);
(b) the presence of possible cognitive disorder (e.g. disorder of automatic cognitive processes, "jumping to conclusions" and emotional biases); and
(c) the context and relationship of their experiences to ongoing and previous events

may assist to prevent them from adopting a fixed view that external agents are the sole cause for their problems. There is also a need to help people to come to terms with the trauma of psychosis (see Jackson & Iqbal, Chapter 3 in this volume). Many existing cognitive therapy strategies are consistent with these aims (see Drury, Chapter 8, and Jackson, Hubert & Henry, Chapter 9, in this volume). Treatment manuals provided by Fowler, Garety & Kuipers (1995) and Chadwick, Birchwood & Trower (1996) provide further details on these strategies.

Awareness of potential stressors is important in developing relapse prevention strategies. All the above patients were assisted by taking neuroleptic medication, and continuing to take medication is to some degree protective. However, there is also emotional vulnerability. For Robbie, the experience of being threatened by others in the future might bring back the feeling of threat thereby triggering psychosis. For Ben, events exacerbating his frustration, loneliness and failure to achieve may lead to a return to a preoccupation with a direct relationship with God. For Sarah, conflicts regarding her sexuality might be a trigger which would weaken her resolve to stay sane. Helping people to become aware of these vulnerabilities is important in the context of developing strategies to manage relapse (see Spencer, Murray & Plaistow, Chapter 10 in this volume).

There is now substantial evidence of an association between duration of untreated psychosis and subsequent relapse rate (Johnstone et al., 1986) and the degree of remission and time to remission after a first psychotic episode (Loebel et al., 1992). Wyatt (1995) has suggested that untreated psychosis may be biologically toxic and responsible for long-term morbidity. While this may be the case, it may also be the case that untreated psychosis is psychologically toxic. What may characterise the development of an increased vulnerability to psychotic symptoms may be an association of episodes of psychosis with an adverse psychological reaction to psychosis characterised by emotional reactions, cognitive biases and behavioural disturbance. Cognitive approaches to prevention in early psychosis should therefore seek to prevent the development of an adverse psychological reaction to the manifestations of psychotic disorder.

REFERENCES

Arieti, S. (1966). Schizophrenic cognition. In Hoch, P.H. and Zubin J. (Eds), Psychopathology of schizophrenia. New York: Grune & Stratton.
Castle, D.J., Phelan, M., Wessely, S. & Murray, R.M. (1994). Which patients with non-affective functional psychosis are not admitted at first psychiatric contact ? *British Journal of Psychiatry*, **165**, 101–106.
Bannister, D. (1983). The psychotic disguise. In W. Dryden (Ed.), *Therapists' Dilemmas*. London: Harper & Row.

Benjamin, L.S. (1989). Is chronicity a function of the relationship between the person and the auditory hallucination? *Schizophrenia Bulletin, 15,* (2), 291–310.

Bentall, R.P. (1990). The illusion of reality: a review and integration of psychological research on hallucinations. *Psychological Bulletin, 107,* 82–85.

Bentall, R.P., Kinderman, P. & Kaney, S. (1994). The self, attributional processes and abnormal beliefs: towards a model of persecutory delusions. *Behaviour Research and Therapy, 32,* 331–341.

Birchwood M., Smith, J., Macmillan, F., Hogg, B., Prasad, R., Harvey, C. & Bering S. (1989). Predicting relapse in schizophrenia: the development and implementation of an early signs monitoring system using patients and families as observers. *Psychological Medicine, 19,* 649–656.

Birchwood, M., Macmillan, F. & Smith, J. (1994). Early Intervention. In M. Birchwood and N. Tarrier (Eds), *Psychological Management of Schizophrenia.* Chichester: Wiley.

Birchwood, M. (1996). Early intervention in psychosis. In G. Haddock & P. Slade (Eds), *Cognitive-Behavioural Interventions with Psychotic Disorders.* London: Routledge.

Birchwood, M. & Chadwick, P. (1997). The omnipotence of voices: testing the validity of a cognitive model. *Psychological Medicine, 27,* 1345–1353.

Bleuler, E. (1950). *Dementia Praecox or the Group of Schizophrenias.* (Originally published 1905; English translation; Zinkin, E.) New York: International Universities Press.

Bannister, D. (1983). The psychotic disguise. In W. Dryden (Ed), *Therapists' dilemmas.* Harper & Row.

Claridge G. (1985). *Origins of Mental Illness.* Oxford: Blackwell.

Chadwick, P.D.J. & Birchwood, M.J. (1994). The omnipotence of voices: a cognitive approach to hallucinations. *British Journal of Psychiatry, 164,* 190–201.

Chadwick, P.D.J. & Birchwood, M.J. (1995). The omnipotence of voices II. The beliefs about voices questionnaire. *British Journal of Psychiatry, 165,* 190–201.

Chadwick, P.D.J. & Lowe, C.F. (1994). A cognitive approach to measuring and modifying delusions. *Behaviour Research and Therapy, 32,* 355–367.

Chadwick, P.D.J., Birchwood, M.J. & Trower, P. (1996). *Cognitive therapy for Delusions, Voices and Paranoia.* Wiley Series in Clinical Psychology. Chichester: Wiley.

Chapman, J. (1966). The early symptoms of schizophrenia. *British Journal of Psychiatry, 112,* 225–251.

Chapman, L.J. & Chapman, J.P. (1988). The genesis of delusions. In T.F. Oltmanns & B.A. Maher (Eds), *Delusional Beliefs,* (pp. 167–183). New York: Wiley.

Ciompi, L. (1988). *The Psyche and Schizophrenia.* Cambridge, MA: Harvard University Press.

Clark, D.M. (1988). A cognitive model of panic attacks. In S. Rachman and J.D. Maser (Eds), *Panic: Psychological Perspectives* (pp. 71–89). Hillsdale, NJ: Applebaum.

Close, H. & Garety, P. (1998). Cognitive assessment of voices: further developments in the understanding the emotional impact of voices. *British Journal of Clinical Psychology, 37,* 173–188.

Cutting, J. (1985). *The Psychology of Schizophrenia.* Edinburgh: Churchill-Livingstone.

Cutting, J. & Dunne, F. (1989). Subjective experience of schizophrenia. *Schizophrenia Bulletin, 15,* 217–231.

Drayton, M., Birchwood, M. & Trower, P. (1998). Early attachment experience and recovery from psychosis. *British Journal of Clinical Psychology, 37,* (3) 269–284.

Drury, V. (1999). Cognitive behaviour therapy in early psychosis. In M. Birchwood, D. Fowler and C. Jackson, (Eds), *Early Intervention in Psychosis: A Practical Handbook.* Chichester: Wiley.

Dudley, R.E.J., John, C.H., Young, A.W. & Over, D.E. (1997). The effect of self referent material on the reasoning of people with delusions. *British Journal of Clinical Psychology, 36,* 575–584.

Federn, P. (1953). *Ego Psychology and the Psychoses*. New York: Basic Books.

Fowler, D.G., Garety, P. & Kuipers, E. (1995). *Cognitive Behaviour Therapy for Psychosis: Theory and Practice*. Chichester: Wiley.

Fowler, D., Garety, P. & Kuipers, E. (1998). Understanding the inexplicable: a cognitive approach to delusions. In C. Perris and P. McGorry (Eds), *A Handbook of Cognitive Psychotherapy for Psychosis*. Chichester: Wiley.

Fowler, D.G., Hadley, C., Garety, P.A., Kuipers, E. & Freeman, D. (in preparation). The relationship between trauma and psychosis.

Freeman, D., Garety, P.A., Fowler, D., Kuipers, E., Dunn, G., Bebbington, P. & Hadley, C. (1998). The London–East Anglia randomised controlled trial of cognitive-behaviour therapy for psychosis. IV: Self esteem and persecutory delusions. *British Journal of Clinical Psychology*, **37**, 415–430.

Freeman, D. & Garety, P.A. (1999). Worry, worry processes and dimensions of delusions: an exploratory investigation of a role for anxiety processes in the maintenance of delusional distress. *Behavioural and Cognitive Psychotherapy*, **27**, 47–62.

Freud, S. (1924/1961). The loss of reality in psychosis and neurosis. In J. Strachey et al. (eds), *Collected Works. Standard Edition* (Vol. 3; p. 176). London: Hogarth.

Frith, C.D. & Done, D.J. (1987). Towards a neuropsychology of schizophrenia. *British Journal of Psychiatry*, **153**, 437–443.

Frith, C.D. (1992). *The Coopritive Neuropsychology of Schizophrenia*. Hove: Lawrence Erlbaum.

Garety, P.A., Hemsely, D.R. & Wessely, S. (1991). Reasoning in deluded schizophrenic and paranoid patients: biases in performance on a probabilistic inference task. *Journal of Nervous and Mental Disorder*, **179**, 194–201.

Garety, P.A. & Freeman, D. (1999). Cognitive approaches to delusions: a critical review of theories and evidence. *British Journal of Clinical Psychology*, **38**, 2.

Garety, P.A. & Hemsley, D.R. (1994). *Delusions: Investigations into the Psychology of Delusional Reasoning*. Oxford: Oxford University Press.

Garety, P.A., Fowler, D., Kuipers, E., Freeman, D., Dunn, G., Bebbington, P.E., Hadley, C. & Jones, S. (1997). The London–East Anglia randomised controlled trial of cognitive behaviour therapy for psychosis. II: Predictors of outcome. *British Journal of Psychiatry*, **171**, 420–426.

Garfield, D.A. (1995). *Unbearable Affect: A Guide to the Psychotherapy of Psychosis*. New York: Wiley.

Gray, J.A. (1998). Integrating schizophrenia. *Schizophrenia Bulletin*, **24** (2), 249–266.

Gray, J.A., Feldon, L., Rawlins, J.N.P., Hemsley, D.R. & Smith, A.D. (1991). The neuropsychology of schizophrenia. *Behavioural and Brain Sciences*, **14**, 1–20.

Haddock, G., Tarrier, N., Spaulding, W., Yusupoff, L., Kinney, C. & McCarthy, E. (1998). Individual cognitive behaviour therapy in the treatment of delusions and hallucinations: a review. *Clinical Psychology Review*, **17**, (7) 821–838.

Harrow, M., Rattenbury, F. & Stoll, F. (1988). Schizophrenic delusions: an analysis of their persistence, of related pre-morbid ideas and of three major dimensions. In T.F. Oltmanns & B.A. Maher (Eds), *Delusional Beliefs*. New York: Wiley.

Hemsley, D. (1993). A simple (or simplistic?) cognitive model for schizophrenia. *Behaviour Research and Therapy*. **31**, 633–646.

Hemsley, D. (1998). The disruption in the sense of self in schizophrenia: potential links with disturbances of information processing. *British Journal of Medical Psychology*, **71**, 115–124.

Jackson, C.E. & Iqbal, Z. (1999). The trauma of psychosis. In M. Birchwood, D. Fowler and C. Jackson, (Eds), *Early Intervention in Psychosis: A Practical Handbook*. Chichester: Wiley.

Jaspers, K. (1963). *General Psychopathology* (trans. J. Hoenig & M.W. Hamilton). Manchester University Press.

Johnstone, E.C., Crow, T.J., Johnson, A.L. & Macmillan, J.F. (1986). The Northwick Park Study of first episode schizophrenia: I. Presentation of the illness and problems relating to admission. *British Journal of Psychiatry*, **148**, 115–120.

Jones, C., Cormac, I., Mota, J., Campbell, C. (1999). Cognitive behaviour therapy for schizophrenia (Cochrane Review). *The Cochrane Library*, Issue 1, Oxford: Update Software.

Jung, C.G. (1907) The psychology of dementia preacox. In *The Psychogenesis of Mental disease. Collected Works of Carl Jung*, Vol. 3, 1960. London: Routledge & Kegan Paul.

Kingdon, D.G. & Turkington, D. (1994). *Cognitive-Behavioural Therapy of Schizophrenia*. New York Guilford Press.

Kingdon, D. (1997). The Wellcome study of cognitive therapy for treatment resistant schizophrenia. Paper presented at 2nd International conference on psychological treatments for schizophrenia. Oxford, UK, June 1997.

Kuipers, E., Garety, P., Fowler, D., Dunn, G., Bebbington, P., Freeman, D. & Hadley, C. (1997). The London–East Anglia randomised controlled trial of cognitive-behavioural therapy for psychosis. I: Effects of the treatment phase. *British Journal of Psychiatry*, **171**, 319–327.

Kuipers, E., Fowler, D., Garety, P., Chisholm, D., Dunn, G., Bebbington, P., Freeman, D. & Hadley, C. (1998). The London–East Anglia randomised controlled trial of cognitive behaviour therapy for psychosis. III: Follow up and economic evaluation at 18 months. *British Journal of Psychiatry*, **173**, 61–68.

Harrow, M., Rattenbury, F. & Stoll, F. (1988). Schizophrenic delusions: an analysis of their persistence, of related premorbid ideas and of three major dimensions. In T.F. Oltmanns, & B.A. Maher (Eds) *Delusional Beliefs*. New York: Wiley.

Harrop, C.E., Trower, P. & Mitchell, I.J. (1996). Does biology go around the symptoms? A copernican shift in schizophrenia paradigms. *Clinical Psychology Review*, **16** (7), 641–654.

Kingdon D.G. & Turkington, D. (1994). *Cognitive-behavioural therapy of schizophrenia*. Hove: Lawrence Erlbaum.

Lauder, I., Thomas, P., McNally, D. & Glinski, A. (1998). What voices can do with words: pragmatics of verbal hallucinations. *Psychological Medicine*, **27**, 885–898.

Loebel, A., Lieberman, J., Mayerhoff, D., Geisler, S. & Szymanski, S. (1992). Duration of psychosis and outcome in first episode schizophrenia. *American Journal of Psychiatry*, **149** (9), 1183–1188.

Maher, B.A. (1988). Anomalous experience and delusional thinking: the logic of explanations. In: T.F. Oltmanns, and B.A. Maher, (Eds), *Delusional Beliefs* (pp. 15–33). New York: Wiley.

McGorry, P.D., Chanen, A., McCarthy, E. et al. (1991) Post traumatic stress disorder following recent onset psyhcosis: an unrecognised postpsychotic syndrome. *Journal of Nervous and Mental Disease*, **179**, 253–258.

McGorry, P.D., McFarlane, C., Patton, G., Bell, R.Q., Dudgeon, P., Hibbert, M., Jackson, H. & Bowes, G. (1995). The prevalence of prodromal features of schizophrenia in adolescence: a preliminary survey. *Acta Psychiatrica Scandanivica*, **90**, 375–378.

Mollon, A.P. (1996). *Multiple Selves, Multiple Voices. Working with Trauma, Violation and Dissociation*. Chichester: Wiley.

Morrison, A.P., Haddock, G. & Tarrier, N. (1995). Intrusive thoughts and auditory hallucinations: a cognitive approach. *Behavioural and Cognitive Psychotherapy*, **23**, 265–280

Morrison, A. (1999). A cognitive analysis of auditory hallucinations: are voices to schizophrenia what bodily sensations are to panic? *Behavioural and Cognitive Psychotherapy*, 289–302.

Mueser, K.T., Osher, F.C., Vidaver, R., Ancillo, P. & Foy, D.W. (1998). Trauma and post traumatic stress in severe mental illness. *Journal of Consulting and Clinical Psychology*, **66** (3), 493–499.

Nayani, T.H. & David, A.S. (1996). The auditory hallucination: a phenomenological survey. *Psychological Medicine*, **26**, 177–189.

Neale, J.M. (1988). Defensive functions of manic episodes. In T.F. Oltmanns, and B.A. Maher (Eds), *Delusional Beliefs*. (pp. 138–156) New York: Wiley.

Newman-Taylor, K. (1998). *Examination of the role of agency in individuals responses to auditory hallucinations*. Unpublished D.Clin.Psy. thesis, University of East Anglia.

Nisbett, R.E. & Wilson, L. (1977). Telling more than we can know: verbal reports on mental processes. *Psychological Review*, **84**, 231–259.

Perris, C. Fowler, D., Skagerlind Olsson, M. & Thorsson, C. (1998). The development and validation of the dysfunctional working models of the self questionnaire (DWMS): a scale to measure dysfunctional assumptions in schizophrenia and related conditions. *Acta Psychologica Scandinivica*: **98**, 219–223.

Peters, E.R., Joseph, S.A. & Garety, P.A. (1999). The measurement of delusional ideation in the normal population. *Schizophrenia Bulletin*, **25**, 553–576.

Roberts, G. (1991). Delusional belief systems and meaning in life: a preferred reality? *British Journal of Psychiatry*, **159** (14), 19–28.

Romme, M.A.J. & Escher, A D.M. (1989). Hearing voices. *Schizophrenia Bulletin*, **15** (2), 209–216.

Romme, M.A.J., Honig, A., Noodhoorn, E.O. & Escher, A.D. (1992). Coping with hearing voices, an emancipatory approach. *British Journal of Psychiatry*, **16**, 99–103.

Rooke, O. & Birchwood, M. (1998). Loss, humiliation, and entrapment as appraisals of schizophrenic illness: a prospective study of depressed and non-depressed patients. *British Journal of Clinical Psychology*, **37**, (3), 259–268.

Shepherd, M., Watt, D., Falloon, I. & Smeeton, N. (1989). The natural history of schizophrenia: a five-year follow-up in a representative sample of schizophrenics. *Psychological Medicine*, Monograph Supplement 15.

Strauss, J. & Carpenter, W.T. (1977). Prediction of outcome in schizophrenia. III: Five year outcome and its predictors. *Archives of General Psychiatry*, **34**, 159–163.

Strauss, J.S. & Carpenter, W.T. (1981). *Schizophrenia*. New York: Plenum.

Spencer, B., Murray, E. & Plaistow, J. (1999). Relapse prevention in early psychosis. In M. Birchwood, D. Fowler and C. Jackson (Eds), *Early Intervention in Psychosis: A Practical Handbook*. Chichester: Wiley.

Teasdale, J. & Barnard, P. (1993). *Affect, Cognition and Change: Remodelling Depressive Thought*. Hillsdale, NJ: Erlbaum.

Tien, A.Y. (1991). Distributions of hallucinations in the population. *Social Psychiatry and Psychiatric Epidemiology*, **26**, 287–292.

Weirsma, D., Neinhus, F.J., Slooff, C.J. & Giel, R. (1998). Natural course of schizophrenic disorders: a 15 year follow up of a Dutch cohort. *Schizophrenia Bulletin*, **24** (1) 75–85.

WHO (1973). *The international pilot study of schizophrenia*. Geneva: World Health Organisation.

Wyatt, R.J. (1995). Early intervention in schizophrenia: can the course of the disorder be altered? *Biological Psychiatry*, **38**, 1–3.

Yung, A. & McGorry, P. (1996). The prodromal phase of first episode psychosis: past and current conceptualisations. *Schizophrenia Bulletin*, **22**, 353–371.

Zubin, J. & Spring, B. (1977) Vunerability: a new view of schizophrenia. *Journal of Abnormal Psychology*, **86**, 103–126.

Chapter 5

THE EARLY DEVELOPMENT OF EXPRESSED EMOTION AND BURDEN IN THE FAMILIES OF FIRST-ONSET PSYCHOSIS

Elizabeth Kuipers* and David Raune*

> I find myself asking for God to take it from her and give it to me. If I could do anything to take it from her I would prefer that. (Mother of 19-year-old daughter)

> I was so shocked. If I had been that type of person I would have had a heart attack. (Father of 23-year-old son)

> Emotionally I couldn't handle it, it was just tearing me apart. (Mother of 19-year-old son)

As can be seen from the above quotations, the impact on carers of those with first-onset psychosis, and the implications for the care involved, cannot be minimised. First onset is a unique opportunity to look at these processes in families, both to compare them with what we know from research on more long-term groups, to help understand how family reactions are formed and then develop, and finally to consider optimal intervention at this early stage, before attitudes have hardened and rejection, resignation or despair set in. The purpose of this chapter is to address these issues, using data from previous research on long-term families and some new data on first-onset psychosis.

*Institute of Psychiatry, London, UK.

Early Intervention in Psychosis.
Edited by M. Birchwood, D. Fowler & C. Jackson.
© 2000 John Wiley & Sons Ltd.

THE IMPACT OF CARE

We know from previous research that the impact of having to offer care to a relative with psychosis is likely to be severe. Since the 1950s researchers have looked at this area and arrived at a fairly consistent consensus on the burden that the caring role imposes on relatives and on the range and depth of the areas that are affected. (Fadden, Bebbington & Kuipers, 1987; Kuipers, 1993). This burden has been defined most succinctly as the "effect of the patient on the family" (Goldberg & Huxley, 1980). Carers do not choose these roles; they find that they become carers, often in the long term, because of changes in a close relative, who develops psychosis. These changes are usually poorly understood, the person's behaviour often misattributed (Brewin et al., 1991) as "laziness" or "being difficult". It is often extremely difficult to access appropriate help, because the person with psychosis will frequently not agree that there is a problem, as will other professionals at times, and often there has to be quite a severe or dramatic crises before mental health agencies become involved.

The caring role in psychosis frequently requires the carer to take on tasks and roles not normally expected to need supervision in another adult, unless they have a physical disability or dementia. The initial reactions to this can range from bewilderment to denial, anxiety and shock. Most carers will have no idea of what to expect and often make assumptions that this will be an acute and temporary problem which will resolve. Such unrealistic expectations are usually based on lack of information. They include not being aware of the extended time period often required for social recovery in psychosis, and the likelihood that role performance will be severely impaired during this time. Care-givers are likely to be elderly mothers of young adult clients, given the typical age of onset of psychosis (Scazufca & Kuipers, 1997). It is evident that when people take on the role, they are likely to suffer increased levels of worry and strain, and three times the clinical rate of depression and anxiety as the normal population (30% compared to around 10%) (Fadden, Bebbington & Kuipers, 1987). They are also likely to be emotionally upset, primarily because of feelings of loss, but also due to a range of other feelings, from anger, frustration, guilt, anxiety about the future, to over-concern and over-protection. Carers will themselves suffer from reduced social networks (Andersen et al., 1984) and are likely to feel both isolated and stigmatised. This is because mental illness is still both feared and demonised in our society. Typically, negative symptoms such as social withdrawal are found most difficult to deal with, as is disruptive or embarrassing behaviour when it exists (Creer & Wing, 1975; Gibbons et al., 1984).

Thus carers rapidly finds themselves involved in providing care, with few perceived resources, no specialist knowledge, and often no perceived support from services. In particular, emotional support is felt to be lacking, even if services can provide practical help (MacCarthy et al., 1989). Thus, despite being an important and much valued resource for those with psychosis, who can enhance recovery (Kuipers & Bebbington, 1985) carers can easily feel both exhausted and exploited (Noh & Turner, 1987).

EXPRESSED EMOTION

The importance of the quality of the relationships that are part of the caring role has also been examined in considerable detail since the 1950s. While carers may be tolerant and understanding of a client's difficulties, the very nature of psychosis tends to mitigate against this. People with psychosis often have unusual or bizarre beliefs (delusions), may hear or see distressing things that are not apparent to others (hallucinations), have jumbled or unusual thought processes (thought disorder) and suffer from severe levels of apathy, self-neglect or social withdrawal (negative symptoms). They themselves may not agree that there is a problem (poor insight) and may not want to discuss how they are feeling (suspiciousness). All these symptoms typically appear in young adulthood when the individual may also be trying out new relationships, be involved in substance abuse (drugs or alcohol), and starting new and independent lifestyles with all the attendant stresses and demands that these imply. Thus carers are particularly likely to attribute at least some of the symptoms, particularly negative ones, to adolescence, the drug culture, unsuitable friends, or general stress. A typical reaction at this stage, is to feel angry or frustrated at what is perceived to be unmotivated or odd behaviour, and to try to change this by becoming annoyed or critical. An alternative response, particularly in the acute stages of a florid attack, is to "take over" care and every day tasks, in order to protect and look after the individual, who may be perceived correctly as no longer competent. While perfectly understandable, and useful in the acute stage, this over-protective response quickly becomes over involved and intrusive in the recovery stage, when acute symptoms have improved, as it can prevent the adult being able to take back appropriate roles and functioning in the future.

These two coping styles, criticism (critical comments [CC]) and emotional over-involvement (EOI) are the key predictive features of Expressed Emotion [EE]. This has now been reliably measured in a wide variety of studies, and found in a range of diagnoses, not just schizophrenia and manic depression, to be a reliable predictor of outcome. High levels of either or both CC or EOI, predict poor outcome in the ensuing nine months after an acute episode, if the person goes back to live in this environment. Typically, around 50% of those returning to live in high EE families will relapse in the next nine months, compared to 21% returning to low EE environments (Kavanagh, 1992; Kuipers, 1994; Bebbington & Kuipers, 1994). These relationships are not restricted to family carers, but also occur in staff, who in key relationships with clients not only find the same behaviour difficult to deal with (negative symptoms and disruptive behaviour), but show similar (particularly critical) attitudes towards it (Moore, Ball & Kuipers, 1992; Kuipers & Moore, 1996).

Links between burden and expressed emotion

Despite the fact that the literature on the impact of care (burden) in psychosis, and the literature on Expressed Emotion in carers has existed since the 1950s, remarkably few studies have measured them both. Jackson, Smith and McGorry (1990) first completed an exploratory study suggesting that they were linked. Smith et al. (1993) investigated 49 relatives of those with psychosis and found that carers with a high level of EE reported higher levels of disturbed behaviour in clients, more subjective burden and less (perceived) effective coping. Scazufca and Kuipers (1996) looked at 67 relatives (50 key relatives) of 50 clients with psychosis. We found that high EE relatives had significantly higher mean scores for their burden of care than low EE relatives. High EE carers also perceived more deficits in client functioning. In fact, social functioning and symptoms in clients were independent of the EE rating of carers. We also found that relatives who were working were more likely to be low EE, high contact with clients was associated with increased burden and more carers were women. The association between work and low EE was not causal of course, but did suggest that those who worked might also be able to have a different perspective on the problems, because caring was not their only role. It was also clear, in this study, that low EE carers were still burdened, but perceived this as less problematic. We concluded that "the measures of both EE and burden are more dependent on relatives appraisal of the patient's condition than on their actual deficits" (p. 586). Further "that EE is a measure of the quality of the relationship viewed through relatives appraisal of the circumstances" (p. 586).

These findings suggest two things. Firstly, that a consideration of burden might make it easier to identify poor outcome families who might benefit from intervention; secondly, that intervention might be particularly valuable if it was focused on impaired social functioning, and on how to improve a family's ability to negotiate about it.

First-episode studies

Although the research evidence so far appears promising, the effects of these processes are not yet established in first-onset psychosis. For instance, studies of early onset schizophrenia have found much weaker effects for the predictive effects of EE. Leff and Brown (1977) found a 38% relapse rate in first admission high EE families, compared to 69% relapse rates in readmission families. Macmillan et al. (1986), in a first-episode study, claimed that high EE was not predictive of outcome at all. Stirling et al. (1991) found that family EE at first onset was not predictive of outcome in the first nine months, although there was some evidence of an association between EE and the psychiatric status of patients at an 18-month follow-up (Stirling et al., 1993).

Birchwood and Smith (1987) have posited a transactional model for EE. They have suggested that EE develops over time and that families emerge as high EE, depending on their ability to cope with problems. This has put coping responses as a central feature of high or low EE carer responses.

More recently, attribution research has found that, after intervention, there was a shift to more universal attribution for negative behaviours rather than personal blame by carers (Brewin, 1994). Bentsen et al. (1998) found that both criticism and hostility were predicted by a patient's lack of employment, more than three hospital admissions and difficult behaviour. Bertrando et al. (1992) found that high warmth in carers was associated with low admission rates even in high EE families. Thus there seems to be some suggestion that it would be helpful for families to reattribute difficult symptoms, to remain as positive and empathic about the client as possible, and perhaps to intervene before problems become too intractable.

There are thus good reasons to investigate the processes of adaptation to the caring role at first onset in psychosis, when it might be possible to answer the following questions.

- Is EE a relevant factor at first onset and does it relate to outcome at this stage?
- Is EE related to carer burden and distress?
- Is EE associated with particular coping responses and, further, are some coping responses more adaptive than others?

There are also theoretical questions to be answered. These include, how EE develops over time, whether it is a transactional process, and how our understanding of the vulnerability stress model of psychosis (Neuchterlein, Snyder & Mintz, 1992) might become more specific.

Clinically there are several implications. We know from the literature that family interventions in schizophrenia are "an effective and underused treatment" (Anderson & Adams 1996) and have well-attested efficacy (Penn & Mueser, 1996). However, these have tended to be offered to families with long-term problems. We are interested to consider instead whether early intervention could reduce morbidity, distress and outcome for first-onset families, how to engage such families in treatment at a stage when shock and denial may be paramount and, finally, how best to focus any intervention to meet the needs of this group.

In order to investigate these issues a first-onset study was undertaken, and some of the results are included here.

Assessment instruments

Standard social and demographic data were collected from both patients and carers. Patients were further assessed with the SCAN 1.1 (WHO, 1992) in order to measure and classify their psychopathology and associated behavioural problems.

Carers were also were given the Social Isolation Scale (SIS: O'Connor & Brown, 1984); carers were asked about the frequency of contact and the quality of their social ties. The Camberwell Family Inventory (CFI: Vaughn & Leff, 1976) was conducted in order to rate EE. The CFI is a semi-structured interview which asks carers about the start of the patients' problems, focusing on the previous three months, covering how the patients spend their time and how their behaviour has changed. All interviews were tape recorded. A relative was considered high EE if they made six mor more critical comments, revealed any hostility or were rated 3 or more on emotional over-involvement. In order to assess burden the Experience of Caregiving Inventory (Szmukler et al., 1996) was administered. This is a 66 item instrument which asks about the subjective experience of caregiving in eight areas covering difficult behaviours, negative symptoms, stigma, problems with services, effects on the family, need for back up, dependency and loss and two areas of positive experiences of caring, covering positive personal experiences and good aspects of the relationship.

The COPE (Carver et al., 1989, 1994) was administered to measure how often carers had been using each coping style when they experienced stress and problems related to the patient. The scales assessed were: active coping; planning; seeking instrumental social support; seeking emotional social support; suppression of competing activities; turning to religion; positive reinterpretation and growth; restraint coping; acceptance; focus on and venting the emotions; denial; mental disengagement; behavioural disengagement; alcohol/drug disengagement; and humour. Finally, carers were given the Beck Depression Inventory (BDI: Beck et al., 1979) and the General Health Questionnaire (GHQ-28: Goldberg & Hillier, 1979) to look at carer morbidity and stress levels.

Results

There was a 10% refusal rate for patients and a carer refusal rate of 6%. Data were available on 46 key carers and patients.

Patient sample

Diagnosis: Most (70%) patients carried a schizophrenia or schizoaffective diagnosis. The remainder carried the diagnoses of bipolar disorder (13%), or other psychotic disorders (17%). Fifty-eight per cent were male and 42% were female. Patients were aged between 17 and 64 with a median age of 28. Twenty-one per cent were teenagers, half were under 30 and over three quarters (82%) were under 40. As expected, men had an earlier illness onset (means of 28 vs 33), although the difference was not statistically significant. As expected for a first-episode study, patients had recent onset, with illness lengths ranging from 9 to 2,260 days with a median of 19 weeks. Men had a median illness length 10 weeks longer than women. Fifty-four per cent of the sample were white with 17% black Caribbean, 20% black African and 9% other. Twenty-four per cent of the patients lived with a partner and 34% lived alone. Interestingly, nearly a third (32%) of women had made previous psychiatric contact for non-psychotic conditions compared to only 7% of the men. Nearly two-thirds (65%) of patients were unemployed at the time of interview.

CARERS

Carers were mainly a group of parents (61% parental, 20% were partners). They were predominantly middle-aged (mean age 47), and women (72%), of whom over half (60%) worked as well as cared (47% worked full time). About a fifth (21%) were retired and nearly two-thirds (61%) had a partner. Over half (54%) lived with the patient and nearly half (46%) were living with the patient at illness onset. Carers had moderately high face-to-face contact (27 hours per week mean), with nearly a third (32%) in contact for more than 35 hours per week. Just over half the carers were white (56%). At the time of the assessment 44% of patients were in hospital. Most (65%) carer assessments were carried out in their home. Nearly a fifth (19%) described previous experience of caring for someone with a psychiatric problem.

Carers "Needs"

Carers had a range of needs due to social isolation, distress and depression to burden and less constructive coping styles. Nearly half (41%) of carers lived either alone or just with the patient, with the group on average having "some" isolation on the SIS (score of 3.1; 1 = marked isolation, 4 = none). The mean for the sample as a whole was just above the threshold for mild depression (9.4) with 41% showing at least mild depression. Just over a third (35%) of carers were defined as "cases" by the GHQ (bi-modal score of 6). There was a high (0.78) positive correlation between distress and depression total scores, but the number of hours of face-to-face contact was not linked to either of these. As a group, carers had on average six worries on their mind "nearly all the time". Despite this, 7/10 of the most frequent thoughts about aspects of caring were actually about positive experiences. On the other hand, one-third of the carers were relying "a lot" on alcohol or drugs, when they felt stress related to the patient.

Finally, nearly half (44%) of the carers were high EE: 33% were highly critical, 30% hostile and 22% emotionally over involved.

Links between EE, burden and coping

EE and its components were found in the univariate analysis to be linked to increased subjective burden, carers' coping styles, an increased perception by carers of patients' social functioning deficits. In the multivariate analysis, the strongest link with overall EE and with criticism and hostility was coping style, whereas with EOI the strongest links were social isolation score and not living with a partner. The most consistent and strongest link with EE was avoidant coping in the form of behavioural disengagement.

There were quantitative differences between high and low EE carers on the ECI : low EE carers were burdened in all areas, but high EE carers were more burdened. Positive aspects of the caring experience were among those most frequently thought about in both the low and high EE groups, but positive experiences were not significantly higher in the low EE group.

Coping

There were also differences in coping styles. Both high and low EE carers used all the designated styles, but high EE carers used some styles significantly more. High ratings on all four EE components were linked with behavioural disengagement and alcohol/drug disengagement.

Carer perception of social functioning

High CC and hostility both linked with SFS total and with the subscales of interpersonal functioning and recreation. High EOI, however, was not linked with these at all, but was instead linked to withdrawal and the level of independence: competence. Thus, highly critical carers perceived patients as having less interaction and less social success and believed they did not engage much in hobbies and pastimes. High EOI carers, on the other hand, saw patients as more withdrawn and incompetent.

High EE carers were more subjectively burdened than low EE carers overall. Two areas in which the high EE group scored significantly higher were "difficult behaviours" and "loss".

High EE carers used behavioural disengagement, mental disengagement, alcohol/drug disengagement, and "seeking support for emotional reasons" more frequently than low EE carers.

Finally, High EE carers perceived more deficits in all areas of social functioning, but significantly more so in interpersonal functioning, indicating that they thought of patients as having less interpersonal ability and success.

In summary, overall EE was linked most simply and strongly to coping style in a two-variable model. Behavioural disengagement coping was highly significant, and seeking support for emotional reasons was just significant.

Specific links with components of EE

A third of the sample were highly critical. All areas of burden were rated higher in the high CC group, significantly so for overall burden and the two subscales of "difficult behaviours" and "effect on the family". High CC were also linked with coping style. Three forms of avoidant coping were used more frequently by the high CC group: behavioural disengagement, mental disengagement, and alcohol/drug disengagement. Three other types of coping styles were also higher in the high CC group: restraint, seeking support for emotional reasons, and denial. CC were also linked with overall perception of social functioning and the two subscales of recreation and interpersonal functioning. The multivariate analysis revealed that the strongest link with the simplest model for high CC was coping style in the form of behavioural disengagement.

It was also of interest that there was a strong trend for the burden of negative symptoms to be higher in the high EE group. This is consistent both with attributional theory and previous EE studies.

A third of the carers were hostile. Hostility was linked to overall burden. Multivariate analysis revealed that the strongest link with hostility was coping style in the form of behavioural disengagement. There was a strong trend (p=0.08) for carers to be hostile if the patient was presenting with a problem for the first time. Eight out-of 24 of the non-Hostile carers had patients who had presented before, whereas none of the 14 hostile carers had patients who had presented before. It is possible that carers lowered their expectations about the patient after the previous neurotic problem had emerged.

Just over a fifth (21%) of the carers were highly emotionally over-involved. These carers were more burdened overall, particularly on the subscales of dependency, loss, and problems with services. EOI was linked to avoidant coping style, in the forms of behavioural disengagement and alcohol/drug disengagement. It was also linked to the perceived social functioning areas of social withdrawal and level of independence or competence, with a strong trend for high EOI carers to have patients less likely to be working or attending rehabilitation activities. All high EOI carers were women, 80% of them mothers. High EOI carers were also more likely to be in high (more than 35 hours per week) face-to-face contact with their relatives, and to be more socially isolated.

Forty-three per cent of the sample were already high EE at the first onset with a median illness length before the carer interview of only 19 weeks. This finding is more supportive of a triggering than an emergent model of EE. Since coping was so strongly linked to high EE, some carers may become high EE because of less adaptive coping, particularly avoidant coping. This could be developed as an outcome measure for family interventions.

CONCLUSION

The main result of the first-onset study described here is to replicate previous research on the links between high EE, high subjective burden and avoidant coping responses in carers. The appraisal of some behaviour as problematic seems to lead to high EE responses even at this early stage, and is not restricted to a more chronic course. In the long term, avoidant coping seems a particularly ineffective way to manage these problems, and suggests both a specific avenue for intervention and for measuring outcome. This could mean that dealing with the upset, shock and misunderstanding associated with first-onset psychosis is not so different from later reactions in carers. It also suggests that early intervention might be particularly beneficial in reducing depression, stress and distress in carers, and the likelihood of symptoms recurring in the client.

Our results add to our understanding of the particular stresses of caring, which in turn can be stressful for the client. They emphasise the importance of improving the quality of the relationships that form the environment of people with psychosis. They may well remain vulnerable to future episodes, but can be helped to recover in a supportive setting.

The general importance of negotiated and constructive problem-solving in caring environments underlines the value of these interventions, as already described in detail in various published manuals (Anderson, Reiss & Hogarty, 1986; Falloon, 1985; Kuipers, Leff & Lam, 1992; Barrowclough & Tarrier, 1992).

SUMMARY

Evidence is accumulating that, at the time of first onset, psychosis already imposes burdens on family carers who may react in the same way, and find the same sorts of behaviour problematic, as long-term carers. The appraisal of problems appears to be a key issue, as does attribution of blame and a tendency to use avoidant coping. The evidence is thus that particular problems trigger appraisal processes that can lead to high perceived burden and high EE. This is counter to the idea that the development of these phenomena is the result of a much more gradual interactive process. Ineffective coping strategies appear to be rapidly triggered in the early stages of dealing with the problems posed by the emergence of psychosis in a relative. Key interventions for this group would seem to be the facilitation of constructive problem-solving related to the poor social functioning of the patient, as well as an understanding of the emotional loss and isolation that carers are likely to perceive, which may hinder engagement with services.

Thus early intervention would seem to be indicated in psychosis as in other severe and disabling conditions. If it was available it might be able to improve adjustment to perceived problems, as well as longer term reductions in distress and morbidity. This might reduce both the emotional and financial costs for carers and their relatives.

REFERENCES

Anderson, J. & Adams, C. (1996). Family interventions in schizophrenia. *British Medical Journal*, **313**, 505–506.

Anderson, C., Hogarty, G., Bayer, T. & Needleman, R.A. (1984). Expressed Emotion and social networks of parents of schizophrenic patients. *British Journal of Psychiatry*, **144**, 247–255.

Anderson, C., Reiss, D. & Hogarty, G.E. (1986). *Schizophrenia in the Family: A Practical Guide*. New York: Guilford Press.

Barrowclough, C. & Tarrier, N. (1992). *Families of Schizophrenic Patients: Cognitive Behavioural Interventions*. London: Chapman & Hall:

Bebbington, P.E. & Kuipers, L. (1994). The predictive utility of Expressed Emotion in schizophrenia: an aggregate analysis. *Psychological Medicine*, **24**, pp. 707–718.

Beck, A.T., Rush, A.J., Shaw, B.F. & Emery, G. (1979). *Cognitive therapy of depression*. New York: Guilford Press.

Bentsen, B.H., Notland, T.H., Boye, B., Munkvold, O.G., Bjorge, H. et al. (1998). Criticism and hostility in relatives of patients with schizophrenia or related psychoses: demographic and clinical predictors. Acta Psychiatrica Scandinavica, **97**, 76–85.

Bertrando, P., Beltz, J., Bressi, C., Clerici, M., Farma, T., Invernizzi, G. & Cazullo, C. L. (1992). Expressed Emotion and schizophrenia in Italy: a study of a urban population. *British Journal of Psychiatry*, **161**, 223–229.

Birchwood, M. & Smith, J. (1987). Schizophrenia in the family. In J. Orford (Ed.), *Coping with Disorder in the Family*. London: Croom Helm.

Brewin, C.R. (1994). Changes in attribution and expressed emotion among the relatives of patients with schizophrenia. *Psychological Medicine*, **24** (4), 905–11.

Brewin, C.R., MacCarthy, B., Duda, R. & Vaughn, C.E. (1991). Attribution and Expressed Emotion in the relatives of patients with schizophrenia. *Journal of Abnormal Psychology*, **100**, 546–554.

Carver, C.S., Scheier, M.F. & Weintraub, J.K. (1989). Assessing coping strategies: a theoretically based approach. *Journal of Personality and Social Psychology*, **56**, 267–283.

Carver, C.S., Pozo, C., Harris, S.D., Noriega, V., Scheier, M.F., Robinson, D.S. et al. (1993). How coping mediates the effect of optimism on distress: a study of women with early stage breast cancer. *Journal of Personality and Social Psychology*, **65** (2), 375–390.

Creer, C. & Wing, J.K. (1975). Living with a schizophrenic patient. *British Journal of Psychiatry*, **157**, 119–122.

Fadden, G., Bebbington, P. E. & Kuipers, L. (1987). The impact of functional psychiatric illness on the patient's family. *British Journal of Psychiatry*, **150**, 285–292.

Falloon, I.R.H. (1985). *Family Management of Schizophrenia*. Baltimore: Johns Hopkins University Press.

Gibbons, J.S., Horn, S.H., Powell, J.M. & Gibbons, J.L. (1984). Schizophrenic patients and their families: a survey in a psychiatric service based on a DGH unit. *British Journal of Psychiatry*, **144**, 70–77.

Goldberg, D.P. & Hillier, V.F. (1979). A scaled version of the general health questionnaire. *Psychological Medicine*, **9**, 139–145.

Goldberg, D.P. & Huxley, P. (1980). *Mental Illness in the Community: The Pathway to Psychiatric Care*. London: Tavistock.

Jackson, H.T., Smith, N. & McGorry, P. (1990). Relationships between EE and family burden in psychiatric disorders: an exploratory study. *Acta Psychiatrica Scandinavica*, **82**, 243–249.

Kavanagh, D.J. (1992). Recent developments in Expressed Emotion and schizophrenia. *British Journal of Psychiatry*, **160**, 601–620.

Kuipers, L. & Bebbington, P.E. (1985). Relatives as a resource in the management of functional illness. *British Journal of Psychiatry*, **147**, 465–71.

Kuipers, L. (1992). Expressed Emotion research in Europe. *British Journal of Clinical Psychology*, **31**, 429–443.

Kuipers, L., Leff, J., & Lam, D. (1992). *Family Work for Schizophrenia: A Practical Guide*. Royal College of Psychiatrists.

Kuipers, L. (1993). Family burden in schizophrenia: implications for services. *Social Psychiatry and Psychiatric Epidemiology*, **28**, 207–210.

Kuipers, L. (1994). The measurement of expressed emotion: its influence on research and clinical practice. *International Review of Psychiatry*, **6**, 187–199.

Kuipers, E. (1996). The management of difficult to treat patients with schizophrenia using non-drug therapies. *British Journal of Psychiatry* (Suppl. 131), 41–51.

Kuipers, E. & Moore, E. (1996). EE and staff–client relations: implications for community care of the severely mentally ill. *International Journal of Mental Health*, **24** (3), 13–26.

Leff, J.P. & Brown, G.W. (1977). (Letter) Family and social factors in the course of schizophrenia. *British Journal of Psychiatry*, **130**, 417.

MacCarthy, B., Kuipers, L., Hurry, J., Harper, R. & Lesage, A. (1989). Counselling the relatives of the long term adult mentally ill. I: Evaluation of the impact on relatives and patients. *British Journal of Psychiatry*, **154**, 768–775.

Macmillan, J.F., Gold, A., Crow, T.J., Johnson, A.L. & Johnstone, E.C. (1986). The Northwick Park study of first episodes of schizophrenia. IV: Expressed emotion and relapse. *British Journal of Psychiatry*, **151**, 320–323.

Moore, E., Ball, R.A. & Kuipers, L. (1992). Expressed emotion in staff working with the long-term adult mentally ill. *British Journal of Psychiatry*, **161**, 802–8.

Noh, S. & Turner, R.J. (1987). Living with psychiatric patients: implications for the mental health of family members. *Social Science and Medicine*, **25**, 263–272.

Nuechterlein, K.H., Snyder, K.S. & Mintz, J. (1992). Paths to relapse: possible transactional processes connecting patients' illness onset, expressed emotion, and psychotic relapse. *British Journal of Psychiatry*, **161** (Suppl. 18), 88–96.

O'Connor, P. & Brown, G.W. (1984). *The SESS Manual*. Bedford Square.

Penn, D. & Mueser, K. (1996). Research update on the psychosocial treatment of schizophrenia. *American Journal of Psychiatry*, **153**, 607–617.

Scazufca, M. & Kuipers, E. (1996). Links between expressed emotion and burden of care in relatives of patients with schizophrenia. *British Journal of Psychiatry*, **168**, 580–587.

Scazufca, M. & Kuipers, E. (1997). The impact on women who care for those with schizophrenia. *Psychiatric Bulletin*, **22**, 1–3.

Smith, J., Birchwood, M., Cochrane, R. & George, S. (1993). The needs of high and low Expressed Emotion families: a normative approach. *Social Psychiatry and Psychiatric Epidemiology*, **28**, 11–16.

Stirling, J., Tantam, D., Thomas, P., Newby, D. & Montague, L. (1991). EE and early onset schizophrenia: a one year follow-up. *Psychological Medicine*, **21**, 675–685.

Stirling, J., Tantam, D., Thomas, P., Newby, D., Montague, L., Ring, N. & Rowe, S. (1993). Expressed emotion and schizophrenia: the ontogeny of EE during an 18 month follow-up. *Psychological Medicine*, **23**, 771–778.

Szmukler, G.T., Burgess, P., Herman, H., Benson, A. & Colusa, S. (1996). Caring for relatives with serious mental illness: the development of the "Experience of Caregiving Inventory". *Social Psychiatry and Psychiatric Epidemiology*, **31** (3–4), 137–148.

Vaughn, C.E. & Leff, J.P. (1976). The measurement of expressed emotion in the families of psychiatric patients. *British Journal of Social and Clinical Psychology*, **15**, 157–165.

WHO (1992). *Schedules for Clinical Assessment in Neuropsychiatry (SCAN 1.1)*. World Health Organisation, Division of Mental Health, Geneva.

Part II

STRATEGIES FOR EARLY INTERVENTION

Chapter 6

CAN DURATION OF UNTREATED PSYCHOSIS BE REDUCED?

Tor K. Larsen*, Jan Olav Johannessen*, Thomas McGlashan†, Marthe Horneland*, Sigurd Mardal‡ and Per Vaglum§.

INTRODUCTION

While the original Kraepelinian notion of schizophrenia as a deteriorating illness has been challenged, the prognosis remains poor for far too many patients. First-episode psychosis is still a potentially devastating happening for patients and their families (Hegarty et al., 1994; McGlashan, 1988). The schizophrenia-spectrum disorders (schizophrenia and schizophreniform disorder) in particular, are often chronic diseases with pervasive negative impacts on the functional, social and mental status of affected individuals. Despite the development of systematic individual and family therapy, modern neuroleptics, and psychosocial rehabilitation programmes, too many patients do poorly or commit suicide (Johnstone et al., 1990). There is need for improvement in the treatment of first-episode psychosis.

The idea of secondary prevention in psychosis has been focused on during the last decade (Birchwood, McGorry & Jackson, 1997). The question has been raised whether the positive results in somatic medicine with early diagnosis of disorders such as cancer, heart diseases, etc. can be replicated within the field of psychiatry (Larsen & Opjordsmoen, 1996).

A number of studies on first-episode psychosis during the last decades have shown that the Duration of Untreated Psychosis (DUP) is very long. This is reported to be on average between one and two years (Keshavan & Schooler 1992), which means that people can live for a long time in the

*Rogaland Psychiatric Hospital, Stavanger, Norway †Yale Psychiatric Institute, New Haven, CT, USA ‡Rogaland County Hospital in Haugesund, Norway §University of Oslo, Norway.

Early Intervention in Psychosis.
Edited by M. Birchwood, D. Fowler & C. Jackson.
© 2000 John Wiley & Sons Ltd.

society with severe symptoms of mental illness such as delusions, hallucinations or severe thought disorder, without getting treatment. Is this delay in identification of people suffering from mental disorder a major public health problem, or is it simply natural that many patients do not want or need treatment in the early phase of illness?

In the following we will present arguments for early detection of psychosis from different view-points. We will describe in detail an ongoing multi-centre project in Scandinavia with the specific aim to reduce DUP, the TIPS (Early Treatment and Identification of Psychosis) study. Finally, we will discuss the preliminary experiences and early results of this project.

STUDIES OF PATIENTS WITH FIRST-EPISODE PSYCHOSIS AND DUP

In a review of studies on first-episode psychosis and DUP, McGlashan and Johannessen (1996) described retrospective and prospective studies. The retrospective studies provide indirect evidence that long DUP is associated with poor outcome. Wyatt (1991) and Opjordsmoen (1991) both found that earlier treatment with medication was associated with better long-term prognosis. The retrospective study designs contain methodological limitations and at present these studies can be looked upon as forerunners of later prospective studies in which a more accurate description of outcome has been possible. In the following we review some of the important first-episode psychosis studies with a prospective design.

The Northwick Park Study of first-episode schizophrenia studied 253 patients (Johnstone et al., 1986) and reported that the interval between onset of illness and admission varied widely and had a skewed distribution; 28% were admitted within two months after onset, 25% after two to six months, 9% after six months to one year and 26% after more than one year. In the remaining cases the onset could not be ascertained. They found that during this interval between the onset of illness and admission, 41% of the patients made contact with either a hospital, a GP, private medicine faculties, social workers, religious bodies, marriage guidance, etc. Thirteen per cent of the cases made more than nine contacts without receiving treatment. Before admission a substantial number of the patients demonstrated severely disturbed behaviour that was potentially threatening to the patient's life (5% repeatedly, 20% once or twice), threatening to another's life (6% repeatedly, 13% once or twice), or sexually bizarre (6% repeatedly, 8% once or twice). In addition, 30% of the sample showed bizarre or inappropriate behaviour not included in the above categories. Recognising the potentially damaging effect on patients' ability to recover when detected late in their course of illness with such severe symptomatology, the authors write: "It is perhaps unrealistic to hope that admission can always be arranged after no more than three contacts" (p. 119). And they concluded that "appropriate services were not available for these people when they were required" (p. 120).

A subsample of the Northwick Park study ($N = 120$) was included in a randomised placebo-controlled trail of maintenance antipsychotic medication (Crow et al., 1986). They found that duration of untreated illness was a stronger predictor of relapse than maintenance medication status.

Another study on the early course in first-episode psychosis was carried out by Rabiner, Wegner and Kane (1986) at the Hillside Hospital. The duration of untreated illness was defined as the time between "onset of the first signs of noticeable change in behaviour to baseline evaluation". The mean duration of untreated illness in the schizophrenia group ($N = 36$) was 14.5 months compared to 3.6 months in the affective disorder group ($N = 19$). When looking at the outcome after one year the authors report a significant relationship between poor outcome (in episode or relapsed) and long duration of untreated illness.

Keshavan and Schooler published an important paper discussing the use of concepts related to the early course of first-episode psychosis (Keshavan & Schooler, 1992). They reviewed 53 first-episode studies and found marked inconsistencies in the definitions of key variables related to onset. They stressed the importance of defining these variables in such a way that different studies can be compared. They defined *onset of illness* as the first appearance of prodromal symptoms and *onset of episode* as the first appearance of psychotic symptoms (related to a retrospective description of duration and severity). In our review of studies published after 1993 we emphasised the importance of also defining the *onset of adequate treatment* (Larsen et al. 1996a). Finally there are two important intervals; duration of untreated illness (from onset of prodromal symptoms to initiation of adequate treatment) and duration of untreated psychosis, DUP (from onset of psychosis to initiation of adequate treatment).

In 1992–93 Loebel and colleagues published the results of another first-episode study at the Hillside Hospital (Loebel et al., 1992; Lieberman et al., 1993; Szymanski et al., 1995). This study explored the early course of illness in 70 first-episode schizophrenic and schizo-affective patients and found that the DUP was 51.9 weeks (mean). This period was preceded by a substantial period with prodromal symptoms with a duration of 150.8 weeks (mean) before treatment. DUP was significantly associated with time to remission and level of remission. Patients who had been ill for a long time before receiving treatment took longer to respond to treatment. The significance of these findings is unclear however, because it could simply mean that patients who are already more severely ill are detected later.

Haas and Sweeney (1992) studied 71 first-episode patients with schizophrenia, schizophreniform disorder and schizo-affective disorder. They found that 56 % of the sample had a DUP longer than one year. The mean DUP was three years. In a later report on 150 patients with the same diagnosis (Haas, Keshavan & Sweeney, 1994), they found that when treatment with medication was initiated after more than two years of untreated psychosis, treatment response was slower and resulted in more severe symptoms (positive and negative).

A group from Mannheim, Germany (Häfner et al., 1993), thoroughly reconstructed the early course of illness in 165 first-episode patients with schizophrenia. They developed a standardised instrument, the Interview for Retrospective Assessment of Onset of Schizophrenia (IRAOS), compared the patients' own descriptions with the observations of a family member or with available objective data. They found that psychotic symptoms were noticed by relatives or documented in case records 12 months later than they were perceived by the patients. They explain this difference as a consequence of the fact that psychotic symptoms such as hallucinations are subjectively experienced long before they are perceptible to others. They found DUP to be 2.1 years (mean) and duration of the earliest sign of mental disorder until first admission to be 4.6 years (mean). They also found that 70 % of the cases began with negative symptoms.

In a unique study from Iceland, Helgason detected 107 cases of probable schizophrenia during the years 1966–67. At the point of inclusion most of them were not receiving treatment. These cases were detected because the relationship between the patients and their general practitioner is very close in Iceland. The sample was followed for 21–22 years and even at the end of the follow-up period as many as 20% had still not received treatment (Helgason, 1990). Helgason concluded that we do not know whether the prognosis for these untreated patients could have been better had they been treated despite their unwillingness.

Some of the most interesting and extensive studies on the early course of psychosis have been carried out by Falloon (1992), Falloon et al. (1996), McGorry et al. (1996) and Yung et al. (1996). They are described in detail elsewhere in this volume.

In summary, DUP is reported to be very long (1–2 years) and patients with schizophrenia often have a long period with non-psychotic signs of mental illness (prodromal symptoms) before the onset of psychosis (1–5 years). Furthermore, during the time after onset patients and their relatives very often seek help without receiving proper assessment and treatment. Many patients are hospitalised with severe symptoms and bizarre behaviour. Other studies report a relationship between long DUP and poor outcome as well as long DUP and longer time to remission and lower level of remission. Because these studies were correlational, it was not possible to determine whether a reduction in DUP would have an effect on outcome.

DUP IN A ROGALAND SAMPLE; THE TIPS PILOT STUDY

In order test whether DUP in our own area at Rogaland County, Norway, was as long as reported in these studies, we carried out a study of first-episode, non-affective psychosis during the years 1993–94 (Larsen, McGlashan & Moe, 1996; Larsen et al., 1996). Patients between the ages of 15 and 65 were included in the study. We found 43 consecutively admitted patients and the findings regarding DUP are presented in Figure 6.1.

The general characteristics of the sample were: 65% males, mean age 26.3 years and mean DUP 2.1 years. As described in Figure 6.1 there were some patients with a very short DUP, but also many patients with a DUP longer than one year. We studied more closely the pathways to care for the 34 patients in the sample who suffered from schizophrenia and found that active and passive withdrawal, together with poor social networks, seemed to be the main obstacles against being identified and treated earlier (Larsen et al., 1998).

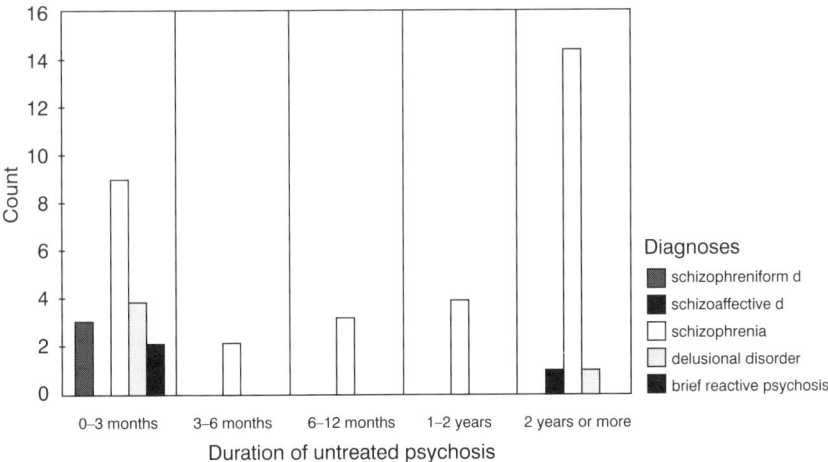

Figure 6.1   DUP results for 43 consecutively admitted patients.

WHY IS IT IMPORTANT TO REDUCE DUP?

Reducing DUP is clearly beneficial by foreshortening psychosis. By analogy, imagine a 17-year-old young man who becomes deaf. Would it make a difference if he learns sign language after two months against two years? Obviously, it would. Living two years without being able to communicate with other people would be very stressful and it is self-evident that early training in sign language would be helpful. Being psychotic is a social and personal disaster. Affected patients very often lose contact with family and friends, and are not able to attend school or work. If a reduction in DUP could be achieved, some of these negative consequences might be minimised. It also seems reasonable to expect that it may be easier to establish a therapeutic alliance with patients detected before their psychosocial "breakdown" has become complete.

Reducing DUP is theoretically beneficial by slowing or preventing the neurobiological deficit processes linked to symptom formation in the early course of psychosis (Lieberman et al., 1993; McGlashan & Johannessen, 1996). McGlashan (1988) introduced the concept of a window of deterioration in schizophrenia, and found through a review of North American follow-up studies that this window ends on average one year after the onset of psychosis. If earlier treatment attenuates this window, then reducing DUP may lead to a better long-term prognosis. Some of the research reviewed above found significant correlations between DUP and outcome, especially the Hillside study (Loebel et al., 1992). The reported correlations could be a selection effect, with those detected later being poor prognosis patients to begin with, and at present we do not know whether an "experimental" reduction in DUP would have a positive influence on outcome. In order to test the effect of such an experimental reduction, we designed the TIPS study.

TIPS: EARLY TREATMENT AND IDENTIFICATION OF PSYCHOSIS PROJECT—AN INTERNATIONAL MULTI-CENTRE STUDY

The main aim of the TIPS project is to explore whether early identification of first episode psychosis leads to a better long term prognosis. Patients treated in first-episode psychosis programmes at three different geographical sites are compared: one in Rogaland (Norway) with an early identification programme and two others in Oslo (Norway) and Roskilde (Denmark), both with normal identification.

Design and methods

The ideal design for testing the causal relationship between DUP and prognosis would be to randomise consecutive cases of first-episode psychosis to active treatment versus a long (e.g. months) no-treatment waiting list control. This strategy is clearly unethical given that active psychosis, especially first psychosis, is a treatable, medical emergency. The next best, realistic design for testing the causal relationship between DUP and prognosis is a non-randomised application of an early detection (ED) system to one population but not to another demographically similar population, receiving a matching treatment programme, and measuring the differences in treatment response and longitudinal outcome. This is "quasi"-experimental, because randomisation is not and cannot be used. A standard treatment protocol is used in all study populations to minimise the effect of treatment on the dependent variables (outcome) and to maximise the effect of differences in the independent variable (DUP) (McGlashan, 1996).

The above design outlines a comparative study with two parallel control groups. We also compare the Rogaland ED sample with the 1993–94 Rogaland first-episode sample described above, a so-called "historical" control sample. The historical control design has the advantage that the demographic variances between samples are likely to be small. Variables such as age, sex, race, socioeconomic status are likely to be stable within the same geographical area, provided that the timespan between the two samples is not too long. The disadvantage of historical control designs are non-measurable sources of variance known as cohort effects. In order to minimise measurement variance in the historical control comparison, we have tried to use the same assessment methods in our new sample.

The study began on 1 January 1997. Patients with a first-episode, non-affective psychosis began to be included and followed for five years. Inclusion criteria are a diagnosis of schizophrenia, schizophreniform disorder, delusional disorder, brief reactive disorder, schizo-affective psychosis, psychosis NOS and affective disorders with mood incongruent symptoms. The total population across all three sites is about 600,000, and altogether we expect approximately 300 patients to be included over four years of sampling. First episode is defined as the first time a patient receives adequate treatment (biologically defined as 16 mg perphenazine daily or equivalent dosage for at least 12 weeks) for psychosis. We define the onset of psychotic symptoms as follows: a score 4 or higher on one of the positive psychotic symptoms items in the PANSS (Positive And Negative Syndrome Scale), and manifestation of psychotic symptoms such as delusions, hallucinations, thought disorder or inappropriate/bizarre behaviour in which the symptoms are not apparently due to organic causes. In addition, these symptoms must have lasted throughout the day for several days or several times a week, not being limited to a few brief moments. The patients must be residents in one of the counties and speak the language satisfactory. The exclusion criteria are as follows; no known contraindication to the use of neuroleptics, no mental retardation (IQ under 70) and no neurological or endocrinological disorders that could cause the psychotic symptoms. Finally, the patient must be able and willing to sign written consent.

Treatment programme

In order to test whether a reduction in DUP will lead to a better outcome, we need to control for other variables that can influence the outcome. Systematic differences in the treatment between the sites could explain different outcomes, and therefore we have developed a treatment programme consisting of three elements that are used and described in detail at all sites. The elements are: supportive psychotherapy, multi-family groups and a medication algorithm. In Table 6.1 the three parts of the treatment programme are briefly described.

Table 6.1   Treatment programme*

Supportive psychotherapy
A trained psychotherapist offers at least one session per week (min. 30 minutes) for at least two years. The attitude should be active and "outreaching", meaning that when the patients fail to appear for therapy, phone calls or home visits are made.

Multi-family group
1. One family session, one introductory session and three (or more) further sessions at least two without the patient.
2. Family workshop, full-day education seminar.
3. Bi-weekly multi-family sessions (5–6 families) for two years.
Patients are motivated to participate. Emphasis is put on problem-solving techniques and psychoeducation.

Medication
Defined algorithm starting with perphenazine (at least 10 weeks), then risperidone (at least 12 weeks) and finally clozapine. Specific doses and administration procedures are described. (Since 1 January 1998 the first drug of choice has been changed to Olanzapine.)

*This table is related to first-episode schizophrenia; treatment programmes for non-schizophrenic first-episode psychosis are described in detail in the study protocol.

Hypothesis tested

The first hypothesis to be tested is whether a system for early detection of psychosis can reduce DUP. This will be tested in two ways; first, as a comparison between the pilot study sample and the TIPS ED sample (historical control study) and, second, as a comparison between the TIPS ED sample and the TIPS non-ED sectors sample (parallel control study).

This chapter will present preliminary data relevant to the first hypothesis using the TIPS and historical control samples.

EARLY DETECTION OF PSYCHOSIS PROGRAMME AT ROGALAND COUNTY

On 1 January 1997 a new health services system for the early detection of first-onset psychosis was established in Rogaland County, Norway, the experimental sector. This detection system will be described after first outlining the Rogaland County's health care system.

ROGALAND COUNTY'S HEALTH CARE SYSTEM SERVICES

Rogaland County is located on the south-western coast of Norway (Figure 6.2). The population at 1 January 1994 consisted of 350,876 people including 175,808 women and 175,068 men.

The health services are organised in the following manner. Each of the 26 communes has its own health system based on general practitioners (GPs), an organisation of home nurses, and most have their own midwives and psychiatric nurses. There are approximately 220 GPs, some in private practice and some working in the communes. The GP's refer patients to the somatic and psychiatric health care services. The psychiatric health care has its own administration separate from the somatic institutions, but the entire health care system is organised under the Rogaland County authorities.

The Psychiatric Services in Rogaland (PSR) are divided into two sectors. The north sector is located in Haugesund Hospital and the second sector is subdivided into (1) the mid-sector located in Stavanger and (2) the south sector, located in Sandnes. These two sectors constitute Rogaland Psychiatric Hospital Departments of Psychiatry.

The early detection programme in Rogaland has two elements: an education programme and Detection Teams (DTs).

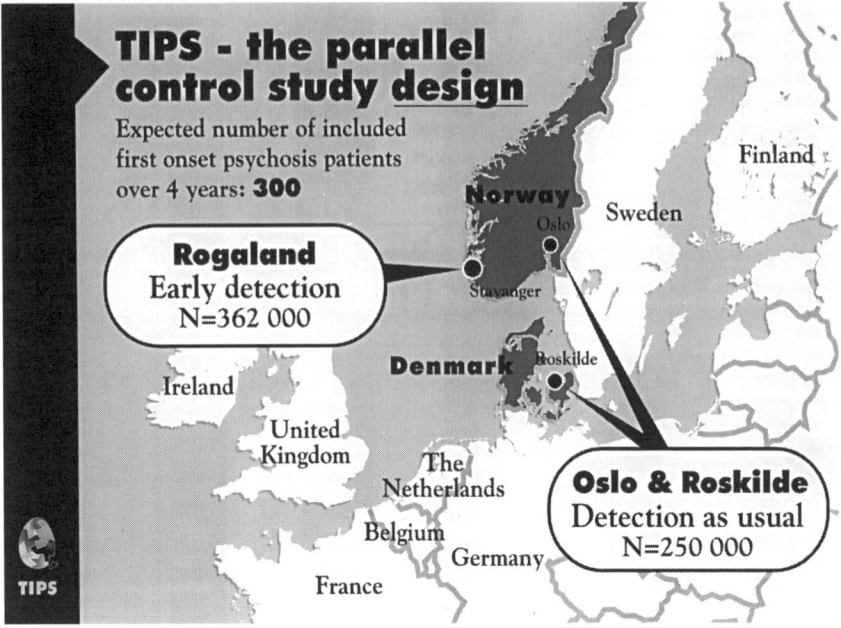

Figure 6.2   Sites in the TIPS study.

THE TIPS EDUCATION PROGRAMME

General population

Public education about psychosis is a tradition in Rogaland. During the last 10 years Rogaland Psychiatric Hospital has arranged so-called Schizophrenia Days. This is a week with several programmes aimed at increasing the awareness among the general population of psychiatric topics. The core elements are:

- A political conference on psychiatry and society
- Art exhibition
- Movie with panel discussion
- Theatre plays
- Public lectures on selective psychiatric topics
- A professional conference on the treatment of various psychiatric disorders, especially schizophrenia.

The conference is held at the Culture House in Rogaland's main city, Stavanger. The main aim of these arrangements has been to challenge popular myths about psychiatry and to increase the knowledge about mental disorders in general. Schools have been invited to participate in art exhibitions, and articles about psychosis appear in the local press. Figure 6.3 presents the programme for 1997.

In December 1996 all households in Rogaland County (180,000) received a 12-page brochure with information about the TIPS project (Figure 6.4). The brochure stated: "Psychiatric disorders have at least one thing common with other diseases—the chance for a good cure is better when treatment is started as soon as possible." The brochure contained a section with general information about the early symptoms of psychosis and a symptom check-list describing different grades of severity. The psychosis Detection Teams (DTs—to be described) are introduced and how to get in touch with them is emphasised.

During the period December 1996 to February 1997 whole page advertisements were initiated in the local newspapers. The first was called "Myths and Reality" and consisted of a series of full-page advertisements, each

Figure 6.3   Schizophrenia Days programme, 1997.

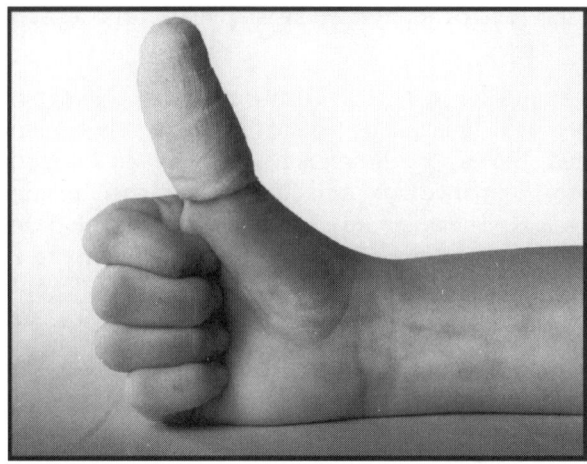

Psychiatric disorders have at least one thing in common with other diseases

– the chance for a good cure is better when treatment is started as soon as possible

Figure 6.4   Household brochure.

having a picture with a scene from the movie "One Flew Over the Cuckoo's Nest" (myth) opposed to a picture with people working in the DT (reality). The series of pictures used in these advertisements were the same as in the brochure sent to all households (Figure 6.5).

In the third week of January 1997 we launched a new information campaign, this time consisting of whole page newspaper advertisements and commercial radio and cinema advertisements. During the remainder of 1997, on a regular basis, this was repeated. In total, 10 different whole page advertisements, three different radio advertisements (where psychiatry were presented in a humorous manner) and a number of smaller newspaper advertisements were presented to the general population of Rogaland. Throughout the project period (the next three years) these campaigns will be repeated regularly.

The Schools

The main elements of the information towards the schools have been:

- Courses and seminars for all teachers, councillors and for the pedagogic schools services (mainly psychologists).

MYTEN   VIRKELIGHETEN

Psychiatric disorders are like other diseases; it is easier to help if you have knowledge about the symptoms.

Figure 6.5 "Myth and Reality".

- Educational programmes for the teachers to use in their teaching on psychology.
- A video illustrating early signs of psychosis.
- Information brochures.

In cooperation with the "Pedagogic-Psychological School service" (PPT) a teaching programme for all teachers at gymnasium level was developed. It was a modified version of the education programme for GPs. The psychologists working in PPT are also organising education seminars in cooperation with the school authorities (Department for Education).

A video, "Something is wrong with Monica", was made by a gymnasium school class. In the 20-minute video, 16-year-old Monica experiences early symptoms of psychosis, withdraws from her friends and is referred to a GP after a consultation with the school nurse. The video is used in teaching sessions at the schools for both teachers and pupils.

In January 1997 all pupils at the gymnasium level received an information brochure regarding early symptoms of psychiatric illnesses, and general information on how to seek help (Figure 6.6).

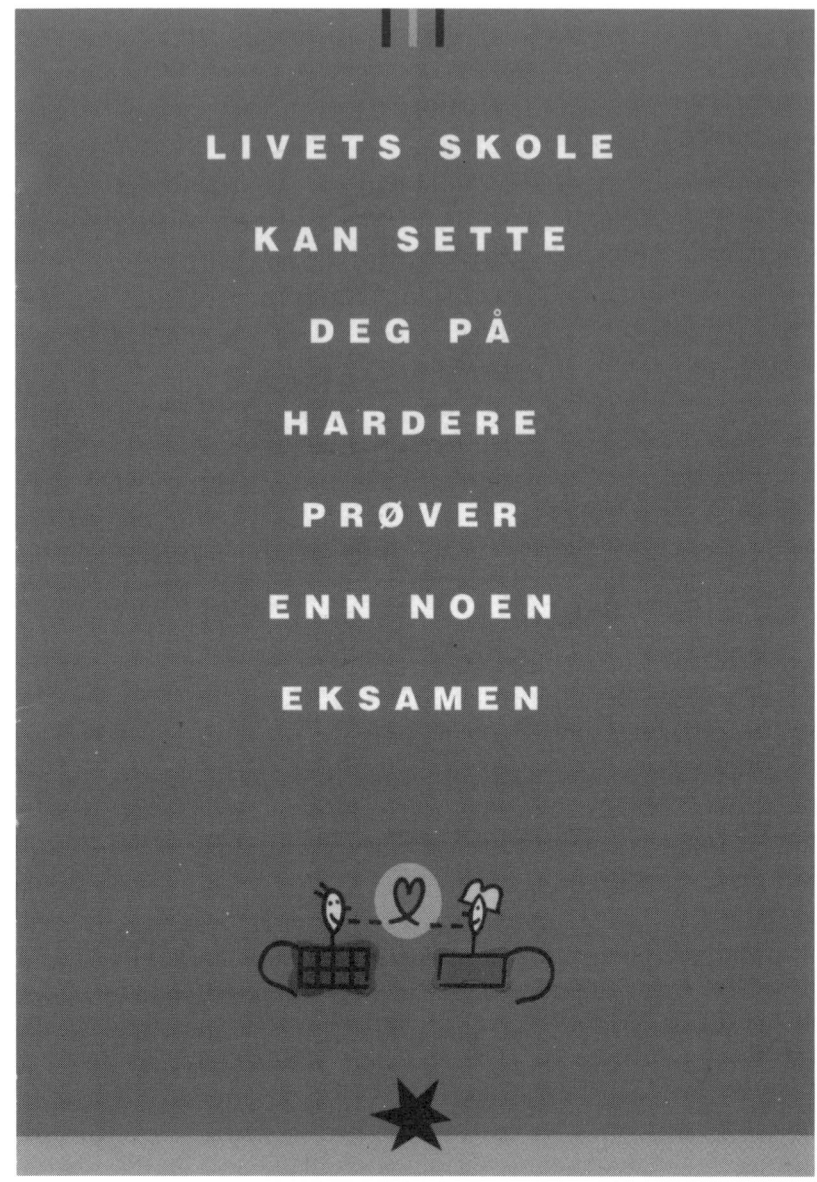

The school of life can put you on
tests harder than any exams

Figure 6.6 Information brochure for the schools.

Primary health services

During the pilot study (1993–94) we started to develop an education programme for the primary health services, especially GPs and social nurses.
We developed a TIPS manual in which the nine DSM-III-R prodromal
symptoms were rated on severity (0 = not present, 1 = uncertain, 2 =
present) and introduced as "warning signs" of psychosis. In addition, the
manual contains detailed description of the seven positive symptoms in
the PANSS which are rated from 1 to 7. The positive symptoms are used to
describe the presence and severity of psychosis. A 30-minute video
demonstrates an actress playing a young woman with emerging symptoms of psychosis. In addition, two lectures were developed on the topics
of early diagnosis of psychosis and the TIPS project. An education session
lasts three hours and starts with the two lectures, then the TIPS manual is
introduced, the video shown and the video rated with use of the TIPS
manual. Finally, half an hour is used to discuss the scoring of the video and
clinical relevance of the early detection work. All GPs in Rogaland
(approximately 220) have received the TIPS manual and general information about the project. Almost 50 other health professionals, such as social
nurses and school nurses, have participated in the sessions.

During the six-month period preceding the start of the project, a number
of educational seminars were held for different groups within the primary
health services. Participants were psychiatric nurses working in the com-
mune, social welfare professionals, teachers, school nurses, etc. This work
has continued as a part of the TIPS programme.

EARLY DETECTION SYSTEM

On 1 January 1997, two Detection Teams (DTs) were established in the
north and south sectors. The DTs are clinically managed by an experienced
psychologist (north) and psychiatrist (south/mid). In the north DT one
psychiatric nurse and one MD are employed, part time. In the south DT
two psychiatric nurses and one social worker are working in the team, also
part time.

Both teams are on call for referrals from 08.00 to 15.30, Monday to Friday.
During weekends the doctors in duty at the psychiatric hospitals take over
the DT function, but they only assess emergency cases. Patients or relatives
who call during nights or weekends are asked to call back on the next
working day.

The pathways from first contact with the DT to final inclusion in the study
is described in Figure 6.7

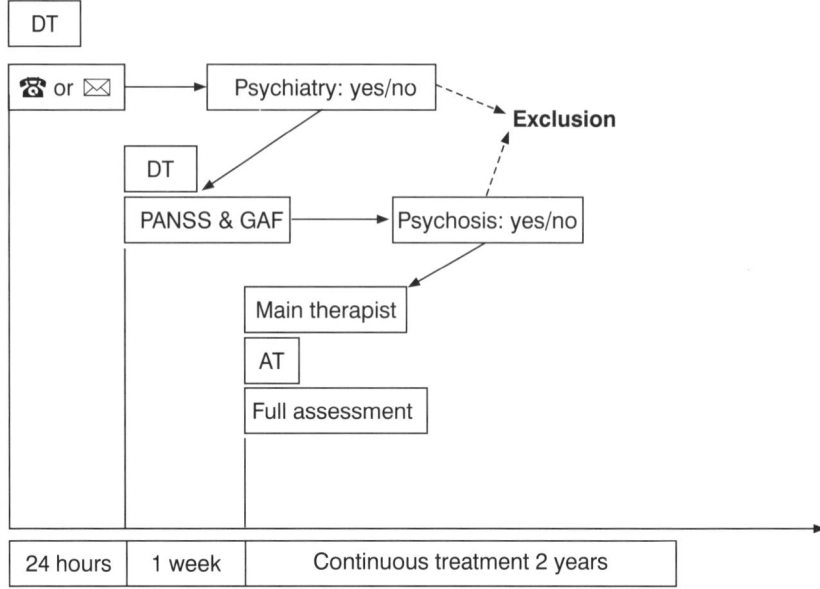

Figure 6.7   DT flow chart.

The DT makes a first assessment over the phone or while reading the referral, and decide whether the case is *psychiatry* or not. The next step is to meet with the patient or the referring persons. This can be done at the patient's home, in the school, in the GPs office, etc., or at the DT office. The teams are mobile and work with an active outreach attitude. They give a "24-hour guarantee", meaning that when reference is made to a patient with probable risk of first-episode psychosis, the DT should be able to offer an assessment within 24 hours. In most cases the assessment is carried out within a few hours, but in some cases, especially when the patient is not motivated, longer time delays are felt to be clinically appropriate. When the DT meet the patient they carry out a PANSS (Kay, Fiszbein & Opler, 1987) interview describing actual symptoms and makes a GAF (Global Assessment of Functioning rating scale: APA, 1987) assessment. All DT members are trained raters in these manuals.

The next step is to decide whether the patient is suffering from a first episode psychosis or not. This decision is made by the Assessment Team (AT), which consists of research scientists carrying out assessments according to the study design, in cooperation with the DT. Patients meeting the inclusion criteria, enter the study and receive the standard treatment protocol, after giving informed consent. Patients who refuse to participate will be offered the same treatment programme. Weekly case conferences with all TIPS clinicians and researchers are organised to discuss difficult cases. When the early assessment by the DT with PANSS and GAF does not clarify diagnostic issues, further assessment is carried out by the AT. A Structured Clinical Interview for DSM-IV Axis 1 disorders (SCID: Spitzer et al., 1990) is carried out as soon as possible. In addition, assessment of premorbid functioning (Premorbid Adjustment Scale, PAS: Cannon-Spoor, Potkin & Wyatt, 1982), social functioning (Strauss & Carpenter, 1974), quality of life, deficit symptoms, drug/alcohol abuse, life events, Expressed Emotions, duration of untreated psychosis and duration of prodromal symptoms is conducted by the AT.

When it is determined that the patient is having a first-episode psychosis, a main therapist either at the outpatient clinic or in the hospital will start treating the patient within a week. Some detected cases are, of course, in need of hospitalisation, and the DT will organise that in cooperation with the GP when necessary. In a few cases, we have experienced that too much "fuss" (too many interviews) at this stage in the treatment process will only make the patient frightened and insecure, the main therapist will then use the necessary time to secure an alliance with the patient. The main therapist has full responsibility for the treatment.

Patients who are not included in the project, because they have a disorder other than psychosis, will receive information on how to secure the help they need. Patients with the tentative diagnosis of "at risk for developing psychosis" are presently not included in the study, but will be offered treatment at the outpatient clinic and be reassessed when their main therapist feels that psychosis may be emerging. For patients who are at risk, but refuse to receive treatment, the DT will phone or see the patient within days, weeks or months, to remain in contact.

PRELIMINARY RESULTS

Early detection work

During the first year (from 1 January to 31 December 1997) 299 patients were referred to the detection teams. Most of the cases were referred by phone (82%), but patients were also referred by letter (14%) and by personal contact (4%). The frequency distribution of all referrals related to time of year is reported in Figure 6.8.

The highest referral rate was at the beginning of the project (28% in January), and the lowest rate was during the summer holidays (3% in July) and in November (2%). During the last six months the referral rate stabilised at approximately 13 cases per month. Altogether 30% of the referrals

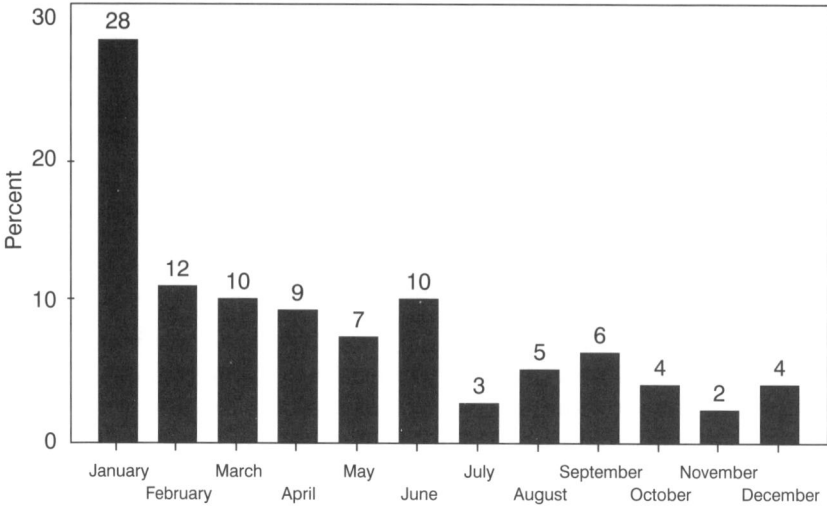

Figure 6.8   Distribution of referrals according to time of year.

were anonymous, but of the 89 anonymous cases 35% were in January, 15% in February and 10% in March. From July and throughout the year only three or four anonymous referrals are received per month.

In Table 6.2 we compare three different groups; all patients referred to the DT ($N = 299$), patients rated as having psychiatric problems by the early DT assessment ($N = 146$) and finally the group of patients that were or could have been included in the project with a first-episode non-affective psychosis ($N = 28$, four patients refused to participate). The last group have all been completely assessed by the assessment teams.

In general, approximately 75% of the patients are male, irrespective of which group we look at. The mean age is 25.6 years for the whole group and 23.6 years for the first-episode group. The prodromal scale sum scores increase (the nine prodromal symptoms from DSM-III-R are rated as 0 = not present, 1 = uncertain and 2 = present), as we go from the group including all patients to the group of detected first-episode patients.

The most important referral sources seems to be the family and GPs. When we look at the group with a first-episode psychosis, 14% are referred from the mother, 7% from the father and 4% from other family members. Twenty-five per cent of the sample with psychosis are referred by the GPs. Also the schools refer patients with psychiatric problems (21%) and with definite first-episode psychosis (14%). Finally, the outpatient clinics refer 21% of the patients with psychosis.

Table 6.2   Comparison of three different groups of referrals.

	All patients N = 299	Patients with psychiatric problems N = 146	Patients with first- episode psychosis N = 28
Gender % male	61	71	75
Age; mean (s.d.)	25.6 (10.5)	23.6 (6.9)	23.6 (5.3)
Prodromal symptoms;			
mean (s.d.)	7.4 (3.5)	8.2 (3.1)	9.8 (3.5)
Percentage referred			
from:			
Patient	17	4	4
Mother	16	14	14
Father	5	6	7
Other family	14	10	4
School	10	17	14
Friends	3	1	–
Social office	3	4	4
Others	9	8	7
GP	13	21	25
Outpatient clinic	10	15	21

A total of 118 patients were referred to the DT and assessed as having psychiatric problems, but were not regarded as having a first-episode psychosis. In 73% of these cases a full PANSS interview was carried out. In Table 6.3 the conclusions made by the DT for these patients are reported.

As can be seen in the table, 18% had a psychosis, but had either been treated earlier or lived outside the county. All these cases were referred for treatment at the responsible institutions such as hospitals or outpatient clinics. The DTs assessed 15% (N = 8) as having emerging psychosis; these

Table 6.3   DT conclusions for psychiatric patients

Diagnostic evaluation by DT	Patients with psychiatric symptoms, but not first-episode psychosis (N = 118) %
Psychosis (not first episode)	16
Emerging psychosis?	15
Depression	33
Drug abuse	9
Not psychosis, but psychiatry	11
Crisis in life	6
Not psychiatry	20

patients were offered treatment at the outpatient clinics and were followed closely in order to see if they would develop psychosis. One-third of the patients had a depression and 9% drug abuse; and 11% had other psychiatric problems such as eating disorders, anxiety disorders, etc. In 6% of the cases the assessment found a life crisis and in the remaining 20% no psychiatric disorders could be diagnosed.

In Table 6.4 preliminary results from the historical comparison between the pilot study sample in 1993–94 and the patients detected during 1997 in the TIPS ED sample are presented. In both samples 65% of the cases were males. The TIPS ED sample is younger both at onset of psychosis and at hospitalisation, but the differences does not reach statistical significance. The DUP is significantly reduced in the ED sample ($p = 0.001$). The mean DUP was 114 weeks in the pilot sample, and 17 weeks in the ED sample. The median values are reduced from 26 to 12 weeks.

CONCLUSIONS

In general, the early experiences from our ED system are positive. The detection teams are functioning well and the clinicians experience the work they are doing as meaningful.

Groups that normally do not refer patients to the psychiatric health services, such as family, teachers, social office etc., do so when they are invited. During the first year 30% of the patients that were detected with psychiatric problems, and 25 % of the detected first-episode psychosis patients, were referred from a close family member. In general it seems that the groups at which the information campaigns were aimed (family, schools, GPs and patients themselves) have responded and helped us to detect patients earlier. The preliminary results are very positive; our system of early detection has reduced the mean DUP from 114 weeks to 17 (median DUP, 26 weeks to 12). This means that earlier detection is achieved.

Table 6.4   Historical comparison of studies in 1993–94 and 1997.

	Pilot study 1993-94 N = 43	TIPS ED 1997 N = 32	p values*
Gender % male	65.1	65.6	n.s.
Age at onset of psychosis (mean, s.d.)	26.3 (8.4)	24.1 (8.7)	n.s.
Age at hospitalisation (mean, s.d.)	28.4 (8.3)	25,1 (7,9)	n.s.
DUP (mean, median)	114.2 (26.0)	17.2 (12,0)	0.001

*T-test for equality of means (2-tailed) for continuous data and chi-square for categorical data.

Schizophrenia and first-episode psychosis is a relatively rare occurrence and, as discussed by van Os et al. (1997), it is to be expected that a large screening of the general population will give few positive findings. Our system of educating the general population, schools, GPs, etc., however, seems to make people aware of psychosis development. The DTs seems to function as a low threshold entrance into psychiatric treatment. They have experienced that approximately 1 in 5 referrals that they assess to have psychiatric problems, actually have a first-episode psychosis.

The information campaigns are quite expensive, the costs are almost 1 million Norwegian kroner per year (~ £100,000). On the other hand, this also equals almost half of the expenses that an average Norwegian grocery shop uses in advertising each year. It may be necessary for the psychiatric health services to think along new lines in order to achieve lasting early identification of first-episode psychosis. Even though the primary findings are positive, only time will show whether these effects are of benefit for the patients in the long term, and the TIPS study should be able to answer some of these questions during the years to come.

REFERENCES

APA (1987). *DSM-III-R: Global Assessment of Functioning Scale*. Washington, DC: American Psychiatric Association.

Birchwood, M., McGorry, P. & Jackson, H. (1997). Early intervention in schizophrenia. *British Journal of Psychiatry*, **170**, 2–5.

Cannon-Spoor, H.E., Potkin, S.G. to Wyatt, R.J. (1982). Measurement of premorbid adjustment in chronic schizophrenia. *Schizophrenia Bulletin*, **8**, 470–484.

Crow, T.J., Macmillan, J.F., Johnson, A.L. & Johnstone, E.C. (1986). A randomised controlled trial of prophylactic neuroleptic treatment. *British Journal of Psychiatry*, **148**, 120–127.

Falloon, I.R.H. (1992). Early intervention for first episodes of schizophrenia: a preliminary exploration. *Psychiatry*, **55**, 4–15.

Falloon, I.R.H., Kydd, R.R., Coverdale, J.H. & Tannis, M.L. (1996). Early detection and intervention for initial episodes of schizophrenia. *Schizophrenia Bulletin*, **22**, 271–282.

Hegarty, J.D., Baldessarini, M.D., Tohen, M., Waternaux, C. & Oepen, G. (1994). One hundred years of schizophrenia: a meta-analysis of the outcome literature. *American Journal of Psychiatry*, **151** 1409–1415.

Haas, G.L. & Sweeney, J.A. (1992). Premorbid and onset features of first episode schizophrenia. *Schizophrenia Bulletin*, **18**, 373–386.

Haas, G.L., Keshavan, M.S. & Sweeney, J.A. (1994). Delay to first medication in Schizophrenia: evidence for a possible negative impact of exposure to psychosis (Abstract). Presented at the American College of Neuropsychopharmacology, San Juan, Puerto Rico, December 1994.

Häfner, H., Maurer, K., Loeffler, W. & Riechler-Roessler, A. (1993). The influence of age and sex on the onset of early course of schizophrenia. *British Journal of Psychiatry*, **162**, 80–86.

Helgason, L. (1990). Twenty years' follow-up of first psychiatric presentation for schizophrenia: what could have been prevented? *Acta Psychiatrica Scandinavica*, **81**, 231–235.

Johnstone, E.C., Macmillan, J., Crow, T. & Johnson, A.L. (1986). The Northwick Park first episode of schizophrenia study. *British Journal of Psychiatry*, **148**, 128–133.

Johnstone, E.C., Macmillan, J.F., Frith, C.D., Benn, D.K. & Crow, T.J. (1990). Further investigation of the predictors of outcome following first schizophrenic episodes. *British Journal of Psychiatry*, **157**, 182–189.

Kay, S.R., Fiszbein, A. & Opler, L.A. (1987). The Positive and Negative Syndrome Scale (PANSS) for schizophrenia. *Schizophrenia Bulletin*, **13** (2) 261–269.

Keshavan, S. & Schooler, N.R. (1992). First-episode studies in schizophrenia: criteria and characterization. *Schizophrenia Bulletin*, **18**, 491–513.

Larsen, T.K. & Opjordsmoen S. (1996). Early identification and treatment of schizophrenia—conceptual and ethical considerations. *Psychiatry*, **59**, 371–380.

Larsen, T.K., McGlashan, T.H. & Moe, L.C. (1996). First-episode schizophrenia: I. Early course parameters. *Schizophrenia Bulletin*, **22**, 241–256.

Larsen, T.K., McGlashan, T.H., Johannessen, J.O. & Vibe-Hansen, L. (1996). First-episode schizophrenia: II. Premorbid patterns by gender. *Schizophrenia Bulletin*, **22**, 257–270.

Larsen, T.K., Moe, L.C., Vibe-Hansen, L. & Johannessen, J.O. (1998). Premorbid functioning, duration of untreated psychosis and clinical outcome in first-episode non-affective psychosis. *Schizophrenia Research 2000* (in press).

Lieberman, J.A., Jody, D., Geisler, S., Alvir, J., Loebel, A., Szymanski, S., Woerner, M. & Borenstein M. (1993). Time course and biologic correlates of treatment response in first-episode schizophrenia. *Archives of General Psychiatry*, **50**, 369–376.

Loebel, A.D., Lieberman, J.A., Alvir, J.M.J., Mayerhoff, D.I., Geisler, S.H. & Szymanski, S.R. (1992). Duration of psychosis and outcome in first-episode schizophrenia. *American Journal of Psychiatry* **149**, 1183–1188.

McGorry, P.D., Edwards, J., Mihalopoulos, C., Harrigan, S.M. & Jackson, H.J. (1996). EPPIC: an evolving system of early detection and optimal management. *Schizophrenia Bulletin*, **22**, 305–326.

McGlashan, T.H. (1988). A selective review of recent North American follow-up studies on schizophrenia. *Schizophrenia Bulletin*, **14**, 515–542.

McGlashan, T.H. (1996). Early detection and intervention in schizophrenia. *Schizophrenia Bulletin*, **22**, 327–345.

McGlashan, T.H. & Johannessen, J.O. (1996). Early detection and intervention with schizophrenia: rationale. *Schizophrenia Bulletin*, **22**, 201–222.

Opjordsmoen, S. (1991). Long-term clinical outcome of schizophrenia with special reference to gender differences. *Acta Psychiatrica Scandinavica*, **83**, 307–313.

Rabiner, C.J., Wegner, J.T. & Kane, N. (1986). Outcome study of first-episode psychosis. I: Relapse rates after 1 year. *American Journal of Psychiatry*, **143**, 1155–1158.

Spitzer, R.L., Williams, J.B.W., Gibbon, M. & First, M.B. (1990). *Structured Clinical Interview for DSM-III-R—Patient Edition* (SCID-P). Washington, D.C.: American Psychiatric Press.

Strauss, J.S. & Carpenter, W.T. (1974). The prediction of outcome in schizophrenia. II: Relationships between predictor and outcome variables. *Archieves of General Psychiatry*, **31**, 37–42.

Szymanski, S., Lieberman, J.A., Alvir, J.M., Mayerhof, D., Loebel, A., Geisler, S., Chakos, M., Koreen, A., Jody, D., Kane, J., Woerner, M., & Cooper, T. (1995). Gender differences in onset of illness, treatment response, course, and biological indexes in first-episode schizophrenic patients. *American Journal of Psychiatry*, **152**, 699–703.

Wyatt, R.J. (1991). Neuroleptics and the natural course of schizophrenia. *Schizophrenia Bulletin*, **17**, 325–351.

van Os, J., Takei, N., Verdoux, H., & Delespaul, P. (1997). Early detection of schizophrenia (letter). *British Journal of Psychiatry*, **170**, 579.

Yung, A.R., McGorry, P.D., McFarlane, C.A., Jackson, H.J., Patton, G.C. & Rakkar, A. (1996). Monitoring and care of young people at risk of psychosis. *Schizophrenia Bulletin*, **22**, 283–303.

Chapter 7

EARLY INTERVENTION IN PSYCHOSIS: PHARMACOTHERAPEUTIC STRATEGIES

*Paul Bebbington**

THE RATIONALE FOR EARLY INTERVENTION

In this chapter, I will examine the arguments for a focused policy of early pharmacological intervention in schizophrenia. It must be acknowledged, however, that many of the arguments apply with equal force to social and psychological treatments. I have not in this review attended to the issue of how *long* drug therapy should be maintained following a first episode of psychosis. This is an issue decided more by clinical opinion (and caution) than by hard evidence. Frances, Docherty and Kahn (1996) advocate treatment for 1–2 years followed by a very gradual tapering off, and many clinicians would view this as reasonable.

There are three main reasons why we might wish to intervene as early as possible in the course of a psychotic illness. The first is that it is humane to do so: the requirement to curtail suffering does not require any special pleading. However, the two other reasons for early intervention do need to be substantiated. First, early treatment may improve outcome both for the episode and for the long-term course. Secondly, effective early intervention may improve the attitudes of patients towards treatment. Early intervention is predicated on two further assertions: our treatments are imperfect, but are more effective if administered earlier. Obviously, if we could treat schizophrenia perfectly, the only grounds for early intervention would be

*Royal Free and University College London Medical School, London, UK.

Early Intervention in Psychosis.
Edited by M. Birchwood, D. Fowler & C. Jackson.

common humanity. In terms of the outcome, it would not matter when treatment was given.

Crucial to this debate is the question of when the course of psychotic disorder becomes set. This can be explored in various ways: examination of the overall course of illness, of the impact of florid relapse on overall course, and of the effect of treatment at different stages of the course.

The old Kraepelinian model of dementia praecox suggested a course characterised by gradual and enduring deterioration (Kraepelin, 1921). However, our current clinical experience is not consistent with this view. Thus we commonly see patients who have a period of considerable disturbance in the early course of their psychotic illness, but who in later years show some amelioration and restitution of function. This topic has been comprehensively and competently reviewed by McGlashan and Johannessen (1996). They concluded that, although some of the studies did show progressive decline, the majority suggested that there is little difference in populations of people with longstanding psychosis in the level of negative symptoms once the illness has lasted for a year or two.

The standard clinical view has been that a majority of patients develop social disabilities before the onset of florid psychotic symptoms and that an acute episode is superimposed against this background (e.g. Häfner & Nowotny, 1995). However, it is apparent that the salience of negative symptoms is greater after a first episode of positive symptoms than before. This suggests that there is some kind of link between the emergence of positive and of negative symptoms. This might be biological, and is usually assumed to be so. However, a psychological or psychosocial connection could be argued with equal plausibility (see David Fowler, Chapter 4 in this volume).

Thus, the early efflorescence of positive symptoms may be a critical period for intervention. In theory at least, it might be possible to reduce the development of negative symptoms and minimise the tendency for positive symptoms to relapse by intervening during this critical period.

There is some evidence that the response to drug treatment is slower and less complete in later episodes (Loebel et al., 1993; Lieberman et al., 1996) although, even in first episodes, 20% are unresponsive to conventional drug treatment. There are, however, methodological problems limiting the strength of this conclusion. In particular, comparison must be made between early and late episodes in the same subjects. Cross-sectional comparisons within a group containing people at different stages in the overall course of disorder will not do. Obviously if the group contains some people with very few episodes, the contrast between early episodes and late episodes will be distorted by the fact that these people, who will on average tend to have better outcomes anyway, have no later episodes for comparison.

JUSTIFYING EARLY TREATMENT

What evidence is there to justify early intervention on pragmatic rather than humane grounds early in the first psychotic episode? There have been a number of studies suggesting that long duration of untreated psychosis (DUP) is associated with poor outcome. This has been found both in retrospective (Fenton & McGlashan, 1987; Coryell & Tsuang, 1982; Helgason, 1990; Haas, Keshavan & Sweeney, 1994) and in prospective investigations (Johnstone et al., 1986; Loebel et al., 1992). Despite attempts to control for other features associated with poor outcome, these studies remain open to the charge that DUP in any case reflects a worse form of disease.

Another approach to establishing a justification for early intervention on heuristic grounds is to examine outcome historically, both before and after the introduction of effective biological treatments. Such studies are suggestive, as outcome genuinely seems to be better in younger cohorts (Wyatt, 1991; Opjordsmoen, 1991). However, these cohort effects could be the result of influences other than better treatment.

The main problem in justifying early intervention is that the key study cannot be done because of ethical restrictions. This would be a randomised-controlled trial of early and late intervention. There is one study where an approximation to this design was followed inadvertently. May and his colleagues (1981) reported on a follow-up study of a randomised-controlled trial of treatment in first-episode psychosis. Some of the patients had been allocated to a psychotherapy only group, and they responded less well in the treatment phase than patients receiving drugs or ECT. This implies that in this first group *effective* treatment was delayed on a random basis. As treatment was not controlled in the follow-up phase, these patients received pharmacotherapy at a later stage. Nevertheless, at follow-up, their clinical state remained worse. This study looks as if it provides quite good evidence of an effect of (effective) early intervention, but unfortunately the subjects from the psychotherapy group still tended to have less in the way of drugs over the follow-up period.

The TIPS project described by Tor Larsen and colleagues in this volume (Chapter 6) is now the nearest approximation to an RCT of early and late intervention that is ethically acceptable. It comprises one experimental sector and two control sectors. In the experimental sector there is an additional resource for early detection. However, in no sector is treatment delayed once a diagnosis of psychosis has been made. Results of this study will obviously be of enormous interest.

The current state of knowledge is thus sufficient only for tentative conclusions. It is possible that early intervention does effect the immediate, medium and long-term outcome of psychosis. Added to the humane argument for early intervention, this, in my view, justifies the investment of resources in preferentially targeting people early in the course of their psychotic illness, partly on the basis of the precautionary principle. Such investment also serves the aim of being as careful as possible in deciding on and implementing treatments, particularly of a pharmacological nature. Even if early treatment, whether biological or psychological, does not directly improve outcome, it may do so indirectly by increasing engagement. This is particularly true for medication, where it may be possible to reduce the dosage required for effective treatment, to improve the experience of medication, and thus increase the likelihood that later treatment will be taken. Relapse rates in schizophrenia may be three times higher than they would be if all patients prescribed neuroleptics actually took them (Kissling, 1994).

This is the compliance argument for intervention. I have reviewed this elsewhere (Bebbington, 1995), but one of the main problems in the dialogue between patients and physicians is that the benefit of neuroleptic medication may only be established over long periods, while side-effects are usually immediately apparent. A number of authors have examined the effect of initial experiences of neuroleptic medication on later compliance. The drugs have a variable but definite capacity for inducing dysphoric reactions to a first dose. This seems particularly associated with the experience of extrapyramidal symptoms (EPS), although weight gain and sexual dysfunction also have major effects on compliance (van Putten, May & Marder, 1984; Buchanan, 1992; Fleischhacker et al., 1994). Even in the context of specific compliance therapy, EPS predicted non-compliance (Kemp et al., 1996). Bad first experiences might be expected to dissuade patients of the virtues of persisting with medication, and many researchers have found this (van Putten et al., 1981; van Putten, May & Marder, 1984; Awad, 1993). While the effect of the initial reaction on the acceptance of treatment later on is much worse if patients continue to have bad subjective responses, it is clear that the possibility of an initial disaffection is a strong argument for introducing medication carefully: using small test doses and gradual increments in dose.

THE TIMING OF EARLY INTERVENTION

Early intervention may be targeted at the prodrome of first episodes of psychosis, or at the episodes themselves. Obviously, in order to intervene effectively during the prodromal stage, it must be possible to recognise it accurately. Some claims have been made to this effect. Thus, Falloon (1992) argues that his catchment area service in Buckingham, England, may have reduced the incidence of schizophrenia through intervention during the prodrome. There are serious problems with this work, based as it is on small numbers and the absence of a control group. Patrick McGorry (see Chapter 1) and his colleagues now claim to be able to recognise psychotic prodromes with a positive predictive value (ppv) of 50%. If so, this is a considerable advance. However, even with a ppv of this magnitude, it would be unethical to introduce treatment with neuroleptic medication, given the high rate of side-effects even with the modern atypical antipsychotics. Thus intervening pharmacologically during a prodrome cannot be justified, although it would be much easier to argue for a psychological intervention.

THE PROBLEM OF SIDE-EFFECTS

The neuroleptic drugs have many side-effects, but the ones that distress the patient most and consequently have most effect on compliance are, as indicated above, extrapyramidal (Buchanan, 1992; Bebbington, 1995).

Not all extrapyramidal disorder is of relevance to the early phases of treatment in neuroleptic medication. These side-effects can be divided into early, intermediate and late varieties. The late extrapyramidal side-effects of neuroleptic medication occur after months or years of treatment, and are covered by the term "tardive dyskinesia". Obviously, side-effects coming on so late are unlikely to affect the initial responses of patients to medication.

However, the early side-effects comprising acute dystonia occur within hours or days of onset of treatment, and the intermediate side-effects occur within days or weeks. The latter include Parkinsonism and akathisia. Both early and intermediate side-effects may affect the patients' views on the utility, benefits, and costs of neuroleptic medication. With conventional neuroleptics, the frequency of acute dystonias is reported as lying between 2 and 60%. Thus, 34 to 36% of patients receiving fluphenazine develop acute dystonias, rising to 60% of those prescribed haloperidol. Predisposing factors include the potency of the drug, the dose, and the rate of increment in drug dose. The frequency is also affected by age, being increased in young men. The experience of dystonia, which may require emergency treatment with an intramuscular anticholinergic drug, can be very distressing indeed, particularly if it has not happened before or is unexpected.

However, as far as patients themselves are concerned, the tendency of neuroleptic medication to induce Parkinsonism is perhaps its major disadvantage. Again, drug-related Parkinsonism is common. Between 40 and 75% of patients who are prescribed neuroleptics will experience such symptoms. Between 15 and 35% will meet criteria for the syndrome of

Parkinsonism (Whitworth & Fleishhacker, 1995). However, as many as 90% of patients will experience the *subjective* symptoms of Parkinsonism. These include fatigue, anergy, apathy, weakness, slowness, dysphoria, depression, stiffness and bradyphrenia (Casey, 1995). Patients will describe these subjective symptoms in characteristic language. They feel washed out, exhausted, lacking in interest, a zombie, and that they just cannot be bothered with things. Clinicians are very poor at recognising these subjective symptoms, but the main way in which they can be picked up is by having a high index of suspicion.

Again, the predisposing factors for the induction of Parkinsonism include the potency of the drug, its dose and the rate at which the dose is increased. There is also some evidence of individual susceptibility.

Dopamine blockade and the problem of side-effects

If we are to develop a rational approach to early neuroleptic intervention, we must consider the implications of the dopamine hypothesis. This proposes that dopaminergic neurones in the brain are linked to the pathogenesis and treatment of schizophrenia, particularly its positive symptoms. Even though it is at best an oversimplification, it is supported by a number of observations. Thus, there are no effective antipsychotic drugs which do not have some antagonistic action at dopamine receptors, and the potency of the older antipsychotic drugs is directly related to their affinity for the D_2 receptor. Moreover, D_2 agonists, for example amphetamines, can cause or exacerbate the positive symptoms of schizophrenia. The modulatory dopaminergic pathways (which are most prominent in limbic, striatal and cortical regions of the brain) are known to be of relevance in schizophrenia.

Studies using Positron Emission Tomography (PET) scans have illuminated this issue further. They suggest that the therapeutic effect of conventional neuroleptics is achieved around 65% blockage of D_2 dopamine receptors. Parkinsonian side-effects are not evident until receptor blockade has reached 80% (Farde et al., 1992). (These figures for blockade depend to an extent on the ligand used, but the principle remains.) Thus there would appear to be a therapeutic window in which it is possible to achieve therapeutic effectiveness without side-effects.

This ought to have a radical impact on clinical psychiatrists responsible for managing neuroleptic medication regimes. There was for some time a debate about the appropriateness of "megadose" therapy (Hirsch & Barnes, 1995). However, patients treated with neuroleptic medication have until recently received doses that guaranteed 100% occupancy of D_2 receptors.

In these circumstances, it is hard to see how increasing the dose further would be of benefit. Moreover, although using relatively low doses may take longer to achieve a therapeutic effect, this delay in the short term may be justifiable if a long-term consequence is that patients are more likely to take medication.

SEARCHING FOR A STRATEGY FOR EARLY INTERVENTION WITH CONVENTIONAL ANTIPSYCHOTIC DRUGS

The principle underlying the use of neuroleptic medication in the early stages of schizophrenia is simple: it is to ensure that the experience of medication is as positive as possible. This means the rapid and effective reduction of the symptoms of the disorder, but it also requires that patients experience the absolute minimum of side-effects. Finally, but perhaps most importantly, the experience of medication can be enhanced in non-pharmacological ways—building a trusting mutual relationship with patients and, in the process, providing information in an amount, sequence and manner that makes them feel safe, valued and involved.

Given that the avoidance of side-effects is a crucial (perhaps *the* crucial) consideration in the treatment of first-episode psychosis, what approaches are available to us?

The first involves the tempered use of a conventional neuroleptic. It is clear that the prescribed doses of these drugs is still often well in excess of what is needed for a therapeutic effects, and well into the range associated with severe extrapyramidal side-effects. Once the priorities of prescribers shift from therapeutic effect at any cost to a trade-off between main and side-effects, strategies can be developed to arrive at dosages inside the therapeutic window. One of these is *neuroleptic threshold dosing*, in which the dose of drug is increased to the point where EPS appear and then reduced by a small amount to what then becomes the established treatment dose (McEvoy, Hogarty & Steingard, 1991).

There are two disadvantages to this. The first is that it requires that the patient experience clear EPS during the process of dose fixing. The other is that it requires the treating clinician to be able to identify EPS quickly and with a low recognition threshold. As many of the symptoms of Parkinsonism are subjective, and as these subjective symptoms are seriously aversive, this strategy may condemn the patient to an experience of appreciable duration and unpleasantness, with all that may mean in terms of reduced compliance.

Embarking on prolonged drug therapy in schizophrenia is predicated on the simple and well-established empirical finding that it reduces relapse rates. For many patients, however, the idea of prolonged or open-ended maintenance therapy is distasteful: it involves a ceding of control to the psychiatrist, and the prolonged use of drugs with unpleasant effects is an unwelcome prospect.

At first sight, the most appealing style of pharmacotherapy would involve *responsive or targeted medication*. Under this regime, patients do not take maintenance medication, but return to medication at times of incipient breakdown. The main problem with such treatment is that it may be difficult to identify relapses early enough to be able to abort them. There is plenty of evidence that the targeting strategy not only involves more relapses, but also more hospitalisations (Pietzcker et al., 1993; Gaebel, 1994). There is a further possible disadvantage: intermittent dosing with neuroleptics may increase the overall incidence of tardive dyskinesia (Glenthoj, Hemmingsen & Bolwig, 1988). It is possible that intermittent targeted regimes may do better where patients can be wholeheartedly engaged with the process of therapy and of identifying potential relapse. Targeted dosing may also work better if it takes place against a background of low dose maintenance medication (e.g. Marder, 1994; Huttunen et al., 1996).

Low-dose therapy with older neuroleptic drugs represents a trade-off between effectiveness and side-effects. Consider first the issue of effectiveness. Because of the relatively small window between the levels of receptor occupancy associated with clinical effect and with extrapyramidal symptoms, it is perhaps inevitable that low dosages are associated with higher relapse rates (Burnett et al., 1993; Bollini et al., 1994). In their meta-analysis, Barbui et al. (1996) confirmed this increase in relapse rate with low-dose regimes: however, it was not great. The increase was significant at 12 months, but not at 24 months into treatment. However, it should be noted that they compared a really low dose with a medium dose (50–100 mg with 200–500 mg in chlorpromazine equivalents), and the differences from patients on higher but still moderate dosages might be greater.

Note now the effect of low-dose therapy with conventional antipsychotics on the emergence of EPS. Barbui and Saraceno (1996) have carried out a metanalysis of the impact of low-dose regimes on extrapyramidal side-effects in schizophrenia. There was some benefit, but the reduction in EPS with low-dosing was only about 0.3 standard deviations, really rather disappointing.

Given these relatively small improvements in side-effects that arise from low-dose therapy with a conventional neuroleptic, there are two further problems. The first is that a given dose administered to different patients may result in a ten-fold variation in serum level of the drug, so attaining the correct dose without causing side-effects is difficult. The other problem in avoiding negative experiences of medication is that clinicians are not very good at recognising them. This was demonstrated in a study by Weiden et al. (1987). Drug-related extrapyramidal disorder was identified by specially trained research workers. Their findings were then compared with the clinicians' ratings of the presence of extrapyramidal symptoms. While the latter were able to identify more than half of cases of Parkinsonism, they were only able to recognise dystonia in a third of patients, akathisia in a quarter, and tardive dyskinesia in a tenth.

This inability to recognise side-effects is reflected in a study by Hoge et al. (1990). These workers compared clinicians' and patients' judgements about the reasons why antipsychotic medication had been refused. In a half of cases the clinicians attributed the patients' refusal of antipsychotic medication as being due to psychotic or idiosyncratic causes. In 11% of cases they identified transference problems, and in 7% side-effects. In contrast, the patients attributed their discontinuation or refusal of medication to side-effects in 35% of cases. In only 12% of cases did they discontinue medication because they felt it to be ineffective. This consistent failure of clinicians to recognise the salience of side-effects of conventional neuroleptic medication can only detract further from its acceptability.

The conclusion from the various strategies for enhancing the clinical performance of conventional antipsychotics is that they lead to some reduction in effectiveness, and that this is offset by some improvement to their side-effects profile. This inevitably obliges us to consider whether better outcomes may be obtained by using the newer antipsychotics, and thus whether they should be prescribed as first-line drugs in early psychosis.

THE ATYPICAL NEUROLEPTICS AND THE ATTENUATION OF THE DOPAMINE HYPOTHESIS

As foreshadowed above, the dopamine hypothesis is now regarded as a gross oversimplification. For many years there was a strong expectation that elevated levels of D_2 receptors would be found in the brains of people with schizophrenia, but there is no evidence from PET studies to suggest a constitutional change in the frequency of D_2 receptors. Moreover, at least 10% of patients with positive symptoms of schizophrenia do not respond to D_2 blockage.

However, the most challenging piece of evidence concerns the newer antipsychotics (e.g. clozapine, olanzapine, ziprazadone), which achieve an antipsychotic effect without high D_2 occupancy. Indeed, clozapine is effective in many patients who have not responded well to typical neuroleptics. This is despite appearing to operate at particularly low levels of occupancy of D_2 receptors. Its action in blocking $5HT_2$ receptors is thought to be of greater significance in its therapeutic effects. Other atypical antipsychotic agents also appear to have an increased affinity for $5HT_2$ receptors, even when, like risperidone, they still appear to mount an effective blockade of dopamine receptors. Thus, it is beginning to appear as if dopamine blockade is not an essential feature of therapeutic effectiveness in neuroleptics.

The first neuroleptic drug used in psychiatry was chlorpromazine. It was named Largactil by the company that produced it, in order to indicate its wide range of actions in human subjects. This attribute was shared by all the early drugs of this type. Their actions are now known to be associated with affinities for an equally extensive range of receptor sites. The efficacy and side-effects of these early drugs varied only in degree.

Clozapine was the first antipsychotic drug that seemed to have a genuinely different therapeutic profile, the first to which the epithet "atypical" could reasonably be applied. It has an interesting history. It was actually synthesised more than 40 years ago, and was withdrawn in most countries in 1975 when its capacity for inducing agranulocytosis was fully appreciated. Its unusual actions and pharmacology, however, led to its later reintroduction under stringent monitoring conditions (in 1990 in the UK).

Its success and its disadvantages led to a renewed interest in drug discovery for the treatment of psychosis (Kerwin, 1996). The target drug would have a similar range of therapeutic effect but lack the serious side-effects. Several new drugs now have product licences in the UK, but none really satisfies the aspirations of those looking for an improved version of clozapine. Nevertheless, they do share features that make it reasonable for them to be regarded as "atypical".

Although there are several different levels at which atypicality can be defined (chemical, pharmacological and clinical: King, 1998), side-effects are central to the commonly accepted definition. Thus, atypical or novel antipsychotics characteristically have low extrapyramidal side-effects within the normal therapeutic dose range (Meltzer, 1991). Other attributes are merely trivial increases in prolactin levels, and (perhaps) effects on symptoms other than positive ones. A number of new drugs fit these characteristics, although they actually vary quite widely in their pharmacological characteristics (Arnt & Skarsfeldt, 1998). Despite their diverse pharmacological effects, they are clinically considerably cleaner drugs than their conventional forebears.

As indicated above, these benefits are regarded as resulting from $5HT_2$ blockade. Thus there is now considerable evidence that blockade of $5HT_2$ receptors reduces the Parkinsonian side-effects that almost inevitably accompany dopamine blockade, acting as a sort of internal antidote to the other effects of the drugs.

Because of their effect on $5HT_2$ receptors, it has also been claimed that these drugs may improve negative symptoms. The impact of neuroleptics on negative symptoms has always been treated with scepticism. In fact there are several potential interrelationships of schizophrenia, neuroleptic drugs and negative symptoms. Thus, negative symptoms may be intrinsic to the schizophrenic process; they may be the direct consequence of positive symptoms; they may result from the psychological responses of patients to their predicament; and they may be caused by the neuroleptic drugs themselves, in the sense that negative symptoms clearly overlap with neuroleptic side-effects.

It is generally felt that the symptoms most likely to be affected are those which are very closely associated with positive symptoms. Thus, impaired concentration and thinking might well be the result of positive symptoms like hallucinations. Obviously, treating the hallucinations would therefore be likely to improve the negative symptoms. However, there is in fact some evidence of direct effects of neuroleptics on negative symptoms. Tollefson and Sanger (1997) carried out a path analysis on data from a study of 335 patients treated in a randomised-controlled trial comparing olanzapine, placebo and haloperidol. Because they measured positive, negative and extrapyramidal symptoms separately, they could thus entangle direct and indirect effects. Their findings indicated at least some direct effect of olanzapine in improving negative symptoms. Note that because the authors had no measure of psychological attitudes, they were unable to distinguish between direct pharmacological effects and those that might be mediated psychologically.

Moreover, this study, though elegant, had the drawback of a sample with relatively high levels of positive symptoms and low levels of negative ones. It might be better to estimate direct effects of neuroleptics on negative symptoms in patients selected as suffering predominantly for such symptoms. This was done by Loo and his colleagues (1997) using amisulpride. Amisulpride ameliorated negative symptoms to a greater extent than placebo. However, placebo also improved the patients to some extent, and this is clear evidence of psychological mechanisms. Although these findings on negative symptoms are of interest, there must be doubt about whether their magnitude leads them to be of clinical significance.

The clinical status of the novel antipsychotics may be overstated if the controlled trials used to establish them are viewed uncritically. The American Food and Drugs Administration (FDA) have stipulated that trials of new antipsychotic drugs should involve comparison with haloperidol. This has the advantage of establishing a common yardstick, aided further by the use of standard instruments such as the BPRS and PANSS. However, the FDA did not stipulate the dose of haloperidol that should be used, reflecting the paucity of dose-ranging studies in relation to the conventional antipsychotics. A consistent problem is that in most studies novel antipsychotics are compared with what would now be regarded as relatively high doses of haloperidol. Thus, Petit and his colleagues (1996) have compared zotepine with 10 and 20 mg daily of haloperidol, Puech et al. (1998) compared three doses of amisulpride with 16 mg daily of haloperidol, while Tandon, Harrigan and Zorn (1997) and Goff et al. (1998) reported placebo-controlled trials with ziprasidone that used haloperidol 15 mg daily as a comparator.

These doses of haloperidol are likely to result in 100% receptor blockage and to produce extrapyramidal symptoms, and in this respect the reported advantage of each of these new drugs may be exaggerated, and will in any case be difficult to interpret. Thus, in the comparison study carried out by Emsley and his colleagues (1995), risperidone was compared with what would normally be regarded as very low doses of haloperidol (a mean dose of 5.6 mg). Twenty of 99 patients on risperidone and 26 of 84 patients on haloperidol did not complete the six weeks of the trial, but side-effects were implicated in 15 cases in the haloperidol group and only six cases in the risperidone group—a significant difference. There was very little difference in outcome in terms of symptom scores at the end of treatment. Thus although there is a clear advantage of risperidone in relation to side-effects, particularly extrapyramidal ones, this is not by an order of magnitude.

It should also be noted that the advice given on the administration of the atypical neuroleptics is designed to minimise the prospect of side-effects. Thus, manufacturers recommend dose regimes quite rigidly, and these regimes are designed to avoid full D_2 receptor blockade. Moreover, they often recommend that the therapeutic dose is introduced gradually, a strategy that also minimises the side-effect rate. If traditional neuroleptics were used in this manner, the very high rates of Parkinsonian and dystonic side-effects would be considerably reduced.

While Tollefson and Sanger (1997) also used haloperidol as the comparator for olanzapine, both drugs could be used according to clinical need, in doses ranging from 5 to 20 mg olanzapine outperformed haloperidol in reduction of symptoms overall and specifically in reduction of negative symptoms. This is an impressive study, but the differences in clinical outcome were not marked between the two drugs. There were, however, considerable differences in dropout rates, and the dosing strategy, in this study at least, did not particularly favour olanzapine.

We now have the advantage of several meta-analyses of the efficacy of the novel antipsychotic drugs carried out specially for the National Schizophrenia Guideline Group of the Royal College of Psychiatrists and

British Psychological Society. I will make use of these analyses in describing the performance of the individual atypical antipsychotic drugs.

As described above, the first of these was clozapine. Many of the trials involving clozapine are actually quite old. A dozen randomised-controlled trials have examined its effectiveness, and 20 have looked at its tolerability. It is appreciably more effective than the other old antipsychotic drugs, although, probably because of the requirement for repeated blood tests, its tolerability is no greater. Several of the trials of clozapine specifically involve people with refractory schizophrenia. Its effectiveness in the long term still requires adequate demonstration (Essock et al., 1996; Rosenheck et al., 1997).

Of the other novel antipsychotic drugs currently licensed in the UK, amisulpride and olanzapine appear to be superior to haloperidol in their effect on symptoms, although this superiority is small and at the margin of clinical significance. It is possible that olanzapine's superiority is more marked in early episodes. Quetiapine, risperidone and sertindole appear no more effective in treating psychosis than haloperidol. However, the selling point of these drugs was never their superior effectiveness, but their reduced side-effect profile, with the implied increase in tolerability. This they certainly have: the use of these drugs may lead to 10% fewer people dropping out of treatment, perhaps fewer still in the case of olanzapine. This increase in compliance is quite likely to be due to their consistently lower tendency to induce dystonia, and especially akithisia. Risperidone has a particular problem in its relatively high binding to striatal dopamine receptors. As a result, it has a greater tendency to induce extrapyramidal side-effects. It seems likely that this will eventually lead to lower recommended dose ranges.

It should be noted that this résumé of results does require qualification, since the superiority of the novel antipsychotics, as we have noted above, is in comparison to relatively high doses of haloperidol. When the dose of haloperidol is controlled for, it is apparent that much of the advantage of the novel antipsychotics disappears. Bech and his colleagues (1998) have recently conducted their own meta-analyses comparing risperidone with conventional neuroleptics, concluding superior effectiveness and side-effect profile. However, they did not include the Emsley et al. (1995) study, nor did they control for dose of the comparator medication.

There seems to be only one study comparing the relative performance of the novel antipsychotics. For this reason, the study is worth reporting in some detail. Tran et al. (1997) compared olanzapine with risperidone in the first RCT to compare two novel antipsychotics with each other. Patients on olanzapine did significantly better in terms of overall response rate, negative symptoms side-effects, adverse events and the maintenance of treatment effects. This was in accord with the authors' predictions based on the different pharmacology and in vivo neuropharmacology of the two drugs. However, the authors used one-tailed tests of significance for which their rationale seems very dubious. Moreover, the study has power problems given the likely effect sizes. Dosing was flexible within limits (10–20 mg per day for olanzapine; 4–12 mg per day for risperidone). Levels of discontinuation were similar for the two drugs, the reasons being indistinguishable. In many respects the response of the various measures differed little between the two drugs. There was less sexual dysfunction with olanzapine.

The other characteristic these drugs have in common is their cost: all are understandably much more expensive than the drugs they replace. However, increased tolerability might have considerable impact on their cost-effectiveness: expensive pills do not make for expensive treatment if they are much more likely to be taken.

There are relatively few actual studies of the cost-effectiveness of novel antipsychotics in comparison with the older drugs. Byrom, Garratt and Kilpatrick (1998) have presented a decision-tree economic model that incorporates estimates of effects in reducing the level of care. Clearly, any expensive drug may recoup its costs if it enables those treated with it to manage with less intensive treatment.

Hamilton and her colleagues (1998), however, have provided actual cost data from the large RCT comparing olanzapine with haloperidol. In overall medical costs, olanzapine was $431 per month cheaper than haloperidol in the acute phase and $345 in the maintenance phase, although only the latter was significant. It certainly sounds on the basis of these data that olanzapine was unlikely to be *more* expensive, although again we must remember that some of the advantage may come from the dose ranges of haloperidol used for comparison. However, the current knowledge of cost–benefit in neuroleptic medication is very inadequate and secure conclusions are not possible.

CONCLUSIONS: RATIONALITY AND HUMANITY IN THE EARLY PHARMACOLOGICAL MANAGEMENT OF PSYCHOSIS

The evidence reviewed above places the prescribing psychiatrist in a difficult position. It is clear that high dosages of conventional antipsychotics should be strenuously avoided because they will cause unpleasant side-effects with little additional benefit. A relatively superficial evaluation of the available research suggests that neither targeted dosing nor low dose treatment with conventional antipsychotics quite fulfils its promise. On this basis, there is a firm argument for using novel antipsychotics (not clozapine) as the first line of treatment in people newly developing psychosis. This is based on their lower rate of unpleasant side-effects, their greater tolerability, and (possibly) their greater overall cost-effectiveness.

However, we have seen that there are various uncertainties about the trials used to substantiate the introduction of the new antipsychotics. These arise because the dose of the comparison drug haloperidol is almost invariably in the range that would be expected to produce side-effects and reduce tolerability. (The safest study in this respect is the as yet under-published multi-centre trial of risperidone.) This design anomaly must reduce the advantage of the novel antipsychotic drugs in terms of tolerability and cost-effectiveness.

What then is the clinician to do? I think that, in the current state of knowledge, the use both of low-dose conventional antipsychotics and of the novel antipsychotics could be justified. The new drugs almost certainly are better, if not as much so as has been claimed, and several authors recommend them as first choice drugs in early psychosis (e.g. Sheitman et al., 1997). However, the acquisition costs of the novel antipsychotics are such that if there were no cost–benefit advantage, their introduction as universal first line drugs would represent an increase of several hundred million pounds a year in National Health spending. The National Schizophrenia Guideline Group have not used the cost–benefit principle in drafting their guidelines but have relied instead on the precautionary principle, appropriate in the context of novel drugs whose own side-effects are not yet fully logged. They have therefore expressed reservations over first usage in new cases of psychosis. However, they also suggest that the dose of typical neuroleptic should be restricted, and that switching to a novel antipsychotic should have a low threshold, being activated immediately there is an indication of side-effects or of ineffectiveness. The draft guideline can be summarised succinctly: it is not unreasonable to use a typical antipsychotic in carefully monitored low doses in people who are early in the course of a psychotic illness; it is unreasonable to move to doses likely to produce side-effects in the face of a poor response; it is reasonable to move quickly to an atypical antipsychotic drug in cases where there is a poor response or side-effects. These recommendations would incidentally tend to discourage somewhat the financial consequences of going directly to first usage of atypicals, but they do leave it fairly open to the clinician to switch, and in our view represent a rational response to the available evidence. Obviously the slant of the evidence is likely to change in the next few years, perhaps more strongly in favour of the atypicals, but the draft recommendations maintain some of the opportunity costs released by sticking to the older drugs. They are nevertheless likely to lead to a gradual escalation of drug costs over the next few years.

I would emphasise that as much thought should be given to monitoring and modifying the dose, and to engaging patients in their own treatment, as to the choice of drug. All guidelines are exactly that, guidelines, and may be modified in the light of negotiation with clients. Meeting patients early in the course of their illness provides great opportunities for optimising the outcome in the long-term. The whole treatment package should be geared towards this.

REFERENCES

Arnt, J. & Skarsfeldt, T. (1998). Do novel antipsychotics have similar pharmacological characteristics? A review of the evidence. *Neuropsychopharmacology*, **18**, 63–101.

Awad, A.G. (1993). Methodological and design issues in clinical trials of new neuroleptics: an overview. *British Journal of Psychiatry*, **163** (Suppl. 22), 51–71.

Barbui, C., Saraceno, B. Liberati, A. & Garattini, S. (1996). Low-dose neuroleptic therapy and relapse in schizophrenia: meta-analysis of randomized controlled trials. *European Psychiatry*, **11**, 306–313.

Barbui, C. & Saraceno, B. (1996). Low-dose neuroleptic therapy and extrapyramidal side effects in schizophrenia: an effect size analysis. *European Psychiatry*, **11**, 412–415.

Bebbington, P.E. (1995). The content and context of compliance. *International Clinical Psychopharmacology*, **9**, (Suppl. 5), 41–50.

Bech, P., Peuskens, JC.J.R., Marder, S.R., Chouinard, G., Hyberg, O.J., Huttunen, M.A., Blin, O. & Claus, A. (1998). Meta-analytic study of the benefits and risks of treating chronic schizophrenia with risperidone or conventional neuroleptics. *European Psychiatry*, **13**, 310–314.

Bollini, P., Pampallona, S., Orza, M. J., Adams, M.E. & Chalmers, T.C. (1994). Antipsychotic drugs: Is more worse? A meta-analysis of the published randomized control trials. *Psychological Medicine*, **24**, 307–316.

Burnett, P.L., Galletly, C.A., Moyle, R.J. & Clark, C.R. (1993). Low-dose depot medication in schizophrenia. *Schizophrenia Bulletin*, **19**, 155–164.

Buchanan, A. (1992). A two-year prospective study of treatment compliance in patients with schizophrenia. *Psychological Medicine*, **22**, 787–797.

Byrom, B.D., Garratt, C.J. & Kilpatrick, T. (1998). Influence of antipsychotic profile on cost of treatment of schizophrenia: a decision analysis approach. *International Journal of Psychiatry in Clinical Practice*, **2**, 129–138.

Casey, D. (1995). Motor and mental aspects of extrapyramidal syndromes. *International Clinical Psychopharmacology*, **10**, 105–114.

Coryell, W. & Tsuang, M.T. (1982). DSM-III schizophreniform disorder. *Archives of General Psychiatry*, **39**, 66–69.

Emsley, R.A., McCreadie, R., Livingston, M., De Smedt, G. & Lemmens, P. (1995). Risperidone in the treatment of first-episode patients with schizophrenia disorder. A double-blind study. (Abstract) Presented at the 8th ECNP Congress, Venice, Italy.

Essock, S., Hargreaves, W.A., Covell N.H. & Goethe, J. (1996). Clozapine's effectiveness for patients in state hospitals: results from a randomised trial. *Psychopharmacology Bulletin*, **32**, 683–697.

Falloon, I.R.H. (1992). Early intervention for first episodes of schizophrenia: a preliminary exploration. *Psychiatry*, **55**, 4–15.

Farde, L., Nordstrom, A.L. Wiesel, F.A. Pauli, S. Halldin, C. & Sedvall, G. (1992). Positron emission topographic analysis of central D_1 and D_2 dopamine receptor occupancy in patients treated with classical neuroleptics and clozapine. Relation to extrapyramidal side effects. *Archives of General Psychiatry*, **49**, 538–544.

Fenton, W.S. & McGlashan, T.H. (1987). Sustained remission in drug-free schizophrenic patients. *American Journal of Psychiatry*, **144**, 1306–1309.

Fleischhacker, W.W., Meise, U., Guenther, V. & Kurz, M. (1994). Compliance with antipsychotic drug treatment: influence of side effects. *Acta Psychiatrica Scandinavica*, **89**, (Suppl. 382), 11–15.

Frances, A., Docherty, J.P. & Kahn, D.A. (1996). Treatment of schizophrenia. The Expert Consensus Guidelines Series. *Journal of Clinical Psychiatry*, **57**, (Suppl. 12B), 1–57.

Gaebel, W. (1994). Intermittent medication: an alternative? *Acta Psychiatrica Scandinavica*, **89**, (Suppl. 382), 33–38.

Glenthoj, B., Hemmingsen, R. & Bolwig, T.G. (1988). Kindling: a model for the development of tardive dyskinesia? *Behavioural Neurology*, **1**, 29–40.

Goff, D.C., Posever, T., Herz, L., Simmons, J., Kletti, N., Lapierre, K., Wilner, K.D., Law, C.G. & Ko, G.N. (1998). An exploratory haloperidol-controlled dose-finding study of ziprasidone in hospitalized patients with schizophrenia or schizoaffective disorder. *Journal of Clinical Psychopharmacology*, **18**, 296–304.

Haas, G.L., Keshavan, M.S. & Sweeney, J.A. (1994). Delay to first medication in schizophrenia: evidence for a possible negative impact of exposure to psychosis. (Abstract.) Presented at the American College of Neuropsychopharmacology, San Juan, Puerto Rico.

Häfner, H. & Nowotny, B. (1995). Epidemiology of early-onset schizophrenia. *European Archives of Psychiatry and Clinical Neuroscience*, **245**, 80–92.

Hamilton, S.H., Revicki, D.A., Genduso, L.A., Tollefson, G. & Edgell, E.T. (1998). Costs of olanzapine treatment compared with haloperidol for schizophrenia: results from a randomized clinical trial. (Abstract.) American Psychiatric Association, 1998 annual meeting, Toronto.

Helgason, L. (1990). Twenty years' follow-up of first psychiatric presentation of schizophrenia: what could have been prevented? *Acta Psychiatrica Scandinavica*, **81**, 231–235.

Hirsch, S.R. & Barnes, T.R.E. (1995). The clinical treatment of schizophrenia with antipsychotic medication. In S.R. Hirsch & D.R. Weinberger (Eds) *Schizophrenia* (pp. 443–468). Oxford: Blackwell Science.

Hoge, S.K., Appelbaum, P.S., Lawlor, T., Beck, J.C., Litman, R., Greer, A., Gutheil, T.G. & Kaplan, E. (1990). A prospective, multicenter study of patients' refusal of antipsychotic medication. *Archives of General Psychiatry*, **47**, 949–956.

Huttunen, M.O., Tuhkanen, H., Haavisto, E., Nyholm, R., Pitkanen, M., Raitasuo, V. & Romanov, M.. (1996). Low- and standard-dose depot haloperidol combined with targeted oral neuroleptics. *Psychiatric Services*, **47**, 83–85.

Johnstone, E.C., Crow, T.J., Johnson, A.L. and Macmillan, J.F. (1986). The Northwick Park study of first episodes of schizophrenia. I: Presentation of the illness and problems relating to admission. *British Journal of Psychiatry*, **148**, 115–120.

Kemp, R., Hayward, P., Applewhaite, G., Everitt, B. & David, A. (1996). Compliance therapy in psychotic patients: randomised controlled trial. *British Medical Journal*, **312**, 345–349.

Kerwin, R.W. (1996). An essay on the use of the new antipsychotics. *Psychiatric Bulletin*, **20**, 23–29

Kissling, W. (1994). Compliance, quality assurance and standards for relapse prevention in schizophrenia. *Acta Psychiatrica Scandinavica*, **328** (Suppl.), 16–24.

King, D.J. (1998). Atypical antipsychotics and the negative symptoms of schizophrenia. *Advances in Psychiatric Treatment*, **4**, 53–61.

Kraepelin, E. (1921). *Manic-Depressive Insanity and Paranoia* (trans. R.M. Barclay). Edinburgh: Livingstone.

Lieberman, J.A., Koreen, A.R., Chakos, M., Sheitman, B., Woerner, M., Alvir, J. & Bilder, R. (1996). Factors influencing treatment response and outcome of first episode schizophrenia. Implications for understanding the pathophysiology of schizophrenia. *Journal of Clinical Psychiatry*, **9**, 5–9.

Loebel, A.D., Lieberman, J.A., Alvir, J.M., Mayerhoff, D.I., Geisler, S.H. & Szymanski, S.R. (1992). Duration of psychosis and outcome in first-episode schizophrenia. *American Journal of Psychiatry*, **149**, 1183–1188.

Loebel, A.D., Lieberman, J.A., Alvir, J.M.J. Geisley, S.H., Szymanski, S.R. & Mayerhoff, D.I. (1993). *Consistency of Treatment Response Across Successive Psychotic Episodes in Recent-onset Schizophrenia Research*. Colorado Springs, CO.

Loo, H., Poirier-Littre, M.F., Théron, M., Rein, W. & Fleurot, O. (1997). Amisulpride versus placebo in the medium term treatment of negative symptoms of schizophrenia. *British Journal of Psychiatry*, **170**, 18–22.

May, P.R.A., Tuma, A.H., Dixon, W.J., Yale, C., Thiele, D.A. & Kraude, W.H. (1981). Schizophrenia: a follow-up study of the results of five forms of treatment. *Archives of General Psychiatry*, **38**, 776–784.

McEvoy, J.P., Hogarty, G.E. & Steingard, S. (1991). Optimal dose of neuroleptic in acute schizophrenia: a controlled study of the neuroleptic threshold and higher haloperidol dose. *Archives of General Psychiatry*, **488**, 739–745.

Marder, S.R. (1994). The role of dosage and plasma levels in neuroleptic relapse prevention. *Acta Psychiatrica Scandinavica*, **89**, (Suppl. 382), 25–27.

McGlashan, T.H. & Johannessen, J.O. (1996). Early detection and intervention with schizophrenia: rationale. *Schizophrenia Bulletin*, **22**, 201–222.

Meltzer, H.Y. (1991). The mechanism of action of novel antipsychotic drugs. *Schizophrenia Bulletin*, **17**, 263–287.

National Schizophrenia Guideline Group (1999). Parmacological treatment for schizophrenia and related conditions—an evidence-based clinical practice guideline (submitted to the *Lancet*).

Opjordsmoen, S. (1991). Paranoid (delusional) disorders in the light of a long-term follow-up study. *Psychopathology*, **24**, 287–292.

Petit, M., Raniwalla, J., Tweed, J., Leutenegger, E., Dollfus, S. & Kelly, F. (1996). A comparison of an atypical and typical antipsychotic, zotepine versus haloperidol in patients with acutre exacerbation of schizophrenia: a parallel-group double-blind trial. *Psychopharmacology Bulletin* **32**, 81–87.

Pietzcker, A., Gaebel, W., Koepcke, W., Linden, M., Müller, P., Müller-Span, F. & tegeler, J. (1993). Intermittent versus maintenance neuroleptic long-term treatment in schizophrenia: 2-year results of a German multicentre study. *Journal of Psychiatric Research*, **27**, 321–339.

Puech, A., Fleurot, O., Rein, W. & the Amisulpride Study Group (1998). Amisulpride, an atypical antipsychotic, in the treatment of acute episodes of schizophrenia: a dose-ranging study vs haloperidol. *Acta Psychiatrica Scandinavica*, **98**, 65–72.

Rosenheck, R., Cramer, J., Xu, W., Thomas, J., Henderson, W., Frisman, L., Fye, C. & Charney, D. (1997). A comparison of clozapine and haloperidol in hospitalized patients with refractory schizophrenia. Department of Veterans Affairs Cooperative Study Group on Clozapine in Refractory Schizophrenia. *New England Journal of Medicine*, **337**, 809–815.

Sheitman, B.B., Heidi, L., Rael, S. & Lieberman, J.A. (1997). The evaluation and treatment of first-episode psychosis. *Schizophrenia Bulletin*, **23**, 653–661.

Tandon, R., Harrigan, E. & Zorn, S.H. (1997). Ziprasidone: a novel antipsychotic with unique pharmacology and therapeutic potential. *Journal of Serotonin Research*, **4**, 159–177.

Tollefson, G.D. & Sanger, T.M. (1997). Negative symptoms: a path analytic approach to a double-blind, placebo- and haloperidol-controlled clinical trial with olanzapine. *American Journal of Psychiatry*, **154**, 466–474.

Tran, P.V., Hamilton, S.H., Kuntz, A.J., Potvin, J.H., Andersen, S.W., Beasley, C. & Tollefson, G.D. (1997). Double-blind comparison of olanzapine versus risperidone in the treatment of schizophrenia and other psychotic disorders. *Journal of Clinical Psychopharmacology*, **17**, 407–418.

van Putten, T., May, P.R. Marder, S.R. & Wittmann, L.A. (1981). Subjective response to antipsychotic drugs. *Archives of General Psychiatry*, **38**, 187–190.

van Putten, T., May, P.R. & Marder, S.R. (1984). Response to antipsychotic medication: the doctor's and the consumer's view. *American Journal of Psychiatry*, **141**, 16–19.

Weiden, P.J., Mann, J.J. Haas, G., Mattson, M. & Frances, A. (1987). Clinical non-recognition of neuroleptic-induced movement disorders: a cautionary study. *American Journal of Psychiatry*, **144**, 1148–1153.

Whitworth, A.B. & Fleishhacker, W.W. (1995). Adverse effects of antipsychotic drugs. *International Clinical Psychopharmacology*, **9**, (Suppl. 5), 21–27.

Wyatt, R.J. (1991). Neuroleptics and the natural course of schizophrenia. *Schizophrenia Bulletin*, **17**, (2), 325–351.

Chapter 8

COGNITIVE BEHAVIOUR THERAPY IN EARLY PSYCHOSIS

*Val Drury**

INTRODUCTION

Early acute episodes can have a pernicious impact on the trajectory of psychotic disorders (e.g. Shepherd et al., 1989; Wyatt, 1991) and on the quality of sufferers' lives. They may represent a time when conflicts and issues which cannot be resolved by the individual surface as psychotic symptoms (e.g. Bannister, 1983) and are likely to be the place where residual positive symptoms originate (Shepherd et al., 1989; Wiersma et al., 1998). Furthermore, psychological distress linked to florid symptoms and the ordeal of hospitalisation can present the individual with an extremely demanding and difficult adaptation process (McGorry et al., 1991). It has therefore been suggested that the early years after onset may be a critical time for psychological and other interventions and is "likely to have a disproportionate impact relative to interventions later in the course" (Birchwood, Todd & Jackson, 1996, p. 56).

Attempts to shorten the duration of early acute psychotic episodes and to reduce residual positive symptoms would seem a worthwhile endeavour for several reasons. Firstly, it is claimed that the longer the time spent in acute psychosis the greater the risk of long-term morbidity (Wyatt, 1991; Harrison et al., 1996) and the longer the period of psychosis prior to treatment with medication in first-episode patients, the poorer the short-term outcome (Crow et al., 1986; Loebel et al., 1992). Secondly, it has been demonstrated in follow-up studies of patients with non-affective psychosis that *after* each acute episode the proportion of patients with residual psychotic symptoms

---

*University of Birmingham, UK.

Early Intervention in Psychosis.
Edited by M. Birchwood, D. Fowler & C. Jackson.

increases (Shepherd et al., 1989; Wiersma et al., 1998), suggesting that the acute phase is the source of these residual symptoms. Thirdly, the experience of acute psychosis, pathways to care that involve the police, judiciary or Accident and Emergency departments and inpatient treatment that involves enforced medication and being accommodated on a secure ward are likely to be highly traumatising for the individual and may lead to persisting symptoms of Post-Traumatic Stress Disorder (McGorry et al., 1991) and alienation from services. Consequently, cognitive-behavioural interventions in the acute phase may help to improve engagement with services and reduce the emotional costs of admission. Fourthly, it is suggested the individual may be more amenable to psychological intervention at the commencement of an acute episode. Many early researchers (e.g. Donlon & Blacker, 1973; Sachar et al., 1970) observed that at the height of decompensation a patient's defences are reduced, their coping strategies may be minimal or maladaptive and individuals appear to be pursuing a *disordered* search for an explanation to their predicament. A cognitive behavioural intervention in the acute phase would then attempt to assist the patient in a *structured* search to make sense of his/her experiences. Lastly, acute inpatient care rarely has a theoretical or evidence base, is often limited to provision of medication and varying degrees of asylum and is viewed as a separate rather than an integral part of the overall plan of care (Sensky & Scott,1995). Furthermore, it is unlikely to be geared to the needs of young people suffering from psychosis (McGorry,1996). It has been suggested both in early studies (Kayton,1975) and in recent controlled trials (Hogarty et al., 1995, 1997) that acute care needs to be carefully managed to respond to the specific needs of individual patients in each phase of their recovery. It is therefore suggested that a CBT intervention that aims to integrate information from the acute crisis into a psychological formulation of the genesis and maintenance of psychosis is likely to be beneficial to the patient and promote personal adjustment.

Various reasoning biases have been linked to the formation and maintenance of delusions in some patients (e.g. Garety, Hemsley & Wessely,1991; Bentall, Kaney & Dewey, 1991; Garety & Hemsley, 1994) and problems with the cognitive process of reality discrimination have been implicated in the genesis of auditory hallucinations (Slade & Bentall,1988). This latter difficulty can lead to a blurring between imaginings, dreams and actual experience which may result in bizarre evidence being incorporated into belief systems. On the other hand, normal cognitive processes have been found to operate during the disintegration of delusional beliefs (Sacks, Carpenter & Strauss,1974; Brett-Jones, Garety & Hemsley, 1987; Buchanan et al., 1993).

CBT for psychotic symptoms, as described in this chapter, makes three assumptions: (i) some of the reasoning biases may be overcome by cognitive-behavioural techniques which help patients to re-evaluate the evidence for their beliefs (Garety & Hemsley, 1994); (ii) normal psychological processes evident in the disintegration of delusional beliefs, such as acting on a belief to test its validity and becoming aware of evidence contrary to the belief, may be facilitated; and (iii) there are similarities between mental representations of the self in depressed individuals and those with persecutory delusional beliefs, in particular, latent negative self-representations (Bentall et al., 1994). Core cognitive vulnerability also may be similar (Trower & Chadwick, 1995; Chadwick et al,1996) suggesting that cognitive interventions with known therapeutic efficacy for depression may be suitable for patients suffering from psychosis.

However, complete recovery from an acute episode of psychosis has been shown to involve considerably more than the resolution of florid symptomatology (Breier & Strauss, 1984; Tohen et al,1992). Full restitution includes amelioration of nonpsychotic symptoms (Carr, 1983) and resumption of interpersonal and occupational functioning (Breier & Strauss, 1984) as well as psychological adjustment and the reconstruction of a sense of self (Davidson & Strauss, 1992). The experience of psychosis can lead to a tortuous search for an identity which has been exemplified in the autobiographical writings of Peter Chadwick (1997), an academic psychologist and sufferer from schizo-affective illness. He wondered whether at one point there was "any sense of I-ness present in me at all". He describes his battle for an integrated sense of self as "a journey through deviance and perversion. It was a journey in the style of Dante to a new state of being right through a hole in the middle of Hell itself" (P.K. Chadwick, 1997, p. 37).

Therapeutic interventions for early psychosis must therefore take account of many issues and be multi-faceted. The stage of the individuation–separation process, attachment history and difficulties managing life transitions and change points are important aspects to be aware of when working with an individual experiencing a first episode of psychosis. In particular, it is suggested that opportunities to reduce stigma, raise self-esteem and challenge negative evaluations about the self and psychosis should be integral parts of a CBT programme for early psychosis.

In this chapter I shall describe engagement, assessment, formulation and intervention (individual and group CBT) procedures for young people suffering from psychosis which have attempted to address some of these issues.

ENGAGEMENT

Engagement and rapport building are notoriously difficult problems with people suffering from a psychosis and perhaps more than with any other disorder or client group the development of a sound therapeutic alliance is essential for conducting cognitive behavioural therapy (Fowler, Garety & Kuipers, 1995; Chadwick, Trower & Birchwood, 1996; Nelson, 1997). We have found that the acute phase (particularly of first or early episodes) may provide an unrivalled time in which to establish a therapeutic alliance. Relationships built up at this time are often enduring as shown by the low refusal rate (8%) in our recent five-year follow-up study of 37 patients who engaged in a CBT or activity programme during an acute episode of psychosis (Drury, Birchwood & Cochrane, in press).

Chadwick, Trower & Birchwood (1996) have identified several major factors which may hinder psychotic clients engaging in a therapeutic relationship. These include: an inability of the therapist to empathise with psychotic phenomena because they are outside the realm of the therapist's experience (e.g. auditory hallucinations, delusional beliefs that appear fantastic or ridiculous), restrictive beliefs the therapist holds about psychosis (e.g. delusional beliefs are qualitatively different from other beliefs and hence are not amenable to psychological intervention), beliefs clients hold about therapy (e.g. admission of/or discussions about voices and delusions leads to increases in medication and/or hospitalisation), client's history of interpersonal difficulties, and limited insight/motivation to engage. They conclude that when attempting to engage psychotic clients there is a "need to ease individuals very gradually into therapy" (p. 44).

The initial contacts with a patient suffering from a psychotic breakdown are likely to be critical in setting up the therapeutic relationship. Patients often have difficulty interpreting verbal messages but may be very sensitive to the sincerity of others (Perris, 1989). It is necessary, however, to be mindful of the points of reference in the sufferer's world. It is dangerous to assume that what the therapist thinks are the parameters of the relationship and the rules of the interaction are the same as those experienced by the client, especially during acute episodes (see P.K. Chadwick, 1997). For instance, the author has been mistaken for a chat show host who was conducting an interview for American TV, as a prison officer who was going to help administer ECT to the patient, and as a police officer who was part of a government conspiracy to indoctrinate and control the patient's mind! In another interview the patient thought time had gone back to the 1960s and he was a famous rock star. He felt that the therapist was encouraging him to attend music therapy so that he could practise for several scheduled "gigs". In the first and last examples, unknown to the interviewer at the time, the delusions had facilitating effect on the therapeutic alliance but the patient's disappointment and loss when the actual conditions of the relationship were realised had to be sensitively acknowledged by the therapist. In the other two examples the beliefs had potentially damaging effects on the therapeutic relationship. Considerable persistence, reassurance and patience were required on behalf of the therapist to prevent these misconceptions destroying the building of rapport. Non-delusional misunderstandings about therapeutic encounters can also affect the setting up of a therapeutic relationship. If patients observe that not everyone on a ward or Day Unit sees a psychologist/therapist, they may feel singled out and hence feel "picked on" or "pestered" or, alternatively, feel "special" or "superior". They may also have difficulty understanding the boundaries of the relationship and may confuse it with a friendship or something more intimate.

When attempting to engage a client suffering from psychosis, particularly those in late adolescence or early adulthood, it is important to adopt an informal, flexible and friendly approach to the encounter. It is, however, necessary to adapt one's interpersonal style to the patient. Many psychosis sufferers are wary, mistrustful and avoidant (both behaviourally and cognitively) whilst others can be overfriendly and intrusive. Frequent use of the patient's first name (after checking how they like to be addressed) can help to keep the patient focused on what you are saying and to feel "grounded". Many sufferers do not seek therapy of their own volition nor do they know who they can trust, so it is critical, on the one hand, not to appear aloof or detached, nor on the other to be too inquisitive and to ask too many questions. However, it is likely that the therapist will need to take the initiative, to structure the encounter carefully and to avoid long silences which may be perceived as punitive. As many people suffering from psychosis do not find social interactions reinforcing per se, it is important to try to make the interaction rewarding by spending up to half the session discussing topics they find interesting. Television soaps, pop music, football and sport generally are popular subjects with many younger people. Due to lack of trust it may be necessary to keep note-taking to a minimum whilst trying to engage some patients in the therapeutic process and it may be unhelpful to try to interpret a client's unwillingness or reluctance to see the therapist. The usual psychotherapy practice of weekly therapy sessions of one hour will probably need to be replaced by much shorter, more frequent contacts in an attempt to allow for a client's difficulties, particularly with regard to attention and concentration. The therapist may need to use simple, short sentences and keep checking out the patient is following what is being said. A great deal of flexibility may be necessary in terms of the choice of location for therapy and in trying to make the therapeutic space feel safe. Nelson (1997) makes some practical suggestions about making the space safe, e.g. adding homely touches, increasing the angle and spacing of chairs, using reduced levels of eye contact, having a cup of tea, always using the same room, etc. Some patients, however, prefer less formal settings and are happier talking whilst walking in the hospital grounds or playing a game of pool. It is also worth giving some consideration to dress. As a general guideline it should be fairly neutral and not make any strong statements about the person. Some colours, especially red and yellow, may be aversive to patients when they are acutely disturbed or indeed may be incorporated into their delusional system. During an acute phase, when so much feels chaotic, patients tend to like consistency and predictability and that extends to the way people look—a change of hairstyle or wearing glasses when the therapist usually wears contact lenses can be very disconcerting to them.

Some therapists find that judicious use of self-disclosure helps to build rapport (Fowler, Garety & Kuipers, 1995). The author also find it helpful to tell the client something about how she works when making initial introductions to facilitate the building of trust, e.g. "I am a psychologist who has been working for several years on wards where people have been admitted suffering from acute psychosis. I work with the team of doctors and nurses that are treating you. We have found that people (and their families) tend to find it helpful to talk about their experiences of coming in to hospital and about how they are thinking and feeling. We've also found that completing a few simple questionnaires with patients each week helps us to monitor the changes in their thinking and feelings and to understand their difficulties better. We also encourage patients to attend various activities such as snooker, discussion groups, relaxation, art, cookery and the like." The therapist's self-disclosure may also model the behaviour required of the client during individual and group therapy (Perris, 1989; Yalom, 1970). It can also be useful to discuss therapeutic contact with other clients with similar symptoms (obviously protecting client's identities). This is likely to increase the therapist's credibility and partly reduce the client's sense of isolation and loneliness.

Family members and other carers may play a critical role in helping the sufferer to engage in the therapeutic process. By providing the family with information about the disorder and about the rationale underlying the programme the family will hopefully be able to understand and support the ethos of the programme and the various therapeutic endeavours. It is important to remember that family members and other caretakers of first episode patients are also in crisis and require intervention (McGorry et al., 1996).

We have also found that involving the client in social and recreational activities in informal settings and carrying out monitoring procedures encourages trust and disclosure (Drury et al., 1996a). Indeed, discussions whilst making a cup of tea or travelling to a community-based leisure facility may be far more productive than several sessions in a therapy room.

The following example will demonstrate some of the above points:

Case Study

Michael is a 28-year-old man who was admitted to a psychiatric hospital for the first time, after his worried mother had insisted on taking him to his GP. He had been neglecting himself and making threats to self-harm. On admission, he was preoccupied and avoidant, spending most of the time in his room. He claimed he was a "man of few words", a private person and trusted no one. One of the nurses felt he may have made a reference to abuse issues. He reported that everyone could read his mind, he could hear male voices speaking to him, his mother was not his real mother and his father had been a group of old men who had inseminated a farm animal. He believed he was born in the middle of a famous football ground.

Before admission he had been living alone in a flat in a run-down part of the outer city and had been neglecting himself over the past six months. Prior to this he had been living with his mother and there had been an increasing number of rows. He had been unemployed for the last six years and had previously worked in a factory. He appeared to have a five-year history of increasing social isolation.

Michael's history of lack of trust, interpersonal difficulties, possible abuse issues and avoidant coping strategies indicated that he was likely to be difficult to engage. Furthermore, his bizarre ideas about his parentage indicated it might be difficult to empathise with his beliefs.

Michael reluctantly agreed to talk to the psychologist after agreeing to keep the first session very short (about 10 minutes). He chose a chair in the therapy room at the furthest point possible from the therapist. After a long preamble by the therapist about her role on the ward and her contact with people with similar experiences to his own, she asked Michael about why he thought he had been brought into hospital. He felt his admission to hospital and allocation of a Key nurse were punishments, attempts to remove his freedom and to "programme his mind". Furthermore, he felt he had been singled out to see a psychologist. Empathising with Michael's anger and sense of injustice seemed important at this point but the intention to help and support him was also reiterated. He said he found it difficult to talk and was used to his mother "doing all the talking". He appeared to have few interests now, but in the past he had enjoyed football, watching TV and travelling. He complained that his memory was very poor and he was bored on the ward. It was agreed to meet Michael again the next day.

The engagement process consisted of frequent short meetings to build up trust and encourage Michael to play pool on the ward with other patients, watch TV in the communal lounge and to get involved in cookery and craft classes (for which he had expressed an interest). A fair amount of the early sessions were spent discussing TV and football games and talking about his experiences of travelling on his step-father's lorry as a boy. In an attempt to ascertain his memory difficulties and to build up a stronger sense of his identity he was encouraged to talk about his childhood, his relationship with his parents and siblings and his plans and goals for the future. Interestingly, his first memory was going off on his tricycle frantically in search of his natural father who left home when he was two years old. Later in the assessment this appeared to be a crucial factor in his identity issues.

Michael did not like unstructured sessions and liked to know exactly how long the session would last and what they were going to talk about. It seemed very important, however, not to echo the relationship with his mother and fill all the silences. The use of standardised measures seemed to help to relieve Michael's anxiety, helped to cue his memory and to create a "safe environment", indicating that detailed assessment is another key area for this client group.

ASSESSMENT

We have found that there are four important areas to consider when assessing people suffering from an acute episode of psychosis: (i) taking a background history (including the circumstances leading up to the present period of acute care and how they felt about the admission/referral); (ii) reference to the patient's medical notes to discover the nature and progression of previous episodes and pathways to care; (iii) the use of standardised measures which involves the elicitation of current symptoms and concerns; and (iv) a comprehensive cognitive-behavioural assessment. Although these stages in practice often overlap, we have found in the interests of fostering engagement with the patient that it is best to carry out the assessment at least loosely in this order. Although perhaps obvious, it is worth stating afresh that the therapist must possess sound basic "counselling" skills (e.g. effective listening, reflecting, summarising, possession of empathy, warmth and unconditional regard, etc.) if the assessment process is to be successful.

Background information

Taking a fairly detailed personal and family history can be another way of building rapport and can provide valuable information about the genesis and meaning of psychotic symptoms. It is our experience and that of others (e.g. Kingdon & Turkington, 1994) that the majority of patients are not only able to provide the key facts of this background information at the beginning of a period of acute care but eliciting this information helps to distract them from their psychotic symptomatology for a while. Further details of premorbid functioning such as relationship and occupational history, educational attainment, and previous contact with psychiatric services may be gained from the patient's previous medical and community team notes, or with the patient's informed consent from relatives, friends and other carers. Since the size of the social networks of people experiencing first episodes of schizophrenia have been modestly predictive of functional outcome at 18 months (Erikson et al., 1989) and the availability of good supportive and unconditional relationships are linked to good outcome in schizophrenia (Breier & Strauss, 1984), knowledge of the patient's social network is useful information for care plans. Further valuable information gained from medical notes would include nature and progression of symptoms during past episodes if any (since symptom profiles tend to be repeated at each subsequent acute episode; Winokur et al., 1985), the patient's perception of his/her problems and previous/current treatment and presence of enforced treatment/hospitalisation which might indicate particularly high levels of trauma (McGorry et al., 1991).

It is particularly important to be aware of any discrete stressors which may have triggered the present episode, whether they have been recognised by the patient and their family or not (such as relationship breakdown, bereavement, leaving home, starting at college, job commencement or job loss, etc.) as these may give some indication of the patient's underlying psychological vulnerability. The individual's explanation for his admission (e.g. it's a test, a conspiracy, deserved punishment, because of a failure to cope, hospital is a safe haven/a good place where all good people end up) may also provide useful information for a psychological formulation of the person's difficulties, as might the patient's behaviour and preoccupations soon after admission, e.g. feeling he is being followed by/intruded into by bad forces, feeling his parents aren't his parents, etc. First or early episodes of psychosis are recognised as being traumatic in themselves and attempts should be made to assess the level of trauma and the coping style of the patient (see below). Pathway to care if it involves the police, judiciary, or Accident and Emergency departments because of a self-harming incident is also likely to be traumatic (see Chapters 00 and 00).

Standardised measures

The measurement of positive symptoms (hallucinations, delusions and thought disorder) is a core aspect of monitoring recovery from acute pychosis since exacerbation and remission of these symptoms are used as markers of the beginning and end of acute phases (Tohen et al., 1992). Recent controlled trials of CBT for psychosis have used the ever-popular Brief Psychiatric Rating Scale (Overall & Gorham, 1962) for measuring the severity of positive symptoms (Kuipers et al., 1997; Tarrier et al., 1998). The Psychiatric Assessment Scale (PAS: Krawiezcka, Goldberg & Vaughn, 1977), although originally designed for a chronic population, has also been found to be a quick, reliable measure for assessing hallucinations, delusions and thought disorder (Manchanda, Saupe & Hirsch, 1986). It has been used extensively for patients in acute episodes and for assessing the effectiveness of drug treatments (Johnstone et al., 1978, 1986; Johnstone, 1989). Personal Questionnaires (Shapiro, 1961) and the Maudsley Assessment of Delusions Schedule (Buchanan et al., 1993) have been used for measuring detailed changes in dimensions of individual delusional beliefs (e.g. conviction and preoccupation) in controlled trials of CBT (Kuipers et al., 1997) and in single case studies (Sharp et al., 1997). Intense affect associated with principal delusional beliefs (e.g. anxiety, anger, despair) can also be measured by Personal Questionnaire (see Sharp et al., 1997).

Assessment of first or early episodes of psychosis warrants some additional measures to elicit psychotic symptoms and to detect subtle changes in functioning. The patient is likely to be experiencing extreme terror, confusion, and possibly lost desired roles and/or goals (see Rooke & Birchwood,1998). Patients may fear being labelled "mad", feel their identity is being engulfed either by their symptoms or by the devalued role of "psychiatric patient" or "community care patient" and hence may try to conceal their difficulties. Standardised mental state assessments such as the present State Examination (PSE-9 Wing, Cooper & Sartorius, 1974) or SCAN (WHO, 1992) and checklists which identify features of prodromes of psychotic episodes (e.g. Early Signs Questionnaire (ESQ): Herz & Melville, 1980 or Early Signs Scale (ESS): Birchwood et al., 1989) are likely to be particularly useful assessment tools in early episodes. We have found that completing the ESS often provide points for discussion and elicits comments that wouldn't otherwise be forthcoming, especially in verbally unresponsive individuals. For instance, in response to the question "Have you been feeling violent?", one young man, who found it difficult to express any opinions, answered "I don't like violence, it gets you nowhere. I don't like young lads showing off in front of women in pubs—being big-headed—they've got things I haven't got."

Owing to the high rate of depression and demoralisation in people in early episodes of psychosis, especially young males, it is suggested that depression is assessed using the Calgary Depression Scale (Addington, Addington & Matricka-Tyndall, 1992) and suicide risk is assessed using the Beck Hopelessness Scale (BHS; Beck et al., 1974). Other measures which might be worth considering are: the Psychiatric Admission and PTSD Questionnaire (McGorry et al., 1991) as a measure of ongoing trauma; the Social Functioning Scale (Birchwood et al., 1990) as a measure of pastimes, interests and social networks; and the Premorbid Adjustment Scale

(Cannon-Spoor et al., 1982) as measures of current and premorbid social functioning. Since a person's tendency to "integrate" or "seal over" their psychotic experience has been linked to long-term outcome (McGlashan,1987) we would also suggest that coping style is assessed using the Recovery Style Questionnaire (Drayton, Birchwood & Trower, 1998). A measure of self-esteem (e.g. the Rosenberg Self-Esteem Scale (RSES): Rosenberg, 1965/1989), and the Dysfunctional Attitudes Scale (Weisman & Beck,1978), a measure of negative self-schemata, may be helpful in determining underlying negative representations of the self.

In our trial of CBT in acute psychosis (Drury et al., 1996a, 1996b) we also found it useful to assess insight using the Insight Scale (Birchwood et al., 1994) and negative evaluative beliefs about psychosis using the Personal Beliefs about Illness Questionnaire (Birchwood et al., 1993). Table 8.1 shows a core set of measures that we have found helpful in monitoring the recovery process in a clinical situation. However, it is important when administering these measures to take into account the patient's concentration, attention and motivation for questionnaire completion and to know when to withdraw.

Cognitive behavioural assessment and formulation

Detailed cognitive behavioural assessments of people suffering from psychosis can be found in two recent texts (Fowler, Garety & Kuipers, 1995; Chadwick, Trower & Birchwood, 1996) and therefore only an outline will be provided here as they relate to particular issues with the young client. The most important overall goals are to determine which are the primary symptoms/concerns of the patient (these are likely to have associated troublesome affects and destructive and/or self-defeating behaviours), to identify precipitating events and earlier experiences which led to the development (and maintenance) of the symptoms and to draw up an individualised cognitive formulation of the person's problems. For those patients in an acute phase of psychosis construction of a full developmental cognitive formulation may not be possible until a period of stabilisation of symptoms has been achieved.

Chadwick, Trower & Birchwood, (1996) identify an eight-step approach to cognitive assessment of hallucinations and delusions, much of which, as they point out, has been derived from an integration of the pioneering work carried out by Beck et al. (e.g. 1979) and Ellis (1962, 1994) with emotional disorders. In essence, their approach involves identifying which problem the patient would like to concentrate on first, eliciting a detailed breakdown of the triggering events (A), determining beliefs about the event (images, inferences and evaluations) (B) and identifying the emotional and behavioural consequences of the belief (C). In practice it is

Table 8.1 Core set of measures to assess symptomatic recovery and psychological adjustment in early acute psychotic episodes

Standardised measure	Variable	Frequency
Mental state Psychiatric Assessment Scale (Krawiecka et al., 1977)	Severity of positive, negative and disorganisation symptoms	Weekly
Delusional beliefs Belief and Convictions Scale (Brett-Jones et al., 1987) or	Conviction in, preoccupation with three core delusional beliefs. Response to hypothetical contradiction	Weekly
Maudsley Assessment of Delusions Scale (Buchanan et al., 1993)	Chance of "being mistaken" about belief	
Insight Insight Scale (Birchwood et al., 1994)	Beliefs about awareness of illness, need for treatment, and origins of psychotic symptoms	Weekly
Non-psychotic symptoms Early Signs Scale (Birchwood et al., 1989)	Anxiety, depression, negativity, disinhibition and incipient psychosis	Weekly
Calgary Depression Scale (Addington et al., 1993)	Depression	6 weekly
Beck Hopelessness Scale (Beck et al., 1974)	Hopelessness	6 weekly
Self-esteem Rosenberg Self-Esteem Scale (Rosenberg, 1965).	Self-esteem	6 weekly
Beliefs about psychosis (Birchwood et al., 1993)	Beliefs about psychosis and psychosis sufferers (e.g. perceived control, awareness of stigma)	6 weekly
Coping style The Recovery Style Questionnaire (Drayton et al., 1998)	Integration and sealing recovery style	Baseline and recovery

usual to start with A or C. The therapist needs to demonstrate to the client how A and C are connected and to help the client determine B by the process of thought chaining. Collecting past and present evidence which support and refute the client's delusion beliefs and determining key events which have led up to the belief's formation are critical elements of a cognitive assessment. The use of ABC diaries are often helpful for those clients with residual symptoms, but are unlikely to be suitable for use with individuals in acute episodes because of difficulties with attention, concentration and motivation.

The following case example demonstrates some of the important points in carrying out a cognitive assessment:

Case Study

Avtar is a 20-year-old Asian man who was admitted to an inner city psychiatric hospital during a first episode of acute psychosis. A period of home treatment had failed mainly because Avtar was never at home when the team called, preventing attempts to engage him in a therapeutic relationship and to administer medication. His main concern was that government agents were reading his mind and controlling his thinking and behaviour via a device implanted in his brain.

Avtar was the second eldest of four children and came from a close-knit family with traditional Asian family values. His parents owned a restaurant and were extremely busy and hard working. Over the years they had become increasingly despairing of their children's rebellious behaviour and were finding it increasingly difficult to set appropriate boundaries. Avtar's father was critical and difficult to please whilst his mother was gentle and considerate but somewhat passive. Avtar described himself as a "private" person who found it difficult to build close relationships. He did, however, have a white girlfriend several years his senior and two young sons who lived separately from him. The relationship with his partner tended to be marked by conflict and approach-avoidance relating. His preferred lifestyle up to the psychotic breakdown was attending night clubs and displaying his considerable dancing talents by dancing alone in the middle of the floor until the early hours. He had a history of truanting from school, scholastic failure and recreational drug use from the age of 13 years. He was also hospitalised briefly with a head injury around this time following an assault in the street by a white man. Avtar felt this was a racially motivated attack. He was expelled from school at the age of 14.

His delusional ideas seemed to have begun about a year before his hospitalisation. Around this time two incidents had occurred: he had been badly beaten up by a gang of white youths and found guilty on a drugs charge which Avtar maintained was a "set up". During his three-month prison sentence, he started to reflect on his life and had become very depressed about the future and full of shame about his misspent youth and failure. He also started to feel that people could read his mind and people on the TV and radio were making references to his behaviour.

On release from prison Avtar came to the conclusion that during his prison sentence an electrical device had been implanted in his head by prison officers. He decided that this procedure had been carried out one night whilst he slept and its aim was to allow the government to monitor and restrict his thinking and behaviour. He also believed that there was a remote control device in the factory opposite his house which controlled the electronic device in his head. Furthermore, he felt the mind-reading experiences were designed to punish him for the rest of his life and to prevent him from getting on with his life and having fun.

At assessment it was found that Avtar could quote considerable evidence which he felt supported his belief. The main evidence involved thought-reading experiences which appeared to occur mainly on the street when people in cars (especially police officers) passed by him. He believed that various noises that emanated from the factory, sirens of service vehicles and the switching on and off of central heating thermostats were tapping out the content of his thoughts. He considered that police helicopters and aircraft were continuously going overhead and had surveillance equipment on board. He also believed that his low mood, inability to concentrate, loss of libido and lack of feelings were further evidence for the control being exerted over him.

However, evidence was elicited which Avtar felt might question his belief. He had asked members of his family about the noises from the factory and they all felt they had been going on for years in much the same way. He had also questioned a security guard at the factory who looked puzzled and said the noise was due to the ventilation system. Furthermore, he sometimes queried why he had not woken up when the device had been inserted into his brain and why there was no visible operation scar. This led him to suspect that the device had been inserted at the age of 13 when he was hospitalised and had only recently been activated. (This is an example of how past events can be reinterpreted under the influence of strongly held delusions.) He did wonder to himself sometimes why "they" had waited so long to activate it and how they would install new batteries. Also a fellow patient on the ward who had held a similar belief for many years had been given a CT scan which had showed no foreign structures in his brain.

The cognitive formulation attached significance to Avtar's early experience of being criticised by his father and being unable to please him and feeling that his elder brother was preferred by his parents. His experiences of educational underachievement, marginalisation, victimisation and imprisonment further reinforced the idea that he was flawed, inferior to others and a failure. It was hypothesised that he experienced strong conflict between the part of him that enjoyed being a rebel, impulsive and irresponsible (which earned him respect from his white friends) and the part of him that wanted to conform to the strict religious and moral codes of his parents and his ethnic group. His parents had always found it difficult to set appropriate limits for his behaviour and there was a sense that all of their children were engaged in self-defeating behaviours and had been unable to develop a capacity to delay gratification. His period in prison had provided him with time to think and reflect on his truancy from school, his drug taking, limited scholastic performance and his early parenthood. He became full of shame and regret about his past misdemeanours and felt despairing and defeated when he thought about how he could carve out a future for himself. His behaviour became very submissive.

It was hypothesised that he had a longstanding need for the respect of others and to be independent and autonomous. Consequently, he had become somewhat hedonistic and self-absorbed and had developed a wary and mistrustful interpersonal style that attempted to defend him against other people's intrusions, control and judgement. It appeared that being found guilty on a drugs charge and being sent to prison (A) were the triggers for various affects: namely shame, despair, frustration and defeat (C). Evaluative beliefs (B) about being flawed and a total failure were found to link the A to the C. It was hypothesised that the delusion represented, on the one hand, his fear of being controlled by others but, on the other, a desire to be able to delay gratification and to set appropriate limits for his self-defeating behaviours.

CONDUCTING THERAPY

Individual cognitive behavioural therapy

In our controlled trial of cognitive therapy the primary aim was to accelerate the decay of hallucinations and delusions and to reduce the number and severity of residual positive symptoms (Drury et al., 1996a, 1996b).The individual work tended to be limited to cognitive therapy for delusional beliefs, beliefs about voices and ideas of reference. Only in a few cases, where the delusional belief proved resistant to verbal challenge and empirical testing and/or where the individual requested more in-depth exploration of his difficulties, was work with dysfunctional assumptions about the self carried out.

A rationale for discussion about the beliefs was presented to the patient, i.e. that the therapist was interested in helping the patient reduce the distress and concern associated with the belief and that the belief was only one of several ways of making sense of some of the strange happenings and experiences that had been going on. Other explanations considered were in terms of stress, fatigue, biochemical imbalances and that the belief may be functional because it reduced negative affect and psychological conflict. An agreement for the therapist and patient to differ about the credibility of these explanations without it affecting the relationship, however, was also accepted. A detailed documentation of the evidence which had led to the formation (and, where appropriate, maintenance of the belief) was completed. In line with Chadwick and Lowe (1990), the patient was asked to place this evidence in a hierarchy of importance to the belief. Alternative ways of making sense of this evidence was then considered. Verbal challenges were offered for the pieces of evidence (starting with the least important piece of evidence first and working up the hierarchy) and then finally for the belief itself. In some cases where the belief was still held following a period of verbal challenge, a reality test of the belief was carried out.

The following case example demonstrates these above points:

Case Study

Julie is a 25-year-old Caucasian post-graduate university student. She was found in the early hours of the morning wandering the streets in a confused state by the police and taken to the police station where she was unable to give an account of herself. After a night in a police cell, where she was troubled by critical voices and visions of the devil, she was released and a friend offered to take her to the local psychiatric hospital where she agreed to accept help. This was her first contact with psychiatric services. During her hospital stay she was given a diagnosis of schizophrenia.

She was the youngest of three daughters and believed she was favoured by her father. Her mother tended to be over-protective, whilst her father tended to be remote and emotionally unavailable. She was a shy and anxious child who suffered with recurrent nightmares. It was reported that her father suffered from depression and anxiety following a suicide attempt and had received some counselling but no other treatment. He could be unpredictable, hostile and angry and there were many rows between Julie's parents. Her father was interested in West Indian culture and blues music. He was a freelance artist who found it difficult to find employment in England and was often absent from home working abroad. Her mother, who worked in the caring professions, was the main breadwinner.

Julie had a difficult adolescence with few friends. She could be irritable, angry and sometimes uncaring and tended to fantasise a lot about pretend lovers. She was very sensitive to rejection—for instance would be inconsolable if her penfriend didn't write—and suffered with bouts of depression. She started an on-off relationship with a West Indian boy at 17 who was suffering from a psychotic disorder and felt it was her job to "save" him.

Her parents went through an acrimonious divorce just after she left home for university and her father moved abroad. At university she tended to be rather isolated but enjoyed going to night clubs and liked to flirt with the DJs. She also became involved with a group of left-wing activists and tended to get very angry about oppression of vulnerable groups.

For the few months before hospitalisation, she had become obsessed with a pirate radio station and had listened to it 24 hours a day. She had slept very little and had been neglecting herself and her flat. She believed that she was having an intimate relationship with one of the West Indian DJs on the pirate radio station. This was despite never having met the DJ or knowing for sure what he looked like. It is interesting how much of the DJs behaviour (the records he played, the flirtatious, ambiguous comments he made, the times he appeared on the radio) was interpreted as evidence to support the belief. (In fact, later on as the belief started to disintegrate and she stopped being preoccupied with the radio, the DJ coincidentally stopped doing his regular programme. She felt this was a direct consequence of her not listening to the radio enough.)

The following evidence was elicited in support of this belief:

(i) I met, talked and had sexual relationship with him (later understood as a dream-like experience).
(ii) I heard his voice in my room and had a conversation with him across the airwaves. He played records just for me.
(iii) He knew what I was thinking and knew so much about me.
(iv) I met a certain man in a railway station and we exchanged meaningful looks. This meeting was later confirmed by a record the DJ played.
(v) A record he played regularly mentioned my full name.
(vi) Certain girls' and boys' names that he mentioned were coded messages for me.

The last three pieces of evidence all involved ideas of reference. The verbal challenge centred around the idea that ambiguous communications were being misinterpreted to support her belief. It was explained to Julie that DJs commentaries and pop records are aimed at a wide audience and, like astrological predictions, are intended to be meaningful to a lot of people. It is therefore easy to believe that popular songs have personal meaning and relevance The majority of pop records have falling in love as a main theme, which Julie recognised had been a preoccupation of hers for a long time. This made her hyperalert to the content of these songs and she was tending to hear what she expected and wanted to hear. With regard to hearing her full name in a song, it was explained that all speech sounds (especially electronic sound emerging from the radio and TV) are inherently ambiguous and therefore easily misinterpreted. It was also explained that the spoken word does not exist of itself but rather exists as a set of vibrating air molecules. The spoken word has to be reconstructed by the brain. When the brain is under stress as in a psychotic breakdown, it is believed that sets of nerve cells may isolate themselves and generate their own outputs which can become superimposed on incoming external sound so distorting it (Hoffman & McGlashan, 1993). It was also explained to Julie that experiences like hers are very common in people with mental health problems. For instance, many get ideas of reference on the street, on buses or from the TV and radio. Furthermore, they tend to persist for a long time and be resistant to treatment.

The mind-reading, auditory hallucinations and hypnogogic experiences were all explained in this instance in terms of a brain disorder which Julie found acceptable and stress reducing. It seemed to help her to know that in those who suffer with a psychosis there can be a difficulty in discriminating reality, i.e. deciding which is an external sound/image and what is a dream, thought, memory, fantasy or daydream. In other words, the boundary between the internal and external worlds can become blurred. As people with psychosis tend to have an intolerance of ambiguity, deciding on a fixed explanation helps to reduce anxiety. In line with Kingdon and Turkington (1991, 1994), to some extent these experiences were also normalised. It is well known that some people who are fatigued and sleep deprived (which Julie was) can hear auditory hallucinations and that some intimate partners feel "so in tune with each other" that they can predict what their lover will say and do.

As a final manoeuvre, because the belief kept re-emerging with low levels of conviction at times of stress and when Julie felt very lonely, it was decided to test the belief by trying to obtain a photograph of the DJ. Julie also decided independently to write to the DJ asking him if he knew her. The photograph of the DJ looked nothing like Julie's fantasy of him and the DJ replied to her letter denying ever having met her. This evidence helped her to finally let go of her belief but it left her with a deep sense of loss and emptiness which she needed to work through in therapy over several months.

Group cognitive behavioural therapy

Meddings (1998) has outlined some of the difficulties in running therapy groups for people suffering from psychosis. She suggests that therapists must employ flexibility and ingenuity if they are to overcome problems such as participants' irregular attendance, occasional disrespect for ground rules and difficulties with concentration and attention. Difficulties with group CBT highlighted by Gledhill, Lobban and Sellwood (1998) included lack of confidentiality and lack of individual formulations. The idea of a group can often be threatening to people with psychosis as many experience severe social anxiety. It is therefore important to prepare people carefully for group work so they will know what to expect. The group should feel a "safe" environment in which to disclose personal information. In other words, a place where respect, empathy and understanding for each other's symptoms, feelings and experiences is fostered but also somewhere that is fun, informal and has a sense of group bonding. We have found that not only should facilitators have the opportunity to debrief after each session of the group, but ideally keyworkers should be on hand to see discuss with group members any issues that may have arisen for them which they could not address in the group.

THE AIMS OF GROUP CBT IN ACUTE PSYCHOSIS

The group work described below is carried out in acute psychosis and aims to reduce the patient's sense of isolation and bewilderment through sharing of experiences and the provision of information about the aetiology, course and management (including medical and psychological techniques) of psychotic disorders. The negative cultural stereotypes of severe mental illness are highlighted and questioned, and blame-free acceptance of illness is encouraged in order to reduce stigma. Feelings of control, mastery and empowerment are fostered through improved management of symptoms (including utilising medication, self-control and coping strategies), integration of psychotic experiences, relapse prevention work and improved medication adherence. The cognitive aspects of the group work looks particularly at individuals' beliefs about the origins and maintenance of psychotic symptoms, the appraisals of loss and reduced control associated with developing a psychosis (and possible negative self-schemas), subjective assessment of risk and benefits of treatment in context of personal goals and values and the negative automatic thoughts and beliefs about stressors and anxiety-provoking situations.

Setting up and running CBT groups

We have found that groups of six people with two or three facilitators (representing different disciplines and including former patients if possible) provides an optimum learning environment for sufferers. We have also found that those patients who are engaged in individual therapy and a social programme at the same time as the group therapy are more likely to attend the group regularly and "stay the course". An individualised formulation highlighting the relevant cognitive vulnerability will also have been drawn up and shared with the client. It is important that a *range* of symptoms (particularly a variety of delusional beliefs) are represented in the group, rather than all members of the group presenting with one particular symptom, e.g. delusional beliefs about possession by evil forces/the devil. This facilitates reflection and discussion rather than collusion and further anxiety. Careful use of humour by the facilitators can often diffuse difficult situations. Our groups are particularly geared to the needs of young people and focus on identity issues, the problems of negotiating the transition from adolescence to adulthood and the problems of stigma associated with mental illness. The ending may be particularly difficult for some, especially those with rejection sensitivity. To help with this, a support group led by sufferers may be set up.

The content and aims of each of the eight session will now be briefly described.

Session 1: Introductory session

The most important tasks for the first session are the setting of ground rules and an agenda for the eight weeks (e.g. what people would like to know about their disorder and its management, identifying participants' personal goals for the group) and beginning to dispel the myths and negative stereotypes the public hold about psychosis and psychosis sufferers. As an ice-breaker exercise we have found it useful to include certain experiments with visual illusions to demonstrate the principles of reality testing and consensual validation and how these relate to belief formation. Participants' beliefs about what caused their illness are ascertained. Although the list will inevitably include some delusional ideas, the principal explanatory frameworks offered are usually stress (e.g. leaving home, starting college, family pressure, fear of being myself) and interpersonal issues (isolation, misunderstandings by others including racism and jealousy). The stress–vulnerability model is introduced as a means of explaining how the disorder develops.

Session 2: Making sense of experiences and symptoms

This aim of this session is to get people talking about their symptoms and sharing experiences to reduce fear and bewilderment. Recurrent themes of the content of voices and delusions are highlighted, e.g. persecution, control, grandiosity, changed identity, concerns about parentage and sexuality. Various psychological and biological explanations for symptoms are introduced: i.e. in terms of a continuum with normality, they are functional because they reduce negative affect, they are the result of a brain disorder which involves biochemical changes and nerve receptor site changes. The stress–vulnerability model is once again offered as a way of combining and understanding these different approaches. Individuals are encouraged to see their voices as internally generated and are phenomena that other people cannot hear. Finally, participants are encouraged to place their symptoms into an historical context and to make connections between relevant beliefs/concerns in childhood or adolescence, e.g. a young man who believed he had taken on the identity of a deceased rock star who was notorious for being rebellious said "from the age of 14 I was always staring in the mirror worried my hair was too thin and that I wouldn't get a girl. When I was ill I thought I was a famous pop star who had a thick head of hair and a 'way with women'. I think this was the way I coped with my poor self-confidence and lack of success with the opposite sex."

Session 3: The role of medication in managing psychosis. Adherence, self-medication and non-compliance

This session aims to inform people about the role of medication in managing psychotic disorders, to discuss how medication works, to explore ambivalence towards medication, to itemise the benefits and the drawbacks of taking medication and to encourage sufferers to have an active role in negotiating medication levels and exploring opportunities for self-medication where appropriate.

Session 4: Stress and anxiety management

The session begins with a reminder that the previous session was about medication and the next five sessions will be about the use of self-help techniques ("how you can control your own problems"). In Session 4 we aim to define stress and anxiety, to describe the origins and function of anxiety and to discuss the role of stress in psychosis. Other aims are to teach participants to learn how to recognise their own signs and symptoms of anxiety and stress, to learn about the fight-and-flight response, to get clients to talk about stressful life events that may have triggered an episode of illness, to identify situations and thoughts that trigger anxiety reactions (especially social anxiety) and to learn more effective ways of coping with stress.

Session 5: Early warning signs, relapse signatures and relapse prevention

The emphasis of this session is that learning that one's early warning signs of relapse can be a means of *controlling* the course of the disorder (see Chapter 00). Participants are encouraged to see that relapse can sometimes be prevented, or the severity of the relapse reduced, so that people feel less at the "mercy of their illness". The following points are made: it is important to recognise one's own pattern of relapse and become familiar with it; relapse prodromes may last from days to months; everyone has a bad day or two and this doesn't mean that a relapse is imminent; if a relapse is occurring the symptoms will tend to get worse and become more noticeable as time passes. Useful strategies to use when people notice early signs of relapse are discussed: e.g. first and foremost, getting in touch with the patient's doctor or nurse who may suggest increasing medication for a time; using relaxation and stress reduction techniques; seeking supportive help from family, friends and other carers; and using self-medication if this has been previously agreed with the doctor.

Session 6: Coping strategies for delusional beliefs and voices

The aim of this session is to help participants to share ideas with each other about helpful and unhelpful ways of coping with positive and negative symptoms. The helpful coping strategies for positive symptoms are divided into behavioural change (active and passive distraction, change of environment, physical activities, immobility and indulgences), cognitive control, socialisation and general strategies. Participants also learn new ways of coping and are encouraged to plan to try them out. Finally, some personal accounts of recovery from psychotic illness that convey hope and optimism are read out. The idea of a support group led by users is promoted strongly.

Session 7 and Session 8: Cognitive therapy for beliefs about voices, delusional beliefs and ideas of reference in a group setting

The aim of these sessions is to ask for volunteers to discuss past or present delusional beliefs and beliefs about voices and to show how some of these are supported by feelings or subjective assessment only (e.g. I feel so bad/persecuted, someone must be after me), or by flimsy, inconsistent sometimes contradictory evidence and irrationalities. There is a clear rule imposed by the facilitators about these discussions that no one should feel personally attacked and that it is only that person's belief that is being considered in a gentle, reflective way. The proposed sequences in the decay of delusional beliefs and beliefs about voices (pointing out the "normal" processes involved in belief disintegration) are described. Ways people have tested or could test delusional beliefs are considered, and how some of the predictions made by voices could be tested. Finally, the prevalence of ideas of reference and why they tend to be treatment resistant and persist are discussed. Ways of challenging them in everyday social situations are suggested.

General strategies

We have found that there are several general helpful strategies for running CBT groups for young people with psychosis. These include the use of handouts about the previous session, circulation of poems and personal accounts by sufferers (both from outside and within the group) to engender understanding and hope, the use of a video for feedback about certain beliefs people have about themselves (e.g. I look odd and "stone faced", that is why people stare at me) and for making educational material for other sufferers, and the setting up of a support group to consolidate the new experience of "togetherness" and to further develop interpersonal skills. With regard to facilitators, there can be a burden on them to contain and limit chaos and to draw together disparate threads of discussion. There can be strong countertransference experiences and, therefore, it is recommended that debriefing and good supervision are carefully planned for therapists.

CBT FOR ACUTE PSYCHOSIS: A CONTROLLED TRIAL

Our CBT intervention package which has been evaluated in a controlled trial (Drury et al., 1996a, 1996b) consisted of individual cognitive therapy, group cognitive therapy, family psychoeducation/support and meaningful activities delivered as an addition to standard care. We chose group work as part of our intervention for several reasons. Previous research by Smith, Birchwood and Haddrell (1992) has shown that individuals suffering from schizophrenia were able to assimilate information about their illness in a group setting, particularly with regard to demography and coping strategies. Smith and colleagues also record qualitative evidence that participants welcomed the chance to share their experiences with other sufferers and some participants viewed themselves less negatively in relation to others as a result of the group (see also Gledhill, Lobban & Sellwood, 1998). Many patients have limited experience of group membership (e.g. adolescent peer groups, sports teams) and it has been suggested that the successful negotiation of a group can be therapeutic in itself (Yalom,1970). Yalom has defined several "curative factors" provided by therapy groups irrespective of the group's theoretical underpinnings. Provision of information, instillation of hope and universality (the realisation that others have similar anxieties and experiences to one's own) and opportunities for corrective emotional experience are just some of the benefits he has described. We also suggest that since longstanding interpersonal difficulties occur in at least a third of patients with schizophrenia (Watt, 1978) many sufferers will have had limited interpersonal experiences.

Results from our controlled trial of CBT for acute psychosis (where 60% of patients were suffering from first or second episodes of acute psychosis) showed that applying CBT during the acute phase of a psychotic illness is not only feasible but produces significant symptomatic benefits at discharge and at nine-month follow-up (Drury et al., 1996a). When compared with a group receiving recreational activities and standard care, our CBT intervention led to a 25–50% reduction in recovery time (depending on the stringency of the definition used) and a 50% reduction in time spent in hospital (Drury et al., 1996b) Furthermore, enduring benefits at five-year follow-up are evident if relapse can be avoided or minimised (Drury, Birchwood & Cochrane, in press). We suggest that these benefits may be even greater if CBT is applied to first-episode patients (when secondary disabilities associated with schizophrenia have not had time to develop) and an intensive relapse prevention programme is included in treatment strategies.

CONCLUSIONS

In this chapter, I have argued that CBT programmes for early acute episodes of psychosis need to be multi-component and flexible. Individual and group sessions running in parallel with an emphasis on highlighting and challenging negative evaluative beliefs about the self and psychosis may help to address some of the many complex needs of younger psychosis sufferers. There is increasing evidence that attempts to ameliorate psychotic symptoms with CBT techniques can be successful and bring about speedier recoveries from acute episodes. However, improvements in positive symptoms do not generalise to other areas of functioning, e.g. standard CBT does not bring about changes in social or occupational functioning, self-esteem or depression (Tarrier et al., 1998) or in relapse rates (Drury, Birchwood & Cochrane, in press). The challenge, therefore, for the next decade would seem to be to develop more comprehensive programmes that facilitate a more robust integrated sense of self, and address issues to do with self-esteem, hopelessness, social roles and loss whilst maintaining an air of realistic optimism. In other words, CBT must not be implemented in a vacuum but as part of an integrated approach to the young person.

REFERENCES

Addington, D., Addington, J. & Matricka-Tyndall, E. (1993). Rating depression in schizophrenia: a comparison of a self-report and observer report scale. *Journal of Nervous and Mental Disease*, **181**, 561–565.

Bannister, D. (1983). The psychotic disguise. In W. Dryden (Ed.) *Therapists' Dilemmas*. London: Harper & Row.

Beck, A.T., Weissman, A.W., Lester, D. & Trexler, L. (1974). The measurement of pessimism: the Hopelessness Scale. *Journal of Consulting and Clinical Psychology*, **42**, 861–865.

Beck, A.T., Rush, A.J., Shaw, B.F. & Emery, G. (1979). *Cognitive Therapy of Depression*. New York: Guilford Press.

Bentall, R.P., Kaney, S. & Dewey, M.E. (1991). Paranoia and social reasoning: an attribution theory analysis. *British Journal of Psychology*, **30**, 13–23.

Bentall, R.P., Kinderman, P. & Kaney, S. (1994). The self, attributional process and abnormal beliefs: towards a model of persecutory delusions. *Behaviour Research and Therapy*, **32**, 331–341.

Birchwood, M.J., Smith, J., Macmillan, F., Hogg, B., Prasad, R., Harvey, C. and Bering, S. (1989). Predicting relapse in schizophrenia: the development and implementation of an early signs monitoring service system using patients and families as observers—a preliminary investigation. *Psychological Medicine, 19*, 649–656.

Birchwood, M., Smith, J., Cochrane, R., Wetton, S. & Copestake, S. (1990). The Social Functioning Scale. *Psychological Medicine, 28*, 397–405.

Birchwood, M.J., Mason, R., Macmillan, F. & Healy, J. (1993). Depression, demoralisation and control over psychotic illness: a comparison of depressed and non-depressed patients with a chronic psychosis. *Psychological Medicine, 23*, 387–395.

Birchwood, M.J, Smith, J., Drury, V., Healy, J. & Slade, M. (1994). A self report insight scale for psychosis: reliability, validity and sensitivity to change. *Acta Psychiatrica Scandinavica, 89*, 62–67.

Birchwood, M.J., Todd, P. & Jackson, C. (1996). Early intervention in psychosis: the critical period hypothesis. *British Journal of Psychiatry, 172* (Suppl. 33), 53–59.

Hoffman, R.E. & McGlashan, T. H. (1993). Parallel distributed processing and the emergence of schizophrenic symptoms. *Schizophrenia Bulletin, 19*, 119–140.

Breier, A. & Strauss, J. (1984). The role of social relationships in the recovery from psychotic disorders. *American Journal of Psychiatry, 141*, 949–955.

Brett-Jones, J., Garety, P. & Hemsley, D. (1987). Measuring delusional experiences: a method and its application. *British Journal of Clinical Psychology, 26*, 257–265.

Buchanan, A., Reed, A., Wessely, S., Garety, P.A., Taylor, P., Grubin, D. & Dunn, G. (1993). Acting on delusions. II: The phenomenological correlates of acting on delusions. *British Journal of Psychiatry, 163*, 77–81.

Cannon-Spoor, H.E., Potkin, S.G. and Wyatt, R.J. (1982). Measurement of premorbid adjustment in chronic schizophenia. *Schizophrenia Bulletin, 8*, 470–484.

Carr, V.J. (1983). Recovery from schizophrenia: a review of patterns of psychosis. *Schizophrenia Bulletin, 9*, 95–121.

Chadwick, P.D.J. & Lowe, C.F. (1990). Measurement and modification of delusional beliefs. *Journal of Consulting and Clinical Psychology, 58*, 225–232.

Chadwick, P.D.J., Trower, P. & Birchwood, M. (1996). *Cognitive Therapy for Delusions, Voices and Paranoia.* Chichester: Wiley.

Chadwick, P.K (1997). *Schizophrenia: the Positive Perspective in Search of Dignity.* London: Routledge.

Crow, T. J., Macmillan, F., Johnson, A. & Johnstone, E. (1986). Northwick Park study. II: A randomised controlled trial of prophylactic neuroleptic treatment *British Journal of Psychiatry, 148*, 120–127.

Davidson, L. & Strauss, J. (1992). Sense of self in recovery from psychosis. *British Journal of Medical Psychology, 65*, 131–145.

Donlan, P.T. & Blacker, K.H. (1973). Stages of schizophrenic decompensation and reintegration. *Journal of Nervous and Mental Disease, 157*, 200–209.

Drayton, M., Birchwood, M. & Trower, P. (1998). Early attachment experience and recovery from psychosis. *British Journal of Clinical Psychology, 37*, 269–284.

Drury, V. Birchwood, M., Cochrane, R. & Macmillan, F. (1996a). Cognitive therapy and recovery from acute psychosis: a controlled trial. I: Impact on psychotic symptoms. *British Journal of Psychiatry, 169*, 593–601.

Drury, V., Birchwood, M., Cochrane, R. & Macmillan, F. (1996b). Cognitive therapy and recovery from acute psychosis: a controlled trial. II: Impact on recovery time. *British Journal of Psychiatry, 169*, 602–607.

Drury, V., Birchwood, M. & Cochrane, R. (in press). Cognitive therapy and recovery from acute psychosis: a controlled trial. III: Five year follow-up.

Ellis, A. (1962). *Reason and Emotion in Psychotherapy.* New York: Lyle Stuart.

Ellis, A. (1994). *Reason and Emotion in Psychotherapy: Revised and Expanded Edition.* New York: Lyle Stuart.

Erikson, D.H., Beiser, M., Iacono, W.G., Fleming, J. & Lin, T. (1989). The role of social relationships in the course of first-episode schizophrenia and affective psychosis. *American Journal of Psychiatry,* **146**, 1456–1461.

Fowler, D., Garety, P.A. & Kuipers, L. (1995). *Cognitive Behaviour Therapy for Psychosis: Theory and Practice.* Chichester: Wiley.

Garety, P. & Helmsley, D. (1994). *Delusions: Investigations into the Psychology of Delusional Reasoning.* Oxford: Oxford University Press.

Garety, P., Hemsley, D. and Wesseley, S. (1991). Reasoning in deluded and paranoid subjects: biases in performance on a probabilistic inferencing task. *Journal of Nervous and Mental Disease,* **179**, 194–201.

Gledhill, A., Lobban, F. & Sellwood, W. (1998). Group CBT for people with schizophrenia: a preliminary evaluation. *Behavioural and Cognitive Psychotherapy,* **26**, 63–75.

Harrison, G., Coudace, T., Mason, P. Glazebrook, C. & Medley, I. (1996). Predicting the long-term outcome of schizophrenia. *Psychological Medicine,* **26**, 697–705.

Herz, M.I. & Melville, C. (1980). Relapse in schizophrenia. *American Journal of Psychiatry,* **137**, 801–805.

Hoffman, R.E. & McGlashan, T.H. (1993). Parallel distributed processing and the emergence of schizophrenic symptoms. *Schizophrenia Bulletin,* **19**, 119–140.

Hogarty, G.E., Kornblith, S.J., Greenwald, D., Dibarry, A. L., Cooley, S., Flesher, S. Reiss, D., Carter, M. & Ulrich, R. (1995). Personal therapy: a disorder-relevant psychotherapy for schizophrenia. *Schizophrenia Bulletin,* **21**, 379–393.

Hogarty, G. E., Kornblith, S. J., Greenwald, D. et al (1997). Three-year trials of personal therapy among schizophrenic patients living with or independent of family. I: Description of study and effects on relapse rates. *American Journal of Psychiatry,* **154**, 1504–1513.

Johnstone, E. (1989). The assessment of positive and negative features in schizophrenia. *British Journal of Psychiatry,* **155** (Suppl. 7), 41–44.

Johnstone, E., Crow, T., Frith, C., Carney, M. & Price, J. (1978). Mechanism of the antipsychotic effect in the treatment of acute schizophrenia. *Lancet, i,* 848–851.

Johnstone, E., Crow, T., Johnson, A L. & Macmillan, J.F. (1986). The Northwick Park study of first episode schizophrenia. I: Presentation of the illness and problems relating to admission. *British Journal of Psychiatry,* **148**, 115–120.

Kayton, L. (1975). Toward an integrated treatment for schizophrenia. *Schizophrenia Bulletin,* **12**, 60–70.

Kingdon, D. & Turkington, D (1991). The use of cognitive-behavioural therapy with a normalising rationale in schizophrenia: a preliminary report. *Journal of Nervous and Mental Disease,* **179**, 207–211.

Kingdon, D. & Turkington, D (1994). *Cognitive-Behavioural Therapy of Schizophrenia.* Brighton: Earlbaum.

Krawiezcka, M., Goldberg, D. & Vaughn, M. (1977). Standardised psychiatric assessment scale for chronic psychiatric patients. *Acta Psychiatrica Scandinavica,* **36**, 25–31.

Kuipers, E., Garety. P., Fowler, D., Dunn, G., Bebbington, P., Freeman, D. & Hadley, C. (1997). London–East Anglia randomised controlled trial of cognitive-behavioural therapy for psychosis. I: Effects of the treatment phase. *British Journal of Psychiatry,* **171**, 319–327.

Loebel, A., Lieberman, J., Alvir, J., Meyerhoff, D., Geisler, S. & Szymanski, S. (1992). Duration of psychosis and outcome in first-episode schizophrenia. *American Journal of Psychiatry,* **149**, 1183–1188.

Manchanda, R., Saupe, R. & Hirsch, S. (1986). Comparison between the brief psychiatric rating scale and the Manchester scale for the rating of schizophrenia symptomatology. *Acta Psychiatrica Scandinavica*, **74**, 563–568.

McGlashan, T.H. (1987). Recovery style from mental illness and long-term outcome, *Journal of Nervous and Mental Disease*, **175**, 681–685.

McGorry, P. (1992). Recovery and secondary prevention in psychotic disorders. *Australian and New Zealand Journal of Psychiatry*, **26**, 3–17.

McGorry, P. (1996). Preventative strategies in early psychosis; verging on reality. *British Journal of Psychiatry*, **172**, (Suppl. 33), 1–2.

McGorry, P., Chanen, A., McCarthy, E., Van Reil, R., McKenzie, D. & Singh, B. (1991). Post traumatic stress disorder following recent onset psychosis: an unrecognised postpsychotic syndrome. *Journal of Nervous and Mental Disease*, **179**, 253–258.

McGorry, P., Edwards, J., Mihalopoulos, C., Harrigan, S. & Jackson, H. (1996). EPPIC: an evolving system of early detection and optimal management. *Schizophrenia Bulletin*, **22**, 305–326.

Meddings, S. (1998). A hearing voices group for people who are cognitively disorganised: challenges to group work. *Clinical Psychology Forum*, **112**, 14–17.

Nelson, H. (1997). *Cognitive Behavioural Therapy with Schizophrenia. A Practice Manual*. Cheltenham: Stanley Thornes.

Overall, J. & Gorham, D. (1962). The brief psychiatric rating scale. *Psychological Reports*, **10**, 799–812.

Perris, C. (1989). *Cognitive Therapy with Schizophrenic Patients*. New York: Cassell.

Rooke, O. & Birchwood, M. (1998). Loss, humiliation and entrapment as appraisals of schizophrenic illness: a prospective study of depressed and non-depressed patients. *British Journal of Clinical Psychology*, **37**, 259–268.

Rosenberg, M. (1965/1989) *Society and the Adolescent Self-Image*. Middleton, CT: Wesleyan University Press.

Sachar, E.J., Kanter, S.S., Buie, D., Engle, R. & Mehlman, R. (1970). Psychoendocrinology of ego disintegration. *American Journal of Psychiatry*, **126**, 1067–1078.

Sacks, M.H., Carpenter, W.T. Jr & Strauss, J. (1974). Recovery from delusions: three phases documented by patients' interpretations of research procedures. *Archives of General Psychiatry*, **30**, 117–120.

Sensky, T. & Scott, J. (1995). Acute in-patient wards. In Phelan et al. (Eds), *Emergency Mental Health Services in the Community*, pp. 320–339. Cambridge: Cambridge University Press.

Shapiro, M.B. (1961). A method of measuring psychological changes specific to the individual psychiatric patient. *British Journal of Medical Psychology*, **43**, 151–155.

Sharp, H.M., Fear, C.F., Williams, M.G., Healy, D., Lowe, C.F., Yeadon, H. & Holden, R. (1997). Delusional phenomenology: dimensions of change. *Behaviour Research and Therapy*, **34**, 123–142.

Shepherd, M., Watt, D., Falloon, I. & Smeeton, N. (1989). The natural history of schizophrenia: a five year follow-up study of outcome and prediction in a representative sample of schizophrenics. *Psychological Medicine* (Monograph suppl. 15).

Slade, P. & Bentall, R.P (1988). *Sensory Deception: A Scientific Analysis of Hallucinations*. London: Croom Helm.

Smith, J., Birchwood, M. & Haddrell, A. (1992). Informing people with schizophrenia about their illness: the effect of residual symptoms. *Journal of Mental Health*, **1**, 61–70.

Tarrier, N., Barrowclough, C., Vaughn, C., Bamrah, J., Porceddu, K., Watts, S. & Freeman, H. (1988). The community management of schizophrenia: a controlled trial of behavioural intervention with families to reduce relapse. *British Journal of Psychiatry,* **153**, 532–542.

Tarrier, N., Yusupoff, L., Kinney, C., McCarthy, E., Gledhill, A., Haddock, G. & Morris, J. (1998) Randomised controlled trial of intensive cognitive behaviour therapy for patients with chronic schizophrenia. *British Medical Journal,* **317**, 303–307.

Tohen, M., Stoll, A.L., Stakowski, S.M., Faeddda, G.L., Mayer, P., Goodwin, D.C., Kolbrener, M. & Madigan, A. (1992). The McClean First-episode project: six-month recovery and recurrence outcome. *Schizophrenia Bulletin,* **18**, 273–282.

Trower, P. & Chadwick, P. (1995). Pathways to defense of the self: a theory of two types of paranoia. *Clinical Psychology: Science and Practice,* **2**, 263–277.

Watt, N.F. (1978). Patterns of childhood social development in adult schizophrenics. *Archives of General Psychiatry,* **36**, 160–165.

Weissman, A.N. & Beck, A.T. (1978). The Dysfunctional Attitudes Scale. In J.M.G. Williams (Ed.), *The Psychological Treatment of Depression. A Guide to Theory and Practice of Cognitive Behaviour Therapy* (pp. 100–104). London: Routledge.

Wiersma, D., Nienhuis, F.J., Slooff, C.J. & Giel, R. (1998). Natural course of schizophrenic disorders: a 15 year follow-up of a Dutch incidence cohort. *Schizophrenia Bulletin,* **24** (1), 75–85.

WHO (1992). *Schedules for Clinical Assessment in Neuropsychiatry.* World Health Organisation: Geneva.

Wing, J.K., Cooper, J.E. & Sartorius, N. (1974*). Measurement and Classification of Psychiatric Symptoms.* An instruction Manual for the PSE and Catego Program. Cambridge University Press.

Winokur, G., Scharfetter, C. & Angst, J. (1985). Stability of psychotic symptomatology (delusions, hallucinations), affective syndromes, and schizophrenic symptoms (thought disorder, incongruent affect) over episodes in remitting psychoses. *European Archives of Psychiatry and Neurological Science,* **234**, 303–307.

Wyatt, R.J. (1991). Neuroleptics and the natural course of schizophrenia. *Schizophrenia Bulletin,* **17**, 325–351.

Yalom, I.D. (1970). *The Theory and Practice of Group Psychotherapy.* New York: Basic Books.

Chapter 9

THE TREATMENT OF SECONDARY MORBIDITY IN FIRST-EPISODE PSYCHOSIS

Henry J. Jackson*, Carol A. Hulbert* and Lisa P. Henry*

INTRODUCTION

The Neo-Kraepelinian paradigm continues to dominate psychiatry, being embodied in the DSM-III (APA, 1980) and its subsequent versions, DSM-III-R (APA, 1987) and DSM-IV (APA, 1994). Explicit within the DSM-III/-R/IV criteria for psychosis are the triple assumptions that schizophrenia is a true "entity" consisting of a coherent grouping of signs and symptoms with good convergent and discriminant validities, and that it inherently possesses both an inevitably deteriorating course and a poor outcome. Within this Neo-Kraepelinian model (Andreasen, 1984) there is little discussion of the person per se being able to influence the severity and intensity of their symptoms, let alone their being able to moderate the course and outcome of their disorder. The considered treatment is almost exclusively medical in nature, primarily pharmacological (Andreasen, 1984). After all, by the end of the 1970s proponents of this essentially fatalistic biological view were able to point to the demonstrable failure of psychodynamic therapy in producing positive change for the individual suffering from psychosis (Jackson et al., 1999). There was an additional problem—one which directly bears on the content of this chapter. Within the clinical and diagnostic practices of the time, if the psychotic person experienced the symptoms of an additional condition, say anxiety, then usually the latter went untreated (with the possible exception of depression). The prevailing view was that the symptoms were part and parcel of

*University of Melbourne, Australia

Early Intervention in Psychosis.
Edited by M. Birchwood, D. Fowler & C. Jackson.
© 2000 John Wiley & Sons Ltd.

the dominant condition. Little effort was spent in unpacking the "secondary" symptoms, and in determining whether they truly preceded the psychotic condition, but rather occurred concurrently or subsequent to the emergence of the psychosis.

Our treatment for secondary morbidity was developed within a number of contexts—within the therapy known as COPE (this being an acronym for Cognitively-Oriented Psychotherapy for Early Psychosis: Jackson et al., 1996, 1998, 1999) which was developed within a particular service delivery and geographic context and within a particular historical context and theoretical context. The first third of this chapter is devoted to describing the historical context, the theoretical context and the geographical and service delivery context. The chapter also contains a brief description of COPE and the four constituent "phases". (For more details of the various contexts see McGorry et al., 1996; McGorry & Edwards, 1997.)

In the second two-thirds of this chapter we describe the various forms of "secondary" or "co-extant" psychopathologies that we see in our clinical practice, explain the techniques used to treat patients, and provide three case illustrations where we illustrate the application of techniques to "secondary" conditions. We conclude with a brief description of our research findings to date, and the directions we think this area of treatment should pursue within the immediate future.

PSYCHOLOGICAL APPROACHES TO THE TREATMENT OR MANAGEMENT OF PSYCHOSIS: THE HISTORICAL CONTEXT

On reading the relevant literature one concludes that there have been three eras in the treatment of psychosis, or more accurately, schizophrenia. The first era was dominated by psychodynamic approaches but their lack of efficacy, combined with the introduction of neurolepetics in the 1950s, led to the eventual demise of this approach. The 1960s and 1970s witnessed the ascendancy of behavioural approaches as adjunctive to the prescription of neuroleptic medication, these approaches including social skills training, living skills training, and family psychoeducational interventions (Jackson, et al., 1999; Smith, Bellack & Liberman, 1996). These have proved useful, notwithstanding questions concerning the generalization and maintenance of treatment effects induced by social skills training (Jackson, et al., 1999). The 1970s and 1980s saw the introduction of cognitive methods within the psychosis field: those approaches focused on remediating information-processing deficits; those aimed at either challenging the delusional beliefs underpinning delusions and hallucinations, or helping the individual to cope with the emotional and behavioural consequences of the same; or those approaches intended to help the client to adapt to the consequences of having a psychotic disorder by actively involving clients in their own recovery (Chadwick, Birchwood & Trower, 1996; Fowler, Garety & Kuipers, 1995; Haddock & Slade, 1996; Kingdon & Turkington, 1994; Perris, 1989).

THE THEORETICAL CONTEXT

In the lead-up to the establishment of the Early Psychosis Prevention and Intervention Centre we found little available information that could directly inform one's clinical practice with first-presentation psychotic patients. We were forced to develop our own guidelines. We did this on the basis of our clinical practice, on reading or listening to first-hand accounts of patient experiences, from adapting extant empirical literature focused on more chronic patients that appeared relevant, and from widely ranging theoretical material. At the time we developed COPE, the literature which has since emanated from the United Kingdom concerning the treatment of positive symptoms was sparse. However, unlike the researchers behind those developments, we were not dealing with treatment-resistant chronic patients; instead we were dealing with patients who in the main were responsive to neuroleptics. Given this, our focus turned to the patient's adaptation *subsequent to* the initial first episode.

We found the reports of Davidson and Strauss (1995) to be highly pertinent, focusing as they did on the patients being instrumental to their own recovery, with emphasis being given to ways in which individuals could develop a sense of self-efficacy, utilise various coping or control methods, and elicit the assistance of members of their social network. In the view of Davidson and Strauss (1995), illness can afford opportunities to enhance, not only impair, one's future development. Perris (1989) also emphasised the need to respect and enhance patients' autonomy and competence. More recently, Hogarty et al. (1997a,1997b) have defined and described a phase-oriented approach they label "Personal Therapy"—included within this therapy are a range of cognitive-behavioural approaches. The therapy is conducted over a lengthy period of time and is aimed at enhancing the person's adjustment and functioning. Encouraging results were reported for mostly chronic psychotic patients at three years following discharge. For example, personal therapy led to continuing improvement in the social adjustment of patients in the second and third years after discharge (Hogarty et al., 1997b).

In selecting from theoretical perspectives, we found the most useful to be the notion of "critical constructivism" (see Jackson et al., 1999; Mahoney, 1991, 1995) with acknowledgement to "realist" philosophers that there is "furniture in the universe" (Whitehead 1957—cited in

Mahoney, 1991, p. 38), thereby distinguishing it from solipsism with its denial of an external reality. "Critical constructivism" can be construed as an overarching theory which can accommodate more specialised and narrower theories such as life-span development, trauma theory, cognitive therapeutic principles, attributional theory and social learning theory (Jackson et al., 1999). Within limits imposed by external reality, "critical constructivism" (Bruner, 1986; Mahoney, 1991, 1995) views the person as the architect of his own destiny and reality. In short, there is an emphasis on self and the notion of development occurring over time (Bruner, 1986; Kelly, 1955; Mahoney, 1991, 1995).

The developmental emphasis is of paramount importance, given the age of the patients presenting to us for treatment. There are self- and other expectations of the young person tackling certain tasks at this stage, forming an identity, moving away from the family, maintaining and intensifying peer group involvement, beginning intimate relationships, developing occupational and leisure interests, and so forth. Although not adhering to a strictly epigenetic Ericksonian model (Erickson, 1968), we do view the accomplishment of developmental tasks at certain stages as building a platform for future development. We view the psychosis as having the potential to derail the young person's developmental trajectory, impacting on their attempts to form an identity, develop relationships, obtain employment, maintain hobbies, and so forth. Psychologically speaking, we perceive the psychosis as potentially becoming entwined with the person's identity and impairing their sense of self-efficacy and self-directedness. In our determinations, a useful therapy would be one which imparted a message of hopefulness, helped protect the person from being overwhelmed by the psychosis, and protected and bolstered the person's sense of self-efficacy and self-directedness, encouraging them to pursue their goals and aspirations. In brief, it would help them to adapt following the psychosis and would involve them in dealing with their own illness.

THE GEOGRAPHIC AND SERVICE DELIVERY CONTEXT

The COPE model of therapy was developed in the context of the Early Psychosis Intervention and Prevention Centre (EPPIC). This is a "front-line" service that deals with psychotic disorders in young persons aged between 16 and 30 years of age. It is responsible for a particular catchment area (containing 800,000 persons), this being the Western metropolitan region of Melbourne. Approximately 250 or more cases present to EPPIC each year. The entry requirement for EPPIC is that they must have a psychosis, primarily not due to organic factors. COPE therapy is delivered by one of six trained therapists, four of whom are clinical psychologists, and two of whom are psychiatrists. Individual and group supervision is conducted on a weekly basis to ensure some degree of treatment integrity.

COPE AND ITS "PHASES"

COPE consists of four "phases". They are assessment, alliance, adaptation, and secondary morbidity. In reality the therapist may shift between these "phases" both within and between sessions. To aid comprehension they are described herein under four separate headings.

Assessment

Within the province of assessment there are various tasks that need to be undertaken by the COPE therapist. Because symptoms may fluctuate over time, mental state examinations are undertaken at regular intervals. Additionally, the various parameters of symptoms are examined, i.e. intensity, preoccupation, conviction, frequency, and so on. A more avowedly phenomenological stance can be assumed in order to discern the individual's explanatory model for what has happened to them and the putative meaning symptoms may have for the particular person (Roberts, 1991; Roberts, 1999). This latter line of investigation may inform us about how patient preoccupations and concerns are "wrapped up" in the psychotic content.

A detailed discussion needs to occur around the onset of the disorder, the first emergence of dysfunction, precursor non-psychotic and "quasi"-psychotic symptoms, and florid psychotic symptoms. It is important to gauge functioning in the various life domains—social, intimate, occupational, study, leisure/hobbies, and so on, before, during, and after the episode, to determine: length of the total period of "unwellness", level and duration of highest and best period of functioning, and impact of psychosis on functioning and developmental tasks. Allied to this is the necessity of ascertaining the person's prior aspirations, hopes and goals and the impact of the psychosis on the same (thus invoking the social psychological notion of "possible selves"; Markus & Nurius, 1986). Besides direct questioning, we have found useful supplementary assessment methods in diaries, self-monitoring sheets, essays, audio-tapes, the empty-chair technique, and role-plays.

Alliance

A good patient–therapist relationship is an important facilitative factor for conducting a thorough assessment and for achieving good patient outcomes

(Luborsky et al., 1997). The general psychotherapy literature has identified the following therapist characteristics as being important in forging the therapist–client relationship, e.g. warmth, empathy, tolerance and the capacity to inspire trust (see, amongst others, Mohr, 1995; Weinberger, 1995). Factors assisting engagement in treating young psychotic clients include sensitivity to the client's mental state and relational capacity, patience and persistence, and flexibility regarding such matters as the duration, frequency and location of sessions.

From our experience in working with early psychosis patients one needs to bear in mind the youth of these patients, their inexperience with individual therapy and their greater experience with group-based learning in school situations, the degree of social support they enjoy, their phase of development, their intelligence level and a specific factor which is emerging in other areas of psychosis, this being cognitive flexibility (Garety et al., 1997). In overcoming difficulties in engagement, we have found that focusing on the resolution of a practical problem, e.g. how to deal with an inquisitive relative, may be helpful in promoting the therapist–patient relationship. Humour, used appropriately, together with careful challenging of faulty thinking, can be effective in countering resistance and in encouraging a more reflective and collaborative approach to a problem.

Adaptation

The model

In previous publications (Jackson et al., 1996, 1999) we detailed a model of adaptation which outlined a number of "elements"—all of which required consideration during assessment. We highlighted the need to assess the person's experience of the psychosis (which may be traumatic) and identify distortions in their thinking. The latter are seen as reflective of "deeper schemas" and "attributional style", and may be reflective of personality traits like perfectionism, self-directedness, etc., that may in themselves require consideration by the therapist. All of the aforementioned "elements" may have consequences for the way in which the person perceives their self-worth, their capacity to adapt, and their life goals. We also noted the importance of assessing the person's repertoire of coping skills, their social supports and the strength and breadth of their goals, and critically, their developmental stage (Jackson et al., 1996, 1999). All afford potential targets for COPE therapy.

Interventions

Our interventions are adapted from the work of Davidson and Strauss (1995) who outline four stages to their work. In Stage 1, instilling hope in the patient forms the major therapy focus, with the therapist attempting to improve the patient's self-efficacy or belief that they can influence their course and outcome, that a better life is possible, and that at least some of their goals and aspirations are achievable.

In Stage 2 the "real" cognitive work begins. Employing a variety of modalities, psychoeducation and first-person accounts centre on helping to detoxify stereotypes. Cognitive interventions focus on challenging distortions in the client's thinking, both about psychosis itself, what it means for the person, and the person's beliefs in their capacity to deal with the psychosis and its consequences. Video-tapes, information sheets, booklets, and other visual tools comprise useful supplementary aids to assist this process. Looking at the person's goals and aspirations and examining the "cognitive roadblocks" to realisation of the same, is an essential precursor to the person taking action. Cognitive restructuring, role-plays, and imagery projection may be useful in challenging those "roadblocks". Likewise, the examination, broadening and deepening of coping strategies. In some cases it is imperative that the therapist directly focuses on changing the severity of a person's "perfectionism" or attributional style, e.g., "pessimism" (Jackson et al., 1999).

Stage 3 involves taking action. Graded tasks may be used to assist the client in making steps towards the realisation of goals using the cognitive strategies mentioned above to facilitate attempts. Contacting friends, tackling new goals, e.g. obtaining one's car licence, organising a party, resuming work, or recommencing studies, are all examples of taking action. Stage 4 involves conducting a "review" of one's progress, taking stock of the fact that one has accomplished a number of goals and is able to set and tackle new goals for oneself. This is about improving self-efficacy and self-directedness.

SECONDARY MORBIDITY

Secondary morbidity is the fourth "phase" of COPE, but since it is the focus of the chapter it is discussed at length, initially in terms of the prevalence of secondary conditions, its manifold presentations, vulnerabilities to the same, and then finally in terms of assessment and treatment.

Prevalence of secondary morbidity

Empirical evidence of the prevalence of secondary morbidity in early psychosis populations is limited, with most of the available data relating to those patients with more established schizophrenic disorders. Depending on the study of interest, the rates reported for specific secondary conditions in schizophrenia vary considerably, for example, for depression from 7 to 75% (Bermanzohn & Siris, 1991, 1992), for panic attacks from 28 to 63% (Argyle, 1990; Boyd, 1986) and for obsessive-compulsive disorder from 13 to 30% (Bermanzohn, Porto & Siris, 1997; Fenton & McGlashan, 1986).

The prevalence rate of alcohol or drug abuse in the chronic schizophrenic population is suggested to be as high as 60% (Bland, Newman & Orn, 1987). A study by Hambrecht and Häfner (1996) examined the prevalence rates of alcohol and drug abuse in a representative sample of 232 people with first-episode schizophrenia. Alcohol abuse prior to onset was found in 24%, drug abuse in 14%. This is twice the rate of the general population. Alcohol abuse tended to occur after the first symptoms of schizophrenia, whereas drug abuse showed no consistent pattern. This study raised the question whether one disorder is a consequence of the other, but did not support a unidirectional causality.

Strakowski et al. (1995) examined psychiatric comorbidity in 71 first-episode psychotic patients. For each specific comorbid diagnosis, the percentage of patients in whom that comorbidity was *antecedent* to the psychosis, was as follows: drug abuse 89%, alcohol abuse 81%, anxiety disorders 73%, PTSD 69%, and obsessive-compulsive disorder, 33%. Yet no significant differences were found in the ratio of *antecedent* to *total* comorbidity diagnoses. Strakowski et al. (1995) found that post-traumatic stress disorder *prior* to onset of psychosis might be a risk factor for the development of psychotic depression. These findings suggest the existence of psychiatric syndromes prior to the onset of psychosis, which begs consideration of early intervention in certain high-risk populations.

However, obtaining convincing evidence as to the incidence and prevalence of *all of the "secondary" conditions* necessitates the undertaking of large-scale epidemiological studies for both general psychiatric and first-episode populations (Jackson et al., 1999).

Working with a defined early psychosis population within a specified catchment area, we have found a number of these conditions to be highly prevalent in the early psychosis population, especially depression and social phobia (Mooney & Pica, 1997). Also, we have observed that these conditions may present in subthreshold forms. We would argue that treatment should be offered even when diagnostic criteria are not fully met as the condition may still complicate or impede the recovery process.

The psychopathologies of secondary morbidity

In the first-episode population, "secondary" depression may be conceptualised as a grief reaction with the person mourning what they believe to be their lost identity and life direction due to the psychotic illness. The person may feel that they have lost their key roles and status in life and view their life as now uncontrollable and worthless. Feelings of low self-esteem, hopelessness and worthlessness are reflected in depressive schemas such as: *"My life has been irreversibly changed"*; *"I have no future now"*; *"I am unlovable"*; *"I've lost my job, I'll never work again"*; *"I'll never be able to study again"*.

Social anxiety usually takes the form of individuals reporting the experience of feeling alienated from, or actively shunned by their peer group during both the psychotic and recovery phases of their illness. This can engender feelings of unremitting despair and loneliness for the sufferer. Anxiety schemas may include concerns about stigmatisation such as: *"Will my friends/family/colleagues still accept me?"*; *"Do they think that I'm mental?"*; *"They are thinking that I'm dangerous"* ; *"They think that I'm no good at my job now that I've been in a psychiatric hospital."*; *"I cannot see my friends anymore."*

Becoming psychotic and forcibly admitted to a psychiatric hospital, where one is restrained and injected with a psychotropic medication, can be traumatic and has implications for the recovery and successful adjustment of the patient (Jeffries, 1977). The significance of the psychotic episode or the circumstances surrounding it might be underestimated by clinicians (McGorry et al., 1991). Sounds, smells, places or people might be triggers for anxiety and dissociative symptoms. Flashbacks, sleep disturbance, nightmares, and concentration and memory difficulties are not only disturbing, but they may inhibit social or occupational integration.

A minority of early psychosis clients present with disorders such as obsessive-compulsive disorder, panic disorder and generalised anxiety disorder. The initial presentation of the disorder may appear to be intertwined with symptoms of the psychotic illness. Examples include generalised anxiety or panic symptoms related to paranoid ideation, and compulsive rituals created to neutralise delusional beliefs, as with the young male client who believed a family member was using telepathic forces to bombard him with arrows and who used the placement of objects in his bedroom to protect himself. In this case, however, clear examples of obsessions and compulsions were evident long after resolution of the psychosis. For others, panic or generalised anxiety symptoms may arise in the course of the client's resumption of their usual activities. These "secondary" conditions may be associated with beliefs about the client's inability to independently handle previously straightforward tasks such as shopping in supermarkets or using public transport. We argue that prompt and judicious use of cognitive behavioural intervention for these disorders can greatly assist the recovery process. Prior to discussion of relevant treatment approaches, factors contributing to vulnerability to secondary morbidity and the assessment of secondary morbidity are considered.

Vulnerability to the development of "secondary" psychopathology

While the presence of "true" secondary morbidity is seen to indicate a failure in adaptation to the psychotic episode, a number of potential vulnerability factors for such conditions may well predate the onset of psychosis. Contributing factors include genetic predispositions (for example, family history of depression), neurological impairment, personality style and prior exposure to traumatic life events (DeLisi, 1997; Hulbert, Jackson & McGorry, 1996; McGorry et al., 1991). For example, a small number of COPE clients presented with PTSD symptoms relating to previously experienced trauma such as rape, observing violent armed robberies, and involvement in a motor vehicle accident leading to a fatality. For these clients, the experience of psychosis appeared to trigger, or in one case mask, post-traumatic symptoms (for example, flashbacks, nightmares) specifically related to the trauma that in some cases had occurred years before.

For some clients, pre-existing neurological impairment may be associated with continuing cognitive impairment and persisting positive symptoms. This subgroup of clients may be more prone to self-stigmatisation and hopelessness and to secondary disorders such as substance abuse and depression.

It has been suggested that during the period of acute illness less adaptive aspects of personality may become more prominent, complicating recovery and leaving the individual vulnerable to the development of secondary conditions (Bronisch & Klerman, 1991). Younger clients still engaged in negotiating the developmental challenges of adolescence and early adulthood may be especially at risk in this regard (Bernstein et al., 1993). The limited available evidence indicates that it is those dimensions of personality that compromise social involvement and help seeking, for example, either schizotypal or antisocial traits, that are most influential in this context (Hulbert, Jackson & McGorry, 1996). Conversely, we found the five-factor model personality traits of Extroversion and Agreeableness (as measured at six-month follow-up), and also, Openness to Experience (as measured at post-acute and six-month assessments), to be correlated with better outcome at the 12-month follow-up (Hulbert, McGorry & Jackson, 1997).

COPE is predicated on the notion that, for most individuals, the experience of psychosis is likely to impact on the person's sense of self in negative and unhelpful ways. Psychologically, vulnerability to secondary psychiatric disorders is understood in terms of the individual's information-processing style and their underlying preoccupations and thematic content. These are seen to interact with common sequelae of the psychosis such as the experience of stigma, a reduction in available competence, roles and life opportunities, frequently leading to demoralisation and loss of self-efficacy and self-esteem.

Assessment of Secondary Morbidity

Current diagnostic practice encourages a hierarchical approach which can result in comorbid and secondary disorders being left undiagnosed and untreated.

Distinguishing pre-existing and secondary disorders in the context of a psychotic illness, even when the latter is well managed, is a complex and difficult task (Hulbert, Jackson & McGorry, 1996; Strakowski et al., 1993, 1995). To circumvent these diagnostic complexities, Bermanzohn, Porto and Siris (1997) suggested that the term "associated psychiatric syndromes" be utilised. We have opted to rely on reports by clients and informants (if available) regarding the onset of symptoms, nominating conditions "secondary" if they developed after the onset of the psychosis and appeared to be directly associated with failed adaptation to the psychotic illness. As regards treatment, however, in some cases we have treated conditions that clearly preceded the psychosis; strictly speaking, these are not "secondary" conditions (see our case of Sam—a case of previous trauma unmasked).

In the context of psychosis, comprehensive assessment of secondary morbidity requires both accurate diagnostic investigation and examination of dimensions of psychological and social functioning, and of life circumstances. A complex case formulation is developed in which information regarding the onset, duration, severity, intensity and frequency of both psychotic and any secondary symptoms is integrated with data relating to the individual's history and experience.

Assessment of psychological and social functioning requires detailing of the client's current beliefs and cognitive style and the range of coping responses and social skills, including help-seeking skills and attitudes—both adaptive and maladaptive. Of particular importance is the client's construal of the psychotic disorder, including their subjective experience of psychosis, their explanatory model of illness and their perception of the impact on their life and sense of self. Effective employment of behavioural strategies in treatment necessitates a knowledge of the client's social network and their role functioning in domains such as family, work and study.

General approaches to treatment of secondary morbidity

The treatment of secondary morbidity draws on a wide repertoire of cognitive and behavioural strategies, although currently, published tests of these approaches with psychotic patients are typically limited to isolated case reports (e.g. Sarron & Lelord, 1991). In treating specific "secondary" conditions clinicians should make use of interventions with established efficacy for that "primary" disorder, e.g. depression, in the non-psychosis domain. A useful reference in this regard is DeRubeis and Crits-Christoph (1998) who describe the empirically supported individual and group psychological treatments for adult mental disorders. The disorders of interest include all the anxiety disorders, major depressive disorder, and alcohol and substance abuse.

For the more prevalent disorders in this population, that is, depression and anxiety disorders, the use of a range of both cognitive and behavioural interventions is essential (DeRubeis & Crits-Christoph, 1998). Following on from the work of Beck and his colleagues (Beck et al., 1979; Beck & Emery, 1985; Beck, Freeman & Associates, 1990) the earlier phase of treatment should be based around appropriate behavioural strategies and less challenging cognitive techniques. For depression these might include activity scheduling, mastery and pleasurable activities and graded task assignments. At this time it is usually appropriate to introduce basic monitoring of mood, the identification of automatic thoughts and the use of self-instruction and self-statements, for example, to counter amotivation and increase homework compliance.

Early phase work with anxiety disorders such as social phobia and panic disorder might involve relaxation training, distraction, role-plays and imaginal and in vivo exposure. Exposure and response prevention has been established as the psychological treatment of choice for obsessive compulsive disorder (DeRubeis & Crits-Christoph, 1998) and with appropriate consideration for the mental state of the client is effective with this population. Early psychosis clients often report troubling imagery as a component of their anxiety response. Techniques such as time projection, substitution of imagery and decatastrophising the image have proved helpful.

At this stage in particular, the use of psychoeducation materials including videos, handouts and selected readings, can help to improve both understanding of the disorder and engagement in treatment (see, e.g., McGorry, 1995). As the client's mental state and cognitive functioning stabilises, the introduction of more complex cognitive strategies can proceed. Monitoring of mood can be expanded to incorporate detection of dysfunctional beliefs and thinking styles. Then empirical disputation, including the collection and testing of evidence related to significant beliefs, can be implemented.

Working with post-traumatic stress disorder (PTSD), the therapist should endeavour to provide a safe place for the patient to describe their fears, anxiety, flashbacks, avoidance, nightmares, sleep-disturbances or emotional numbness. This necessarily depends on the formation of a strong therapeutic alliance, especially the element of trust. The therapist should allow and encourage the patient to experience emotional intensity when recalling the trauma (and all its elements) within the therapy session. (For more information on PTSD treatment see McCann & Pearlman, 1990, and for early intervention work with PTSD see Creamer, 1996.)

At all times, the clinician should be mindful of the client's mental state and relational capacity and adopt a flexible attitude to the use of these techniques. With the psychotic client the intervention may need to be deferred on occasion or proceed at quite a slow pace. Interventions may need to be modified, with the therapist taking a more active and involved role, for example, with in vivo exposure and the role-playing of homework tasks.

Illustrative case vignettes

The following three cases illustrate common secondary morbidities. They also demonstrate our approach to working with such patients, drawing on the more general techniques outlined previously.

Social anxiety

Tina was a 19-year-old apprentice chef admitted for approximately two months to a psychiatric hospital for treatment of a psychotic illness. Six months prior to admission Tina had become increasingly distressed by the belief that the neighbours were spying upon her and talking about her. She believed that they could read her thoughts and put thoughts into her head. About three months after this, Tina become noticeably disorganised and was unable to attend to her usual daily routine. She began hearing voices saying she was "a bad person". She was admitted to hospital after visiting her General Practitioner to obtain sleeping pills in an attempt to escape from these voices.

In hospital Tina was initially treated with 200 mg daily of chlorpromazine, which, with a marked improvement in her mental state, was later reduced to 100 mg, then 50 mg daily. Following discharge from hospital she returned to live with her family. One month later Tina resumed work on a part-time basis. The job involved late nights, and after work Tina and her coworkers would usually go out to a café to relax and socialise before going home. Reportedly not socially anxious previously, Tina found herself feeling very uncomfortable, both in the workplace and social settings. Tina felt that her friends stared at her when she walked into the café. She became increasingly anxious and withdrawn at work and eventually stopped going out after work. She also expressed concerns regarding her reduced confidence and self-esteem since hospitalisation.

With Tina's social anxiety the agreed-upon focus of treatment, the therapist explored her thoughts about why she felt awkward around her friends and work colleagues. She reported the belief that people would think she was now "tainted" because she had been admitted into a "mental hospital". The four-column technique of Beck et al. (1979) was utilised to examine Tina's thinking processes and highlight the relationship between the client's thoughts, emotions and behaviours. The four-column technique details the situation in which the feeling/thought occurred, which is usually the trigger component; the thought, which is usually negative, irrational and self-disparaging; the emotional response; and then an alternative rational thought which challenges the original way of interpreting a situation.

Using the columns, it was determined that, for Tina, one *activating event* was walking into the café and seeing her friends stare at her. Tina's *belief* about this event was "My friends don't like me anymore because they think I'm loony". The *consequential feeling* Tina had to this thought was a rush of anxiety and a subsequent inability to enjoy herself in the café. This *resulted* in Tina deciding not to go to the café after work.

The four-column technique is most useful when used over a period of time as an ongoing homework task which is reviewed in the therapy sessions. It takes time for people to learn and then understand the relationship between thoughts, feelings and behaviours. As in Tina's case, role-plays can be used to reinforce the four-column technique by assisting the patient in formulating and practising coping plans "in vitro". The aim is to achieve a shift in the patient's belief system by assisting the patient to recognise that her thoughts are merely one of many possible interpretations and outcomes of an event. This technique can often give a patient the style of self-dialogue, as well as the courage, to embark upon a task.

Initially, the therapist focused on examination of Tina's thought content and her thought processes and then later asked her to consider other rational hypotheses. Role-plays allowed rehearsal of anxiety-provoking situations, with Tina being asked to practise a number of social initiations and responses. To counter her increasing social avoidance, Tina agreed to undertake graded homework tasks. Ongoing review of Tina's monitoring of her homework and the use of role-plays allowed her and the therapist to examine her dysfunctional thoughts and behaviour strategies, and to assist her in developing alternative thoughts regarding problematic situations. As a parallel process, the therapist also carefully explored and challenged any evidence of stigma related to the psychosis, thereby allowing Tina to develop a less negative view of her episode of psychotic illness. At the end of therapy Tina indicated that she was able to socialise with little or no anxiety and that she now believed her friends had been concerned for her and that they were happy to see her back at work and well again.

A case of previous trauma unmasked

Sam was a 28-year-old male who developed an acute-onset psychosis characterised by delusions of reference and grandiose and paranoid delusions. Two weeks prior to Sam's admission, his parents observed deterioration in his personal appearance, hygiene and tidiness around the house. He developed paranoid ideation in relation to a recently televised piece of music, which he believed he had composed. He implicated a television presenter and family members in what he believed was a plot to steal his music. Unable to make sense of what Sam was saying, his father brought him to hospital.

The psychotic disorder appears to have occurred in the context of chronic post-traumatic symptoms, including flashbacks, nightmares, severe anxiety, anhedonia, decreased social contact and phobic avoidance of venues that reminded Sam of banks (e.g. cinemas and shopping centres). Sam related the onset of these symptoms to a period six years before, when, while employed as a bank teller, he had been the victim of two violent armed robberies that occurred within a two-week period. On each occasion, a gun was pointed at his head and the offender threatened to shoot him. Sam described being paralysed with fear, experiencing an overwhelming sense of helplessness. Soon after the robberies, Sam resigned because of his continuing experience of intense fear in the workplace. His employer offered no professional counselling at that time. The traumatic-related symptoms continued but became masked by the emergence of the florid psychotic symptoms.

Initially admitted as an involuntary patient, Sam was quiet and withdrawn on the ward. His delusions improved rapidly with antipsychotic medication (2.5 mg haloperidol) and after 14 days Sam was discharged to the care of his supportive family. Sam was readmitted 19 days later with a one-week history of depressive features in the absence of any psychotic symptoms. He felt empty and believed that there was nothing to look forward to in his future. Sam experienced anhedonia, sleep and appetite disturbance, poor concentration, anergia and suicidal ideation, although without specific suicidal plans. Sam was commenced on antidepressant medication (20 mg fluoxetine) and with the abatement of his suicidal ideation, he was discharged three days following this re-admission. The traumatic symptoms continued during and after the depressive episode.

The cognitive therapy agenda was initially focused on discussion of Sam's experience during, and following, the bank robberies; the therapist and Sam conceptualised the psychotic episode as having masked and compounded the PTSD symptoms. Subsequent to his psychotic episode, Sam noted that he felt exposed, vulnerable, and subject to the ridicule of his friends and colleagues; these thoughts and feelings reminding him of the horror and helplessness he felt following the bank robberies.

Imaginal exposure was used, with the contextual and emotional experiences of the bank robberies being confronted systematically. Additionally, an in vivo exposure hierarchy was constructed, with this ranging from least anxiety-provoking situations through to the most anxiety-provoking situations. These included, for example, thinking about a shopping centre or bank; walking past a shopping centre or bank; walking into a shopping centre or bank; standing in a short queue at a shop check-out or bank-line.

The commencement of imaginal exposure to the memory of the armed robberies provoked intense anxiety and some avoidance of this topic. Discussion ensued regarding the nature of avoidance as a post-trauma response and, also, Sam's thoughts and fears about experiencing anxiety. After three sessions, Sam indicated that he believed himself capable of confronting his memories and the associated fears. While initially very fearful, the client was able to acknowledge a significant lowering of his anxiety over the 12 sessions of imaginal exposure. Between each session Sam reinforced the gains he was achieving in the therapy sessions by completing in vitro and in vivo homework. Using his exposure hierarchy, he assigned himself exposure tasks working methodically from the least to the highest anxiety-provoking situation. This intervention resulted in the cessation of avoidance of feared situations and some reduction of anxiety and other PTSD symptoms.

A further component of treatment involved interventions to increase social activity and strengthen Sam's social network. Cognitive techniques were used to help him to identify and challenge his distorted thinking regarding people's motives and intent towards him. Techniques such as the four-column technique reported by Beck et al. (1979) were essential to this process. Subsequently, Sam commenced socialising and became more focused on realising a positive future—one which involved family and work commitments.

A case of post-psychotic depression

Lucy was a 27-year-old woman who had experienced an insidious onset of more than two years duration before the emergence of a florid psychotic episode. Her symptoms included systematised paranoid delusions about her family and her neighbours watching her and video-taping her. During this time she was unable to work as nurse as she was increasingly distracted by auditory hallucinations which informed her that she was being watched because she was a worthless nurse. Her family and friends became concerned about her and eventually Lucy was admitted as an inpatient to a psychiatric hospital. Her medical treatment included 2 mg of risperidone daily, which resulted in her psychotic symptoms swiftly abating.

Soon after her discharge Lucy returned to nursing part time. At first she found the transition exhilarating but one month after her return to work she reported feeling depressed with low self-esteem, overeating, sleeping, amotivation and lethargy. She indicated that she was not attending work regularly and that she started to believe that she was an ineffectual person. It was apparent that Lucy was experiencing a post-psychotic depression.

One of the strengths of cognitive behaviour therapy for depression lies in the prevention of further deterioration. Since Lucy was amotivated and lethargic, it was crucial to engage her attention and counteract her withdrawal from life. An activity schedule (Beck et al., 1979) was used to offset Lucy's loss of motivation and preoccupation with depressive ideas. Initially, Lucy kept a diary of her activities and this was reviewed in the therapy session. The activity schedule involved graded tasks, beginning with getting out of bed in order to make her breakfast and eventually progressing to grocery shopping and visiting her parents. This also provided an opportunity for the therapist to assist Lucy in challenging the underlying reasons for her inactivity through Socratic questioning and challenging.

Once Lucy was more active, the next step in her treatment was to assess her current cognitive framework. Using the cognitive triad, as described by Beck et al. (1979), the therapist was able to discuss and evaluate Lucy's current distorted and negative perceptions of herself, the world and her future, including cognitions regarding her sense of her own inadequacy and worthlessness. The cognitive behavioural model of depression, as described by Beck and his colleagues (1979), was used to elucidate the relationship between cognitions, emotions and behavioural consequences.

Cognitive challenging (Beck et al., 1979) based on the four-column technique, was used to explore the rationale for Lucy's avoidance of work and social situations. Her fears and other dysfunctional thoughts relating to avoided situations were closely examined and challenged. After a number of sessions Lucy recognised that she was misinterpreting events and feedback from people, which resulted in her believing that she was disliked and that she was seen as not coping in her nursing position. Also, she was able to recognise the reinforcing negative cycle of her thought processes and how these had contributed to social and occupational withdrawal and the onset of depression. She provided an example of how she had interpreted events to suit her negative view of herself and subsequently used these to support her disparaging feelings about herself; she recalled the charge nurse on her ward suggesting that she have a rest during her lunch break. Lucy took this to signify that the Charge Nurse thought she needed a rest because she was ineffectual as a nurse. Via the four-column technique, alternative, rational solutions or beliefs were constructed.

This discussion also highlighted Lucy's lack of self-confidence and beliefs about her perceived loss in role functioning following the psychotic episode. Lucy reported that she feared life would never be the same as it had been prior to the onset of the psychosis. She noted that previously she had enjoyed challenges and responsibilities and had considered herself competent and successful. This provided an opportunity to challenge Lucy's self-blame and overturn her misconceptions about recovery from psychosis. Lucy was seen to be mourning her premorbid sense of self and to be placing herself under enormous pressure to *succeed immediately* without regard to her current phase of illness (Strauss, 1992). Psychoeducation regarding the expected progress through the recovery phase of psychosis provided her with a rationale for a more graduated return to work. Accurate empathy and sensitive discussion of feelings about what might indeed prove to be enduring changes, assisted adjustment to the current situation.

RESEARCH OUTCOMES TO DATE

To date there have been two trials of COPE. The first trial of COPE—an open uncontrolled trial which is now complete—included three groups of patients. The first group consisted of those patients who were offered and accepted COPE. The second group were those patients who were offered COPE but refused that therapy (the Refuser group) and the third group of patients were those who were never offered COPE because they belonged to another geographic region and were therefore considered to be out-of-area (Control group). It is of note that patients who refused COPE (the Refuser group) could continue to receive the usual range of outpatient services from the EPPIC service, as could the first group (the COPE acceptors), but the third group of patients were never offered the range of EPPIC outpatient services. COPE acceptors received from 2 to 40 sessions, with a mean of 18 and a median of 19 sessions. Patients were assessed at entry and at the end of treatment. Patients who received COPE obtained significantly superior scores ($p<0.05$) to the Control group on four of the seven measures, but only outperformed the Refuser group on one of the seven measures ($p<0.05$). The COPE group performed significantly worse on one of the measures than the Refuser group ($p<0.05$), although on five of the seven measures, the end-of-treatment raw means for the COPE group were better than the raw means of the Refuser group. Effect sizes were also provided (Jackson et al., 1998). A one-year follow-up study is completed and the report is in preparation.

One point is worthy of comment. In our pilot study (Jackson et al., 1998) and in a related study (Henry et al., 1997), we found that mean levels of secondary morbidity were lower than expected. Arguably, there are two possible explanations. First, the result reflects the true state of affairs and secondary morbidity is not particularly prevalent in this population. Second, the measures we used, namely the SCL-90-R (Derogatis, 1983) and the BDI (Beck & Beck, 1972), were not adequately capturing the phenomena of interest. Henry et al. (1997) note that the SCL-90-R and BDI are dimensional, not categorical, measures. Possibly these dimensional ratings were not sensitive enough to detect the changes. This, in our collective view, is the most convincing explanation. Put another way, patients were presenting with a *diverse range of secondary conditions and no one condition dominated to any great extent*. Given the dimensional nature of the measures (SCL-90-R and BDI), high scores for particular individuals suffering from, say, social phobia, were averaged out across the COPE sample and the prominence of any particular secondary condition was lost in the averaging procedure. Certainly clinically, we did treat "secondary" conditions such as those described earlier in the three vignettes. In the future, it would seem essential that researchers report the *numbers and types of all clinically significant* secondary conditions in their psychotic populations to provide readers with some idea of the diagnostic profile of their samples, even if the conditions did not fully meet diagnostic criteria for a *disorder*. This would permit more of a direct comparison with Strakowski et al.'s (1995) finding of comorbidity being present in 69% of their first-episode psychosis patients.

Unfortunately, since only 51 of the 80 patients in the pilot study of COPE were available for the one-year follow-up, the Refuser and Control groups were combined, each having lost approximately 50% of their patients. Yet, the results again favoured COPE in a similar, albeit weaker, way to those obtained at the end of treatment. Results will be forthcoming. Also, a second trial of COPE which involves a randomised-controlled design (COPE versus No-COPE/EPPIC case management), has been completed. Data are now being analysed.

SUMMARY, CONCLUSIONS AND FUTURE DIRECTIONS

In this chapter we have outlined our methods for treating secondary conditions in first-presentation psychosis. We have attempted to put this in various contexts (i.e. historical, theoretical, geographic and service delivery), explicitly acknowledging that all therapies are to some extent products of time and place. It has been our collective view, developed over a period of time, that first-presentation psychotic clients require a different form of treatment—one that takes into account their developmental "space". We have described COPE and its four phases with a strong emphasis on the secondary morbidity phase. We described the prevalence and psychopathologies of secondary morbidity, vulnerabilities to the same, and assessment and treatment issues. The three vignettes provide some illustrations of our approach which stems from the ground-breaking work of Beck and his colleagues (Beck & Emery, 1985; Beck et al., 1979). We note that only fairly recently has this work been applied to the problems of individuals suffering from first-episode psychosis.

We have undergone some change in our collective thinking since devising COPE. Although the data are yet to all come in, and will require replication in other settings, our current view is that COPE is a useful addition to our armentarium but that it needs to be combined with the treatment of positive symptoms. We have moved towards this already with patients who continue to have persisting positive symptoms following an adequate course of low-dose medication for a period of three months (Maude et al., 1997) but we believe that there are grounds for extending this combined treatment to first-episode patients, even granted that the positive symptoms of up to 80–90% of our patients may respond to neuroleptic treatment. Our view is that such treatment may help patients to see that they may have control over their delusions and hallucinations, rather than as viewing them as discretely separate phenomena which are not comprehendable from a psychological perspective nor amenable to psychological treatment. Obviously the sheer amount of resources required constitutes the major limitation of extending combined COPE/psychological treatment of positive symptoms to all first-episode psychotic patients. Such an approach needs to be easily learnt and dispensed by front-line practitioners of various disciplines. Developing a simplified yet comprehensive treatment which can address the medical and psychological treatment of positive symptoms, assist the adaptation of the person following the first psychotic episode, *and deal with secondary morbidities*, represents a pressing challenge—one which should assume the utmost priority if we are to promote optimal recovery and adjustment for young persons presenting with their first episode of psychosis.

REFERENCES

Andreasen, N.C. (1984). *The Broken Brain: The Biological Revolution in Psychiatry.* New York: Harper & Row.

APA (1980). *Diagnostic and Statistical Manual of Mental Disorders* (3rd edn) (DSM-III-R). Washington, DC: American Psychiatric Association.

APA (1987). *Diagnostic and Statistical Manual of Mental Disorders* (3rd rev. edn) (DSM-III-R). Washington, DC: American Psychiatric Association.

APA (1994). *Diagnostic and Statistical Manual of Mental Disorders* (4th edn) (DSM-IV). Washington, DC: American Psychiatric Association.

Argyle, N. (1990). Panic attacks in chronic schizophrenia. *British Journal of Psychiatry,* **157,** 430–433.

Beck, A.T. & Beck, R.W. (1972). Screening depressed patients in family practice: a rapid technique. *Postgraduate Medicine,* **52,** 81–85.

Beck, A.T., Rush, A.J., Shaw, B.F. & Emery, G. (1979). *Cognitive Therapy of Depression.* New York: Guilford Press.

Beck, A.T. & Emery, G. (1985). *Anxiety Disorders and Phobias: A Cognitive Perspective.* New York: Basic Books.

Beck, A.T., Freeman, A. & Associates (1990). *Cognitive Therapy of Personality Disorders*. New York: Guilford Press.

Bermanzohn, P.C. & Siris, S.G. (1992). Akinesia: A syndrome common to parkinsonism, retarded depression and negative symptoms. *Comprehensive Psychiatry*, 33, 221–232.

Bermanzohn, P.C., Porto, L. & Siris, S.G. (1997). Associated psychiatric syndromes (APS) in chronic schizophrenia: Possible clinical significance. Paper presented at the XXVIII Congress of the European Association for the Behavioural and Cognitive Therapies, Venice, Italy, 24–27 September, 1997.

Bernstein, D.P., Cohen, P., Velez, N., Schwab-Stone, M., Siever, L. & Shinsato, L. (1993). Prevalence and stability of the DSM-III-R personality disorders in a community-based sample of adolescents. *American Journal of Psychiatry*, 150, 1237–1243.

Bland, R.C., Newman, S.C. & Orn, H. (1987). Schizophrenia: lifetime co-morbidity in a community sample. *Acta Psychiatrica Scandinavica*, 75, 383–391.

Boyd, J.H. (1986). Use of mental health services for the treatment of panic disorder. *American Journal of Psychiatry*, 143, 1569–1574.

Bronisch, T. & Klerman, G.L. (1991). Personality functioning: change and stability in relationship to symptoms and psychopathology. *Journal of Personality Disorders*, 5, 307–317.

Bruner, J. (1986). *Actual Minds, Possible Worlds*. Cambridge, MA: Harvard University Press.

Chadwick, P.J., Birchwood, M. & Trower, P. (1996). *Cognitive Therapy for Delusions, Voices and Paranoia*. Chichester: Wiley.

Creamer, M. (1996). The prevention of post-traumatic stress. In P. Cotton & H.J. Jackson (Eds), *Early Intervention and Prevention in Mental Health*, (pp. 229–246). Melbourne: Australian Psychological Society.

Davidson, L. & Strauss, J.S. (1995). Beyond the biopsychosocial model: Integrating disorder, health, and recovery. *Psychiatry*, 58, 44–55.

DeLisi, L.E. (1997). Is schizophrenia a lifetime disorder of brain plasticity, growth and aging? *Schizophrenia Research*, 23, 119 -129.

DeRubeis, R.J. & Crits-Christoph, P. (1998). Empirically supported individual and group psychological treatments for adult mental disorders. *Journal of Consulting and Clinical Psychology*, 66, 37–52.

Derogatis, L.R. (1983). *SCL-90-R: Administration, Scoring & Procedures Manual-II for the R(evised) Version*. Towson, Maryland, USA: Clinical Psychometric Research.

Erickson, E.H. (1968). *Identity: Youth and Crisis*. New York: Norton.

Fenton, W.S. & McGlashan, T.H. (1986). The prognostic significance of obsessive-compulsive symptoms in schizophrenia. *American Journal of Psychiatry*, 143, 437–441.

Fowler, D., Garety, P. & Kuipers, E. (1995). *Cognitive Behaviour Therapy for Psychosis: Theory and Practice*. Chichester: Wiley.

Garety, P., Fowler, D., Kuipers, E., Freeman, D., Dunn, G., Bebbington, P., Hadley, C. & Jones, S. (1997). London–East Anglia randomised controlled trial of cognitive-behavioural therapy for psychosis: Predictors of outcome. *British Journal of Psychiatry*, 171, 420–426.

Haddock, G. & Slade, P.D. (Eds) (1996). *Cognitive-behavioural Interventions with Psychotic Disorders*. London: Routledge.

Hambrecht, M. & Häfner, H. (1996). Substance abuse and the onset of schizophrenia. *Biological Psychiatry*, 5, 56–62.

Henry, L., McGorry, P.D., Jackson, H.J., Hulbert, C.A. & Edwards, J. (1997). Cognitive psychotherapy and the prevention of secondary morbidity in first episode psychosis. Paper presented at the XXVIII Congress of the European Association for the Behavioural and Cognitive Therapies, Venice, Italy, 24–27 September, 1997.

Hogarty, G.E., Kornblith, S.J., Greenwald, D., DiBarry, A.L., Cooley, S., Ulrich, R.F., Carter, M. & Flesher, S. (1997a). Three-year trials of personal therapy among schizophrenic patients living with or independent of family: I. Description of study and effects on relapse rates. *American Journal of Psychiatry*, **154**, 1504–1513.

Hogarty, G.E., Greenwald, D., Ulrich, R.F., Kornblith, S.J., DiBarry, A.L., Cooley, S., Carter, M. & Flesher, S. (1997b). Three-year trials of personal therapy among schizophrenic patients living with or independent of family: II. Effects on adjustment of patients. *American Journal of Psychiatry*, **154**, 1514–1524.

Hulbert, C.A., Jackson, H.J. & McGorry, P.D. (1996). Relationship between personality and course and outcome in early psychosis: A review of the literature. *Clinical Psychology Review*, **16**, 707–27.

Hulbert, C.A., McGorry, P.D. & Jackson, H.J. (1997). Personality as a comorbidity factor for treatment outcome in cognitively-oriented psychotherapy for early psychosis (COPE). Paper presented at the XXVIII Congress of the European Association for the Behavioural and Cognitive Therapies, Venice, Italy, 24–27 September, 1997.

Jackson, H.J., McGorry, P.D., Edwards, J. & Hulbert, C. (1996). Cognitively oriented psychotherapy for early psychosis (COPE). In P. Cotton & H.J. Jackson (Eds), *Early Intervention and Prevention in Mental Health*, (pp. 131–154). Melbourne: Australian Psychological Society.

Jackson, H.J., McGorry, P.D., Edwards, J., Hulbert, C., Henry, L., Francey, S., Maude, D., Cocks, J., Power, P., Harrigan, S. & Dudgeon, P. (1998). Cognitively-oriented psychotherapy for early psychosis (COPE): Preliminary results. *British Journal of Psychiatry*, **172** (Supplement), 93–100.

Jackson, H.J., Edwards, J., Hulbert, C. & McGorry, P.D. (1999). Recovery from psychosis: Psychological interventions. In P.D. McGorry & H.J. Jackson (Eds), *The Early Recognition and Management of Early Psychosis: A Preventive Approach* (pp. 265–307). Cambridge: Cambridge University Press.

Jeffries, J.J. (1977). The trauma of being psychotic: a neglected element in the management of chronic schizophrenia. *Canadian Psychiatric Association Journal*, **22**, 199–206.

Kelly, G. (1955). *The Psychology of Personal Contructs*. New York: Norton.

Kingdon, D.G. & Turkington, D. (1994). *Cognitive-Behavioral Therapy of Schizophrenia*. New York: Guilford Press.

Luborsky, L., McLellan, A.T., Diguer, L., Woody, G. & Seligman, D.A. (1997). The psychotherapist matters: comparison of outcomes across twenty-two therapists and seven patient samples. *Clinical Psychology: Science and Practice*, **4**, 53–65.

Mahoney, M.J. (1991). *Human Change Processes: The Scientific Foundations of Psychotherapy*. New York : Guilford Press.

Mahoney, M.J. (1995). Continuing evolution of the cognitive sciences and psychotherapies. In R.A. Neimeyer & M.J. Mahoney (Eds), *Constructivism in Psychotherapy*, (pp. 39–67). Washington, DC: American Psychological Association.

Markus, H. & Nurius, P. (1986). Possible selves. *American Psychologist*, 41, 954–969.

Maude, D., Edwards, J., McGorry, P.D., Cocks, J., Bennett, C., Burnett, P., Pica, S., Bell, R., Harrigan, S. & Davern, M. (1997). A randomised controlled trial using cognitive-behavioural therapy and clozapine in the early treatment of persisting positive symptoms in first-episode psychosis: Preliminary results. Paper presented at the Second International Conference on Psychological Treatments for Schizophrenia, 2 and 3 October, Oxford, England.

McCann, L. & Pearlman, L.A. (1990). *Psychological Trauma and the Adult Survivor: Theory, Therapy and Transformation.* New York: Brunner/Mazel.

McGorry, P.D. (1995). Psychoeducation in first-episode psychosis: a therapeutic process. *Psychiatry,* **58**, 329–344.

McGorry, P.D. & Edwards, J. (1997). *Early Psychosis Training Pack.* Cheshire: Gardiner-Caldwell Communications.

McGorry, P.D., Chanen, A., McCarthy, E., van Riel, R., McKenzie, D. & Singh, B.S. (1991). Post-traumatic stress disorder following recent-onset psychosis. An unrecognized postpsychotic syndrome. *The Journal of Nervous and Mental Disease,* **179**, 253–258.

McGorry, P.D., Edwards, J., Mihalopoulis, C., Harrigan, S.M. & Jackson, H.J. (1996). EPPIC: An evolving system of early detection and optimal management. *Schizophrenia Bulletin,* **22**, 305–326.

Mohr, D.C. (1995). Negative outcome in psychotherapy: a critical review. *Clinical Psychology: Science and Practice,* **2**, 1–27.

Mooney, M. & Pica, S. (1997). Social phobia in psychosis. Detection and treatment. Paper presented at the XXVIII Congress of the European Association for the Behavioural and Cognitive Therapies, Venice, Italy, 24–27 September, 1997.

Perris, C. (1989). *Cognitive Therapy with Schizophrenic Patients.* New York: Guilford Press.

Roberts, G. (1991). Delusional belief systems and meaning in life: a preferred reality? *British Journal of Psychiatry,* **159** (Suppl. 14), 19–28.

Roberts, G. (1999). Introduction: a story of stories. In G. Roberts & J. Holmes (Eds). *Healing Stories: Narrative in Psychiatry and Psychotherapy* (p. 3–26). Oxford: Oxford University Press.

Sarron, C. & Lelord, F. (1991). In vivo exposure of a schizophrenic patient with agoraphobic symptoms. *European Psychiatry,* **6**, 107.

Siris, S.G. (1991). Diagnosis of secondary depression in schizophrenia: Implications for DSM-IV. *Schizophrenia Bulletin,* **17**, 75–98.

Smith, T.E., Bellack, A.S. & Liberman, R.P. (1996). Social skills training for schizophrenia: review and future directions. *Clinical Psychology Review,* **16**, 599–617.

Strakowski, S.M., Tohen, M., Stoll, A.L., Faedda, G.L., Mayer, P.V., Kolbrener, M.L. & Goodwin, D.C. (1993). Comorbidity in psychosis at first hospitalization. *American Journal of Psychiatry,* **150**, 752–757.

Strakowski, S.M., Keck, P.E., Jr, McElroy, S.L., Lonczak, H.S. & West, S.A. (1995). Chronology of comorbid and principal syndromes in first-episode psychosis. *Comprehensive Psychiatry,* **36**, 106–112.

Strauss, J.S. (1992). The person-key to understanding mental illness: towards a new dynamic psychiatry, III. *British Journal of Psychiatry,* **161** (Suppl.), 19–26.

Weinberger, J. (1995). Common factors aren't so common: the common factors dilemma. *Clinical Psychology: Science and Practice,* **2**, 45–69.

Whitehead, A.N. (1957). *Process and Reality.* New York: Macmillan. (Cited in Mahoney, M.J. (1991). *Human Change Processes: The Scientific Foundations of Psychotherapy* (p.38). New York: Guilford Press.)

Chapter 10

RELAPSE PREVENTION IN EARLY PSYCHOSIS

Elizabeth Spencer*, Eleanor Murray* and James Plaistow*

INTRODUCTION

Despite high remission rates after a first episode of psychosis, the risk of subsequent relapse is also high (Shepherd et al., 1989; Mason et al., 1996; Wiersma et al., 1998), reaching 81.9% in one recent study at five-year follow-up (Robinson et al., 1999).

Prevention of relapse early in the course of psychosis is important as most first-episode psychosis patients are young (Johnstone et al., 1986; Lieberman et al., 1993) and are, therefore, likely to be pursuing important social and occupational goals which will be disrupted by the symptoms and treatment associated with psychotic relapse. Furthermore, as Birchwood has considered in Chapter 2 of this volume, each relapse may result in the growth of residual symptoms (Shepherd et al., 1989; Wiersma et al., 1998) and in accelerating social disablement (Hogarty et al., 1991). Indeed, as he has argued, the combination of a high rate of relapse and the plateauing of psychopathology and disability in the early course of psychosis make this time a "critical period" for intervention. Many psychosis sufferers themselves also feel "entrapped" by their symptoms (Birchwood & Chadwick, 1997) or in a relapsing illness and its associated treatment procedures (Birchwood et al., 1993). This sense of entrapment in the illness has been found to be highly correlated with depression among people suffering from schizophrenia (Birchwood et al., 1993; Rooke & Birchwood, 1998). Little wonder, then, that many psychosis sufferers have expressed an interest in learning to recognise the early signs of impending relapse and the skills to prevent its occurrence (Mueser, Bellack & Blanchard, 1992).

*North Birmingham Mental Health Trust.

Early Intervention in Psychosis.
Edited by M. Birchwood, D. Fowler & C. Jackson.
© 2000 John Wiley & Sons Ltd.

THE "EARLY WARNING SIGNS" APPROACH TO RELAPSE PREVENTION

The early warning signs approach to relapse prevention seeks to identify the earliest signs of impending psychotic relapse and to offer timely and effective intervention to arrest their progression towards frank psychosis.

Investigations, including case reports (Docherty et al., 1978), retrospective interviews with sufferers of schizophrenia and their families (Herz & Melville, 1980; Birchwood et al., 1989), and prospective studies (Subotnik & Nuechterlein, 1988; Birchwood et al., 1989; Jørgensen 1998; Tarrier, Barrowclough & Bamrah, 1991) have consistently determined that "subtle pathological deviations in thought, affect and behaviour ...precede the initial onset of overt psychosis" (Bustillo, Buchanan & Carpenter, 1995, p. 553). "Dysphoric" symptoms (depressed mood, withdrawal, sleep and appetite problems) are the most commonly reported, while psychotic symptoms (for example, a sense of being laughed at or talked about) are mentioned less frequently (Herz & Melville, 1980; Birchwood et al., 1989). Furthermore, these symptoms generally occur in a predictable order, with non-psychotic phenomena occurring early, followed by increasing levels of emotional disturbance and, finally, the development of frankly psychotic symptoms (Docherty et al., 1978). The progression occurs, most frequently, over a period of less than four weeks (Herz & Melville, 1980; Birchwood et al., 1989; Jørgensen, 1998).

These symptoms have sometimes been referred to as the psychotic "prodrome" (Norman & Malla, 1995). There is reason to believe, however, that they may be more adequately conceptualised as "early warning signs" of psychotic relapse (Bustillo, Buchanan & Carpenter, 1995).

The term "prodrome", derived from the medical literature, refers to the non-specific symptoms which precede the appearance of symptoms specific to a particular disease and which may indicate the onset of one of a variety of illnesses. Applying this concept strictly to psychosis, therefore, prodromal symptoms must be distinguished from the specific or definitive psychotic features of the illness. Furthermore, the medical concept of prodrome implies a progression from non-specific symptoms to frank psychosis that is unable to be interrupted.

However, studies have found that non-specific prodromal symptoms alone have poor sensitivities and/or specificities in predicting psychotic relapse (Hirsch & Jolley, 1989; Jolley et al., 1990; Gaebel et al., 1994). Furthermore, contrary to the notion of irreversibility implied in the concept of psychotic "prodrome", investigators have found that people with psychosis are actively involved in using coping strategies to intervene in the onset of psychosis (McGandless-Glimcher et al., 1986). Indeed,

Birchwood (1995) has proposed that early warning signs may represent symptoms intrinsic to the illness combined with a psychological response that centres on a search for meaning and control which may contribute to whether the relapse is arrested or accelerated.

Thus, Bustillo, Buchanan & Carpenter (1995) have argue that restricting the definition of early warning signs to non-psychotic symptoms may be conceptually flawed, is irrelevant to clinical action and may reduce the predictive power of the signs. What is important is that psychosis builds up slowly over several weeks. They propose that the concept of a psychotic "prodrome", therefore, be replaced by that of "early warning signs" of psychosis.

Prospective studies (Subotnik & Nuechterlein, 1988; Birchwood et al., 1989; Tarrier, Barrowclough & Bamrah, 1991; Jørgenson, 1998) have shown that psychotic relapse can be predicted with a sensitivity of 50–79% and a specificity of 75–81% from standardised measures of low-level psychotic symptoms combined with "neurotic" or "dysphoric" symptoms, conducted at least fortnightly.

Furthermore, a large percentage of the sufferers of schizophrenia and their relatives have been found to be aware of these early signs of impending relapse. Herz and Melville (1989), for example, found that 70% of schizophrenia sufferers and 93% of their families were aware of changes that indicated that the individual was becoming unwell, while in another study 63% of schizophrenia sufferers were shown to maintain insight into their deteriorating mental state until the day of their relapse (Heinrichs, Cohen & Carpenter, 1985). Interestingly, while Jørgensen (1998) was able to predict psychotic relapse with a high degree of sensitivity (81%) and specificity (79%) from changes in a composite measure of self-reported and observed early warning signs, he found that the self-report instrument (Birchwood et al., 1989) yielded equally acceptable figures (i.e. a sensitivity of 74% and a specificity of 79%) when used alone.

Importantly also, the retrospective (Kumar, Thara & Rajkamar, 1989) and prospective studies (Subotnik & Nuechterlein, 1988; Birchwood et al., 1989; Jørgensen, 1998) have identified considerable variability between individuals in the nature and timing of their early warning signs, which may lower estimates of the predictive power of early warning signs in studies using standardised scales and group design. Higher estimates of sensitivity and specificity in predicting relapse were also found when changes in early warning scores were evaluated against the individual's own baseline scores rather than compared with those of other patients (Subotnik and Nuechterlein, 1988; Jørgensen, 1998). Thus, this suggests that to be clinically relevant, methods of identifying early warning signs of psychotic relapse must take into account this individual variation.

For these reasons, research attention has recently been directed towards identifying and managing each psychosis sufferer's "relapse signature" (Birchwood, 1995): that is, their unique pattern of early warning signs likely to indicate impending psychotic relapse. In a later part of this chapter we will present a methodology used in our clinical practice for this purpose.

There is evidence that timely intervention delivered shortly after the onset of early warning signs of impending relapse may prevent or attenuate the relapse. The recent success of cognitive-behavioural interventions in reducing the positive symptoms of psychosis suggests that such techniques might be used to support the cognitive and behavioural coping methods already used by individuals to deal with impending relapse (McCandless-Glimcher et al., 1986). Similarly, while intermittent medication has been shown to be inferior to continuous medication in preventing psychotic relapse (Jolley et al., 1989, 1990; Carpenter et al., 1990; Gaebel et al., 1993), medication initiated on the development of early warning signs in combination with maintenance medication (usually low dose) has been shown to reduce psychotic relapse rates to 12–23% over two years (Marder et al., 1984, 1987; Jolley et al. 1990; Gaebel et al., 1994). Marder et al. 1994, for example, demonstrated a significant reduction in the risk of relapse and time spent in psychosis from the second year of treatment with a combination of low-dose maintenance medication plus medication targeted at early warning signs, when compared with treatment with low-dose maintenance medication only.

THE IDENTIFICATION AND MANAGEMENT OF THE RELAPSE SIGNATURE

The above theoretical considerations have stimulated the development of a structured methodology for the identification and management of individual relapse signatures, known as the "Back in the Saddle" (BITS) approach to relapse prevention (Plaistow & Birchwood, 1996).

This methodology takes into account individual differences in the early warning signs of psychotic relapse; it recognises that non-specific signs are likely to precede low-level psychotic signs in the progression of the relapse signature; it implies a management strategy leading directly from the relapse signature; and it emphasises the empowerment of individuals in managing their risk of relapse.

This approach involves five stages:

- Engagement and education
- Identification of the relapse signature

- Development of a relapse drill
- Rehearsal and monitoring
- Clarification of the relapse signature and relapse drill

Engagement and education

The identification of the relapse signature and the development of a plan for its management form an ideal medium through which to establish common ground with the client, acknowledge their point of view and engage client and family in working collaboratively with services on the shared goal of relapse prevention.

Initial sessions focus on understanding the individual's attitude towards illness, especially their perception of the risk and controllability of relapse. As an aid to this, a 14-item interviewer-assisted questionnaire assessing the client's fear, catastrophisation of early signs and perceived control in relation to relapse (The Attitude to Relapse Scale) (Davis, Birchwood & Chadwick, in submission-a) is administered. This process allows for a deepening therapeutic alliance as the health worker attempts to come to terms with the unique perception of the individual and especially with their fears of becoming unwell again. It also facilitates identification of possible factors that may exacerbate the relapse process, for example, poor perceived control over illness causing the individual to panic or fail to act on the occurrence of early signs. It also allows for the measurement of helpful changes in the individual's attitude towards illness following the intervention.

Information is provided to the client and their family about the possibility of coping with the fear of relapse through skill learning and the analogy of a "safety net" is used to describe how early detection and intervention can decrease the risk of the progression of early warning signs to a full psychotic relapse. Such a discussion draws upon the positive steps already being taken by the individual to remain well, and occurs in the context of general psychoeducation concerning preventable risk factors of psychotic relapse (e.g. discontinuation of medication and illicit drug abuse). Thus, the client's sense of control over the illness is fostered. An example of a completed relapse prevention sheet, containing completed relapse signature, drill and service contact numbers is shown to support their understanding (see Figure 10.1)

Identification of the relapse signature

The aim of the next part of the process is to construct an hypothesis about the individualised relapse signature: that is, a set of general and idiosyncratic

---

RELAPSE PREVENTION SHEET

Name: Example

Date:

RELAPSE SIGNATURE

Feeling stressed out because I haven't had enough time to do things.

Preoccupied with other people's and my own problems.

Losing interest in appearance and housework
Not sleeping
Not wanting to go out
Feeling superstitious
Thinking people are against me.

Hearing voices
Hearing messages from TV
Thinking people are conspiring to kill me.

Keyworker:

Co-worker:

Present medication:

Carer contacts:

Triggers:

RELAPSE DRILL

Step 1: Contact keyworker
         Make more time for self
         Take a bath, go to bed early
         Visit friends/family
         Talk about feelings

Step 2: Contact and go out with keyworker

Step 3: Try not to panic
         Contact doctor
         Arrange increase in medication
         Ignore voices; let them take their course
         Consider referral to home treatment

Hours of contact: Monday–Friday (9.00–5.00)
                    Tel.:

                    Saturday-Sunday (10.00—5.00)
                    Tel.:

Out-of-Hours Contact: Tel.:

Figure 10.1.   Relapse Prevention Sheet: Example

symptoms, occurring in a specific order, over a particular time period, that serve as early warning signs of impending psychotic relapse.

Clients are first introduced to examples of early warning signs of psychotic relapse. Examples are then used to illustrate the concept that a relapse signature consists of such symptoms, plus idiosyncratic symptoms unique to the individual, occurring in a particular order and escalating potentially, but not inevitably, to psychosis. They are then encouraged to review, either alone or with the support of their key worker or family, any noticeable changes in their thoughts, perceptions, feelings and behaviours leading up to their most recent episode of illness, as well as any events which they think may have triggered these.

Two structured exercises are then used to expand and order this set of early warning signs.

The time line exercise

The individual is supported in constructing a time line of significant external events, proceeding backwards in time from the date of referral to mental health services. These events may include activities, special events, weather conditions and current affairs. Early warning signs that the client identified in the previous part of the process are "pegged" to these external events and the external events are also used as retrieval cues to further expand on the changes in thoughts, feelings and behaviours that the client experienced in the lead-up to the onset of their recent psychotic episode.

The card sort exercise

Similarly, 55 cards describing non-specific and psychotic symptoms, constituting early warning signs of psychotic relapse drawn from the empirical literature, are presented to the client. The client selects any cards describing early signs that they have experienced in the process of becoming unwell, and places them in order of onset. Using the time line to encourage the client to see the illness in terms of a beginning, middle and end facilitates such a task. If most cards are used it can be useful to have the individual select those experiences which are the most recognisable to form the basis of their relapse signature.

The early signs thus retrieved and arranged in order of onset form the basis of the individual's relapse signature. Clients are then encouraged to personalise their signatures through the use of any idiosyncratic early warning signs not already mentioned and through personalised descriptions of symptoms identified from the card sort. Discussion of these exercises is then used to clarify possible triggers such as periods of stress and underlying difficulties preceding illness. Additional information, for example, at what part the individual feels that they lose insight, is also gained. Emphasis is placed on supporting the individual in understanding the meaning of these experiences within his or her own life context.

Development of a relapse drill

Following the identification of the relapse signature, clients are supported in constructing a three-stage action plan known as a "relapse drill".

An essential feature of the relapse drill is that it is staged. It follows directly from the early warning signs, which are stratified into three levels, from those occurring earliest in the relapse signature, to those occurring immediately prior to the psychotic relapse. Since, in general, the earliest warning signs in the relapse signature tend to be non-specific symptoms, with low power to predict psychotic relapse (Hirsch & Jolley, 1989; Jolley et al., 1990; Gaebel et al., 1993), interventions which may have potential risks as well as benefits (such as increases in antipsychotic medication) are generally used after the relapse signature has clearly progressed on its course towards potential psychotic relapse.

The drill is developed collaboratively and focuses on the strengths of the client, their carers and the services they are engaged with. Past coping strategies and therapeutic interventions that have been found to be helpful in preventing relapse are reviewed collaboratively by the individual, their keyworker and their doctor and incorporated into the drill. The nature of the early warning signs in the individual's relapse signature may suggest to the keyworker and client new skills that may offer further protection against relapse. For example, anxiety, dysphoria and other affective changes may respond to techniques incorporating stress management (Hogarty et al., 1997). Similarly, clients suffering from low-level psychotic phenomena may benefit from techniques designed to challenge delusional and dysfunctional thinking drawn from the cognitive therapy literature (Chadwick, Birchwood & Trower, 1996).

Thus, at each stage, the relapse drill draws from three areas of intervention:

- *Pathway to support*: Clients and carers are provided with details of how to contact the mental health services 24 hours a day, including weekends.
- *Service interventions*: These may include increased contact with the keyworker, anxiety/stress management, negotiated temporary increase in medication, respite care, counselling, cognitive therapy and home treatment.
- *Personal coping strategies*: These consist of successful coping strategies that have been applied in the past by the individual or new ones that have been suggested in the recall of the relapse signature.

Rehearsal and monitoring

Having identified an individual's relapse signature and drill, the client and relevant carers involved in the plan are provided with their own copies of the relapse prevention sheet and monitoring is outlined as a shared responsibility between the individual, carers and mental health services. Effective use of the relapse drill is rehearsed using personalised scenarios and role-plays concerning what the client should do if they detect early warning signs. Hypothetical situations are used to discuss any difficulties that might arise (for example, denial or panic responses) and how to deal with these.

Clarification of the relapse signature and relapse drill

Clarifying the relapse signature and refining the relapse drill are other important areas of monitoring. Individuals are encouraged to replace existing coping strategies, forms of support and service interventions with more effective ones learned from ongoing therapy or experience. In this way, impending or actual relapse is used as a positive opportunity to refine the relapse signature and improve the relapse drill, thus increasing control over the illness.

The following case illustrate the process.

Case Study

PF, a 30-year-old married mother of two, was referred to mental health services following a psychotic episode of five months' duration. Her symptoms had involved a brief period of elevated mood with mood congruent delusions, followed by a prolonged period of persecutory and guilty delusions accompanied by a less prominent depressed mood. The episode had occurred approximately six months after the birth of her second child. There had also been a similar, less severe, episode following the birth of her first child six years previously, but this had not resulted in contact with mental health services. At the time of commencement of relapse prevention work, PF's symptoms had successfully responded to a combination of haloperidol and tricyclic antidepressants but she took these only intermittently, in response to minor recurrences of symptoms.

PF: Engagement and education

At initial interview it was clear that PF had found her psychotic episode very traumatic, was fearful of the possibility of another relapse and demonstrated good understanding of the fact that she had been ill and the desirability of preventing a recurrence.

PF: *The identification of the relapse signature*

Working closely with her keyworker and using the "Back in the Saddle" (BITS) relapse, PF obtained a good understanding of the concepts of early detection and intervention and was able to relate these to her own experience.

Figure 10.2 shows PF's relapse signature, identified using a combination of the timeline and card sort exercises, and progressing from feelings of inadequacy and dysphroia (usually in the context of social stressors) through symptoms of elation to the development of frank persecutory and guilty delusions.

PF: The development of a relapse drill

The earliest stage of the drill focused on PF's own coping strategies to deal with low mood, on obtaining early support, and, given the important role of stressors in onset of her symptoms, on stress management (see Figure 10.2). The second stage focused on strategies that she had found helpful in decreasing elation in the past (e.g. listening to sad music, reducing activity, eating regular large meals) and on pharmacological interventions. PF was very reluctant to take maintenance medication although she recognised its benefits in controlling her symptoms. After negotiation discussing the pros and cons of medication use, it was agreed that she would recommence her regular dose of haloperidol if her sleep pattern deteriorated or if she became suspicious. She would then contact her doctor to determine if additional medications were needed. Similarly, for the third stage of the relapse drill, based on previous experience, PF expressed a preference to be treated in hospital or a respite unit in the event of frank psychosis. It was thus agreed in advance that if at all possible her wishes in this matter would be respected.

PF: *Rehearsal and monitoring*

PF and her keyworker then rehearsed the use of the relapse drill using the following scenarios:

You have a bad day with your youngest child throwing a tantrum. You start to feel quite stressed and agitated. Your friend phones because she has to attend an urgent appointment and wants you to look after her two children for her. You agree to this, but they play up and make you more stressed to the point that you have the automatic thought "I can't cope".

What do you do?

You notice that you have been stressed and restless for a number of days. You try relaxation, meditation and yoga but you are still unable to relax.

What do you do?

RELAPSE PREVENTION SHEET (INITIAL)

Name: PF

Date:

RELAPSE SIGNATURE

Increased feelings of inadequacy
Preoccupied about self improvement
Constantly monitoring yourself for faults
Increased feelings of anxiety, restlessness

Racing thoughts feeling very elated/spiritual (laughing and singing)
Suspicious of people close to you
Feeling like you don't need sleep
Not want to eat

Horrific thoughts and paranoia
Beliefs of being punished by God or possessed by the devil
Severe paranoia
Tactile hallucinations (feel like you're burning)

Keyworker:

Co-worker:

Present medication:

Carer contacts:

Tel.:

Trigger of relapse: Summer
                      After childbirth

RELAPSE DRILL

Step 1:   Yoga/meditation, dance and happy music
          Make time for yourself, use Mum for support and to discuss feelings
          Contact keyworker

Step 2:   Strategies to decrease elation
          Increased contact with keyworker
          Reality testing with keyworker (examine beliefs)
          Contact doctor re recommencing or increasing medication

Step 3:   Admission to hospital or respite care

Hours of contact: Monday–Friday (9.00–5.00)
                    Tel.:

                    Saturday–Sunday (10.00–5.00)
                    Tel.:

Out-of-hours contact: Respite and Recovery Unit
                        Tel.:

Figure 10.2.   Relapse Prevention Sheet: PF

You have been preoccupied with a problem and have noticed you have been arguing with your partner more than usual and this caused you not to sleep last night.

What do you do?

PF: *Clarification of the relapse signature and relapse drill*

Approximately two months later PF's partner contacted her keyworker with concerns about PF. An emergency visit revealed that PF was approximately halfway down her relapse signature, had not slept for two nights and was experiencing extreme anxiety and religious and persecutory ideation. She had tried to implement a number of coping strategies but had not taken any medication. As a result of this emergency visit, PF agreed to recommence haloperidol 5 mg twice daily to improve her sleep. During a four-day period of respite care, antidepressant treatment was added to her treatment regime and she was discharged, much improved, to be supported by the local psychiatric home treatment service. After six weeks PF's symptoms had entirely resolved and she had returned to her previous level of functioning.

Although the development of psychotic symptoms and the need for respite care had not been avoided, the speed of her recovery was fed back to PF positively and she was encouraged to review her signature and drill.

Figure 10.3 shows the revised relapse signature and drill incorporating information that had been gained as a result of this relapse.

Thus, PF concluded that she might have avoided a fully developed psychotic episode by making earlier contact with psychiatric services, by involving her partner in a more constructive way, by an earlier review of her medication, and by modifying her tendency to catastrophise problems and to ruminate on intrusive thoughts.

She decided to contact her keyworker informally if at all concerned about her health. Her partner was also educated about the nature of PF's illness, her early warning signs and on possible coping methods. PF received increased cognitive therapy on coping with intrusive thoughts, problem-solving and anxiety management from her keyworker and techniques from this therapy were incorporated into her relapse drill (see Figure 10.3). Finally, the point in her relapse signature at which she should resume psychiatric medication was made objective and an emergency supply of haloperidol was arranged with her doctor.

Over the next few months PF remained well. Lithium carbonate was added to her treatment regime, the neuroleptic was gradually phased out and she was continued on antidepressant medication.

Some months later PF herself rang to request an urgent visit. She reported insomnia, loss of appetite, increased anxiety, low level ideas of reference and

---

RELAPSE PREVENTION SHEET (REVISED)

Name: PF

Date: (revised)

RELAPSE SIGNATURE

Increased feelings of inadequacy
Preoccupied about self-improvement inc. constantly monitoring yourself for faults
Increased feelings of anxiety, restlessness

Racing thoughts/intrusive thoughts
Feelings of elation/spirituality
Do not need to sleep (1 night or more)
Suspicious of people close to you
Not wanting to eat

Horrific thoughts and paranoia
Beliefs of being punished by God repossessed by the devil
Severe paranoia
Tactile hallucinations

Keyworker:

Co-worker:

Present medication:
Carer contacts:
Triggers:

RELAPSE DRILL

Step 1:   Stay calm—yoga, meditation
          Contact keyworker/services to go out and discuss feelings (PF or partner)
          Make time for yourself, use partner and mum for support
          Coping with thought/problems

Step 2:   Distraction techniques (PTO)
          Take   mg   from emergency supply
          Daily contact with services if necessary (discuss feelings, reality testing)
          Contact Doctor re recommencing or increasing medication

Step 3:   Admission to hospital or respite care

Figure 10.3.   Relapse Prevention Sheet PF (revised)

Hours of contact: Monday–Friday (9.00–5.00)
                    Tel.:

                    Saturday–Sunday (10.00–5.00)
                    Tel.:

Out-of-hours contact: Respite and Recovery Unit

Name: PF

Date: June 97

(A)
Coping with automatic thoughts

(1) What is the thought—write it down
(2) What is the evidence?
(3) Are there any other explanations/ways of viewing the thought?
    (evidence to disconfirm this—use others to support) e.g.: "burning up" or
    "extremely anxious"

(B)
Distraction techniques

(a) Count backwards from 100 in 13's
(b) Concentrate on positive images - nature,greenery

Coping with problems/stressors

(1) State problem - write it down
(2) Write down all possible strategies
(3) Pros's and con's of each strategy
(4) select the best solution

Additional Techniques:

Figure 10.3 (*Continued*)   Relapse Prevention Sheet: PF (revised)

a weakly held belief that she might be the devil. She identified that these had been precipitated by a fight with her partner and a by a self-initiated reduction in her maintenance medication. She had successfully initiated stress management and distraction techniques and had enlisted social support from her sister; however, on the night before the visit she had felt increasingly anxious and had taken five antidepressant tablets in an attempt to calm down. As a result of the emergency visit, she was advised to recommence her previous dose of maintenance medication and to continue her stress management techniques and her symptoms quickly resolved. The fact that she had successfully acted on the relapse drill and prevented the progression of her mild psychotic symptoms was seen as a triumph and the relapse signature and drill were again reviewed for potential areas that could be clarified or improved.

COMMON PROBLEMS AND SOME SOLUTIONS

Ideally, the above procedure provides an opportunity for engagement with services as well as a methodology by which appropriate therapeutic interventions can continue to be identified, discussed and implemented. Clients are encouraged to reflect on their own experiences of being unwell and the relapse prevention sessions are used as an opportunity for the client to "integrate" the experience of psychosis into their experience of themselves and to develop a blame-free acceptance of illness. In addition, a high degree of personal involvement in illness management is encouraged through the acquisition and rehearsal of self-control strategies and the use of prearranged treatment decisions. The resultant increase in sense of control over illness may be hypothesised to be associated with decreased feelings of "entrapment" in the illness process and, thus, depression (Birchwood et al., 1993; Rooke & Birchwood, 1998). Furthermore, as the case history shows, the process is particularly suitable for individuals who will not take maintenance medication consistently, as is frequently the case in young clients (Davis & Casper, 1977).

Despite these advantages, our experience has shown that there may be a number of problems in conducting relapse prevention in this population, which may be summarised as follows.

Lack of "insight"

Insight in psychosis is a multi-dimensional and continuous construct (McGorry & McConville, 1999). David (1990), for example, has conceived of insight as involving three independent but overlapping dimensions: an ability to relabel certain mental events (e.g. delusions and hallucinations) as pathological; a recognition by the individual that they are suffering from an illness and that this illness is mental; and a willingness to accept treatment. Similar multi-dimensional models have also been proposed by other authors (Greenfeld et al., 1989; Amador & Strauss, 1993) and McGorry and McConville (1999), in their review of the relevant literature also draw attention to the fact that correlations between measures of awareness of illness and treatment adherence are generally only in the moderate range; they also conclude that in the early stages of psychotic illness, people will often be judged as showing poor insight due to divergent attributions concerning the change in themselves and its causes which will, in turn, be influenced by factors such as the need to protect the self-esteem from the stigma of mental illness.

It may still be possible to construct a relapse signature among individual's who are unable to label their past psychotic ideation as pathological, as the following case history exemplifies.

Case Study

A 24-year-old man was identified for relapse prevention work on recovery from a psychotic episode, although he continued to believe that the major delusion characterising this episode (i.e. that his musical compositions had been stolen by a famous rock band) had, in fact, occurred. However, he and his keyworker were able to agree that his illness had been characterised by prominent depressed mood and he was successfully able to identify the changes in his mood, thoughts and behaviours that led up to development of frankly psychotic experiences, without conceding these experiences to be psychotic symptoms. The following relapse signature was constructed:

- Feeling down and lethargic.
- Unable to take much in when people talking to me.
- Difficulty sleeping.
- Preoccupied thinking about my future, things that are making me feel down.
- Not wanting to go out with mates.
- Neglecting appearance.
- Not washing, showering or shaving.
- Feeling anxious and restless.
- Feeling irritable towards family, friends and girlfriend.
- Saying and doing things out of character.

Alternatively, on other occasions such individuals may consent to their family being involved in relapse prevention work and most efforts to develop a relapse drill can be undertaken here. Thus, a 17-year-old man with mild learning disabilities, was referred for relapse prevention work after having experienced a psychosis in which he believed that he was at risk of being kidnapped. On recovery he still believed that he had been in some real danger, although he was able to accept that his fear had been "paranoid", or excessive. He, therefore, accepted monitoring of early signs by his mother who was able to contact services at a prearranged intervention point.

Similarly, individuals with psychotic illness have a wide variety of explanatory models for their symptoms and their aetiology (Greenfeld et al., 1989). Particularly in the case of those with early psychosis, these models are unlikely to coincide with those of the treating team, with clients emphasising environmental or situational factors to a greater degree than do clinicians (Greenfeld et al., 1989; McGorry & McConville, 1999).

Conguence between the explanatory model of client and clinician is not necessary for relapse prevention work to begin. Indeed, McGorry (1995) notes that adjusting to psychotic illness while maintaining identify and self-esteem usually occurs over several episodes. He thus warns against the overzealous challenging of denial of illness which may serve a protective function in adolescents recovering from an initial psychotic episode.

Case Study

A 26-year-old man was identified for relapse prevention work 12 months after the remission of a prolonged first episode of psychosis. This had been characterised by persecutory ideation concerning his family, formal thought disorder and some episodes of aggression. For the first 18 months of his treatment he had engaged poorly with services, and treatment and remission of symptoms were only secured following an involuntary admission and the commencement of depot neuroleptics.

Subsequently relapse prevention work was initiated. At initial interview it emerged that this young man disliked the concept of submitting to the control of mental health professionals but responded well to the opportunity to adopt the expert role in describing his experiences from his own perspectives. He stated that he had had unusual mental experiences but did not believe that the word "illness" or "psychosis" applied to them. Rather, he saw them as the combined effects of excessive alcohol, personal conflicts, guilt feelings and some spiritual phenomena.

Despite this he was able successfully to categorise his experiences into what he thought would be termed "well"/"not sure"/"unwell". He produced a highly individualised list of experiences that corresponded well with medical understanding of psychosis from which he was able to construct a relapse drill involving increasing support from family and friends, and, with the goal of preventing rehospitalisation, a temporary increase in medication.

Finally, a distinction has been made between "past insight" (awareness of past illness) and "present insight" (awareness of current illness), the former being more easily acquired than the latter (McGorry & McConville, 1999). The percentage of individuals with early psychosis who are unable to prospectively identify their early warning signs in the event of a relapse is unknown. Heinrichs, Cohen & Carpenter, (1985) found that 63% of their sample had insight into their deteriorating mental state on the day on which relapse was said to have begun by their treating physician. The figure may have been higher if the subjects had been investigated earlier in the relapse process. Indeed, Jørgensen's (1998) results suggest that prospective monitoring of early warning signs by patients themselves is as accurate in predicting relapse as is that done by health professionals.

In our clinical experience, however, there is a subgroup of people who, while able to retrospectively construct a relapse signature, have difficulty in prospectively identifying them or lose insight early in the relapse process. Factors such as comorbid learning difficulties and substance abuse may increase these difficulties. There is no easy solution to this problem. While families may be involved in the relapse drill in this group, we have employed prospective monitoring using the Early Signs Scale (Birchwood et al., 1989) in this population. This scale measures early warning signs within the four areas of anxiety/agitation, depression/withdrawal, disinhibition and incipient psychosis and has been found to have an acceptable sensitivity (74%) and specificity (79%) in predicting psychotic relapse (Jørensen, 1998). Completed fortnightly by the client and a family member, it has been used to help to teach the individual to discriminate the changed perceptual, cognitive or affective processes which constitute the relapse signature.

"Sealing over"

A concept related to, but separate from insight (Drayton, Birchwood & Trower, 1998) is that of recovery style. McGlashan, Levy & Carpenter, (1975) argue that there are two recovery styles in psychosis: "integration" and "sealing over". A recovery style characterised by "integration" is one in which the individual is aware of the continuity of their mental activity before, during and after the psychotic experience, assumes responsibility for their psychotic productions, is curious about the experience and has flexible ideas about recovery (McGlashan, Levy & Carpenter, 1975). On the other hand, an individual who "seals over", tends to isolate the psychotic experience, views it as alien and seeks to encapsulate it. He or she maintains an awareness of its negative aspects and therefore is therefore is disinclined to investigate the experience. Recovery by "integration" has been associated with improved prognosis in terms of relapse and social functioning relative to recovery by "sealing over" (McGlashan, 1987)

Chadwick, Birchwood & Trower, (1996) and Drayton, Birchwood & Trower, (1998) have argued that the process of adaptation to psychosis is medicated by the meanings and evaluations that the person attaches to their psychosis, and that, furthermore, "sealing over" is more common in those individuals with developmental histories characterised by insecure attachments to parental figures and who, therefore, have developed vulnerable personalities. For these people the examination of psychosis poses a major threat and sealing over becomes an adaptive strategy. Indeed, "sealing over" has been found to be associated with early experiences of poor parental care and current negative self-evaluations (Drayton, Birchwood & Trower, 1998) in people recovering from psychosis.

Individual's whose recovery style is that of "sealing over" may find the early warning signs approach, with its focus on examination of the illness within an individual's life context, anxiety provoking. Furthermore, for young people, the experience of psychosis may contain a host of meanings. For example, one 23-year-old woman, became increasingly anxious early into the process of developing a relapse signature and refused to continue with the process. This young woman's background was characterised by inconsistent care from a mother who, herself, suffered from an intermittent psychotic illness (bipolar affective disorder) and the early separation of her parents. Her attitude towards her parents was highly ambivalent and this was reflected in her similarly ambivalent approach to involvement with mental health services. At times she would seek contact and reassurance and at times withdraw and cancel appointments. Furthermore, it became clear that her illness was invested with meanings involving shame based on her experiences of her mother's behaviour when manic and on her fear of becoming like her. This resulted, for example, in the young woman refusing to take the same mood stabiliser as her mother.

McGlashan (1987) has argued that a goal of treatment should not be to alter a person's particular recovery style but rather to tailor the treatment programme to match or not conflict with it. Thus, in the case of this young woman the process of establishing a relapse signature was temporarily suspended and attention was paid to helping her establish a secure and trusting relationship with mental health services through working with her to establish vocational and social interests. Similarly, her preferences were respected and she was prescribed a mood stabliser other than that used by her mother. Relapse prevention work, undertaken in conjunction with her keyworker and a clinical psychologist focused on stress management and the challenging of her cognitions of low self-worth. The construction of a formal relapse signature was postponed to a future time, when, following the above interventions, she felt ready to face the task.

Lack of syndrome stability

As McGorry (1994, 1995) has argued cogently, there is evidence of a considerable lack of diagnostic clarity and stability early in the course of psychotic illness, with around 50% of patients with first-episode psychosis changing diagnostic category between their first and second hospitalisation, generally due to a genuine change in the pattern of psychopathology within illness episodes (Stanton & Joyce, 1993; McGorry, 1995). Furthermore, factors such as the presence of substance abuse, the individual's psychological reaction to the illness, the rate of onset of symptoms, and the age and developmental stage at which symptoms occur, differentially influence the clinical presentation at various times during the illness (McGorry, 1994, 1995; Birchwood, 1995). McGorry (1994) has argued that the clinical picture in functional psychosis may become clearer over time, although the findings on this matter are incomplete and difficult to interpret.

Thus, a similar instability in the clinical presentation of the early warning signs of psychotic relapse may be expected over the early course of psychotic illness, although this has not been subjected to formal study. This may pose significant problems in identifying the relapse signature and relapse drill as the following study illustrates.

Case Study

A 23-year-old woman was able to successfully construct a relapse signature after her first episode of psychosis which had been manifested by persecutory delusions, thought broadcasting, delusional memories and passivity phenomena. Her relapse signature involved the onset of irritability, liability of mood and disinhibition and proceeded through suspiciousness to the development of frank persecutory delusions accompanied by a mildly irritable mood. Her second episode of psychosis, however, involved a much clearer elevation in mood accompanied by mood congruent and incongruent delusions and was proceeded by symptoms of increasing euphoria with the early onset of racing thoughts and disinhibited behaviour. In reviewing her relapse signature, this young woman identified the importance of symptoms indicative of irritability or elevated mood which had been noted but not emphasised in the initial construction of the signature. Her case illustrates the unavoidable paradox inherent in this work: increasing clarity of the relapse signature, and therefore, potential increased control of the process of relapse, only emerges with the additional information gained through each psychotic relapse.

THE RELAPSE SIGNATURE PROMISES AND PITFALLS

McGorry (1995) has drawn attention to the relative dearth of psychoeducational interventions aimed at the sufferer of psychosis. Indeed, despite clear evidence that people with psychosis can, and do monitor their own illness (Breier & Strauss, 1983; McCandless-Glimcher et al., 1986; Kumar, Thara & Rajkamar, 1989) relatively little attention has been paid to helping them to refine methods to do so. The evidence reviewed early in this chapter indicates that early signs monitoring is feasible in a large proportion of individuals with psychosis. Furthermore, recent formal evaluative work points towards the usefulness of the relapse signature approach to relapse prevention.

Perry et al. (1999) recently reported on a randomised-controlled trial among 69 patients with bipolar disorder in which the experimental group received training in the identification of their individualised early warning signs of manic or depressive relapse and an action plan was then produced and rehearsed. The methods involved in identification of the relapse signature were much the same those detailed earlier in this chapter, including, for example, a card sort exercise. The experimenters found that, over an 18-month follow-up period, the event curves for time to first manic relapse differed significantly between the experimental and routine care control group. Specifically, the 25th centile time to first manic episode was 65 weeks in the experimental group and 17 weeks in the control. The number of manic episodes over the 18 months' period were also significantly lower in the experimental group but the treatment condition had no effect on time to depressive relapse or number of depressive relapses. There was, however, a significant difference in overall social functioning and employment favouring the group who had received the instruction in identification of relapse signature. In a similar study by another research group, an intervention involving psychoeducation, early signs monitoring and mood induction also resulted in a significant prolongation in time to major relapse relative to the control condition among a group of people with rapid cycling bipolar affective disorder (George & Birchwood, in preparation).

Despite the promise of this method of intervention, some reservations need to be expressed. Some of the difficulties of conducting this sort of work have already been considered. Furthermore, evaluation of the method among individuals with schizophrenia and related disorders and among those in the early phases of psychotic illness is currently in progress but not complete. Preliminary results indicate that individuals with recent onset psychosis who have been treated in a service delivery setting emphasising the early detection of impending psychotic relapse describe their early warning signs with greater clarity and use a wider range of coping mechanisms than do similar individuals with no such exposure (Davis et al., in submission-b).

Importantly also, as Birchwood has discussed in Chapter 2 of this volume, there is evidence that psychosocial interventions are only effective in preventing psychotic relapse for the period during which they are being actively delivered (Hogarty et al., 1991; Linszen et al., 1998). The relapse signature approach to relapse prevention provides a methodology that the client may employ throughout their illnesses to progressively increase their control over relapse without the need for intensive monitoring by mental health services. Assistance with ongoing monitoring may be provided by members of the client's social network and their primary care health resources. Future research may demonstrate, however, that, like other psychosocial interventions, its continued effectiveness depends on ongoing monitoring and reinforcement by the involved mental health practitioners.

However, even if the methodology is not suitable for all people with recent onset psychosis, for many it offers the promise of a substantial reduction in the total duration of untreated psychosis over the course of the illness. With this comes the hope of a reduction in the negative biological and psychological consequences of untreated psychosis, a state which is both harmful and demoralising to clients and frustrating to clinicians.

REFERENCES

Amardor, X.F. & Strauss, D.H. (1993). Poor insight in schizophrenia. *Psychiatric Quarterly*, **64**, 305–318.

Birchwood, M. (1995). Early intervention in psychotic relapse: cognitive approaches to detection and management. *Behaviour Change*, **12**, 2–19.

Birchwood, M. & Chadwick, P. (1997). The omnipotence of voices: testing the validity of a cognitive model. *Psychological Medicine*, **27**, 1345–1353.

Birchwood, M., Smith, J., Macmilllan, F., Hogg, B., Prasad, R., Harvey, C. & Bering, S. (1989). Predicting relapse in schizophrenia: the development and implementation of an early signs monitoring system using patients and families as observers. *Psychological Medicine*, **19**, 649–656.

Birchwood, M., Mason, R., Macmillan, F. & Healey, J. (1993). Depression, demoralisation and control over illness: a comparison of depressed and non-depressed patients with a chronic psychosis. *Psychological Medicine*, **23**, 387–395.

Breier, A. & Strauss, J.S. (1983). Self control in psychiatric disorders. *Archives of General Psychiatry*, **40**, 1141–1145.

Bustillo, J., Buchanan, R.W. & Carpenter, W.T. (1995). Prodromal symptoms vs early warning signs and clinical action in schizophrenia. *Schizophrenia Bulletin*, **21**, 553–559.

Carpenter, W.T., Hanlon, T.E., Summerfelt, A.T., Kirkpatrick, B.M., Levine, J. & Buchanan, R.W. (1990). Continuous versus targeted medication in schizophrenic outpatients. *American Journal of Psychiatry*, **147**, 1138–1148.

Chadwick, P., Birchwood, M. & Trower P. (1996). *Cognitive Therapy for Delusions, Voices and Paranoia*. Chichester: Wiley.

David, A.S. (1990). Insight and psychosis. *British Journal of Psychiatry*, **15**, 798–808.

Davis, E., Birchwood, M. & Chadwick, P. (in submission- a). The Attitude to Relapse Scale: the development and validation of a new scale measuring the perception of relapse among schizophrenics.

Davis, E., Birchwood, M. & Chadwick, P. (in submission-b). Attitude to relapse an ability to discriminate a prodrome: a controlled study of individuals engaged in an early signs service for schizophrenia.

Davis, J.M. & Casper, R. (1997). Anti-psychotic drugs: clinical pharmacology and therapeutic use. *Drugs*, **14**, 260–282.

Docherty, J.P., Van Kammen, D.P., Siris, S.G. & Marder, S.R. (1978) Stages of onset of schizophrenic psychosis. *American Journal of Psychiatry*, **135**, 420–426.

Drayton, M., Birchwood, M. & Trower, P. (1998). Early attachment experience and recovery from psychosis. *British Journal of Clinical Psychology*, **37**, 269–284.

Gaebel, W., Frick, U., Köpcke, W., Linden, M., Müller, P., Mülller-Spahn, T., Peitzcker, A. & Tegeler, J. (1993). Early neuroleptic intervention in schizophrenia: are prodromal symptoms valid predictors of relapse? *British Journal of Psychiatry*, **163** (Suppl. 21), 8–12.

George, S. & Birchwood, M. (in preparation). A cognitive behavioural approach to the treatment of manic depression.

Greenfeld, D., Strauss, JS., Bowers, M.B. & Mandelkern, M. (1989). Insight and interpretation of illness in recovery from psychosis. *Schizophrenia Bulletin*, **15**, 245–252.

Heinrichs, D.W., Cohen, B.P. & Carpenter, W.T. (1985). Early insight and the management of schizophrenic decompensation. *Journal of Nervous and Mental Disease*, **173**, 133–138.

Herz, M. & Melville, C. (1980). Relapse in schizophrenia. *American Journal of Psychiatry*, **137**, 801–812.

Hirsch, S.R. & Jolley, A.G. (1989). The dysphoric syndrome in schizophrenia and its implications for relapse. *British Journal of Psychiatry*, **155** (Suppl. 5), 46–50.

Hogarty, G.E., Anderson, C.M., Reiss, D.J., Kornblith, S.J., Greenwald, DP., Ulrich, R.F. & Carter, M. (1991). Family psychoeducation, social skills training and maintenance chemotherapy in the aftercare treatment of schizophrenia, II. Two-year effects of a controlled study on relapse and adjustment. *Archives of General Psychiatry*, **48**, 340–341.

Hogarty, G. E., Kornblith, S.J., Greenwald, D., DiBarry, A.L., Cooley, S., Ulrich, R.F., Carter, M. & Flesher, S. (1997). Three-year trials of Personal Therapy among schizophrenic patients living with or independent of family, I: description of study and effects on relapse rates. *American Journal of Psychiatry*, **154**, 1504–1513.

Johnstone, E.C., Crow, J.T., Johnston, A.L. & Macmillan, J.F. (1986). The Northwick Park study of first episodes of schizophrenia. I: Presentation of the illness and problems relating to admission. *British Journal of Psychiatry*, **148**, 115–120.

Jolley, A.G., Hirsch, S.R., McRink, A. & Manchanda, R. (1989). Trial of brief intermittent neuroleptic prophylaxis for selected schizophrenic outpatients: clinical outcome at one year. *British Medical Journal*, **298**, 985–990.

Jolley, A.G., Hirsch, S.R, Morrison, E., McRink, A. & Wilson, L. (1990). Trial of brief intermittent neuroleptic prophylaxis for selected schizophrenic outpatients: clinical and social outcome at two years. *British Medical Journal*, **301**, 837–842.

Jørgensen, P. (1998). Early signs of psychotic relapse in schizophrenia. *British Journal of Psychiatry*, **172**, 327–30.

Kumar, S., Thara, R. & Rajkamar, S. (1989). Coping with symptoms of relapse in schizophrenia. *European Archives of Psychiatric Neurological Science*, **239**, 213–215.

Lieberman, J., Jody, D., Geisler, S., Alvir, J., Loebel, A., Szymanski, S., Woerner, M. & Borenstein, M. (1993). Time course and biologic correlates of treatment response in first-episode schizophrenia. *Archives of General Psychiatry*, **50**, 369–376.

Linszen, D., Lenior, M. & De Haan, L., Dingemans, P. & Gersons, B. (1998). Early intervention, untreated psychosis and the course of early schizophrenia. *British Journal of Psychiatry*, **172** (Suppl.), 84–89.

Marder, S.R., Van Putten, T., Mintz, J., McKenzie, J., Lebell, M., Faltico, G. & May, R.P. (1984). Costs and benefits of two doses of fluphenazine. *Archives of General Psychiatry*, **41**, 1025–1029.

Marder, S.R., Van Putten, T., Mintz, J., McKenzie, J., Lebell, M., Faltico, G. & May, R.P. (1987). Low and conventional dose maintenance therapy with fluphenazine decanoate. *Archives of General Psychiatry*, **44**, 518–521.

Marder, S.R., Wirshing, W.C., Van Putten, T., Mintz, J., McKenzie, J., Johnston-Cronk, K., Lebell, M. & Liberman, R.P. (1994). Fluphenazine vs placebo supplementation for prodromal signs of relapse in schizophrenia. *Archives of General Psychiatry*, **51**, 280–287.

Mason, P., Harrison, G., Glazebrook, C., Medley, I., Dalkin, T. & Croudace, T. (1995). Characteristics of outcome in schizophrenia at 13 years. *British Journal of Psychiatry*, **167**, 596–603.

McCandless-Glimcher, L., McKnight, S., Hamera, E., Smith, B.L., Peterson, K. & Plumlee, A.A. (1986). Use of symptoms by schizophrenics to monitor and regulate their illness. *Hospital and Community Psychiatry*, **37**, 929–933.

McGlashan, T.H. (1987). Recovery style from mental illness and long-term outcome. *Journal of Nervous and Mental Disease*, **175**, 681–685.

McGlashan, T.H., Levy, S.T. & Carpenter, W.D. (1975). Integration and sealing over: clinically distinct recovery styles from schizophrenia. *Archives of General Psychiatry*, **32**, 1269–1272.

McGorry, P.D. (1994). The influence of illness duration on syndrome clarity and stability in functional psychosis: does the diagnosis emerge and stablilise with time? *Australian and New Zealand Journal of Psychiatry*, **28**, 607–619.

McGorry, P.D. (1995). Psychoeducation in first-episode psychosis: a therapeutic process. *Psychiatry*, **58**, 313–328.

McGorry, P.D. & McConville, S.B. (1999). Insight in psychosis: an elusive target. *Comprehensive Psychiatry*, **40**, 131–142.

Mueser, K.T., Bellack, A. & Blanchard, J. (1992). Comorbidity of schizophrenia and substance abuse: implications for treatment. *Journal of Consulting and Clinical Psychology*, **60**, 845–855.

Norman, R.J.G. & Malla, A.K. (1995). Prodromal symptoms of relapse in schizophrenia: a review. *Schizophrenia Bulletin*, **21**, 527–539.

Perry, A., Tarrier, N., Morris, R., McCarthy, E. & Limb, K. (1999). Randomised controlled trial of efficacy of teaching patients with bipolar disorder to identify early symptoms of relapse and obtain treatment. *British Medical Journal*, **318**, 149–153.

Plaistow, J. & Birchwood, M. (1996) *Back in the Saddle: A Guide to Relapse Prevention*. Unpublished Manual.

Robinson, D., Woerner, M., Alvir, J.M.J., Bilder, R., Goldman, R., Geisler, S., Koreen, A., Sheitman, B., Chakos, M., Mayerhoff, D. & Lieberman, J.A. (1999). Predictors of relapse following response from a first episode of schizophrenia or schizoaffective disorder. *Archives of General Psychiatry*, **56**, 241–247.

Rooke, O. & Birchwood, M. (1998). Loss, humiliation and entrapment as appraisals of schizophrenic illness: a prospective study of depressed and non-depressed patients. *British Journal of Clinical Psychology*, **37**, 259–268.

Shepherd, M., Watt, D., Falloon, I. & Smeeton, N. (1989). The natural history of schizophrenia: a five-year follow-up in a representative sample of schizophrenics. *Psychological Medicine,*. Monograph Supplement 15.

Stanton, M.W & Joyce, P.R. (1993). Stability of psychiatric diagnoses in New Zealand psychiatric hospitals. *Australian and New Zealand Journal of Psychiatry*, **27**, 2–8.

Subotnik, K.L. & Neuchterlein, K.H. (1998). Prodromal signs and symptoms of schizophrenic relapse. *Journal of Abnormal Psychology*, **97**, 405–412.

Tarrier, N., Barrowclough, C. & Bamrah, J.S. (1991). Prodromal signs of relapse in schizophrenia. *Social Psychiatry and Psychiatric Epidemiology*, **26**, 157–161.

Wiersma, D., Nienhuis, F.J., Slooff, C.J. & Giel, R. (1998). Natural course of schizophrenic disorders: a 15-year followup of a Dutch incidence cohort. *Schizophrenia Bulletin*, **24**(1), 75–85.

Chapter 11

THE EARLY PHASE OF PSYCHOSIS AND SCHIZOPHRENIA: A CRITICAL PERIOD FOR PATIENTS, FAMILIES AND THE PROFESSION

Don Linszen* and Max Birchwood [†]

Schizophrenia remains a frightening disorder of the mind of the patient and a burden for the family. The years of productivity of young people are interrupted with the typical onset of the first psychotic episode of schizophrenia in adolescence or early adulthood. In the phase of life where parents generally expect their children to become adult and independent, deterioration of functioning starts, even before the first psychotic episode (Jones et al., 1993; Hafner et al., 1995). Eighty per cent of people with first episode schizophrenia or related disorders relapse at least once within five years (Shepherd et al., 1989, Robinson et al., 1999). There is a decline in social contacts with the peer group (Levinson, 1986), especially with young men. They have an earlier age of onset than females (mean: 5 years, Angermeyer and Kühn, 1988). In this period the severity of schizophrenia will be established, i.e. in the early phase five years after the first psychotic episode (Bleuler, 1972; McGlashan, 1988). Moreover, in this transition phase the adjustment of the family to the first psychotic episode takes place (Birchwood, 1999). Recognition and intervention at the earliest possible stage of florid psychosis in schizophrenia and related disorders could contribute to earlier psychotic and negative symptom remission, delay of psychotic relapse and prevention of psychosocial deterioration (Wyatt, 1991; Birchwood & Macmillan, 1993; McGlashan, 1996). The early phase of psychosis and schizophrenia could thus be seen as a "critical period" with

*Adolescent Clinic, Amsterdam, The Netherlands. [†]Early Intervention Service, Birmingham.

Early Intervention in Psychosis.
Edited by M. Birchwood, D. Fowler & C. Jackson.
© 2000 John Wiley & Sons Ltd.

major implications for the prevention of disease and psychosocial deterioration (Birchwood, Todd & Jackson, 1998), as well for the patients and their families as for the profession. In this chapter the role of the families of adolescents and young adult patients with a first psychotic episode will be discussed taking their age and the early phase of the illness into account.

Two main concepts about/of schizophrenia have exerted their influence on the role of the family and the attitude towards the family until recently. In the first concept the family has been seen from the medical point of view: a good example is that the family is generating genetic risk factors for schizophrenia. The other point of view has always been represented by approaches integrating medical and psychosocial factors Both points of view will be discussed and their implications and applications in the past and present. Finally, an integration of both concepts and application in prevention programmes with families in the recognition and intervention of first-episode psychosis will be applied to the critical period.

THE FAMILY AND SCHIZOPHRENIA: THE PAST

Interest in the family of patients with schizophrenia has been fluctuating with differences in two basic concepts that can be traced back to the start of this century. Kraepelin (1897) unified a number of psychiatric conditions (hebephrenia, catatonia and paranoia) in one disease: "dementia praecox". The disease had its onset in adolescence and young adulthood and was initially thought to lead inevitably to intellectual deterioration, from which they inevitably failed to discover. Later Kraepelin recognised that a small group of hebephrenic and catatonic patients recovered fully. One should realise that Kraepelins emphasis was on negative symptoms, and not so much on psychotic episodes in actual terminology. The family played its role in the genetic field: genetic factors and metabolic changes by "autotoxins", independent from the family environment, were thought to cause this early dementia type. This disease concept of schizophrenia has been influential in the diagnostic research efforts of the last and current decade. The duration of untreated psychosis longer than one year has been found to predict more severe forms of schizophrenic illness, e.g. more psychotic relapses (Crow et al., 1986) and delay in symptom remission, representing the feature of deterioration (Loebel et al., 1992). Antipsychotic medication has been successfully applied in the acute and maintenance treatment of all forms of schizophrenia and related disorders Kane, 1989). Compliance to antipsychotic medication has been found the major predictor of a favourable outcome over a 5 year follow up period (Robinson et al., 1999). Kraepelin's views on the today still unknown aetiology of schizophrenia are reflected in the studies of molecular genetics of extended families, in looking for structural and functional brain (including neurochemical, neurophysiological and neuropsychological) abnormalities with modern technologies and in pharmacotherapeutical research. According to this concept the emotional reactions of the family will be the same -or even worse because of the young age of the patient- as those of any other family with a more or less genetically determined chronic disease: mourning, denial, despair and anger, being frightened because of the genetic loading and feeling burdened in the case of inadequate care (Hatfield, 1987).

Bleuler (1911) introduced the second concept with the term schizophrenia instead of dementia praecox. He noticed that the slow progression in a demented state was only true in a subset of the patients with the symptoms of dementia praecox. Also the age of onset was not always precocious. According to his view schizophrenia should be seen a group of disorders, differing in (also genetic) causes, clinical picture and outcome. With Jung he pointed out the psychological and social aspects, including family life factors, influencing the course of schizophrenia (Bleuler & Jung, 1908). His efforts can be seen as the basis for psychological and social theories about schizophrenia and by trying to integrate both the biological and the psychosocial views as a forerunner of the vulnerability/stress models (Zubin & Spring, 1977; Nuechterlein & Dawson, 1984). The role of the family in the second concept of schizophrenia has been much more complex and also a conflicting one, especially with young patients. The idea of a non-genetic ætiological role of the family in the development of schizophrenia and of the family climate acting as a stressor affecting the severity of the course of this frightening disorder alienated families from professionals and hindered in a useful cooperation.

THE PRE-EMPIRICAL PAST: THE FAMILY AS CAUSE OF SCHIZOPHRENIA

A non-genetic family theory was developed in the late 1940s and the 1950. Bateson et al. (1956) improvised on the theme of ambivalence in relationships, expanded the concept of the schizophrenogenic mother of Melanie Klein to a family level and developed the "double bind" theory. This theory hypothesised conflicting overt verbal and more abstract non-verbal communication patterns of parents towards their child. The child was not able to distinguish the conflicting message correctly and could not withdraw from the conflicting situation. The thought and communication disorders of adolescents and young adults with schizophrenia were thought to arise from this situation. Lidz and his colleagues (1957) used the term "marital schism" (overt conflicts between the parents) and "marital skew" (in which the disturbed functioning of one parent was compensated by distorted communication of the other) as the underlying condition of schizophrenia. Wynne et al. (1958) described "communication deviance", "pseudomutuality" and "pseudohostility" as the characteristically disordered communication patterns and emotional relation of parents of schizophrenic patients. One must realise that in those days the adaptational aspect of symptoms was in the centre of interest and that antipsychotic medication did not exist. Based on these theories many family therapies for schizophrenic patients were developed and applied to families with young first-episode patients (Lidz, 1973; Selvini et al., 1978; Haley, 1980).

The goal of the ætiologically oriented family therapy was to alter the described pathological family systems, thus improving the course of schizophrenia or even curing the disease. At the same time acute and maintenance antipsychotic medication appeared to be effective against psychotic signs and symptoms and as prevention against relapse. The ætiological oriented family therapists tended to see these medical interventions, such as the use of antipsychotic medication, as inflicting the "sick role" on the schizophrenic family member.

However, despite their attractiveness for many professionals, the results of these family therapy approaches turned out to be disappointing, mainly because of a lack of empirical evidence. Moreover, Terkelsen (1983) and Lefley (1992) have convincingly argued that families and patients experienced negative "side" effects from this type of family intervention. Relatives felt they were being made scapegoats for the cause of the illness and experienced therapy sessions as a burden.

Professionals who are in contact with families with young patients today should be aware of the need of the family, including the patient, for genuine support and empathy. Otherwise the families can feel that they are blamed for the disorder during the intervention. Other developments made this kind of family intervention redundant, especially the efficacy of antipsychotic acute and maintenance medication (Davis, 1975), the increased evidence for genetic factors in the aetiology of schizophrenia (Gottesman & Shields, 1972) and the results of an important WHO study (1975). In this study, with strictly defined symptoms and signs, schizophrenia was found to be present in 17 countries, ranging from highly developed countries to the least developed countries. Symptoms and signs appeared to be culture independent.

FAMILIES AND THE COURSE OF SCHIZOPHRENIA: THE EMPIRICAL PAST AND PRESENT

The interest for the families of patients with schizophrenia changed its focus again during the 1970s to the course, instead of the cause, of the disease. Another WHO study revealed heterogeneous course patterns: patients with schizophrenia from non-western countries appeared to have a better prognosis than patients from western countries (Sartorius et al., 1978). Other differences with the causal family model were the orientation on empirical research as a reaction to the lack of empirical data from earlier family theories and interventions and the use of antipsychotic medication in the expressed emotion (EE) based intervention studies. The original EE finding dated back to the 1950s (Brown, Carstairs & Topping, 1958), showed the same interest in ambivalent emotions as the family theorists from that time, and was replicated in 1972 (Brown, Birley & Wing, 1972). Patients with schizophrenia who returned from the hospital and who lived with relatives expressing themselves in a critical, hostile or emotionally over-involved way about the patient and his/her disease or behaviour in a standardised interview (high EE), experienced psychotic relapses more often than patients who lived on their own or with relatives who expressed themselves less or not emotionally (low EE). Since then numerous studies have supported the value of high EE in predicting substantially higher rates of psychotic relapses and thus the severity of schizophrenia (Kavanagh, 1992; Barrowclough & Tarrier, 1992). At the start the main reason for the addition of family intervention to antipsychotic medication was the incomplete protection of antipsychotic maintenance medication against psychotic relapse (Vaughn & Leff, 1976). Seventy per cent of the studies found a significant difference in relapse rate in high EE environments compared with low EE environments. Low EE is as valuable clinically as maintenance medication, as EE and medication each accounted for about a 30% of the relapse rate (Bebbington & Kuipers, 1995).

The classical interpretation of the EE finding has been that a high EE was an indicator of stressful family interactions. As stressful life events, high EE attitudes of relatives were thought to contribute to a high level of environmental stress, which then interacted with the biological vulnerability factors, and increased the likelihood of relapse, thus influencing the course and severity of schizophrenia.

Family intervention programmes, which were superimposed on maintenance antipsychotic drug treatment, were developed to change the critical, hostile or over-involved climate of the family of the patient with schizophrenia, thus reducing stress and the risk of a psychotic relapse. Four family intervention programmes, all tested against maintenance pharmacotherapy, and all with high EE families, succeeded in their goal of relapse reduction (Leff et al., 1982; Falloon et al., 1982; Hogarty et al., 1986; Tarrier et al., 1988). They reduced the level of negative family interaction (Falloon et al., 1985), high EE (Lam, 1991), in particular the high emotional involvement (Mari & Streiner, 1994). Most of the high EE and intervention studies used psychoeducational and behavioural models and studied older patients with relapsing, non-remitting and chronic outcomes of schizophrenia. Authors emphasised that EE as a predictor in the epidemiological sense could also be interpreted as an expression of burden on the family by a severe mental disease. The Jackson group in Melbourne examined the relation between EE and family burden. High levels of criticism corresponded with the burden felt by disease and patient characteristics (Jackson, Smith & McGorry, 1990).

Theories of ætiological family factors and of family stress factors affecting the severity of schizophrenia, both followed by family intervention after discharge from the hospital, resulted in a negative opinion about families of patients with schizophrenia. This 40-year old attribution by professional people and the lack of acknowledgement of their burden by the same professionals (Hatfield, 1983), the de-institutionalisation and outpatient treatment of schizophrenia (partly possible by the efficacy of antipsychotic medication), led to the establishment of associations of family members in several countries. Giving each other support, looking for information about the latest developments in schizophrenia research and for structured paid work or rehabilitation appeared to be important activities. These associations were advocates of seeing schizophrenia as a disease with an unknown ætiology and were rightly very sensitive to processes of blame and stigmatisation.

FIRST-EPISODE PSYCHOTIC PATIENTS AND EXPRESSED EMOTION

In mixed or in more chronic populations of patients with schizophrenia, high EE has been found to be a robust predictor; controlled clinical trials with high EE families revealed a significant reduction in relapse rates in the family intervention condition in contrast with the control condition (always including antipsychotic medication). In studies with patients with a first psychotic episode of schizophrenia or related disorder, the results of EE research have been more controversial. In some studies of first-episode patients EE was not found to be a predictor at 12 months follow-up (Barrelet et al., 1990; Stirling et al., 1991; Rund et al., 1995; Huguelet et al., 1995). In the Northwick Park study (the last placebo-controlled study with first-episode psychotic patients) EE turned out to be a significant but spurious predictor with duration of untreated psychosis and medication use being better predictors of relapse (Macmillan et al., 1986). Interesting findings of these non-replicating first-episode studies were the high occurrence of emotional over-involvement (EOI) compared with criticism and hostility expressed by the parents with a tendency of EOI to turn into criticism (Stirling et al., 1991). Jackson's team raised the interesting question of this finding being an appropriate reaction to the psychotic disorder (Gleeson et al., 1999). In their non-predicting study after 12 months EE was found to be predictive only after three year follow-up. EE was associated then with a group of first-episode patients that had become more relapsing or chronic patients in the critical period (Huguelet et al., 1995). They lost a third of their patients at follow-up, a finding that could be associated with a finding that low or no family social contacts predicted early relapse (Johnstone et al., 1990). Their other interesting finding was that high EE parents lived significantly more together with substance-using patients than low EE parents. Last, but not least, the Northwick Park team found in the last double-blind placebo-controlled antipsychotic medication study—with first-episode psychotic patients—a significant but marginal difference in psychotic relapse rate: 40% and 60% relapse in the active versus placebo medication group respectively (Johnstone et al., 1986). Untreated duration of psychosis more than a year appeared to be the better predictor of poor outcome.

In two other first-episode studies parental high EE had prognostic value and predicted psychotic relapse within a year. The group from Los Angeles interpreted their finding as underlining the importance of the vulnerability stress model (Nuechterlein & Dawson, 1984). Again they assumed an interaction between a biological (genetic and neuropsychological) vulnerability and environmental stressors (EE) in precipitating a psychotic relapse during the short-term course of first-episode schizophrenia. Alternatively, in a separate analysis the authors found that severity of illness could have elicited high EE, an early onset and living at home.

In a study in Amsterdam, high EE in families with young patients was found to be a predictor as well in a one-year family intervention trial. In this cohort the short-term course was not confounded by repeated admissions or by more than one year's duration of untreated psychosis. Compliance with antipsychotic medication was deemed high throughout the trial. The relapse rate was found low (13%). In patients with high EE families, cannabis abuse was the major relapse predictor (Linszen et al., 1997). However, in a larger sample of this cohort ($n=97$) the Amsterdam group found a relation between cannabis abuse, i.e. heavy abuse and psychotic relapse, with all cannabis abuse preceding the onset of the first psychotic symptoms (Gleeson et al., 1999) by at least one year (Linszen et al., 1994). As in the Melbourne group, the high EE of the parents of these young adolescent and young adult patients in the early phase of their disease could be considered as an acute emotional reaction (a state factor) to the crisis elicited by the recent onset episode disease and admission.

FIRST EPISODE PSYCHOTIC PATIENTS AND FAMILY INTERVENTION

The family intervention studies used a select sample of patients with different ages and in different phases of schizophrenia, namely those from families rated as high in expressed emotion (high EE) and with a mixed sample of first-episode and more chronic patients. Recently a new shift took place in the interest in first-episode schizophrenia and the family, this time with a preventive approach, since early recognition and intervention were thought to lead to a better outcome. In the Northwick Park study, a duration of untreated psychosis of more than a year had shown to be the main relapse predictor (Crow et al., 1986).

Only in three intervention trials have young patients with first psychotic episodes and their families been evaluated. One of these studies did not use duration of untreated psychosis as a predictor variable (Goldstein et al., 1978); another one described a long duration of untreated psychosis of nearly three years (Zhang et al., 1994), a period nearing the "critical period", thus excluding the early intervention aspect. In contrast, in the Amsterdam study by Linszen et al. (1996) the duration of untreated psychotic illness of the young patients (mean age 20.6) turned out to be short, compared with the Nottingham Park study (Crow et al., 1986). Seventy one of the patients appeared to have untreated psychotic symptoms between 0 and 6 months (74%), 14 between 7 and 12 months (14%) and 12 of the patients more than 12 months (12%). Duration of untreated psychotic illness as a risk factor, categorised in less and more than 12 months, appeared not to be predictive of psychotic relapse either. Moreover, in the first two studies EE was not reported (Goldstein et al., 1978; Zhang et al., 1994) and in the last study a full sample of high and low EE families was used (Linszen et al., 1996).

Goldstein and coworkers added a six-week supportive and stress-reducing family therapy to high- and low-dose antipsychotic depot medication, contrasted with individual sessions with the patient. After six months follow-up they found a favourable effect of the family intervention and high-dose depot medication. In the family sessions the acceptance of psychosis was an important issue, as was acquiring active control of stressors. The main weakness of the Goldstein study was the relatively short duration of six months. In the Chinese study family group therapy or individual family therapy, all with patients, was applied over 18 months in a flexible way and contrasted with a "standard care" control group. The experimental group had a significant lower readmission rate than the control group, a shorter hospital stay and a better overall level of functioning. A weakness were the ill-defined outcome criteria, i.e. hospitalisation. Education and stress reduction were the main ingredients of both family interventions with the aim of preventing chronicity of the patients and reducing the burden on the family (Zhang et al., 1994).

In all the empirical family intervention approaches, whether psychoeducational or behavioural, with first episode or with more chronic patients, the families were considered to be allies in the treatment and rehabilitation of patients with schizophrenia. The approaches gave support when relatives experienced burden and educated the family about the illness (i.e. the genetic role in schizophrenia). An attempt was made to avoid making scapegoats of the relatives of patients, but the question remained whether the therapists succeeded in their effort to avoid stress- and guilt induction. In Falloon's family behavioural therapy (1982) and in the Amsterdam study (Linszen et al., 1996), communication training and problem-solving skills followed psychoeducation. An unresolved issue regarding this family programme was how much of the efficacy was due to the provision of support and education and how much to the specific behavioural interventions. This question turned out to be relevant for the results of the Amsterdam controlled clinical trial. The experimental behavioural family intervention of that study (including two supportive and education sessions) did not influence the relapse rate when contrasted with the standard treatment condition. This result turned out to be the first failure of finding an effect of family intervention in the high EE condition. The finding was seen in the following perspective: the inpatient treatment plus the two family sessions and the continuity of care, provided such a "high" baseline that family intervention could not manage to show an additional increment in effectiveness. Also interesting was the slightly higher incidence of relapses in the low EE/standard + family treatment group.

Some additional remarks can be made when the results of our study are compared with the methods and findings of similar studies in the UK and the United States. The inpatient phase of the treatment programme continued for a relatively long period (three months), while in the United States insurance policies typically necessitate discharging the patients after two or three weeks. Compared with the United States, the inpatient treatment programme with both the patients and the families appeared to be close to optimal. Furthermore, an active "needs led" family-oriented treatment programme had already taken place during inpatient care before the start of the trial. This made the programme different from the cited EE-family intervention studies in which only incidental family treatment was undertaken during the inpatient phase. One can assume that the inpatient programme influenced the outpatient results for the entire sample. Although this is speculative, one may hypothesise that the inpatient programme with a few supportive and education sessions was all the help that the low-EE families needed. Cozolino et al. (1988) found that a brief psychoeducational module, along the lines developed by Anderson, Reiss and Hogarty, (1986), did produce a number of positive effects on family sense of support of the treatment team. The follow-up behavioural family intervention phase may have put pressure on the low-EE families to look for and produce clinical changes in the patient, thus increasing the relapse rate. Post hoc analysis revealed that the behavioural family intervention was implemented with significant difficulty in 60% of the low-EE families and 32% of the high-EE families. Besides the interference with the "grief process", there may have been other "adverse" labelling effects in what may be an essentially "good prognosis population". This is a criticism increasingly frequently levelled at EE interventions that may have some validity. There may be a danger of using EE as a criterion for family intervention, rather than a "needs led" family approach (Smith & Birchwood, 1990). In a further study of a smaller sample the Amsterdam group found that with 27% of the families remaining low in expressed emotion and 25% remaining high and with 40% moving in either direction, unstable expressed emotion was linked to relapse in this young sample (Nugter et al., 1997). Expressed emotion as measured by the Five Minutes Speech Sample (Magana et al., 1986) could then be seen as a characteristic of a process of adjustment to psychosis, perhaps at its zenith in this early critical phase (Birchwood, 1999). However, one should be cautious with this interpretation, since only two patients relapsed in the low-EE/family plus standard intervention contrasted with no relapses in the low-EE/standard treatment group. As mentioned earlier standard treatment patients received psychoeducational components regarding their illness, their prodromal signs, coping strategies, three months of post-hospital day treatment, assistance with employment, education and finances, a well-organised medication protocol and home visits when the patients appeared to be non-complying. Compliance with antipsychotic medication was deemed high throughout the study. This therapeutic package may have had an effect on the low relapse rate of the entire sample. Additional family intervention sessions could then not conceivably add anything to the standard treatment.

A crucial question was whether the favourable effect lasted after the end of the intensive 15-month intervention programme with this young population with a short duration of untreated psychosis. Therefore data were gathered from these patients, who were carefully transferred to other agencies and whose follow-up period varied from 17 to 55 months. Psychotic relapses and exacerbations could be rated for 63 patients during the follow-up period after the 15- month transmural intervention. The median survival time, the time at which 50% survives, turned out to be 19 months. Forty patients (63.5%) suffered from at least one psychotic relapse or exacerbation, despite the short duration of illness in the sample. The only way to prevent poor outcome is to continue medication and stress management for a period up to five years, which approaches the "critical period", as articulated by Birchwood, Todd & Jackson (1998). In a similar first episode study from the Hillside hospital, maintenance antipsychotic medication was found to diminish the relapse rate in more than 80% of the patients who suffered from at least one relapse within five years of recovery from a first psychotic episode of schizophrenia or schizo-affective disorder (Robinson et al., 1999).

THE CRITICAL PERIOD OF SCHIZOPHRENIA, THE PATIENT, THE FAMILY AND THE PROFESSIONAL: AN INTEGRATIVE EFFORT

Professionals should be aware that the first psychotic episode of schizophrenia or a related disorder of an adolescent or young adult patient can herald a "critical period" with a high risk of psychotic relapse or psychosocial decline (Schepherd, 1991; Robinson et al., 1999). Recognition and active intervention at the earliest possible stage of florid psychosis could contribute to earlier symptom remission, delay of psychotic relapse and prevention of suicide and psychosocial deterioration (Wyatt, 1991; Birchwood & Macmillan, 1993; McGlashan, 1996). Family members, most of them parents, should be approached as actively as their psychotic child, whose psychotic episode reveals itself in the period where other children, including in their own family, are in the process of becoming independent.

 The basic attitude of professionals should be to approach the parents of first-episode patients as allies in the fight against a potentially severe but treatable mental disease. After admission they can provide a protective shelter that can give the patient time to recover, grieve and integrate the psychotic experience. Professionals in the mental health sector can support the family in this task, but they should also be aware that every, even well-meant, activity could be considered as stigmatising.

Aetiological family oriented approaches have shown that families and patients experienced negative "side" effects from this type of family intervention. Relatives felt they were being made scapegoats or the cause of the disorder and experienced therapy sessions as a burden. Also the classical interpretation of the EE finding has been that a high EE was an indicator of stressful family interactions and that these, as stressful life events, increased the likelihood of relapse. Owing to the negative opinion about families of chronic patients with schizophrenia of some therapists, and to the lack of acknowledgement of their burden by the same professionals (Hatfield, 1983), the de-institutionalisation and outpatient treatment of schizophrenia led to the establishment of associations of family members in several countries. In the Amsterdam study the low-EE families of first psychotic episode patients evaluated behavioural therapy negatively, especially the training in communication skills. This development gives important clues for the needs of the family not only of patients with more chronic forms of schizophrenia, but also of patients with first episodes, since they are advocates of seeing schizophrenia as a disorder with an unknown aetiology. They should be seen as very sensitive for processes of blame and stigmatisation.

In first psychotic episode studies, Expressed Emotion has been found to be of no predictive value (with more over-involvement than criticism (Stirling et al., 1991), spurious (with duration of untreated psychosis as a better indicator: (Macmillan et al., 1986) as predictor related with cannabis abuse (Linszen et al., 1997) or as a relapse predictor over a three-year period (Huguelet et al., 1995). In the Amsterdam study an instable EE pattern for low EE and from high to low and from low to high, was related to relapse. Expressed emotion as measured by the Five Minutes Speech Sample (Magana et al., 1986) could then be seen as a characteristic of a process of adjustment to psychosis, perhaps at its zenith in this early critical phase (Birchwood, 1999). After the critical period, EE could become a robust and stable burden indicator.

In the Amsterdam family intervention, adolescents and young adult patients had a duration of untreated psychosis of less than half a year. Support, relief of burden, facilitating mourning and psychoeducation during inpatient treatment, followed by an individual educational and stress management treatment with a continued relationship with the treatment staff, appeared to be the effective intervention for a limited period. The effectiveness of the programme was reflected in the excellent drug compliance during the intervention.

This may not have been the case in the period after the intervention programme. One may presume that the favourable effect of the intervention programme would last after the intensive 15-month treatment programme. The results of the follow-up study were in sharp contrast with that expectation. The relapse findings during follow-up underline McGlashan's (1996) remark that interventions in schizophrenia are effective as long as they are active, as much towards the families as to the patients. After the intervention study all patients were referred to other mental health facilities, such as community mental health centres or rehabilitation centres. The favourable effects of the family intervention on relapse and a possible effect of the relatively short duration of untreated psychosis disappeared rapidly, underlining that early age of onset of schizophrenia is associated with a poor symptomatic and functional outcome (Häfner et al., 1995; Kessler et al., 1995). The only way to prevent relapse and psychosocial decline after the symptom remission and relapse delay after the first psychotic episode of schizophrenia seems to be continuation of medication compliance and case management with the active ingredients of disease management, medication management and stress management for a minimum period of five years, a period that approaches the critical period (Birchwood & Macmillan, 1993). All these professional intervention ingredients should be fine-tuned with the family.

The two-year results from the Hogarty study (1988) have shown a beneficial effect of the educational family intervention part. Therefore, a follow-up study of the patients and families of our sample is being carried out to look for effects of specific and non-specific family interventions in mixed high- and low-EE parent groups for a five-year intervention period. Follow-up studies can also resolve the issue of whether the standard treatment programme actually prevented relapse or merely delayed the natural course of schizophrenia..

Also, further research efforts are needed to evaluate the contribution of the non-specific (support, relief of burden, facilitating mourning) and specific components (psychoeducation and problem-solving skills) of family intervention programmes. Research on family burden (Hatfield, 1983; Jackson, Smith & McGorry, 1990) of first-episode psychotic patients should be extended.

Finally, family research on the coping skills of the family with the patient's disorder (for example, medication compliance) or the patient's drug abuse, on their emotional adjustment to the disorder and on their effort in supporting the psychological adjustment and rehabilitation of the patient, should be developed during the critical period. Low or non-family contacts are major indicators of relapse as well. With the support of the parents the chances of changing the risk of a chronic course and a better psychosocial outcome for a larger group of patients are high.

REFERENCES

Anderson, C.M., Reiss, D.J. & Hogarty, G.E. (1986). *Schizophrenia and the Family*. New York and London: Guilford Press.

Angermeyer, M. & Kühn, L. (1988) Gender differences in age of onset of schizophrenia. An overview. *European Archives of Psychiatry and Neurology Science*, **237**, 351–364.

APA (1987). *DSM-III-R: Diagnostic and Statistical Manual of Mental Disorders* (3rd edn, revised). Washington, DC: American Psychiatric Association.

Barrelet, L., Ferrero, F., Szigethy, L., Giddey, C. & Pellizer, G. (1990). Expressed emotion and first-admission schizophrenia; nine-month follow-up in a French cultural environment. *British Journal of Psychiatry*, **156**, 357–362.

Barrowclough, C. & Tarrier, N. (1992) *Families of Schizophrenic Patients. Cognitive Behavioral Intervention*. London: Chapman & Hall.

Bateson, G., Jackson, D.D, Haley, J. & Weakland, J.H. (1956) Toward a theory of schizophrenia. *Behavioral Science*, **1**, 251–264.

Bebbington, P.E. & Kuipers, E. (1995). Predicting relapse in schizophrenia: gender and expressed emotion. *International Journal of Mental Health*, **24**, 7–22.

Birchwood, M., Todd, P. & Jackson, C. (1998). Early intervention in psychosis: the critical period hypothesis. *British Journal of Psychiatry*, **172**, (Suppl. 33), 53–59.

Birchwood, M. & Macmillan, J.F. (1993). Early intervention in schizophrenia. *Australian and New Zealand Journal of Psychiatry*, **27**, 374–378.

Birchwood, M. (1999) Psychological and social treatments: course and outcome. In J.M. Kane & H Hafner (Eds), *Current Opinion in Psychiatry*, vol. 12, no 1, *Schizophrenia* (pp. 61–66).

Bleuler, E. *Dementia Praecox or the Group of Schizophrenias*. (1911); translated by Zinkin, J. 1950, New York: International Universities Press.

Bleuler, E. & Jung, C.G. (1908). Komplexe und Krankheitsursachen beim Demetia Praecox. *Zeitbild von Nervenheilkunde und Psychiatrie*, **31**, 220–227

Bleuler, M. (1972). *Die schizophrenen Geistesst"rungen im lichte langjähriger Kranken- und Familien-geschichten.* Stuttgart: Thieme Verlag.

Brown, G.W., Carstairs, G.M. & Topping, G.C. (1958). The post hospital adjustment of chronic mental patients. *Lancet,* **ii**, 685–689.

Brown, G.W., Birley, J.L.T. & Wing, J.K. (1972) Influence of family life on the course of schizophrenic disorders: a replication. *British Journal of Psychiatry,* **121**, 241–258.

Cozolino, L.J., Goldstein, M.J., Nuechterlein, K.H., West, K.L. & Snijder K.S. (1988) The impact of education about schizophrenia on relatives varying in expressed emotion. Schizophr. Bulletin, **14**: 675–687.

Crow, T.J., Macmillan, J.F., Johnson, A.L. & Johnson, E.C. (1986). A randomised clinical trial of prophylactic neuroleptic treatment.

Davis, J.M. (1975). Overview: maintenance therapy in psychiatry: I. Schizophrenia. *American Journal of Psychiatry,* **132**, 1237–1245.

Davis, J.M., Kane, J.M., Marder, S.R., et al. (1993) Dose response of prophylactic antipsychotics. *Journal of Clinical Psychiatry,* **54**, 24–30.

Falloon, I.R.H., Boyd, J., McGill, C.W. Razani, J., Moss, H.B. & Gilderman, A.M. (1982). Family management in the prevention of exacerbations of schizophrenia—a controlled study. *New England Journal of Medicine,* **306**, 1437–1440.

Falloon, I.R.H., Boyd, J.L., McGill, C.W., Williamson, M., Razani, J., Moss, H.B. & Gilderman, A.M. (1985). Family management in the prevention of morbidity of schizophrenia: clinical outcome of a two-year longitudinal study. *Archives of General Psychiatry,* **42**, 887–896.

Gleeson, J., Jackson, H.J., Stavely, H. & Burnett, P. (1999). Family intervention in early psychosis. In P.D. McGorry & H.J. Jackson (Eds.). *The Recognition and Management of Early Psychosis: A Preventive Approach* (pp. 376–406). Cambridge, Cambridge University Press.

Goldstein, M.J., Eliot, H., Evans, J.R., May, P.R.A. & Steinberg, M.R. (1978). Drug and family therapy in the aftercare of acute schizophrenics. *Archives of General Psychiatry,* **35**, 1169–1177.

Gottesman, L.I. & Shields, J. (1972). *Schizophrenia and Genetics: A Twin Study Vantage Point.* New York, Academic Press.

Häfner, H. & Maurer, K. (1995). Epidemiology of positive and negative symptoms in schizophrenia. *Contemporary Issues in Psychiatry,* **55**, 314–335.

Häfner, H., Maurer, K., Löffler, W., Bustamante, S., van der Heiden, W., Riecher-Rössler, A. & Nowotny, B. (1995). Onset and early course of schizophrenia. In H. Häfner & W.F. Gattaz (Eds), *The Search for the Causes of Schizophrenia* (Vol. III, pp. 43–66). Berlin: Springer-Verlag.

Haley, J. (1980). *Leaving home: The Therapy of Disturbed Young People.* New York: McGraw-Hill.

Hatfield, A.B. What families want of family therapists. In W.R. McFarlane (Ed.), *Family Therapy in schizophrenia.* (pp. 41–65). New York and London, Guilford Press.

Hatfield, A.B. Spaniol, L. & Zipple A.M. (1987). Expressed emotion: a family perspective. Schiz. Bull., **13**, (2), 221–226.

Hogarty, G.E., Anderson, C.M., Reiss, D.J., Kornblith, S.J., Greenwald, D.P., Javna, D. & Madonia, M.J. (1986). Family psychoeducation, social skills training and chemotherapy in the aftercare treatment of schizophrenia. *Archives of General Psychiatry,* **43**, 633–642.

Hogarty, G.E., MacEvoy, J.P., Munetz, M., DiBarry, A.L., Bartone, P., Cather, R., Cooley, S.J., Ulrich, R.F., Carter, M. & Madonia, M.J. (1988). Dose of fluphenazine, familial expressed emotion, and outcome in schizophrenia, results of a two-year controlled study. *Archives of General Psychiatry,* **45**, 797–805.

Huguelet, Ph., Favre, S., Binyet, S., Gonzalez, Ch. & Zabala, I. (1995). The use of the Expressed Emotion Index as a predictor of outcome in first admitted schizophrenic patients in a French-speaking area of Switzerland. *Acta Psychiatrica Scandinavica*, **92**, 447–452.

Jackson, H.J, Smith, N. and McGorry, P. (1990). Relationship between expressed emotion and family burden in psychotic disorders: An exploratory study. *Acta Psychiatrica Scandinavica*, **82**, 243–249.

Johnstone, E.C., Crow, T.J., Johnson, A.L. et al. (1986). The Northwich Park Study of first episode of schizophrenia. I: Presentation of the illness and problems relating to admission. *British Journal of Psychiatry*, **148**, 115–120.

Johnstone, E.C., Macmillan, J.F., Frith, C.D. et al.(1990). Further investigation of the predictors of outcome following first schizophrenic episodes. *British Journal of Psychiatry*, **157**, 182–189.

Jones, P.B., Bebbington, P., Foerster, A., Lewis, S.W., Murray, R.M., Russell, A., Sham, P.C., Tone, B.K. & Wilkins, S. (1993). Premorbid social underachievement in schizophrenia: results from the Camberwell Collaborative Psychosis Study. *British Journal of Psychiatry*, **162**, 65–71, 1993.

Kane, J.M. (1989). The current status of neuroleptics. *Journal of Clinical Psychiatry*, **50**, 322–328.

Kavanagh, D.J. (1992). Recent developments in expressed emotion and schizophrenia. *British Journal of Psychiatry*, **160**, 601–620.

Kessler, R.C., Foster, C.L., Saunders, W.B. & Stang, P.E. (1995). Social consequences of psychiatric disorders. I: Educational attainment. *American Journal of Psychiatry*, **152**, 1026–1031.

Kraepelin, E. (1897). *Dementia Praecox and Paraphrenia*. Translated by R.M. Barclay, 1919, Edinburgh: E. & S. Livingstone, Reprinted in 1971 by Krieger Publishing Co., Huntington, New York.

Lam, D. (1991). Psychosocial family intervention in schizophrenia: a review of empirical studies. *Psychological Medicine*, **21**, 423–441.

Leff, J., Kuipers, L., Berkowitz, R., Eberlein-Vries, R. & Sturgeon, D. (1982). A controlled trial of social intervention in the families of schizophrenic patients. *British Journal of Psychiatry*, **141**, 121–134.

Lefley, H.P. (1992). Expressed emotion: conceptual, clinical, and social policy issues. *Hospital and Community Psychiatry*, **43**, 591–598.

Levinson, D.J. (1986) A conception of adult development. *American Psychologist*, **41**, 3–13.

Lidz, T., Cornelissen, A., Fleck, S. & Terry, D. (1957). The intrafamilial environment of schizophrenic patients: II Marital schism and marital skew. *American Journal of Psychiatry*, **114**, 241–248.

Lidz, T. (1973). *The Origin and Treatment of Schizophrenic Disorders*. New York: Basic Books.

Linszen, D.H., Dingemans, P.M. & Lenior, M.E. Cannabis abuse and the course of recent-onset schizophrenic disorders. *Archives of General Psychiatry*, **51**, 273–279, 1994.

Linszen, D.H., Dingemans, P.M., Lenior, M.E., Nugter, M.A., Scholte, W.F. & Van der Does, A.J.W. (1994) Different relapse criteria in schizophrenic disorders. *Psychiatry Research*, **54** (3), 273–281.

Linszen, D.H., Dingemans, P.M., Scholte, W.F., Van der Does, J.W., Nugter, M.A. Lenior, M.E. & Goldstein, M.J. (1996), Treatment, expressed emotion and relapse in recent onset schizophrenic disorders. *Psychological Medicine*, **26**, 333–342.

Linszen, D.H., Dingemans, P.M.A.J, Nugter, M.A., Van der Does, A.J.W., Scholte, W.F. & Lenior, M.E. (1997). Patient attributes and expressed emotion (EE) as risk factors for psychotic relapse. *Schizophrenia Bulletin*, **23**, 119–130.

Loebel, A.D., Lieberman, J.A., Alvir, J.M. Mayerhoff, D. J., Geister, S. H. & Szymanski, R. (1992). Duration of psychosis and outcome in first episode schizophrenia. *American Journal of Psychiatry*, **149**, 1183–1188.

Mari, de J. & Streiner, D.L. (1994). An overview of family interventions and relapse on schizophrenia: Meta-analysis of research findings. *Psychological Medicine*, **24**, 565–578.

Macmillan, J.F., Crow, T.J., Johnson, A.L. & Johnstone, E.C. (1986). The Northwick Park Study of first episodes of schizophrenia. IV: Expressed emotion and relapse. *British Journal of Psychiatry*, **148**, 133–143.

Magana, A.B., Goldstein, M.J., Karno, M., Miklowitz, D.J., Jenkins, J. & Falloon, J.R.(1986). A brief method for assessing Expressed Emotion in relatives of psychiatric patients. *Psychiatry Research*, **17**, 203–212.

McGlashan, T. (1988). A selective review of North American longterm follow-up studies of schizophrenia. *Schizophrenia Bulletin*, **259**, 515–542.

McGlashan, T.H. (1996). Early detection and intervention in schizophrenia. *Schizophrenia Bulletin*, **22**, 197–200.

Nuechterlein, K.H. & Dawson, M.E. (1984). A heuristic vulnerability/stress model of schizophrenic episodes. *Schizophrenia Bulletin*, **10**, 300–312.

Nugter, A., Dingemans, P., Van der Does J.W., Linszen, D., Gersons, B. (1997). Family treatment, expressed emotion, and relapse in recent onset schizophrenia. *Psychiatry Research*, **72**, 23–31.

Robinson, D., Woerner, M., Alvir, J.A., Bilder, R., Goldman, R., Geisler, S. *et al.* (1999). Predictors of relapse following response from a first psychotic episode of schizophrenia or schizoaffective disorder. *Archives of General Psychiatry*, **56**, 241–247.

Rund, B.R., Aeie, M., Borchgrevink, T.S. & Fjell, A. (1995). Expressed emotion, communication deviance and schizophrenia. *Psychopathology*, **28**, 220–228.

Sartorius, N., Jablensky, A., Shapiro, R. (1978). Cross-cultural differences in the short-term prognosis of schizophrenic psychoses. *Schizophrenia Bulletin*, **4**, 102–113.

Schepherd, G. (1991). Rehabilitation and the cure of the long-term mentally ill.*Current Opinion in Psychiatry*, **42**, 288–294.

Selvini, M., Boscolo, L., Cecchin, E. & Prata, G. (1978). *Paradox and Counterparadox*. New York: Jason Aronson.

Smith, J. Birchwood, M. (1990). Relatives and patients as partners in the management of schizophrenia. The development of a service model. *Brit. J. of Psychiatry*, **56**, 654–660

Stirling, J., Tantam, D., Thomas, P., Newby D., Montague, L., Ring, N. & Rowe, S. (1991). Expressed emotion and early onset schizophrenia: a one year follow-up. *Psychological Medicine*, **21**, 675–685.

Tarrier,N., Barrowclough, C., Vaughn, C., Bamrah, J.S., Porceddu, K., Watts, S. & Freeman, H. (1988). The community management of schizophrenia. A controlled trial of behavioral intervention with families to reduce relapse. *British Journal of Psychiatry*, **153**, 532–542.

Terkelsen, K.G. (1983). Schizophrenia and the family. II: Adverse effects of family therapy. *Family Process*, **22**, 191–200.

Vaughn, C.E. & Leff, J.P. (1976). The influence of family and social factors on the course of psychiatric illness, a comparison of schizophrenic and depressed neurotic patients. *British Journal of Psychiatry*, **129**, 125–137.

WHO (1975). *Schizophrenia. An International Follow-up Study*. Chichester: Wiley.

Wyatt, R.J. (1991). Neuroleptics and the natural course of schizophrenia. *Schizophrenia Bulletin*, **17**, 325–351.

Wynne, L., Ryckoff, I., Day, J. & Hirsch, S. (1958). Pseudomutuality in the family relations of schizophrenics. *Psychiatry*, **21**, 205–230.

Zhang, M., Wang, M., Li, J. & Philips, M.R. (1994). Randomised-control trial of family intervention for 78 first-episode male schizophrenic patients: an 18-month study in Suzhou Jiangsu. *British Journal of Psychiatry*, **165**, 96–102.

Zubin, J. and Spring, B. (1997). Vulnerability: a new view of schizophrenia. *Journal of Abnormal Psychology,* **86**, 103–126.

Part III

IMPLEMENTATION

Chapter 12

MODELS OF EARLY INTERVENTION IN PSYCHOSIS: AN ANALYSIS OF SERVICE APPROACHES

Jane Edwards,* Patrick D. McGorry* and Kerryn Pennell*

> *Bringing treatment more rapidly to a person who has become psychotic is in itself enough to justify early detection efforts*
> (MCGLASHAN & JOHANNESSEN, 1996, P. 217).

Early intervention strategies in first-episode psychosis include one or more of the following aims: reduce the duration of untreated psychosis; provide comprehensive expert treatment of the first episode of psychosis; reduce the duration of active psychosis in the first episode and beyond; and maximise recovery, community involvement, and quality of life (McGorry, Edwards & Pennell, 1999; McGorry, 1998a). A more radical subset of the "early intervention movement" has proposed that intervention could be possible before the first episode of psychosis (Yung & McGorry, 1997). While the momentum behind the notion of early intervention in first-episode psychosis is growing, it is striking how difficult it can be to apply the rapidly developing expertise in the detection and treatment of first-episode psychosis in the "real world". Impediments include mind set, money, morale, lack of specific skills, ill defined focus, inappropriate service organisation, age barriers, and poor primary care systems (McGorry & Edwards, 1997). In this chapter a number of models of early intervention, which are currently being applied in various countries around the world,

---

*North Western Health and University of Melbourne, Australia

Early Intervention in Psychosis.
Edited by M. Birchwood, D. Fowler & C. Jackson.
© 2000 John Wiley & Sons Ltd.

are described with a view to enhancing the development of early psychosis service initiatives.

It has been argued that the evidence suggests, rather than demonstrates, that early biological and psychosocial intervention can improve the natural history of schizophrenic disorders (McGlashan & Johannessen, 1996). McGlashan has indicated that this evidence is not strong enough for extensive investment in early detection programmes (or for declarations that ignoring early detection is unethical) and cautions against letting "enthusiasm outstrip the data" (McGlashan, 1996). The serious and relevant research that is warranted with representative samples and proper controls will hopefully be facilitated by the advancement of "real world" models that are described in this chapter. To this end, it will be necessary for clinicians to become political in health care and to augment scientific evidence with the experience of consumers and families. Enthusiasm may actually generate and shape the data.

EVALUATION AND QUALITY CONTROL

The efficacy and effectiveness, including cost-effectiveness, of specific phase-related treatments needs extensive and rigorous research (Kane, 1997; McGorry - 1998a). Evaluation of outcome and quality control in service provision are important in early psychosis not only for their intrinsic value but also as tools to influence policy-makers and other clinicians. Controversy exists over whether treatment effects in clinical research settings equate with the efficacy of similar procedures used in naturalistic settings (cf. restructure of the NIMH, see Psychiatric Research Report, 1997). Effectiveness of interventions needs to be determined in controlled studies and naturalistic studies. Ideally, effectiveness is measured in several ways, including patient (psychopathology, social functioning, and quality of life) and wider community and service system (cost analyses, service utilisation) indices.

The development of clinical practice guidelines can help direct resources and smooth out inappropriate variation in clinical practice (Grimshaw & Hutchinson, 1993). Clinical guidelines also play a role in providing parameters by which clinicians working in a new field can monitor and adjust practice. The Early Psychosis Prevention and Intervention Centre (EPPIC) "Standards of Quality" (EPPIC Information Package, 1998), achieved by consensual clinical committees, were designed to achieve a streamlined and structured approach to the implementation of clinical practice. The Australian Clinical Guidelines for Early Psychosis have been developed through the National Early Psychosis Project (1998). The New Zealand Early Intervention Interest Group have drafted a consensus statement regarding early psychosis services with the purpose of influencing national policy and purchasing decisions and regional developments—encouraging the right people to do the right thing in the right place at the right time (Codyre, 1997). The TIPS Project (see below) has developed treatment guidelines for the purpose of articulating the intervention component of their research. The newly formed International Early Psychosis Association will develop an international consensus statement on early psychosis. The adoption of clinical guidelines is another matter (Rush, 1993): implementation requires a determined "task force" management approach with an active and ongoing education program accompanied by routine outcome measurement (Andrews, 1998); monitoring necessitates regular clinical audit and quality assurance activities (see Tobin et al., 1998).

With regard to an early psychosis service, evaluation should focus on first, how well the program is being delivered, i.e. *process* evaluation and second, whether the program is achieving its specified outcomes or effects, i.e. *impact* and *outcome* evaluation. The evaluation model should be realistic and achievable and is dependent on a number of issues including resources, program design, and the constraints of naturalistic settings (see Thornicroft & Tansella, 1996). McGlashan (1996) provides an overview of issues to consider in outcome research in this field.

MODELS OF EARLY INTERVENTION

The programmatic engineering of early detection and intervention is a relatively new endeavour. During the early to mid 1980s groups in Melbourne and Berne were specialising in first-episode inpatients (see below), a Los Angeles group were focusing on first-episode patients within an outpatient clinical research setting (see below), a Nordic multicentre investigation of psychodynamic psychotherapy for individuals with first-episode schizophrenia (NIPS project; Alanen et al., 1994) was underway, and a public health initiative to detect and treat psychosis in the prodromal phase of onset was initiated (Falloon, 1992; Falloon et al., 1996). However, the mid 1990s has witnessed a "boom" in the development of early psychosis service initiatives.

In some settings, where historical and/or local political factors have been favourable, it has been possible to attempt reform of the service system (e.g., EPPIC; Early Psychosis Service, Birmingham). Elsewhere features commonly found in most service systems have been built upon in creating an early intervention strategy (e.g., FEPP, Avro, see below; National Early Psychosis Project). The coincidence of the epidemiological emergence of psychotic disorder and the developmental phase of adolescence provides the rationale for such a strategy (McGorry, 1996). It has been possible to create an early psychosis focus through enhanced service endeavours (see

Australian National Early Psychosis Project, New Zealand Early Psychosis Interest Group) such as detection and assessment services, staff training programs, high-risk clinics, or recent-onset family interventions. Other models have been possible through research funding which has acted as a catalyst to restructure the service system and enhance clinical expertise (e.g. the Parachute project; the TIPS project).

Twenty-six approaches to early intervention in first-episode psychotic disorders, which are currently in operation in Australia, New Zealand, Western Europe, and North America are described below and summarised in Table 12.1. These programmes are relatively new—published programme descriptions and preliminary evaluation data are limited and constrain the ability to evaluate service models, at this stage. The models covered are not exhaustive and the present authors are aware of a number of other substantial projects (e.g. the Early Intervention Service, Wellington; Department of Child and Adolescent Psychiatry, University of Heidelberg; Clinic for Child and Adolescent Psychiatry, Olgahospital Stuttgart)—not included due to time constraints only. The line between first-episode studies and service delivery models is not clear, and there is certainly much early intervention research currently being undertaken that is not represented here (e.g. the Hillside First Episode Project; University of Edinburgh high-risk project; the *Socrates* trial, Lewis et al., 1996). The services included in this chapter tend to be somewhat advanced in terms of their development, include a specified treatment component, and/or research and evaluation are integral to the service model.

Australasia

Australia and New Zealand have an active approach to early intervention which includes networks/interest groups, attempts to influence health policy, and strong and diverse service initiatives. Interest has been fuelled by national (September 1994) and international (June 1996) early psychosis conferences held in Melbourne; a second national conference focusing on service developments occurred in Hobart in September 1998 at which more than 50 papers were presented.

Early Psychosis Prevention and Intervention Centre (EPPIC), Melbourne, Australia

The Melbourne early psychosis programme has undergone significant evolution over a 14-year period—the most recent descriptions of EPPIC service components and operational details are contained in Edwards and McGorry (1998) and the biannual EPPIC Information Package (February, 1998). The Youth Access Team (YAT; incorporating EPACT; Yung, Phillips &

Drew, 1999), a mobile assessment and community treatment team, is the first point of contact with EPPIC. YAT is a 24-hour seven-days-per-week service which provides assessment for first presentations and, if required, intensive home-based treatment. The Personal Assessment and Crisis Evaluation Clinic (PACE) was established to identify and treat individuals who are thought to be at imminent risk of developing a psychotic disorder (Yung et al., 1996a, 1996b). Research components include examining characteristics of the PACE group for predictive purposes (Yung 1998a, 1998b) and evaluating the effectiveness of a combined psychological therapy/medication intervention in reducing pre-psychotic symptomatology and delaying or preventing the onset of psychosis.

Two geographical teams provide outpatient case management (OCM) and medical treatment for the individuals with first-episode psychosis (Edwards, Cocks & Bott, 1999). Adaptation to the illness and prevention of secondary morbidity (Jackson et al., see Chapter 9 in this volume) are incorporated into the OCM role. The focus of the 16-bed inpatient service is symptom reduction and containment—the average length of a first admission is 18 days. Low doses of neuroleptics are used during the acute phase and disturbed behaviour is managed by intensive nursing, benzodiazepines and lithium as "neuroleptic-sparing" agents, and minimal seclusion (Power et al., 1998). The group programme provides acute and recovery groups (Albiston, Francey & Harrigan, 1998; Francey, 1999) across four "streams": vocation, creative expression, recreational, and personal development. The needs of families for crisis support and practical education about psychosis are addressed through multi-family groups and individual family sessions, supported by specialist family workers (EPPIC, 1997; Gleeson et al., 1998). Other clinical sub-programs cater to accommodation needs, target prolonged recovery (Edwards et al., 1998), and focus on suicide prevention (McGorry, Henry, & Power, 1998; Power, 1999).

Clinical staff number the equivalent of 60 full-time positions (EFT); an additional 30 EFT work in research and education. Programme management is supported by clinical subcommittees which seed ideas and drive new initiatives. Weekly professional development sessions are organised in four cycles: research and evaluation, clinical audit, theory and issues. Additionally, treating teams present at weekly cases conferences rotating through four phases—pre-psychotic, acute, recovery and prolonged recovery.

Each subprogramme undertakes process and impact evaluation; overall outcome is assessed through the formal follow-up of patients. A naturalistic effectiveness study with multi-dimensional outcome measures was undertaken to evaluate the EPPIC programme on 12-month outcome, in contrast to a previous model of care (McGorry et al., 1996). Results suggested that EPPIC clients experienced a significantly better outcome than their counterparts in

Table 12.1   Current models of early intervention

	Commenced	Contact	Focus	Age
AUSTRALASIA				
Early Psychosis Prevention and Intervention Centre (EPPIC), Melbourne	1992 (inpatient unit since 1984)	e-mail: eppic@vicnet.net.au website: http://www.eppic.org.au	Service delivery to individuals with first-episode psychosis in defined catchment area for 18 months and prodrome clinic	15–30
Statewide Services, Victoria	1995	as above	Service development within Victoria	Determined by each service
Psychological Assistance Service (PAS), Hunter Valley, New South Wales	1997	fax: +61 49 297959	Prodrome clinic	14–30
First Episode Psychosis Program (FEPP), Western Australia	1995	avro@iinet.net.au	Service delivery to individuals with first-episode psychosis in defined catchment area for 2 years	16–30
National Early Psychosis Project (NEPP)	1996	e-mail: eppic@vicnet.net.au website: http://ariel.unimelb.edu.au/~nepp	National network	N/A
Totara House, Christchurch, New Zealand	1996	e-mail: Totara@hsl.co.nz	Outpatient service for 2 years for individuals living in Christchurch area	18–30 (flexibility <18)
New Zealand Early Psychosis Interest Group	1996	e-mail: CODYRED@whl.co.nz	National network	N/A
EUROPE				
Early Treatment and Identification of Psychosis (TIPS) project, Norway and Denmark	1997	email: tklarsen@online.no	Reduce DUP in individuals with schizophrenia spectrum and affective disorder with incongruent delusions/hallucinations	18–65
"The Parachute Project", Sweden	1996	fax : +46 8 429 3090 @ Unit for Psychosis Research	Does reducing DUP improve outcome? Needs-adapted treatment research project for non-organic, non-drug-related psychosis	18–45

Service catchment area	New cases per year	Estimated standing caseload	Evaluation	Funding for clinical programme/ network	Emphasis in summary
800,000 (208,000 in 16–30 age range)	200	340	Process; impact; 1 and 2 year outcome for sub-samples	Recurrent	Inpatient, outpatient, prodrome
3.5 million (state of Victoria)	N/A	N/A	Process; 6 and 12 month outcome for pilot projects	Recurrent	Clinical expertise and enhanced service models
500,000 (120,000 in 16–30 age range)	TBD	TBD	Outcome (pre, post and 12 month follow-up using diagnostic, psychosocial, and cognitive indices)	Recurrent	Prodrome
90,000	30	32	Process, community awareness, satisfaction surveys	Annual	Outpatient
N/A	N/A	N/A	Monitoring	2 years	Enhanced service models
350,000	70	Funded for 75 (seeking funding for 120)	Outcome 6-monthly	Recurrent	Outpatient
N/A	N/A	N/A	–	–	Policy
370,000 Rogaland 200,000 Oslo 100,000 Roskilde	100	N/A	Outcome at 3 months, 1, 2 and 5 years; intervention group compared with 2 non-intervention groups in other areas	Intervention = 2 years	Prodrome and outpatient
1,200,000 (19 clinics; 3 provided new cases for 12 months only)	200	Final cohort = 250+	Outcome at 1, 3 and 5 years; historical and prospective comparison groups	Intervention= 2 years	Outpatient

Table 12.1 Current models of early intervention (*continued*)

	Commenced	Contact	Focus	Age
OPUS, Denmark	1998	fax: 4535313953 e-mail: merete.nordentoft@ dadlnet.dk	Reduce DUP, randomised optimal treatment (outpatient) trial for individuals with non-affective first-episode psychosis in two cities for 2 years	18–45
Berne First Episode Psychosis Program, Berne, Switzerland	1989	fax: +41 31 93094 04 e-mail: merlo@puk.unibe.ch website: http: //www.ubeclu.unib e.ch/puk/cp/CP.html	Inpatient unit (D1 ward), day hospital, aftercare family treatment	15–40
Early Intervention Service (EIS), Birmingham, UK	1995	e-mail: m.j.birchwood.20@ bham.ac.uk	Service delivery for individuals with first-episode psychosis in a defined catchment area for a 3 years' policy formulation at regional level	17–30
Initiative to Reduce the Impact of Schizophrenia (IRIS), UK	1996	e-mail: m.j.birchwood.20@ bham.ac.uk website: http: //dialspace.dial.p ipex.com/david-iris		N/A
Early Recognition and Early Intervention Centre for Psychotic Crisis (FETZ), Cologne	1998	e-mail: martin.hambrecht@ medizin.uni-koeln.de	Prodrome clinic	18+ (Younger in cooperation with child service)
Adolescent Clinic, Netherlands	1997	e-mail: J.R.vandeFliert@AMC. UVA.NL	Psychosocial intervention study for individuals with first or second episode of non-affective psychosis (who have >35 hours contact with parents per week) for 3 years	16–28
NORTH AMERICA Development Processes in Schizophrenic Disorders, Los Angeles	1980	fax: 310 206 4310 e-mail: KNuechterlein@ MEDNET.ucla.edu	Outpatient service for individuals with non- affective psychoses <2 years in duration for a 3 years	18–45
Program for Assessment and Early Schizophrenia (PACES), Pittsburgh	1989	e-mail: Keshavanms@msx.upmc .edu website: http: //brains2.wpic.pit t.edu	Service delivery to individuals with first episode psychosis in a defined catchment for a 5 years	14–45

Service catchment area	New cases per year	Estimated standing caseload	Evaluation	Funding for clinical programme/ network	Emphasis in summary
560,000 Copenhagen (C) 500,000 Århus (A)	140-C 100-A	400	Outcome at 3 months, 1, 2 and 3 years	Intervention= 2 years	Outpatient (input commences during inpatient phase)
350,000	30–40	12–14 beds 3–5 day-hospital places	Process, outcome	Recurrent	Inpatient
300,000	120	150	Outcome at 1, 2 and 3 years	Recurrent	Outpatient
N/A	N/A	N/A	–	–	Policy
1 million (city of Cologne)	120	150	Monthly assessment for 2 years	Recurrent	Prodrome
3 million (north-holland and northern part of south-holland; 600,000 16–20 age range)	100 (150–200 referrals)	150	5 year follow-up	Recurrent	Inpatient & outpatient
4 million	10–20	40–60	Repeated assessments for 1 year post outpatient stabilisation	NIMH grants (renewed 1993)	Outpatient
1 million (greater Pittsburg area)	70–100	100	Initial evaluation and follow-up for up to 4 years	Recurrent & NIMH grants	Inpatient, outpatient

Table 12.1 Current models of early intervention (*continued*)

	Commenced	Contact	Focus	Age
Prevention through Risk Identification, Management, and Education (PRIME), New Haven, CT	1997	e-mail: thomas.mcglashan@yale.edu	Prodrome clinic	14–45
Recognition and Prevention of Psychological Problems (RAPP clinic), New York, NY	1997	e-mail: cornblat@lij.edu	Prodrome clinic	14–28
Early Psychosis Program, Nova Scotia, Canada	1995	fax: 920464 6057 e-mail: nshp.dzwhiteh@gov.ns.ca	Assessment and outpatient treatment for new cases of psychosis for province residents and resource for 4 neighbouring provinces	12–54
Early Psychosis Treatment & Prevention Program, Calgary, Canada	1997	e-mail: jmadding@acs.ucalgary.ca	Outpatient service[a] to individuals with non-affective first-episode psychosis in a defined catchment for a 3 years and prodrome clinic	16–45
Psychotic Disorders Team (PDT), Hamilton, Ontario, Canada	1990	Fax: team coordinator 905 521 2628	Outpatient service to individuals with first episode psychosis	16–70
Prevention & Early Intervention Program for Psychoses (PEPP), London, Ontario, Canada	1996	e-mail: akmalla@julian.uwo.ca	Service delivery to individuals with non-affective first-episode psychosis in a defined catchment area for a 2 year period	16–50
First Episode Psychosis Program, Toronto, Canada	1992	e-mail: aco@clarke-inst.on.ca	Service delivery to individuals with non-affective first episode psychosis for unspecified period	18–45
INTERNATIONAL International Early Psychosis Association	1997	fax: 613 9342 2941 e-mail: iepa@vicnet.net.au website: www.iepa.org.au	International network	N/A
Optimal Treatment Project for Schizophrenic Disorders (OTP)	1994	e-mail: 100130.3310@ compuserve.com	Schizophrenia within 10 years of onset for 4–5 years	15–60

Note. Diagnoses refer to DSM-IV. TBD=to be determined.
[a] Continuity of treating psychiatrist for inpatient admissions available to patients at Foothills Hospital.
[b] Catchment areas: Auckland, Wellington (New Zealand); Warrnambool (Australia); Tokyo (Japan); Los Angeles (USA); Ottawa and Montreal, (Canada); Bonn, Frankfurt on Oder (Germany); Trondheim (Norway); Gothenburg, Svenlunga, Lysekil (Sweden); Como, San Daniele, Trieste, Fabriano, Arezzo, Perugia, Benevento, Salerno, L'Aquila, Rome (Italy); Athens (Greece); Valentia (Spain); Anarka (Turkey); Budapest (Hungary); Bratislava (Slovakia)

Service catchment area	New cases per year	Estimated standing caseload	Evaluation	Funding for clinical programme/ network	Emphasis in summary
4 million (CT)	tbd	tbd	Outcome, cross-sectional and longitudinal	Proportional to recruitment	Prodrome
3.26 million (borough of Queens & Nassau County; 453,385 aged 14–28)	50	50	Protocol in progress	Insurance & self-payments on sliding scale	Prodrome
950,000	90	90 (50=active; 40=consultation)	Outcome – 3, 6 12 and 24 month follow-up	Recurrent	Outpatient
750,000	80	Expected=180 individuals and 120 families	Impact outcome – 3 and 6 months, 1, 2, and 3 years	Recurrent	Outpatient, prodrome
120,000	50–60	80 active 75–100 alumni	Process and impact, 2-year outcome	Recurrent	Outpatient
400,000	50	100	1- and 2-year Outcome	Recurrent	Inpatient, outpatient
4 million (primarily Metropolitan Toronto area—no catchment area restrictions)	200	155	–	Recurrent	Inpatient, outpatient
N/A	N/A	N/A	–	Multiple sources	Network
28 centres across 14 countries[b]	N/A	2 cohorts of 1,000 cases; 50–100 from each centre	3 monthly assessment of clinical, social, carer and economic benefits	Multiple sources	Outpatient

non-EPPIC services with regard to overall quality of life, including social and role functioning. The level of post-traumatic stress, previously associated with hospitalisation, was reduced and the experience of psychosis was reported as less traumatic. The average length of hospital stay and the mean dose of neuroleptics had both decreased, though recovery had not been compromised. Increased community costs were more than covered by the reduction in inpatient costs (Mihalopoulos, Carter & McGorry, 1999). Current research focuses on suicide prevention, prolonged recovery, low-dose antipsychotic medication, treatment delay, pre-psychotic samples, and comorbid cannabis use. Service evaluation is assisted by the employment of an evaluation officer—protocols in progress include examination of a new EPPIC group with concurrent comparison cohorts and longer term follow-up of the individuals described in McGorry et al. (1996) and Power et al. (1998). There are constraints on evaluating programme effectiveness due to current funding agreements. However, opportunities to undertake a ran-domised-controlled trial through a partnership with a local adult area mental health service are being actively pursued.

Statewide Services, Victoria

A subprogramme of EPPIC, Statewide Services, has developed a model of professional training, development and consultation that aims to ensure that all mental health agencies in the state of Victoria, Australia, can have access to clinical skills, expertise and knowledge in the field of early psychosis. The team focuses on providing assistance to other mental health teams through a range of specific services that include: secondary and tertiary consultation, professional education and training, resource development, community education, and the facilitation and development of Early Psychosis Projects. These projects make effective use of low staffing levels in the Statewide Services by providing a concentrated and intensive exposure over six months to a discrete region. Statewide Services work in collaboration with local services to develop models of practice and protocols of care that are responsive to local needs and mesh with the regional service's organisation and direction. The effectiveness of the model is being evaluated in a metropolitan area mental health service (the Central East and Northern Early Psychosis Projects) using process and clinical outcome data and including economic indices (Haines et al., 1997).

Psychological Assistance Service (PAS), Hunter Valley, New South Wales, Australia

PAS identifies young people at risk of developing a psychotic disorder, provides case management to those defined as high risk, assesses clients who have experienced a first episode of psychosis, and advises case managers regarding treatment. Assessment includes diagnostic interview, self-reports, informant interview, neuropsychological soft signs, and neuropsychological functioning. Within the Hunter Valley a senior nurse specialises in early psychosis—this person provides ongoing education and skills development for staff, coordinates a recovery group, and audits the relevant clinical files. This service model grew out of a pilot undertaken during 1995 to 1997 which adopted a staff education approach to first-episode psychosis.

First Episode Psychosis Program (FEPP), Avro Community Health Centre, Western Australia.

FEPP operates as a specialist service provided within an adult mental health service. Dedicated clinical staff number 2.5 EFT; medical staff and after hours care are drawn upon from the other Avro services. The programme has four modules: a biopsychosocial *assessment* is undertaken; a keyworker as allocated to provide *support*, including post-traumatic stress debriefing, home visits, goal setting, therapy and community linkages; *treatment* is provided within the person's home if possible, a low-dose medication policy is negotiated, and the keyworker is involved in the management plan if inpatient admission is required; and *education* takes place at the client/family level and within the broader community—a comprehensive information folder is given to the patient and the family, videos are made available and support groups provide education for individuals and families. A day programme specifically for first-episode clients is offered in a local hall with participants encouraged to be involved in the programme selection, identification of topics for guest speakers, and outings; attendance can continue while a person is in hospital. Each aspect of the programme has an objective and defined strategies which provide guidelines to staff; all support and education programme are evaluated. A system enabling early identification of individuals experiencing a first-episode psychosis is in place at the local psychiatric hospitals enabling Avro to become quickly involved. Education which aims to increase community awareness of the importance of early intervention is ongoing with programme staff providing presentations to universities, counsellors, general practitioners, mental health staff, emergency services and the media.

National Early Psychosis Project (NEPP), Australia

NEPP is a collaboration between the Commonwealth, State, and Territory Governments of Australia to promote a national model of best practice in early intervention in psychosis as part of the National Mental Health

Strategy (Pennell et al., 1997). The project has three foci: (a) service and policy development including the provision of tertiary consultation, ongoing support, advice, information, and access to expertise; (b) professional education and training which involves provision and distribution of a range of professional development resources and activities facilitated by project coordinators; and (c) provision of information and promotion of best practice policies. The role of the eight project coordinators, based in each state and territory, has been to progress the project in conjunction with government departments, mental health professionals, consumers and carers and other key stakeholders. Data to assess and monitor the activities of the project has been collected via interviews with all key players, participant observation at key meetings, and regular communication between the project manager and the evaluators (Joyce & Hurworth, 1998). The project has resulted in a high level of activity across all states (see *Early Psychosis News*, numbers 5–8; http://ariel.unimelb.edu.au/~nepp), with an emphasis on development and training activities. In each of the five most populated states there are at least three early psychosis projects in operation. For example, in New South Wales, Sydney-based services have developed early intervention models—the Acute Adolescent Unit, Redbank House, Westmead; Brookvale Early Intervention Centre, Northern Beaches area; the Young Peoples Program, Parramatta; and the Early Psychosis Outreach Community Health (EPOCH), Darlinghurst; Program for Early Intervention and Prevention of Disability (PEIPOD), St Vincent's Mental Health Services; the Blacktown Early Assessment Team (BEAT), Blacktown City Mental Health Service; the Richmond Fellowship Young People's Program, outer western suburbs; while rural areas have also been active with the Hunter Valley (see below) and the Young People and early Psychosis Intervention Programme (YPPI), Gosford, being well advanced in terms of early psychosis initiatives.

Totara House, Christchurch, New Zealand.

Totara House offers outpatient services to individuals experiencing first-episode psychosis including intensive case management and individual sessions with members of the multi-disciplinary team. An extensive group programme focuses on problematic drug and alcohol use, illness management, gender issues, recreation and creativity, relapse prevention, and anxiety management. Family interventions include weekly support groups and individual contact. Medication management aims to treat individuals with the lowest possible dose and atypical neuroleptics are most frequently used. The team comprises eight staff and there is access to a Maori health worker. Difficulties have been experienced in encouraging referrals beyond acute psychiatric sources (Campbell, 1997), indicating a need for more intensive community education.

New Zealand National Early Intervention Interest Group

This group has developed a document to guide service funders about the clinical and organisational steps needed to provide specialist early psychosis programmes. A consensus has been developed concerning the need for service structures to maximise service access, comprehensive assessment, optimal treatments with clearly specified outcomes, and adequate resourcing. The five-year aim is for all patients developing a first episode of psychosis to have ready access to expert early identification and treatment of their illness. This to be achieved through an active programme of lobbying for funding, training forums, education of primary practitioners and the general public, regular sharing of information on service developments (via newsletters, a national database, and meetings) and fostering of research. Funding has been secured for five dedicated early psychosis services in New Zealand to date, with sizeable projects being undertaken in both Wellington and Auckland.

Europe

As with Australia and New Zealand, early psychosis initiatives are widespread in Europe with considerable activity evident in the Scandinavian countries and interest increasing in the Netherlands and German-speaking countries. Early psychosis conferences have been held in Stavanger (April, 1995), Amsterdam (November, 1996), and Stratford-upon-Avon (June, 1997).

Early Treatment and Identification of Psychosis (TIPS), Norway and Denmark

TIPS is a prospective longitudinal five-year study designed to investigate whether early identification and optimal treatment of first-episode psychosis leads to better outcomes. Research support and collaboration occurs via the University of Oslo and Yale University. First-episode patients at three different sites are being compared: one test site (early detection) in Rogaland County (Norway; Johannessen, Bloch Thorsen & Larsen, in press, provides details of treatment context) and control sites in Ullevål sector (Norway) and Roskilde (Denmark). Information on an historical control group, treated in Rogaland, will also be examined. The test programme includes (a) an extensive public education programme informing the public about early signs of psychosis, (b) educating teachers, youth and general practitioners, and (c) clinical early detection teams whose primary responsibility is the early detection of individuals with untreated first-episode psychosis. The treatment protocol, provided at all sites over a two-year period, includes: weekly supportive psychotherapy (trained therapist) with active outreach; a standard low-dose medication regimen (defined algorithm starting with olanzapine, then respiridone and finally clozapine); and family work (individual family sessions, family workshop, and bi-weekly family sessions) focusing on problem-solving and psychoeducation, supervised by Professor William McFarlane (Maine, USA). Evaluation occurs at baseline, three months, and one, two and five years. Assessment includes diagnosis, premorbid functioning, duration of untreated psychosis, level of symptoms, social interaction quality of life and global functioning, and neuropsychological assessment. Preliminary data (J.O. Johannesen, personal communication, 6 March, 1998) suggests that DUP has been significantly reduced in Rogaland ($n=26$; DUP=20 weeks) compared with the historical controls ($n=43$; DUP=141 weeks).

The Parachute Project, Sweden

The Parachute Project is a two-year research project involving 19 psychiatric clinics collecting data on their first-episode psychosis patients (Cullberg & Levander, 1997) which commenced following a pilot period of investigation. Participating clinics aim to fulfil the following six therapeutic and care principles: (a) early intervention—specific treatment begins immediately a first-episode patient has been identified; (b) crisis and psychotherapeutic approach—each patient is treated as being in an acute crisis situation and, therefore, while acknowledging the biological aspects of psychosis, the possible environmental stress factors and the stressful nature of psychosis are also addressed; (c) family approach—the family is invited to weekly "family meetings" in the early stages of a family member's illness, becoming less frequent as recovery proceeds, which aim to assess ongoing stressors, provide support and information, and promote constructive relationships; (d) continuity and easy accessibility—change of treatment team is avoided as far as possible so that knowledge of a patient's history, abilities, and specific problems is retained allowing optimal chance for constructive help if the patient relapses; (e) lowest effective neuroleptic medication—immediate neuroleptic medication is avoided if the clinical situation allows (i.e. in individuals with a diagnosis of schizophreniform and brief reactive psychosis where the distress is not too high with daily home visits undertaken for monitoring and support) and benzodiazepines are used for anxiety symptoms; (f) flexible, home-based treatment—if supervised accommodation is needed, a special more personal unit and mobile team is available in several clinics.

The research programme includes a naturalistic long-term follow-up study designed to differentiate between clinical and personality subgroups with different background factors, treatment needs, and prognosis. A large set of baseline diagnostic tools are used including symptom check lists, neuropsychological tests, projective tests, family climate scales, MRI or CT scan, EEG, and records from the referring clinic. A comparison will be undertaken with "ordinary care" using a group of patients from the same sectors who had their first episode of psychosis three years earlier, and a prospective control group from an adjacent geographical area. These cases will be compared with project cases in terms of diagnosis, consumption of care and prescription of neuroleptic medication. The collection of new cases was completed in January 1998 (note that most of the participating clinics continue the work after finishing the project). The number of individuals included in the study is approximately 300, with a drop-out rate of 29%. Between 40 and 60% of patients are prescribed antipsychotic medication and the mean dose is equivalent to 2–3 mg haloperidol. Mean GAF values at baseline are 32 and at one year follow-up are 62. These results are preliminary (J. Cullberg, personal communications, 27 February and 12 March, 1998) and information on the comparison groups is not, as yet, available.

Early identification and treatment of young psychotic patients (OPUS), Denmark.

The Ministry for Health, the Ministry for Social Affairs, and the Danish Medical Research Council have funded a study in Copenhagen and Århus to examine whether DUP can be shortened by intensified community collaboration and public education and whether early detection leads to better outcomes in individual experiencing first-episode psychosis. A quasi-experimental design is being used whereby these two cities are divided into (a) areas where detection will be improved (via education of general practioners, social services, and teachers in high schools) and (b) areas where usual practice will continue. In addition, outpatients in both detection areas are being randomised to treatment as usual or integrated care with a psychosis team to evaluate whether the latter intervention improves the clinical and social course of the disorder. The "Optimal Treatment Package" (not part of Falloon's project, see below) includes assertive case management (continuity in care, flexibility in frequency of contact, home visits, and outreach), individual family sessions (based on McFarlane's manual) and psychoeducative multi-family groups, medication, and social skills training (based on Liberman's manual) including symptom and medication management. When an individual requires inpatient admission the team plays a consultative role. For inpatients in Copenhagen a third possibility is included in the randomisation[1]—admission to a special unit (U7) for young patients with first-episode psychosis at Sct. Hans Hospital, 30 km out of Copenhagen.

---

[1] Two different conditions are used in Copenhagen. The first is for outpatients who are about to leave the hospital: standard treatment versus treatment with the psychosis team. The second (Danish National Schizophrenia Project, DNS) is for inpatients aged 18–35: standard treatment versus treatment with the psychosis team versus treatment in U7. For more information about DNS and U7 contact Søren Bredkjær on e-mail: <Soeren.Bredkjaer@syhh.hosp.dk>.

Treatment at U7 comprises 6–8 month inpatient stay with weekly supportive/dynamic psychotherapy, psychoeducative multi-family groups, low-dose medication regimen and milieu therapy. To date 150 patients have been recruited (M. Nordentoft, personal communication, 27 August, 1998). Eighteen clinical staff, four researchers and a project leader are employed in the outpatient component of the project.

Berne First Episode Psychosis Program, Berne, Switzerland

This service focuses on early diagnosis, treatment, and rehabilitation of first-admission psychotic patients provided, for the most part, within an inpatient setting (average length of stay is 60 days). The goals for inpatient treatment of the first-episode patient include promoting social competence, autonomy, self-esteem, socialisation and early rehabilitation, with the overall aim being to improve the patient's subjective and objective quality of life (Merlo & Hofer, in press). Psychotic disorganisation is assisted by smoothly and gradually restructuring the biological, psychological and social domains of functioning. An integrated pharmacological and psychotherapeutic approach is utilised, with the psychosocial therapy aimed at providing the capacity to reconnect with the interpersonal world in an autonomous manner (Merlo, in press). Treatment includes individual, family, group, milieu, occupational, and music therapy as well as physiotherapy and sociotherapy. Group dynamics are regularly assessed and careful consideration is given to the amount of stimulation provided. Pharmacological intervention aims at a minimal effective dose of neuroleptics (i.e. 2–4 mg fluphenazine or respiridone) and, if negative symptoms or extrapyramidal symptoms occur, early use of clozapine (thus avoiding ECT). Family therapy (which also includes significant others if indicated, e.g. employer, teacher) is initiated from the beginning of hospitalisation and provided during aftercare. The unit is staffed by 2.5 medical doctors, 10 nurses, and three allied health professionals. A comprehensive clinical and scientific diagnosis is applied with EEG, MRI, neuropsychological examination, computerised cognitive testing, and regular psychopathological evaluation. Preliminary data suggest that patients from non-specialised psychiatric wards are treated with significantly higher doses of medication and experience longer readmissions (Merlo & Hofer, in press). A retrospective two-year follow-up showed three groups of patients on acute wards to have a mean relapse rate of 50% compared to 27% for the Early Psychosis Program participants (M.C.G. Merlo, personal communication, 6 April 1998).

Early Psychosis Service (EIS), Birmingham, UK

EIS focuses on young people in the early stages of psychosis and considered to be at high risk of early relapse and disability. Originally commencing at the Archer Centre in 1990, a psychosocial programme based within a large state psychiatric hospital, the programme focused on younger people, including many with more established psychosis. Since 1995, EIS has developed into a dedicated service for young people experiencing first-episode psychosis; providing vocational, cognitive and psychosocial interventions, embedded within a broader assertive outreach programme (Birchwood, 1997; Jackson & Farmer, in press). The service is now located on a housing estate which is very accessible for clients. The aims of the service concern (a) early identification, (b) promotion of early recovery, (c) prevention of residual primary and secondary symptoms and (d) prevention of relapse. The service operates in an inner-city area with a known high morbidity of psychosis, social deprivation, and a wide ethnic mix. It is part of the Northern Birmingham National Health Service Mental Health Trust which includes Psychiatric Emergency/Home Treatment Teams, Assertive Outreach, and Continuing Needs Services. EIS draws clients from Home Treatment Teams and Primary Care Liaison Services and has two core components—the Assertive Outreach Team and the Residential/Respite Unit. The former comprises 10 case managers (nurses), with maximum case loads of 15 individuals. The treatment protocol includes: low-dose neuroleptic regimes; cognitive therapy for delusions and hallucinations; and specific psychosocial interventions aimed at recovery and perceived control over the illness provided via specialist discipline input. An intake team screens and assesses new referrals. Each client is assigned a keyworker who is responsible for the coordination of care. Interventions are managed through five clinical subprogrammes: vocational and pre-vocational training; cognitive therapy; recovery; social recovery; and family intervention. Subprogramme staff meet on a weekly basis for supervision and training purposes, which also allows a forum for discussion of difficult cases, monitoring the standard of care, and resource development. Emphasis is placed on identifying early warning signs of relapse. The Residential/Respite Unit is a small community-based unit for up to eight individuals requiring intensive input due to prolonged recovery or who cannot be managed within the community (i.e. high suicide risk, major interpersonal problems). Individuals requiring acute care are admitted to the general adult psychiatric facility and visited daily by the case manager. Pathways to care and DUP are monitored and recovery is assessed (e.g. symptoms, quality of life, depression, relapse, suicidal thinking) at intake, and at one, two and three years. Early indications are that EIS has reduced DUP by up to 50% and analysis of outcome data (collected since January 1997) is underway (C. Jackson, personal communication, 4 March 1998). EIS contributes to service-wide training and regional postgraduate programmes.

Initiative to Reduce the Impact of Schizophrenia (IRIS), UK

IRIS has been developed by the West Midlands Early Psychosis Group with the aim of pursuing positive outcomes for young people with psychosis, their families and carers through supporting and developing initiatives (Macmillan & Shiers, 1997). This policy group has drafted standards of care which aim to achieve: early detection and initiation of therapy; low-dose neuroleptics and use of benzodiazapines during the acute phase; cognitive therapy to promote recovery from psychosis and trauma; facilitated access to training/employment; family support; relapse prevention; and use of home treatment where possible.

Early Recognition and Intervention for Psychotic Disorders (FETZ), Cologne, Germany

Based on a solid foundation of longitudinal research (see Klosterkötter et al., 1997a; Klosterkötter et al., 1997b), FETZ aims to recognise and intervene in prodromal states of psychosis. Individuals are included on the basis of symptoms, family history and neurobiological abnormalities (e.g. CPT, evoked potentials). Referrals are made through a variety of sources and a public education campaign is underway. The focus is on a multimodal assessment including psychopathology, neurophysiology, neuropsychology, and family history. Participants will be randomly assigned to treatment (combination of pharmacological and psychosocial therapy) or a control group. The clinical component of FETZ is to be managed by three part-time staff in an outpatient department of a university hospital.

Adolescent Clinic, Amsterdam Medical Clinic (AMC), Netherlands

Within this clinical service a three-year intervention study is underway, informed by the results on a previous intervention study (see Linszen et al., 1998), which compares (a) specialised intervention for first- and second-episode non-affective psychosis to (b) specialised intervention plus monthly family peer support groups led by a social worker and (c) specialised intervention during the inpatient and day hospital phase and referred back to a mental health service near the patients home for the outpatient phase (community care and case management). The specialised intervention involves: continuity of care from inpatient (6–8 weeks), day hospital (6–8 weeks), to outpatient treatment (33 months); family education (psychoeducation, mourning and acceptance, problem-solving and practical assistance) which commences during the inpatient stay; and individual therapy with a focus on relapse prevention through psychoeducation, medication monitoring and compliance; relapse prodrome recognition; and stress management. Staff in the "non-specialised" services receive instruction on the specialised method of treatment, with a focus on relapse prevention through psychoeducation, medication monitoring and compliance, relapse prodrome recognition, and stress management. The instruction operates as more of a "hand over" than actual training. The aim of this condition is to evaluate the effect of discontinuity of care of relapse rates and to teach other mental health professionals about the approach adopted at AMC. Evaluation focuses on symptoms, relapse and suicide rates, negative symptoms, and the psychosocial functioning of the individual and family over the three-year period of the intervention. There are 12 places available in each of the inpatient and day care units and 130 outpatients; two other beds are available on a closed unit if required. Most admissions are inpatient, but it is possible to commence treatment in the day clinic. The service operates on a waiting list system, which tends to result in less acute patients being admitted, and operates on a Monday to Friday basis with clients returning home or housed in the acute ward on the weekends. The programme is quite large with more than 25 clinical staff, six research staff and four support staff.

North America

As one would expect, North American centres have contributed significantly to the momentum in early intervention with ideas, data, and clinical programmes. The latter have been more widely established across Canada with integrated research programmes; however several key centres have also been established in the USA.

Developmental Processes in the Early Course of Illness, Los Angeles

This research group has completed two large treatment and research protocols (see Nuechterlein et al., 1992) and two others have been underway since 1993. The first-episode study is a component of the project titled "Development Processes in Schizophrenic Disorders". One of the current protocols involves an 8–10 year follow-up of the 104 recent-onset schizophrenia patients seen in the initial protocol (1980–1992, "Developmental Processes in Outcome"). The second current protocol ("Developmental Processes in the Early Course of Illness") involves a new sample of patients and is an intensive follow-through study for one year after outpatient stabilisation (i.e. usually three months following intake). Participants are drawn from four major public hospitals. Treatment includes antipsychotic medication, individual case management, behavioural group therapy, and family psychoeducation. Evaluation involves repeated assessments focusing on cognitive and psychophysiological vulnerability factors, psychosocial stressors, and symptomatic, vocational and social outcome. Over a 15-month period 4–5 major assessment batteries are administered (intake, outpatient stabilisation, full remission, psychotic exacerbation if it occurs, and 12 months after stabilisation), functional outcome ratings are completed three-monthly, life events interviews are completed four-weekly, and the BPRS and SANS global items are completed bi-weekly. The

"Aftercare Program" is staffed by two part-time psychiatrists and three case managers with outpatient clinics run on two weekdays; clinicans are on-call (24 hours a day) and extra clinic visits are arranged as needed; a driver is available to transport patients to appointments.

Program for Assessment and Care of Early Schizophrenia (PACES), Pittsburgh.

The goal of PACES is to provide a comprehensive, "state-of-the-art" assessment and treatment programme for patients in their first episode of psychotic illness, which is predicated on the specific needs at the early as well as subsequent stages of the illness. Originally conceived as a service for patients enrolled in neuroscientific studies PACES has grown into a specialised Center within the Comprehensive Care Division of the Western Psychiatric Institute and Clinic (WPIC). The service provides care to first-episode patients referred from the inpatient and outpatient services of WPIC; consultation, diagnostic evaluations, and/or brief therapeutic interventions are also provided for patients referred by mental health clinicians in the greater Pittsburgh and surrounding communities. A comprehensive assessment is undertaken and careful attention is paid to the initiation of treatment. PACES is integrated within the inpatient and outpatient services of WPIC and acute phase treatment may involve admission to the Schizophrenia Inpatient Unit and/or the Partial Hospitalisation Program of WPIC. The outpatient team comprises a psychiatrist and a master's level nurse specialist who meet with each patient periodically for individual and family sessions. A range of therapeutic interventions are offered—pharmacology, education about the illness, supportive psychotherapy, clinical case management, and ongoing groups (focusing on communication, problem-solving, and coping). When the acute symptoms have subsided vocational issues are emphasised. Community supports and other services provided by WPIC (e.g. medical) are drawn upon as required. A 24-hour 7-days-a-week psychiatric coverage is provided through on-call arrangements by the PACES clinicans to ensure a rapid delivery of services to potential programme participants. The service also provides an infrastructure for a variety of diagnostic and treatment-related research studies (see Keshavan et al., 1998).

Prevention through Risk Identification, Management, and Education (PRIME), New Haven, CT

The PRIME research clinic is a collaborative effort between the Yale Psychiatric Institute and the Connecticut Mental Health Center. The treatment study involves a double blind randomised trial of olanzapine versus placebo in people prodromal to psychosis. The catchment area is the State of Connecticut, and the number of cases accepted per year is yet to be determined.

Recognition and Prevention of Psychological Problems (RAPP) Clinic, New York, NY

This clinical service provides a range of interventions during the prodromal stage of schizophrenia—individual and group therapy, social skills training, alternate schooling and medication (when indicated). Support services and psychoeducation are provided for family members. Evaluation involves characterising the sample clinically and neurocognitively, establishing clinical predictors of psychosis, and evaluating best early treatments for preventing or lessening the impact of psychosis. Jointly sponsored by Hillside Hospital and Schneider Children's Hospital of Long Island Jewish Medical Center, the clinic is located at the Children's Hospital. RAPP has a close association with the Hillside First Episode project, with some shared staffing and an inter-change of referrals where appropriate. Individuals in need of treatment are seen every two to four weeks; those who make the transition into psychosis are referred to the Hillside First Episode project or other appropriate treatment facilities. Adolescents who show improvement will not be followed as intensively, but will continue to maintain contact for an as-yet undefined period of time (minimum will be five years). RAPP is currently staffed by one full-time psychologist and 15 part-time clinicans.

Early Psychosis Program, Nova Scotia, Canada

The Early Psychosis Program was established as a partnership between the Nova Scotia Hospital and the Dalhousie University School of Medicine. Clinical consultation is provided and a subgroup of those referred are provided with ongoing clinical care. Key components of treatment have been identified as: (1) an attitude of hope, optimism and respect, (2) early treatment with effective antipsychotic medications used in a manner that minimises side-effects, (3) psychoeducation and counselling regarding the personal meaning of having a psychotic disorder, (4) return to vocational and educational activities and (5) involvement of families as key members of the treating team (Whitehorn, Lazier & Kopala, 1998). Research focuses on improved detection, early course, optimising family supports, cognitive functioning and medication. Educational activities for mental health professionals are provided via the "Early Psychosis Mentorship Program" (bi-monthly workshops), site visits and an annual conference. The programme is staffed by three part-time psychiatrists, three coordinators (clinical, research, community education), and three research nurses plus additional research support staff. The numbers of referrals are somewhat lower than expected, which may reflect detection issues, a lack of community awareness of this relatively new service, or a reluctance to use the service (D. Whitehorn, personal communications, 27 and 28 March 1998). The team is operating at maximum case load given current resources—establishing a maximum time period for working with individuals could assist with the "front end" problem. Following initial assessment consultation is provided for almost 50% of those referred as many patients live substantial distances from the Halifax location and/or have formed alliances with local mental health teams. A formal liaison system has been developed with nurses from the adult teams taking on a coordinating role with the Early Psychosis Program.

Early Psychosis Treatment and Prevention Program, Calgary, Alberta, Canada

This programme offers a comprehensive range of services to individuals experiencing a first-episode non-affective psychosis (less than three months of previous treatment) for a three-year period. Patients are assigned a psychiatrist and a case manager who undertake assessment and monitoring functions plus provision of pharmacotherapy—offering several of the newer neuroleptics. The group programme includes modules on psychoeducation, personal support and coping skills, coping with psychotic symptoms, anger and stress management, good health, substance use, social anxiety, vocation, and psychotherapy. Individual cognitive therapy is aimed to help adaptation to the psychotic illness and the effect on life circumstances, address secondary psychological problems, and treat persistent symptoms. Family workers offer education about psychosis, recommendations for coping with the disorder, communication skills and problem-solving training. An assessment, monitoring, and treatment service is also provided to young people considered to be at imminent risk of developing a psychotic disorder. The multi-disciplinary team comprises 8.7 clinicans. During the first 15 months of operation 100 referrals were received and 80 individuals were engaged in treatment. Evaluation includes assessment of symptoms, side effects, quality of life and substance use, and neurocognitive functioning.

Psychotic Disorders Team (PDT), Hamilton, Ontario, Canada

The team of five clinicians create an alliance between the patient, family and clinical team ("therapeutic partnership"—see Hamilton Wilson & Hobbs, 1995) focusing on short-term treatment goals. Once the goals have been achieved the client returns to the care of the family physician. The PDT offers intense clinical involvement during the early phase of the psychotic illness focusing upon early intervention, helping people to maintain social roles (e.g. student, worker), reduction of trauma and stigma, psychoeducation, and judicious use and careful monitoring of low-dose neuroleptics. Clients who are discharged are referred to as "Alumni" and ongoing shared care is provided by the PDT with the family physician. A study is underway examining outcomes of 30 individuals aged 16–45 who receive services from the PDT for a period of 18 months and 30 controls matched for age, sex, diagnosis, and IQ treated by the community's usual network of psychiatric care providers. Clinical ratings will be obtained at 1, 6 and 12 months including measures of positive and negative symptoms, quality of life, bed utilisation, suicide and employment rates.

Prevention and Early Intervention Program for Psychoses (PEPP), London, Ontario

This programme comprises a 16-bed inpatient unit and an outpatient service. The latter utilises an intensive/assertive clinical case management model—psychiatrists, psychologists and occupational therapists providing direct or indirect specific interventions, while the primary responsibility for patient care lies with the case manager. All case managers have a qualification in nursing and another social science discipline and provide individual, group and family interventions, supervise medication and undertake community liaison. Novel antipsychotics are used almost exclusively. An eight-week group intervention directed at the 16–25 age group addresses issues of working through the psychotic episode, stigma, identity, peer pressure, and drug and alcohol use; skills training follows. Individuals who are symptomatic participate in an activity orientated transition group. The programme is staffed by 15.5 clinicians, five researchers, and inpatient nursing staff. Screening is provided within 24–48 hours of referral and, if psychosis is indicated, a full assessment is undertaken within one week. Individuals considered to be prodromal receive an open trial of stress management and problem-solving with regular review (although a formal prodrome clinic is not in operation). A pilot case detection project is underway in high schools and tertiary counselling services and there are plans for a large-scale community case detection initiative to be undertaken.

First Episode Psychosis Program, Clarke Institute of Psychiatry, Toronto, Canada

The priority in the development of this service has been to facilitate the development of an academic schizophrenia programme. This occurred within the context of an awareness that there was no system in place within Metropolitan Toronto to facilitate optimal treatment of individuals with a first episode of schizophrenia. The clinical base for the programme was a 12-bed inpatient unit and additional resources were secured for a multi-disciplinary outpatient team. Referrals are received from a wide variety of services and are seen within two weeks. Patients are initially assessed by a psychiatrist and a psychiatric resident, usually in the outpatient service, and the family is seen simultaneously for collateral history by another member of the treating team. The mean length of inpatient stay, should it be required, is approximately 30 days. Outpatients are followed up by a case manager (either a psychiatric nurse, social worker, or occupational therapist) and a psychiatrist in the First Episode Psychosis Clinic until it can be determined that needs can be met by other services in the community (i.e. there is no maximum follow-up period). If additional support is required, a variety of community supports including a Home Nurse can be utilized. Outpatients can also be referred to the Home Based Treatment Program where they are visited by a psychiatric nurse on a daily basis for six weeks post-discharge. The programme has not undergone a comprehensive evaluation to date. Research carried out in this clinic has led to a stronger neurobiological basis for the low-dose neuroleptic strategy in first-episode psychosis (Kapur et al., 1996; Remington, Kapur & Zipursky, 1998). The programme is staffed by 12 people.

Other Canadian centres include the Polyclinique Saint-Anne and the Hotel Dieu de Levi, both in Quebec city. The former is an interesting blend of public and private funding sources and a genetic research focus, while the latter has good links with adolescent psychiatry and a cognitive-behaviour therapy focus.

International

International Early Psychosis Association (IEPA)

The IEPA was conceived at the First International Conference for Preventive Strategies in Early Psychosis (Melbourne, 1996) in recognition of the need for an international organisation to facilitate collaborative initiatives and promote best practice in the field of early psychosis. An Advisory Group has been formed to establish the organisation and two groups have been proposed: the Research Group will explore the opportunities for multi-centred trials, cross-cultural research, common assessment instruments, and shared databases; and the Clinical Practice Group will develop an international consensus statement for assessment and treatment of early psychosis. The IEPA is establishing a web site which will provide details and contact information on current early psychosis initiatives and will convene the Second International Early Psychosis Conference which is to be held in New York in the year 2000. To date, approximately 3,500 people have expressed interest in membership of the association.

Optimal Treatment Project for Schizophrenic Disorders

This trial aims to: evaluate the clinical, social, carer and economic benefits of applying integrated drug and psychosocial treatments (Falloon & Fadden,

1993) for relatively recent-onset cases of schizophrenic disorders (onset < 10 years) over a five-year period; compare the outcome of integrated treatment with a randomly selected control group receiving standard care; and examine predictors of the long-term course of schizophrenic disorders including those associated with clinical and social recovery. Treatment involves the minimal effective dose of neuroleptics, assertive case management, carer-based stress management, social and work skills training, and specific cognitive behavioural and drug strategies for residual symptoms and other problems. Multi-disciplinary teams are trained to competence and practice is regularly reviewed for fidelity, with retraining and updates annually. The protocol is continued until full clinical and social recovery is sustained for 24 months. Whilst not a "first-episode" project, there is encouragement to recruit new referrals, followed by the most recent-onset cases already receiving care. First-year results of a cohort show substantial reductions in hospital utilisation when compared with the year prior to entering the project (I. Falloon, personal communication, 19 March 1998)

SYNTHESIS

The focus of the projects described in Table 12.1 can be assigned to one of three categories: research clinic or study (prodromal and/or first-episode), mental health service delivery (i.e. the public agency funded to provide the routine mental health service), and network (local, national or international). Pre-psychotic intervention needs to be clearly distinguished from the early detection and treatment of schizophrenia (Morice, 1997). The six pre-psychotic high-risk or prodrome clinics (PACE at EPPIC, PAS, FETZ, PRIME, RAPP, and the Calgary clinic) are relatively recent developments and research driven. Each draws participants from large catchment areas, are generally managed by small teams, and are yet to tackle issues such as the duration of treatment and follow-up. While there is informal communication between these projects, it may be timely for formal dialogue regarding entry criteria and follow-up measures given the growing experience with this population.

The first-episode treatment studies differ in the way that "first episode" is defined. This is not a new problem (see Keshavan & Schooler, 1992). The most obvious differences concern (a) age entry criteria (young people, defined as aged 30 or younger, are a focus in only five projects) and (b) whether or not individuals with affective psychosis are included for study. The differences between the services in the lower age range is of interest, with a number of projects overcoming the child/youth age hurdle—the lower age of 18 is unacceptable in an early intervention framework, "missing" an early onset subgroup most likely at greatest risk of psychosocial damage as well as treatment resistance. Service age criteria are, for the most, historical, reflecting the child/adult services age split; arguments for developing "youth psychiatry" services need to be considered in view of the epidemiology of psychiatric disorders in general and psychotic disorders in particular. This is a contentious issue (see Birleson & Luk, 1997; McGorry, 1998b; Parry-Jones, 1995; Patton, 1996; Werry, 1997). Partnership models between child and adult psychiatry in the treatment of early psychosis, such as that described by Resch (1998), may require serious examination. The exclusion of affective psychosis in many of these projects seems to reflect theoretical/construct considerations (Europe), funding constraints (USA), and the existence of competing programmes (two Canadian early psychosis programmes reported neighbouring Bipolar Disorder clinics). Given the diagnostic instability in first-episode presentations (Fennig et al., 1994), particularly evident for individuals diagnosed initially with schizophreniform disorder (Strakowski, 1994), there is tension between these constraints and the goal of early intervention. The representativeness of first-episode samples is an issue, as many of the programmes are tertiary referral centres, and the implications of this will need to be discussed in published research accounts. The intensive public awareness efforts required to increase referral rates is highlighted by TIPS and tempered by the realism of case load capacity (see Nova Scotia project). Clearly TIPS and the Parachute Project are impressive in their scope and design, each emphasising different treatment concerns (DUP *versus* treatment following illness onset), both with five-year follow-ups planned. The Danish project is also substantial and, interestingly, tackles DUP *and* randomised optimal treatment.

The duration of treatment varies amongst these projects, ranging from 15 months (Los Angeles), 18 months (EPPIC), two years (Totara House, TIPS, Parachute, Denmark, PEPP), three years (EIS, Calgary) to four or five years (Falloon). Clearly, follow-up assessments are crucial—research is needed to evaluate the effect of early intervention during the "critical period" (Birchwood & Macmillan, 1993) on short- *and* long-term outcome (i.e. can better outcomes be sustained?) and the 3–5 year follow-up periods adopted in a number of projects hold promise. While TIPS, the Parachute project, and the Danish service are time-limited projects, translations into routine care upon cessation of the formal research components could prove to be a "double-edged sword"—exposure to specialised interventions beyond the time specifications of research protocols could impact on the treatment effects reported in the long-term follow-ups.

Twelve of the first-episode programmes are embedded within a service delivery framework with recurrent funding (EPPIC, FEPP, Totara House, Berne, EIS, Amsterdam Adolescent Clinic, PACE, and the five Canadian projects) and the commonalities in treatment principles are striking—case management, low-dose atypical neuroleptics, family psychoeducation, and group work are common threads. An emphasis on making "psychological sense" of the impact of the illness, the importance of optimism, and the need for flexibility and availability of treating clinicans pervades. There are major differences between the projects regarding whether or not specialised inpatient care is provided and the length of inpatient admissions—both issues, to some extent, reflecting respective service contexts (i.e. philosophy and/or tradition). The emphasis is on outpatient services, reflecting the trend towards a shift in the balance of resources and location of care from hospital to the community. However, it would appear that in a number of programmes that provide specialist inpatient services (e.g. the Berne First Episode Psychosis Program, EIS, and the Amsterdam Adolescent Unit) the *most* disturbed individuals with early psychosis receive inpatient services in other non-specialised units. The potential negative impact of hospitalisation (McGorry et al., 1991) needs to be high on the agenda of early psychosis services, with important preventive opportunities being missed. The scope of the projects differ markedly, with EPPIC, EIS and PEPP seemingly the most richly resourced of these 12 models at this stage. The first-episode services may also benefit from a "think tank" regarding common treatment principles and the development of an international early psychosis forum and consensus statement could assist this process.

Information regarding the outcome measures used in the evaluation components of these projects was limited. Future projects would benefit from recommendations regarding a core group of assessment instruments. Economic evaluation featured in only two service projects (EPPIC, Optimal Treatment), which is surprising given that viewing costs and outcomes simultaneously are gaining increasing recognition as important aspects of mental health services evaluation (Maynard & Bloor, 1995). Interestingly very few services had written material regarding programme descriptions readily available—referrals, community awareness, and funding opportunities would be advanced by the promotion of service delivery information. Of greater concern is that detailed information regarding treatment strategies utilised by the various services are generally lacking. From an evaluation viewpoint the treatment approaches clearly require elaboration (cf. Aitchison, Meehan & Murray, 1999; McGorry & Edwards, 1997); failure to undertake such tasks prior to evaluating early psychosis initiatives increases the risk of a weak treatment effect.

Working relationships, particularly with regard to networks, are apparent on national levels—Australia, New Zealand, the Scandinavian countries and Canada. Certainly, the level of interest in the IEPA suggests that the early psychosis field may be approaching paradigm status (Yung &

McGorry, 1997). Realising the potential of early psychosis *workers* via networks, supervision and training will be critical to the success of early psychosis initiatives.

CONCLUSION

The widespread development of early psychosis service models is still in its infancy. There would appear to be a strong rationale for early intervention and some of the early psychosis teams mentioned in this chapter have gained considerable clinical experience with this population over a 5–15-year period. The diversity in services responses to early intervention in first-episode psychosis are notable, and while there are commonalities the significant differences may render cross study comparisons of outcome data (when available) problematic. Early psychosis service delivery outcome data are some years away and it would seem timely to continue dialogue based upon experience thus far.

The essence of the early intervention approach is that a restructuring of services around the onset phase and early course of psychotic disorders will prove to be more cost-effective. This is likely to require an increase in what is currently being spent on these patients and to result in savings in later phases of life for these patients. Young people in the early phases of disorder already consume greater amounts of resources than those in later phases (Cuffel et al., 1996). It would make sense to invest these funds proactively on a needs basis and evaluate the cost-effectiveness of such an approach, as well as the potential reduction in human suffering. There is clearly a sociopolitical dimension to such reform, but it would benefit from a strong evidence base. This should be built on good scientific evidence, including health services research, a strong consumer voice, and effective advocacy at all levels.

ACKNOWLEDGEMENTS

We are grateful to Jean Addington, Jane Beckman, Søren Bredkjær, David Codyre, Barbara Cornblatt, Johan Cullberg, Heather Hobbs, Ian Falloon, Kay Fletcher, Martin Hambrecht, Chris Jackson, Jan Olav Johannessen, Matcheri Keshavan, Thomas McGlashan, Ashok Malla, Marco Merlo, Keith Neuchterlein, Merete Nordentoft, Sian O'Brien, David Shiers, John Titmus, Reinard van de Fliert, David Whitehorn, Jane Hamilton Wilson, and Robert Zipursky for providing (numerous) written contributions at short notice. Shelly McDonald made helpful comments regarding the three programmes she visited during May/June 1998.

REFERENCES

Albiston, D.J., Francey, S.M. & Harrigan, S.M. (1998). Group programmes for recovery from early psychosis. *British Journal of Psychiatry*, **172** (Suppl. 33), 117–121.

Alanen, Y.O., Ugelstad, E., Armelius, B, Lehtinen, K., Rosenbaum, B. & Sjostrom, R. (Eds) (1994). *Early Treatment for Schizophrenic Patients: Scandinavian Psychotherapeutic Approaches*. Oslo: Scandinavian University Press.

Andrews, G. (1998). Bambi meets godzilla: Or how CBT can survive the health planners. Paper presented at the meeting of the Australian Association for Cognitive Behaviour Therapy, Adelaide, April.

Aitchison, K.J., Meehan, K. & Murray, R.M. (1998). *First Episode Psychosis*. London: Martin Dunitz Ltd.

Birleson, P. & Luk, E.S.L. (1997). Continuing the debate on a seperate adolescent psychiatry. *Australian and New Zealand Journal of Psychiatry*, **31**, 447–451.

Birchwood, M. (1997). The Birmingham Early Psychosis Service. Paper presented at First UK International Conference on Early Intervention in Psychosis, Stratford-upon-Avon, June.

Birchwood, M. & Macmillan, F. (1993). Early intervention in schizophrenia. *Australian and New Zealand Journal of Psychiatry*, **27**, 374–378.

Campbell, M. (1997). Psychiatric early interventions for psychosis: the Totara House experience. (Audio tape 11). Paper presented at Schizophrenia Fellowship National Conference, Christchurch, New Zealand, September.

Codyre, D. (1997). Early intervention in first episode psychosis. (Audio tape 11). Paper presented at Schizophrenia Fellowship National Conference, Christchurch, New Zealand, September.

Cuffel, B.J., Jeste, D.V., Halpain, M., Pratt, C., Tarke, H. & Patterson, T.L. (1996). Treatment costs and use of community mental health services for schizophrenia by age cohorts. *American Journal of Psychiatry*, **153**, 870–876.

Cullberg, J. & Levander, S. (1997). The parachute project—need-adapted treatment for first episode psychosis: A Swedish multicenter care development and research project. 12th International Symposium for the Psychotherapy of Schizophrenia, London, October.

Early Psychosis News. Available on the EPPIC website: http: /www.vicnet.au/~eppic.

Early Psychosis Prevention and Intervention Centre (1997). *Working With Families in Early Psychosis: No. 2 in a Series of Early Psychosis Manuals*. Victoria, Australia: Psychiatric Services Branch, Human Services Victoria.

Edwards, J., Cocks, J. & Bott, J. (1999). Preventive case management in first-episode psychosis. In P.D. McGorry & H.J. Jackson (Eds.), *Recognition and Management of Early Psychosis: A Preventive Approach*, pp. 308–337. New York: Cambridge University Press.

Edwards, J., Maude, D., McGorry, P.D., Harrigan, S. & Cocks, J. (1998). Prolonged recovery in first episode psychosis. *British Journal of Psychiatry*, **172** (Suppl. 33), 107–116.

Edwards, J. & McGorry, P.D. (1998). Early intervention in psychotic disorders: A critical step in the prevention of psychological morbidity. In C. Perris & P.D. McGorry (Eds), *Cognitive Psychotherapy of Psychotic and Personality Disorders*. Chichester: Wiley.

EPPIC Information Package (1998). Available on the EPPIC website: http: /www.vicnet.au/[squig]eppic.

Falloon, I.R.H. (1992). Early intervention for first episodes of schizophrenia: a preliminary exploration. *Psychiatry*, **55**, 4–15.

Falloon, I.R.H., Kydd, R.R., Coverdale, J.H. & Laidlaw, T.M. (1996). Early detection and intervention for initial episodes of schizophrenia. *Schizophrenia Bulletin*, **22**, 271–282.

Falloon, I.R.H., & Fadden, G. (1993). *Integrated Mental Health Care*. Cambridge: Cambridge University Press.

Fennig, S., Kovasznay, B., Rich, C., Ram, R., Pato, C., Miller, A., Rubenstein, J., Carlson, G., Schwartz, J.E., Phelan, J., Lavelle, J., Craig, T. & Bromet, E. (1994). Six-month stability of psychiatric diagnoses in first-admission patients with psychosis. *American Journal of Psychiatry*, **151**, 1200–1208.

Francey, S. (1999). The role of day programs in recovery from early psychosis. In P.D. McGorry & H.J. Jackson (Eds), *Recognition and Management of Early Psychosis: A Preventive Approach*. New York: Cambridge University Press.

Gleeson, J., Jackson, H.J., Stavely, H. & Burnett, P. (1999). Psychological interventions in first-episode psychosis. In P.D. McGorry & H.J. Jackson (Eds). *Recognition and Management of Early Psychosis: A Preventive Approach*, pp. 376–406 New York: Cambridge University Press.

Grimshaw, J.M. & Hutchinson A. (1993). Clinical Practice Guidelines—do they enhance value for money in healthcare? *British Medical Bulletin*, **51**, 927–940.

Haines, S.A., Gleeson, J.F., Pennell, K.M. & McGorry, P.D. (1997). *Incorporating an early psychosis focus in a mainstream psychiatric setting: early psychosis projects in Victoria*. Poster presented at the First UK International Conference on Early Intervention in Psychosis, Stratford-upon-Avon, England, June.

Hamilton Wilson, J. & Hobbs, H. (1995). Therapeutic partnership: a model for clinical practice. *Journal of Psychosocial Nursing and Mental Health Services*, **33**, 27–30.

Jackson, C. & Farmer, A. (in press). Current evidence and practice relating to psychosis: early intervention. *Journal of Mental Health*.

Johannessen, J.O., Bloch Thorsen, G-R. & Larsen, T.K. (in press). Experiences with early intervention: Experiences from a study in Stavanger, Norway—history, frame, conditions, structure. In B. Martindale (Ed.), *Outcome Studies*. London: Gaskell.

Joyce, C. & Hurworth, R. (1998). *Evaluation of the National Early Psychosis Project: Final report*. Centre for Program Evaluation, University of Melbourne.

Kane, J.M. (1997). The facilitation of early detection and treatment of schizophrenia: Editorial review. *Current Opinion in Psychiatry*, **10**, 3–4.

Kapur, S., Remington, G., Jones, C., Wilson, A., DaSilva, J., Houle, S., & Zipursky, R. (1996). High levels of dopamine D2 receptor occupancy with low-dose haloperidol treatment: a PET study. *American Journal of Psychiatry*, **153**, 948–950.

Keshavan, M.S. & Schooler, W.R. (1992). First-episode studies in schizophrenia: criteria and characterization. *Schizophrenia Bulletin*, **18**, 491–513.

Keshavan, M.S. Schooler, N.R., Sweeney, J.A., Haas, G.L. & Pettegrew, J.W. (1998). Research and treatment strategies in first-episode psychoses. *British Journal of Psychiatry*, **172** (Suppl. 33), 60–65.

Klosterkötter, J., Gross, G., Huber, G., Wieneke, A., Steinmeyer, E.M. & Schultze-Lutter, F. (1997a). Evaluation of the "Bonn Scale for the Assessment of Basis Symptoms—BSABS" as an instrument for the assessment of schizophrenia proneness: a recent review of recent findings. *Neurology, Psychiatry and Brain Research*, **5**, 137–150.

Klosterkötter, J., Schultze-Lutter, F., Gross, G., Huber, G. & Steinmeyer, E.M. (1997b). Early self-experiences neuropsychological deficits and subsequent schizophrenia diseases: an 8-year average follow-up prospective study. *Acta Psychiatrica Scandinavica*, **95**, 396–404.

Lewis, S., Tarrier, N., Haddock., G., Bentall, R., Kinderman, P. & Kingdon, D. (1996). *A Multicentre, Randomised Controlled Trial of Cognitive-Behaviour Therapy in Early Schizophrenia*. Medical Research Council funded grant (number #G9519373).

Linszen, D., Lenior, M., De Haan, L., Dingemans, P. & Gersons, B. (1998). Early intervention, untreated psychosis and the course of early schizophrenia. *British Journal of Psychiatry*, **172** (Suppl. 33), 84–89.

Macmillan, F. & Shiers, D. (1997). Developing services for young people with psychosis. Paper presented at First UK International Conference on Early Intervention in Psychosis, Statford-upon-Avon, June.

Maynard, A. & Bloor, K. (1995). Economic evaluation of mental health services. *Current Opinion in Psychiatry,* **8,** 122–125.

McGlashan, T.H. (1996). Early detection and intervention in schizophrenia: research. *Schizophrenia Bulletin,* **22,** 327–345.

McGlashan, T.H. & Johannessen, J.O. (1996). Early detection and intervention in schizophrenia: rationale. *Schizophrenia Bulletin,* **22,** 201–222.

McGorry, P.D. (1996). The Centre for Young People's Mental Health: blending epidemiology and developmental psychiatry. *Australasian Psychiatry,* **4,** 243–246.

McGorry, P.D. (1998a). "A stitch in time"…the scope for preventative strategies in early psychosis. *European Archives Psychiatry and Clinical Neurosciences,* **166.**

McGorry, P. (1998b). Beyond adolescent psychiatry: the logic of a youth mental health model [letter]. *Australian and New Zealand Journal of Psychiatry,* **32,** 138–140.

McGorry, P.D., Chanen, A., McCarthy, E., Van Reil, R., McKenzie, D. & Singh, B. (1991). Post traumatic stress disorder follwing recent onset psychosis: an unrecognised post psychotic syndrome. *Journal of Nervous and Mental Disease,* **179,** 253–258.

McGorry, P. D. & Edwards, J. (1997). *Early Psychosis Training Pack.* Cheshire: Gardiner-Caldwell Communications.

McGorry, P.D., Edwards, J., Mihalopoulos, C., Harrigan, S. & Jackson, H.J. (1996). Early Psychosis Prevention and Intervention Centre: an evolving system for early detection and intervention. *Schizophrenia Bulletin,* **22,** 305–326.

McGorry, P.D., Edwards, J. & Pennell, K. (1999). Sharpening the focus: early intervention in the real world. In P.D. McGorry & H.J. Jackson (Eds), *Recognition and Management of Early Psychosis: A Preventive Approach* pp. 441–475. New York: Cambridge University Press.

McGorry, P.D., Henry, L. & Power, P. (1998). Suicide in early psychosis. Could early intervention work? In Kosky, R.J., Fesheshkevan, H.J., Goldney, R.D., Hassan, R. (Eds), *Suicide Prevention. The Global Context*, pp. 103–110. New York: Plenum.

Merlo, C.G. (in press). Psychosocial treatment of schizophrenic disorders: Structuring information processing and information exchange. In M.C.G. Merlo, C., Perris & H. D. Brenner (Eds), *Cognitive Therapy with Schizophrenic Patients: The Evolution of a New Treatment Approach.* Bern: Hogrefe & Huber.

Merlo, C.G. & Hofer, H. (in press). Systemic considerations for the inpatient treatment of first-episode, acute schizophrenic patients. In M.C.G. Merlo, C. Perris & H. D. Brenner (Eds), *Cognitive Therapy with Schizophrenic Patients: The Evolution of a New Treatment Approach.* Bern: Hogrefe & Huber.

Mihalopoulos, C., Carter, R.C. & McGorry, P.D. (1999). Is phase-specific, community-oriented treatment of early psychosis an economically viable method of improving outcome? *Acta Psychiatrica Scandinavica,* **100,** 47–55.

Morice, R. (1997). Comment: Should we walk before setting the PACE? *Australian and New Zealand Journal of Psychiatry,* **31,** 799–805.

National Early Psychosis Project Clinical Guidelines Working Party (1998). *Australian Clinical Guidelines for Early Psychosis.* Melbourne: National Early Psychosis Project, University of Melbourne.

Nuechterlein, K. H., Dawson, M.E., Gitlin, M., Ventura, J., Goldstein, M.J., Snyder, K.S., Yee, C. M. & Mintz, J. (1992). Developmental processes in schizophrenic disorders: longitudinal studies of vulnerability and stress. *Schizophrenia Bulletin,* **18,** 387–425.

Parry-Jones, W. (1995). The future of adolescent psychiatry. *British Journal of Psychiatry,* **166,** 299–305.

Patton, G. (1996). A epidemiological case for a separate adolescent psychiatry? *Australian and New Zealand Journal of Psychiatry,* **30,** 453–466.

Pennell, K.M., McGorry, P.D., Haines, S.A., Urbanc, A., Pound, B., Dagg, B., Handley, P., Wigg, C. & Berry, H. (1997). Australian national early psychosis project: The development and promotion of a national best practice model in early intervention in psychosis—a project overview. Paper presented at the Mental Health Services Conference, Sydney, Australia, September.

Power, P. (1999). Suicide and early psychosis. In P.D. McGorry & H.J. Jackson (Eds), *Recognition and Management of Early Psychosis: A Preventive Approach* pp. 338–362. New York: Cambridge University Press.

Power, P., Elkins, K., Adlard, S., Curry, C., McGorry, P., & Harrigan, S. (1998). Analysis of the initial treatment phase in first-episode psychosis. *British Journal of Psychiatry, 172 (Suppl. 33),* 71–76.

Psychiatric Research Report (1997). A Publication of the APA Office of Research, **13** (4).

Remington, G., Kapur, S. & Zipursky, R.B. (1998). Pharmacothrapy of first-episode schizophrenia. *British Journal of Psychiatry, 172* (Suppl. 33), 66–70.

Resch, F. (1998). Developmental view on adolescent psychosis: Pathogenetic apsects and therapeautic approaches. Paper presented at the Second National Conference on Early Psychosis, Hobart, September.

Rush, A.J. (1993). Clinical practice guidelines: good news, bad news, or no news? *Archives of General Psychiatry,* **50,** 483–490.

Rutter, M. (1995). *Psychosocial Disorders in Young People.* Chichester: Wiley.

Strakowski, S.M. (1994). Diagnostic validity of schizophreniform disorder. *American Journal of Psychiatry,* **151,** 815–824.

Thornicroft, G. & Tansella, M. (Eds) (1996). *Mental Health Outcome Measures.* Berlin: Springer-Verlag.

Tobin, M.J., Hickie, I.B., Yeo, F.M. & Chen, L. (1998). Discussing the impact of first onset psychosis programs on public sector health services. *Australasian Psychiatry,* **6,** 181–183.

Werry, J.S. (1997). Comment on "An epidemiological case for a seperate adolescent psychiatry" [letter]. *Australian and New Zealand Journal of Psychiatry,* **31,** 431–433.

Whitehorn, D., Lazier, L. & Kopala, L. (1998). Psychosocial rehabilitation early after the onset of psychosis. *Psychiatric Services,* **49,** 1135–1137.

Yung, A.R. & McGorry, P.D. (1997). Is pre-psychotic intervention realistic in schizophrenia and related disorders? *Australian and New Zealand Journal of Psychiatry,* **31,** 799–805.

Yung, A.R., McGorry, P.D., McFarlane, C. A. & Patton, G.C. (1996a). The PACE clinic: development of a clinical service for young people at high risk of psychosis. *Australasian Psychiatry,* **3,** 345–351.

Yung, A.R., Phillips, L. J., McGorry, P.D., McFarlane, C. A., Francey, S., Jackson, H.J., Patton, G.C. & Rakkar, A. (1996b). Monitoring and care of young people at incipient risk of psychosis. *Schizophrenia Bulletin,* **22,** 283–351.

Yung, A.R., Phillips, L. J. & Drew, L.T. (1999). Promoting access to care in early psychosis. In P.D. McGorry & H.J. Jackson (Eds), *Recognition and Management of Early Psychosis: A Preventive Approach* (pp. 80–114). New York: Cambridge University Press.

Yung, A.R., Phillips, L.J., McGorry, P.D., Hallgren, M.A., McFalane, C.A., & Jackson, H.J., Francey, S. & Patton, C.G. (1998a). Can we predict the onset of first-episode psychosis in a high-risk group? *International Journal of Psychopharmacology,* **13** (Suppl. 1), S23-S30.

Yung, A.R., Phillips, L.J., McGorry, P.D., McFarlane, C.A., Francey, S., Harrigan, S., Patton, C.G. & Jackson, H.J. (1998b). The prediction of psychosis: a step towards indicated prevention of schizophrenia. *British Journal of Psychiatry,* **172** (Suppl. 33), 14–20.

Chapter 13

THE IRIS PROGRAMME

Fiona Macmillan* and David Shiers†

INTRODUCTION

Despite the profoundly distressing changes that accompany a first episode of psychosis, time to first presentation and treatment after the onset of frank psychosis averages approximately a year (Johnstone et al., 1986). The first experience of mental health care for many service users is legal detention in an acute hospital ward. Moving from institutional models to successful community care has often been thwarted, partly by the historical control exerted by secondary mental health over access to its services, and partly through reluctance of primary care to share the risks and difficulties of supporting clients with serious and enduring mental illness. Consequently, community mental health teams (CMHT) may maintain an "all-embracing" approach which can restrict primary care gaining sufficient skills and confidence to deal with psychosis, re-enforced by limitations in GP training and research.

PRIMARY CARE AND THE MANAGEMENT OF PSYCHOSIS

Although it may be the primary responsibility of the psychiatric team to arrange for follow-up and rehabilitation, Melzer (1991) showed that such clients consulted their GP more than any other professional. A House of Commons select committee (1984), referring to community care, concluded" ...it has come to have such general reference as to be virtually meaningless", and went on to recommend "Community care depends to a large extent on the continuing capacity of GPs to provide primary medical

*Walsall Mental Health Trust, Walsall. †West Midlands NHS Executive, Birmingham.

Early Intervention in Psychosis.
Edited by M. Birchwood, D. Fowler & C. Jackson.
© 2000 John Wiley & Sons Ltd.

care to mentally disabled people". In a similar vein, Shepherd suggested (1989) " ...the cardinal requirement for mental health services in this country is not a large expansion and proliferation of psychiatric agencies but rather a strengthening of the family doctor in his (her) therapeutic role."

Primary and secondary care for mentally ill people have traditionally communicated by doctor's letter alone (Pullen & Yellowlees, 1985). This can result in primary and secondary care failing to share care, and interfacing poorly. Goldberg and Jackson (1992) concluded

> Although many psychiatrists now conduct outpatient clinics in primary care, the commonest pattern of work is the "shifted outpatient" model, in which the psychiatrist conducts a normal outpatient clinic in general practice premises, often during a time when the GPs are not in the building and contact with them may be infrequent.

Burns and Kendrick (1997), reviewing the literature, concluded that there was a striking lack of organised research at a primary care level into schizophrenia explaining why there was no agreement on efficacy for primary care assessment and interventions. In contrast, King (1998), referring to current mental health research, concludes the GP to be " ...the central player. It is vital that clinical and administrative burdens do not reduce the inclination to participate in mental health research."

Kendrick et al. (1991), surveying primary care in the South West Thames region of the UK, found almost no specific strategy for the care of their long-term mentally ill clients. Burns and Kendrick (1997) reported the work of a consensus group in developing good practice guidelines in five areas:

- establishing a practice register and organising regular reviews
- comprehensive assessments
- information and advice for users and carers
- indications for using specialist services
- crisis management.

Whilst doubts exist over the capacity of current primary care to meet the challenges of modern mental health care for those with serious and enduring mental illness, one should not underestimate primary care's ability to innovate major advances, as witness for example those occurring currently in diabetes and asthma.

ALTERNATIVE MODELS

Shepherd et al. (1966) advocate integrating mental health services into primary care to achieve better community care. Falloon and Fadden (1995) have developed a radical service in Aylesbury, Oxfordshire, which bases mental health services within primary care—described as integrated mental health care—which attempts to support primary care with its range of mental health needs as well as evolve a service able to treat severe mental illness in a community setting. Falloon, Shanahan and Laporta (1992) demonstrated marked consumer preference for an integrated care system of assessment compared to hospital-based outpatient assessment, backed by attendance rates of around 95% for the former against 50–75% for the latter (Chen, 1991). Falloon, Shanahan and Laporta (1992) observed marked reduction in expected levels of schizophrenia and major affective disorder and concluded that this was due to integrated care achieving earlier intervention combined with optimal combinations of biomedical and psychosocial strategies.

Creed and Marks (1989) have developed a model of liaison-attachment where the psychiatrist regularly meets with primary care staff to discuss management of shared clients, after which the psychiatrist sees several clients, often jointly with the GP. The GP continues to provide the client with treatment, but benefits from joint management plans and the ability to gain advice without necessarily referring a client. This allows a flexible specialist approach according to the needs of the case, reaches a wider variety of clients, and encourages better shar ing of information and perspectives between primary and specialist care. Strathdee (1988) found that GPs participating in liaison-attachment schemes welcomed assessment and short-term treatment by the psychiatrist, but regarded long-term takeover as poor use of specialist time.

In 1992, the Royal Colleges of Psychiatrists and GPs addressed a common mental health problem by collaborating a successful campaign to "defeat depression". This resulted in the RCGP training a network of primary care mental health tutor pairs to disseminate a primary care approach which maximises effective interventions (e.g. full dose antidepressant) with an element aimed at reducing stigma through public health measures, and patients not achieving sufficient health gain being "filtered" to specialist care.

Since over three-quarters of people with a first episode of psychosis pass through primary care and are key players in the pathway to care, the opportunity for improved partnership between primary and secondary care in the early detection and treatment of psychosis is considerable.

IRIS

In the West Midlands (UK), as a response to concerns about services for young people with psychosis, a group with widely differing perspectives have formed to create the IRIS initiative to promote early intervention and improved partnership between primary and secondary care.

Early intervention has appeared in the UK government's mental health strategy (*Modernising Mental Health Services*); IRIS are charged with the responsibility of developing an early intervention strategy initially for the West Midlands and, through the UK's National *Beacon Service* Programme, it will, in conjunction with the Birmingham Early Intervention Service, provide support and assistance to services and approaches developing throughout the UK.

In collaboration with the UK's National Schizophrenia Fellowship, IRIS have produced a framework document, *Early Intervention in Psychosis: Clinical and Service Guidelines*, in which the aims, principles and guidelines for early intervention have been identified.

The core principles include:

- A youth and user focus.
- The importance of early and assertive engagement.
- The embracing of diagnostic uncertainty.
- Treatment to be provided in the least restrictive and stigmatising setting.
- An emphasis on social roles.
- A family-oriented approach

The guidelines, in brief embrace:

- The implementation of a local strategy for early detection and assessment: this will require the auditing of pathways to care.
- Allocation of an assertive outreach keyworker for at least three years (through the critical period).
- A person- and family-led needs assessment.
- The use of low-dose, preferably atypical, neuroleptics and the implementation of "cognitive therapy".
- Family and friends actively involved in the engagement, assessment, treatment and recovery process.
- A strategy for relapse prevention/minimisation to embrace vulnerability/risk factors, prophylaxis and early detection of relapse.
- A strategy to facilitate clients' pathways to training, work and valued occupation.
- The basic needs: housing, money, social networks.
- Assessment, prevention and treatment of comorbidity, particularly: substance misuse, depression/suicidal thinking and problems associated with adjusting to psychosis.
- A *local* strategy to promote a positive image of people with psychosis and to emphasise the treatability of psychosis.

Those wishing to learn more about IRIS and the UK network of early intervention service approaches can contact joanne.mcilraith@GW.nbmht.nhs.uk.

In the remainder of this chapter we focus on our first guideline: the development of an early detection strategy and use as a prototype a IRIS project in North Staffordshire, UK.

In North Staffordshire a multi-professional audit is currently examining pathways to engagement with specialist services for young people with a first episode of psychosis, particularly looking at obstacles within the primary/secondary interface. Five case vignettes are presented from this study to illustrate some of the challenges to achieving earlier interventions. These results are preliminary and will be enhanced by a full sample of 50 cases. The assessment methodology may be obtained from the authors.

Case 1

J is a 21-year-old single mother with a 10-month-old baby. She had been hearing and responding to voices, for much of the previous 18 months. She moved to a new general practice shortly after confinement. The health visitor from the first practice did not assess for depression, reasoning that J appeared stressed and this might skew the result. However when J moved she did telephone to warn the next health visitor that J was "weird"—the flat was chaotic, the curtains always shut, she dressed and behaved strangely and spoke guardedly. The next health visitor too felt J was strange, anxious and withdrawn. J saw her GP because of stress and was reassured that new mothers could expect this. Finally, an elderly neighbour observed her in the road, wandering and confused. She called round J's father, who, after much telephone negotiation with the GP, was able to drive his daughter 10 miles to see a psychiatrist who then admitted her to hospital under a Section 2.

Discussion points:

1. Opportunities for earlier intervention—Primary Health Care Team (PCHT) failing to ask the right questions.
2. Training of health visitors to detect psychosis.
3. GP delay in seeking specialist opinion.
4. Inception to specialist mental health care using hospital admission under section.
5. Safety of child.

Case 2

K is a 33-year-old married mother with a 5-year old child. She was admitted to an acute ward during the night from A&E with an acute psychosis—paranoid thoughts, delusions of control, strange behaviour and physical aggression. Her husband felt she had been unwell from the birth of their child five years previously, when she was diagnosed as suffering post-natal depression. He learned to cope with her increasingly paranoid thoughts by assuming all responsibility for her, feeling it was his place to look after his wife and that the doctor could not be expected to help. She settled quickly on the ward and was discharged home on neuroleptic medication with the only follow-up arrangement being a six-month outpatient appointment. Her husband is now taking antidepressants. In view of his wife's illness he has been surprised that noone has visited them since her discharge.

Discussion points:

1. Opportunities for early intervention as in Case 1 – PCHT failing to ask the right questions.
2. Mental health education of public – this family's tolerance of "oddness" and ignorance of their right to help.
3. Follow-up by primary and specialist care, disregard for family's needs and inadequate monitoring and support after discharge.

Case 3

C is a 17-year-young man living with his mother and siblings, working as a labourer. He consulted his GP with noises in his ear. The next day mother phoned the GP worried about C's level of stress which had been building up for six months. His GP reviewed him one week later, assessed him "possibly psychotic" and asked the primary CPN to review. He was seen at his home after work the next day when the CPN confirmed psychosis and requested urgent psychiatric referral. But C and his mother failed to attend the hospital clinic the following week. (Interestingly she associated the hospital clinic with memories of her brother, who had suffered a protracted mental illness requiring long-term hospitalisation.) Despite a personal phone-call by the CPN, the secretary explained the psychiatrist was extremely busy and couldn't possibly see him for at least two months. The GP has negotiated with a psychiatrist from a different area to provide support and initiated neuroleptic medication with the primary CPN monitoring. The mother has worked well with the primary care CPN, received a rationale for the services offered and has remained in liaison with the CPN. C still refuses to see a psychiatrist but is taking medication and keeping in touch with the CPN.

Discussion points:

1. Rigidity of response from the first specialist and failure to provide time and place to suit client; failure to explore reasons for non-attendance and to prioritise a clearly described psychosis.

2. Primary care : the ability of primary care to work with families as a resource and to provide a setting to minimise stigma. The effectiveness of clinical supervision by psychiatrist to support primary care treatment is highlighted by this case.
3. Benefits of effective early engagement in the client's home setting to offset social disengagement.

Case 4

M was an academically bright and happy teenager who lost interest and became increasingly defiant in school from the age of 15. Unbeknown to her mother, she dropped out of college and finally left home to live in a series of housing association hostels and flatlets. Aged 18 she consulted her GP because of anxiety, thoughts of people following her and insomnia. She was referred to a psychologist who felt she was anxious with over-valued ideas, but after three sessions M declined further help. Her mother noted increasing oddness, paranoid thoughts and preoccupation with food and body, putting this down initially to M's cannabis use Friends suggested that M watch a TV programme about schizophrenia and M agreed there were similarities between herself and the behaviour discussed.

M found life increasingly difficult, eventually moving back home. Her mother assertively requested referral by the GP resulting in an outpatient appointment to see a psychiatrist two weeks later. Hearing voices and depressive mood was documented and Prozac was prescribed with review two weeks later. A week later she attended her GP's surgery acutely psychotic and disturbed. Initially no action was offered until her mother insisted seeing the GP to request immediate psychiatric referral. This occurred later that day resulting in her admission to hospital under Section 3. In hospital her mother remained greatly concerned over M's paranoid thoughts towards the staff and their understanding, particularly when the Section 3 was discontinued without consulting the mother. M was discharged after four months in hospital with minimal follow-up.

Discussion points:

1. Opportunities for early intervention:
   - family knowledge: use of TV/media to impart information
   - risks of blaming all odd behaviour on drug abuse
   - failure to ask the right questions by psychologist.

2. Family as a key resource :
   - necessity for mother to be assertive and knowledgeable to negotiate services
   - limited school liaison with mother
   - Section decisions without consulting the family.

3. Appropriateness of "minimal CPA" (follow-up) in monitoring the progress of a young person with psychosis.

Case 5

G is a 22-year-old from a close-knit family. He was a quiet child but from the age of about 15 he was described as coming out of his shell. At age 17 he went to his GP with nerve trouble, declined the offer of counselling and was prescribed Prozac. Aged 19 he presented back to the GP depressed with suicidal ideation and was referred to psychology. By the time of the appointment five months later he felt better and so did not attend. Over the next year his family became aware of G's religious obsession, calling himself a slave for Jesus. He left the family home to share a flat with a friend, a known drug user, and he also formed a band. Over the next 18 months his family worried over his vulnerability and increasing social withdrawal.

Rapid deterioration coincided with G discovering his brother-in-law had bowel cancer, to be followed three weeks later by his formal disapproval as an associate of the Jehovah's witnesses. For the next few weeks he became frenzied, deluded and unable to sleep. Very concerned, his parents rang the GP who prescribed Temazepam without seeing G. Over the next two days (weekend) the GP was asked by the parents to visit, in turn requesting the duty social worker and psychiatrist. They gave the family the choice in front of G of admission or allowing the situation to continue avoiding the "unpleasantness of police escort". The family declined because of loyalty to G and because he had a gig that evening. The next day, Monday, G was picked up by the police after a shopkeeper reported him causing a disturbance. He was deluded and praising God around some shops. The police took him home where his parents were able to discuss with the police the events of the previous two days. The police removed G to the police station as a place of safety under Section 136 of the Mental Health Act where he was promptly assessed by a police surgeon who then arranged hospital admission under Section 2. The police, out of concern for his parents, visited the family on two occasions following this. The family are concerned for G's future and fear he may disengage with services after discharge.

Discussion points:

1. Opportunities for early intervention:
   - antidepressant usage in young people
   - long wait to see the psychologist as example of the delay and difficulties in obtaining specialist mental health assessment for a young person
   - 18 months' lag between onset of psychosis and treatment.

2. Obstacles to crisis admission:
   - failure to act by all parties on weekend before admission
   - asking family to make decision over admission in front of patient
   - importance of all agencies working together to gain an outcome.

3. Helpfulness of police intervention as example of the potential breadth of people and agencies who can be involved in early detection.

What do these cases tell us about possibilities for reducing untreated illness?

A core requirement is to improve awareness about psychosis by families, community agencies (e.g. police, youth workers, vicars, housing officers), GPs and PHCT professionals. Crucially this should be given in positive and optimistic terms, justified by the potential gains from earlier intervention:

- knowledge of how symptoms and signs emerge
- understanding the importance of early treatment
- how to access services.

Our audit consistently demonstrated that people across traditional agency boundaries were struggling to work effectively in partnership and failing to deliver evidence-based practice. We would advocate the following actions:

1. *GPs and Primary Care Health Team*: we need to raise the possibility of diagnosis and improve the primary care teams' ability to recognise psychosis and to ask the right questions; to seek appropriate help from specialist services, involve and support the family and take responsibility for overview and continuity of care.
2. *Mental Health Professionals* need to be accessible and fast track young people with possible psychosis, use local clinical policies based on the best evidence and involve appropriate colleagues at appropriate times— e.g. clinical psychologist, occupational therapist, social worker. They must involve and trust the carers, especially close family, discharge patients back to community and primary care as soon as appropriate, and resist taking over sole long-term responsibility, thus excluding GP.
3. *Commissioners of Services* need to have knowledge of what their services currently provide and have knowledge of the evidence for early intervention and its cost-effectiveness. They must realise the importance of appropriate commissioning to support innovation and facilitate changes to achieve early intervention and to develop alliances with users and carers working across agencies such as voluntary sector, housing, education and employment

Our interviews of professionals and families revealed a widespread assumption that "medicalisation", recognition, labelling, or treatment will make the psychosis worse. What was particularly worrying was professionals' lack of knowledge - not recognising symptoms and signs, or recognising symptoms but ignoring the need to act on them, or not appreciating evidence for early intervention and the consequences of lack of intervention. Also worrying was primary care professionals' lack of time to manage the case adequately with competing priorities and the convenience of referring to specialist services, thus abdicating continuing responsibility. The lack of skilled professionals in primary care was widespread. The potential of media for imparting knowledge and reducing stigma is clear. The families' tolerance of odd behaviour before seeking help suggests the assumption that most oddness in young people is due to illicit drug-taking. The popularity of the new antidepressants as a panacea for every mental illness was of particular concern and highlights the importance of improved primary care training in psychosis.

THE WAY FORWARD

Care for young people with psychosis should be seen in a wider context of good mental health care. This hinges on confident, well-trained professionals and care-givers who are able to work autonomously, and capable of communicating and developing the networks of care and support around individuals and their families where they live. Gaining good mental health is more than just health and social care: systems of care relying solely on drugs and containment will fail to meet the real needs of their clients if they do not attend to supporting jobs, housing, social networks, etc. Distinctions between primary, secondary and specialist disciplines become increasingly meaningless if we are serious about caring for people in their own communities.

There is a real need to improve access and this will only come about by primary and secondary care radically reviewing its approach. Present UK specialist service configurations—separation of child and adolescent services from adult services at the crucial age when psychosis tends to develop–creates obvious difficulties. To gain greater primary care involvement, specialist services must shift towards a more collaborative approach which empowers primary care, and indeed other services, to obtain timely access to treatment, risk assessment, safety and support. Current difficulties across the primary/secondary care interface are to some extent based on historical boundaries, where secondary care access was a hurdle denying return, despite the most common course being one of relapse with periods of remission lasting months, years or decades.

IRIS is developing a strategy to promote the concept of integrated care pathway analysis to bring together professionals of widely differing backgrounds and perspectives to jointly focus on what their collective services are delivering to young people with psychosis. This local experience will inform more appropriate service development and training provided there is a commitment and agreement by everyone involved—GPs, CPNs, psychiatrists, psychologists, social workers, and not least those receiving the services. Roles and responsibilities must be clear in delivering the individual elements within an agreed integrated care pathway. Pathways should be continually reviewed in the light of new evidence, and address stages that are not working as well as expected.

A full community approach would include measures which educate a whole population about mental health issues, targeting learning and improving collaboration with non-medical agencies such as police, samaritans, college teachers, housing agencies and others.

Rooting mental health care around primary care would reduce stigma, improve access and acceptability, and strengthen links with social services, housing, employment and education around the emerging UK structure of Primary Care Groups. Raising awareness and increasing optimism and confidence within primary care in their response to mental illnesses will require major review of current education and research. Primary care is well placed to work with the family, the greatest unpaid resource we have, hopefully still relatively intact and available before the situation is undermined by the behavioural concomitants of serious and enduring mental illness. By maintaining contact with young people developing psychosis and their families primary care would increase its confidence, develop its skills, and alter its relationship to specialist services.

REFERENCES

Birchwood, M., McGorry, P. & Jackson, H. (1997). Early Intervention in schizophrenia—Editorial *British Journal of Psychiatry* **170**, 2–5.

Burns, T. & Cohen, A. (1998). Item-of-service payments for general practitioner care of severely mentally ill: does the money matter? *British Journal of General Practice*, **48**, 1416–1417.

Burns, T. & Kendrick, T. (1997). The primary care of patients with schizophrenia: a search for good practice *British Journal of General Practice*, **47**, 515–520.

Chen, A. (1991) Non-compliance in community psychiatry: a review of clinical interventions. *Hospital and Community Psychiatry*; **42**, 282–286.

Drury, V., Birchwood, M., Cochrane, R.C. & Macmillan, F. (1996). Cognitive therapy and recovery from acute psychosis. *British Journal of Psychiatry*; **169**, 602–607.

Falloon, I.R.H. & Fadden, G. (1995) *Integrated Mental Health Care.* (pp. 17–18). Cambridge: Cambridge University Press.

Falloon, I.R.H., Shanahan, W.J. & Laporta, M. (1992) Prevention of major depressive episodes: early intervention with family-based stress management. *Journal of Mental Health*, **1**, 53–60.

Froshaug, H. & Ytrehus, A. (1963) The problems of prognosis in schizophrenia. *Acta Psychiatrica Scandinavica*, Supp 169.

Goldberg, D. & Jackson, G. (1992) Editorial—Interface between primary care and specialist mental health care. *British Journal of General Practice*, **42**, 267–269.

Johnstone, E.C., Crow, T.J., Johnstone, A.L. & Macmillan, J.F. (1986). The Northwick Park study of first episode, schizophrenia. I: Presentation of the illness and problems relating to admission. *British Journal of Psychiatry*; **148**, 115–120.

Kendrick, T., Sibbald, B., Burns, T. & Freeling, P. (1991) Role of general practitioners in care of long term mentally ill patients *British Medical Journal*, **302**, 508–510.

King, M. (1998) Editorial—Mental Health research in general practice: from head counts to outcomes. *British Journal of General Practice*, **48**, 1295–1296.

Loebel, A.D., Lieberman, J.A., Alvir, J.M.N., Mayerhoff, D.I., Geisler, S.H. & Szmanski, S.R. (1992) Duration of untreated psychosis and outcome in first episode schizophrenia. *American Journal of Psychiatry*; **48**, 1183–1188.

Mari, J. & Streiner, D. (1996) The effects of family intervention on those with schizophrenia. In C. Adams, J. Anderson & De Jesus Mari (Eds), *Schizophrenia Module, Cochrane Database of Systematic Reviews* (updated 23 Feb 1996).

McGorry, P.D., Edwards, J., Mihalopoulos, C., Harrigan, S.M. & Jackson, H.J. (1996) EPPIC: An evolving system of early detection and optimal management. *Schizophrenia Bulletin*, **22**(2), 305–326.

Melzer, D., Hale, A.S. & Malik, S.J. (1991) Community care for patients with schizophrenia one year after hospital discharge. *British Medical Journal*, **302**, 1023–1025.

Pullen, I. & Yellowlees, A.J. (1985). Is communication improving between GPs and psychiatrists? *British Medical Journal*, **290**, 31–33.

Shepherd, M. (1989). Primary care of patients with mental disorder in the community. *British Medical Journal*, **299**, 666–669.

Strathdee, G. (1988). Psychiatrists in primary care: the general practitioner viewpoint *Family Practice*, **5**, 111–115.

Shepherd, M., Cooper, B., Brown, A.C. & Kalton,G.W. (1966) *Psychiatric Illness in General Practice*. Oxford: Oxford University Press.

Carpenter, W.T. Jr. & Strauss, J.S. (1991). The prediction of outcome in schizophrenia IV: eleven-year follow-up of the Washington IPSS cohort. *Journal of Nervous and Mental Disease*, **179**, 517–525.

Larsen, T. (1997). *TIPS project—Early Treatment In Psychosis*. A comparative study of early intervention with a parallel control group. Psychiatric Hospital of Rogaland, Norway

Westermeyer, J.F., Harrow, M. & Marengo, J.T. (1991). Risk for suicide in schizophrenia and other psychotic and non-psychotic disorders. *Journal of Nervous and Mental Disease*, **179**, 259–266.

Chapter 14

CREATIVE JOURNEYS OF RECOVERY: A SURVIVOR PERSPECTIVE

*Alison Reeves**

INTRODUCTION

In recent years there has been a surge of interest in the User movement both by people using the services and professionals. User and Survivor organisations now play an extensive role in planning, research and also in service delivery in many places across the world. Much of the research and service delivery which have emerged from the Survivor movement in recent years have been very creative and empowering and has focused on recovery through self-help, spirituality and complementary therapies. For example, the Mental Health Foundation have recently published a survey of User views about complementary therapies called *Healing Our Minds* and have set up national conferences and working groups to look at "spiritual" recovery. It is difficult to imagine this happening even a few years ago, but as we enter the Age of Aquarius—the age of self-healing—this movement continues to grow.

It is therefore important that any service, whether for young people or not, is aware of the research being carried out and the success of service models based on holistic recovery models. Such an example is Skallagrigg Crisis House, which is a "user-led" project running successfully for two years in Aston, Birmingham.

This research provides a wealth of valuable information about what helps people to recover. This chapter will look at the User/Survivor perspective

*Skallagrigg Crisis House, Birmingham.

Early Intervention in Psychosis.
Edited by M. Birchwood, D. Fowler & C. Jackson.
© 2000 John Wiley & Sons Ltd.

on what is considered to be a "good" service that is helpful to the individual recovering from psychotic or other distressing experiences.

HISTORY OF THE SERVICE USER/SURVIVOR MOVEMENT

The Service User/Survivor movement can be traced back as far as 1845 to an organisation formed by ex-patients called the Alleged Lunatics Friends Society. However, the contemporary User/Survivor movement emerged roughly at the same time as the antipsychiatry movement, and other liberation movements such as women, gays and black people in the 1960s.

The User/Survivor movement of the 1960s drew inspiration from the writings of Szasz, Foucault and R.D Laing who provided an academic challenge to the biological model of psychiatry.

Although the User/Survivor movement is a disparate group, many of the ideas are shared about the nature and origins of psychosis, and present a challenge to the biomedical model of mental illness. The original meaning of the word "psychosis" is troubled spirit and it is therefore interesting to note that many people are achieving recovery through a spiritual journey. User/Survivor movements exist across the world, where groups of people are trying to change the mental health system and provide alternative support to their peers. The User/Survivor movements also identify themselves as an oppressed group within society, and campaign on issues of civil liberties and individual rights.

Many people join the User/Survivor movement for support from other people experiencing the same problems. Through a common purpose and self-help, people in the User movement are able to help each other to recover and advocate on each other's behalf's. One example of a very successful organisation set up by voice hearers, for example, is the International Voices Network (0161 718 6677).

In more recent years many people are turning to complementary therapies and "New Age" philosophies as sources of healing, and, as previously mentioned, the Mental Health Foundation are now carrying out research into a phenomenon which could be broadly termed "spiritual recovery". This is a fundamentally different phenomenon to involvement in main stream, traditional religion.

There are many approaches to understanding mental health problems, but I shall concentrate on two: the Medical model and the User/Survivor perspective.

The Medical model of psychiatry

The Medical model considers that the nature and cause of mental illness is biological in origin. There is considered to be a vulnerability within the individual which can be precipitated by stress in more radical approaches. However, stress is considered to be a trigger rather than actually part of the development of mental health problems . Otherwise it is understood to be a brain disease not affected by social causes at all. Medication is thought to be the best form of treatment, and even in the most advanced models we can see today in statutory and voluntary services, the focus is on compliance with medication, either through the use of coercion or by more subtle means. In the view of the User movement, the concept of Assertive Outreach, for example, has been distorted to meet the needs of the Medical model, and, in the USA, requires people to take medication before they can receive benefits. In the UK there are also moves to look at similar laws to allow people to be injected forcibly in their own homes and link benefits to compliance. Nearly all mental health workers, apart from occupational therapists, social workers and psychologists, are focused on the Medical model in their training, and, as a result, this reductionist perspective is hardly ever challenged, except by the User/Survivor movement. Mental health professionals who have a more holistic approach in their training and in their personal beliefs find it very difficult to implement innovative ideas in practice due to the constraints imposed by the power structures of the Medical model and ensuing attitudes. Most of the organisations which represent carers in the UK would also subscribe to this understanding of mental health problems, such as the National Schizophrenia Fellowship (NSF) and SchizophreniA National Emergency (SANE). Virtually the only organisations which provide opposition to the Medical model are User/Survivor organisations.

As a result, research in the area of mental health has been very narrowly focused on areas which also do not present any challenge to the status quo and which ignore real issues in people's lives and their experiences. The scientific validity of psychiatric research is doubtful, and certainly does not justify what many survivors would regard as a system of tyranny and abuse against people with mental illness. Mary Boyle's book *Schizophrenia: A Scientific Delusion* explores this issue at some length.

In addition to the power the mental health services have been given by laws such as the Mental Health Act, the enormous power of the pharmaceutical companies ensures that money goes into further research to prove that the Medical model has some scientific foundations. However, in serious mental illness recovery rates, even with the new drugs, are often only surface deep and relapses occur.

The Survivor movement and individuals who suffer with mental illness have therefore had to look for alternatives outside of main stream psychiatry, and have had much success in doing this.

Psychiatry is also the only medical care system where the needs and prejudices of the public are put before that of the individuals seeking help, apart from infectious diseases. This feeds the notion that people with mental health problems really are dangerous and has created a vicious circle, where psychiatrists are now expected to predict dangerous behaviour and lock people away before they have even done anything. People, especially in ethnic minority groups, are often sectioned as a safety precaution rather than on any real threat. This is not based on scientific notions and can only lead to further abuse of patients within the system. It has also led to widespread demoralisation among workers. Despite the fact that since the introduction of community care numbers of violent acts carried out by mentally ill people has diminished, the government and the mental health system still continues to base its policies and practice on the safety of the public. This fear-motivated behaviour by mental health professionals has created a wall between them and their clients, seriously damaging therapeutic relationships and their ability to really help people.

The User/Survivor movement

The User/Survivor perspective considers that there are a number of social, economic, political, psychological and biological factors which effect a person's mental health. This approach, referred to as "holistic", looks at the physical, mental, emotional and spiritual aspects of people within their social setting. Problems such as poverty, housing, sexual or racial discrimination which may be affecting a person's mental health are considered to be social problems, and therefore the problem is not located within the individual. In other words, the problem is not so much the individual, but rather the social situation and network which is effecting the individual's mental health. Some professionals also advocate a similar view, such as Richard Warner in his book *Deconstructing Schizophrenia* (1997); however, he believes schizophrenia is a "brain disease" influenced by social factors with which the User movement would not agree.

In the past century the spiritual nature of people has been repressed, for example, by the materialist Thatcher years in Britain and dogmatic religions which have abused many people. There is an acknowledgement by many people in society now of the widespread "spiritual" damage which human beings all over the world have undergone and they have a desire to reclaim their humanity.

Traumatic life events are also considered to be important in the origin of mental illness. This could include anything from bullying, life-threatening accidents, becoming unemployed or sexual, physical or emotional abuse. Very often the determining factor of how individuals coped with the trauma will be largely determined by the response of their social network around them at the time. Where a person has been ignored or isolated, this could lead to a far worse reaction to the trauma than if that person had been supported. For example, disclosure of sexual abuse which is not believed and "pushed" under the carpet' can lead to more severe trauma.

It is considered that biological changes can follow emotional changes, in a similar way, for example to that in which fear would lead to a racing heart, sweating, etc. The User/Survivor approach is very similar to that used in complementary therapies. The word "dis-ease" came about through the original understanding of both physical and mental health being related to life events which may cause "dis-ease" within the person. Complementary therapists will endeavour to look at the person's life as a whole, his or her past history and present circumstances, and look at "causes" rather than "symptoms". In holistic medicine physical or mental illness is understood to be a manifestation of emotional imbalance.

With the development of powerful drugs in modern times this perspective has been lost, and in most medical fields symptoms, diagnosis and medication are considered to be the most important knowledge needed in helping people to recover. In many fields of medicine the cure is now often worse than the disease for many people and can have devastating effects on the body and the mind. However, in physical medicine the introduction of complementary therapies into areas such as maternity and for cancer patients is happening slowly, whereas virtually no alternatives are available to people experiencing mental illness on the NHS.

EARLY INTERVENTION SERVICES: A NEW PARADIGM?

Broadly speaking, Early Intervention services which focus on the needs of young people, have been welcomed by the Survivor movement and individual service users. Early Intervention has recognised some of the shortfalls of traditional services, and endeavours to provide a far more rounded approach which is individually focused and sensitive to the needs of young people.

Early Intervention services provide information about medication and diagnosis, family work and psychological interventions and so people have in theory a choice of services they can use. Peer support is considered to be important in Early Intervention services, and in many services people who have experienced mental illness work alongside professional staff. However, some of the shortcomings of Early Intervention again go back to coming from a Medical model perspective.

Young people seeking help should receive a service which empowers them to grow as people and Early Intervention services are in a unique position to provide this service and save people from a career in mental health services.

Is it early intervention or better intervention which is required?

Although early intervention is an excellent idea, there are some ideas within it which may be problematic. These problems are much the same as other services who focus on a medical approach.

Two of the questions that are hotly debated regarding early intervention in psychosis are whether it is necessary and whether it can make a difference. Although research seems to indicate that it is better to seek help earlier rather than later in terms of your prospects for recovery, there are two problems with this.

Firstly, it is also the content of the help as well as when you receive it which is the determining factor as to whether it is a "good" thing. Having worked with the Early Intervention service in Birmingham, and met people involved with early intervention services in Australia and Europe, the reason why these services are successful is not particularly because they are good at intervening early, but because they are strongly influenced by psychological approaches and therefore tend to provide a more individually focused or person-centred approach. They also try to look at the needs of young people as a social group, which provides a more holistic approach in and of itself. A psychological approach would at least root out some of the traumatic life events which may lead to a person developing mental health problems, which could be resolved through therapy or self-help.

Early intervention appears to have broken out of the negative approach of traditional psychiatry in so far as it has a far more optimistic view of recovery; however, it is still very much influenced by the Medical model and the main focus of treatment is still trying to control symptoms and relapse through medication. Early intervention at present does not challenges the wisdom of the Medical model, or the measures employed to enforce treatment compliance. It is these measure of coercion, either overtly or covertly, which can be most damaging to individuals and can easily reinforce feelings of helplessness and powerlessness and encourage avoidance of seeking help.

The idea that relapse can be prevented by medication is a good example of how the medical model understands problems. When looking at a relapse situation much attention is paid to the individual about how he or she is feeling and behaving, and very often what is happening in that person's family, partnership or in society is ignored and not considered to be important. This focus on the individual means that when his or her stress levels start to go up the person is offered more medication rather than being helped to resolve the problems that precipitate a crisis in his or her social network.

Between the Survivor movement and psychiatry lies a void of understanding about what recovery is. For the service users, mental illness is the mind's way of coping with extreme trauma and conflict, emotional abandonment and social isolation. Recovery is about being loved and accepted, finding your true self and your gifts and talents. It is about human transformation in the deepest sense.

For psychiatry, recovery is about obliterating or containing a brain disease at whatever cost to the individual. Recovery here means that the symptoms are under control and the person is compliant with treatment. While being on depot medication might be better for your prognosis in psychiatric terms (and less work for the professionals), it is not necessarily better for your recovery prospects.

The research into early intervention has also not looked at the group of people who recover from psychosis without ever coming into contact with psychiatric services, either by themselves or on the psychotherapist's couch. For example, in Turku in Sweden an experiment was carried out by a group of mental health workers, including a psychiatrist, to compare how young people recovered both with and without neuroleptic medication. All the people in the trial were experiencing a first episode of psychosis and all went through a four-week neuroleptic free zone before the trial was to start. However, by the end of the four weeks and with intensive support from the team in that time, it could not be justified placing any of the people on medication, so the trial could not go ahead (Martensson, 1998).

Extensive research was also carried out in the 1970s at Soteria House in America, which compared young people in a crisis house not receiving medication to those on an acute ward. Again the research showed better outcomes both in the short and long-term for those in Soteria House. The research, however, was squashed and the psychiatric journals refused to print the findings (Mosher and Burti, 1994).

Research in Holland carried out by Marius Romme and Sandra Escher showed that two-thirds of the people they interviewed who were hearing voices, were living their lives without using mental health services (Romme & Escher, 1989,1993). In a further study, 77% of the people they interviewed with schizophrenia, and 100% with disassociative experiences, had suffered major life changes or traumatic life events prior to the onset of hearing voices (Romme & Escher, 1996).

Much knowledge of recovery could be gained from research into the group of people who have recovered outside of the mental health system. By incorporating how people manage without medication and mainstream services there would be much more emphasis on self-help, and taking responsibility and ownership of experience. However, the research which has been done is usually ignored or criticised by mainstream psychiatry.

Early Intervention services should take account of the mind's ability to heal itself, and encourage personal growth. This is particularly important for young people who will be trying to come to terms with who they are and their place in the world. Help should be offered not only in symptom management, but in resolving personal problems, building and sustaining relationships and developing identity and status. This requires staff who understand the recovery process and are enthusiastic and can give hope to their clients.

If Early Intervention services are to provide a truly new paradigm of care, the emphasis needs to change from treating symptoms to helping people to "recover". In some ways the two concepts are not compatible with each other, particularly where force and coercion are used to ensure compliance. In order to understand why this is, the next section will look at "recovery" as a concept and process.

WHAT IS RECOVERY?

Recovery is a concept which is unique to each individual and may mean different things to different people. It is also not static, and as the person grows and achieves his or her goals and dreams the person may feel that even greater levels of recovery and understanding of themselves has been reached. Recovery is essentially a transitional state of mind where people feel at one with themselves and can respect, love and appreciate themselves, other people and the world we live in.

One of the most moving stories I read about recovery was a women who had been paralysed from the neck down in a car accident. Prior to the accident she was a model and a very successful career women. Several years on this woman was now taking other people with physical disabilities on adventure holidays such as deep-sea diving with great white sharks and abseiling. It is difficult to imagine how somebody who is totally paralysed could achieve this, and she was no doubt an exceptionally strong human being. She said that she was glad the accident had happened in many ways as it had made her a different and better person. In many people who have experience of recovery there is a common theme of becoming a better and stronger person following a traumatic life event and being able to overcome adversity and illness. With recovery comes a desire to live each minute to the best of one's ability no matter how difficult the circumstances. Through approaching life in this way, circumstances inevitably become better and problems no longer seem irresolvable.

Recovery in this sense has very little to do with symptoms or illness, and has more to do with a personal outlook about the future and having a valued role. There are a number of complex social issues which can influence recovery. These are:

- A sense of security. This may have different meanings for different people. For some it may mean financial security and good housing. However, there are many communities such as travellers who find security living a simple lifestyle in relative poverty. Another example of this could be Bushmen who have very close and supportive communities but nothing in the way of material wealth. Interestingly, mental illness was not experienced in native cultures and this perhaps can provide us with clues as to what causes it in modern society.
- Social networks, may be family or friends. The ability to sustain and resolve conflicts within relationships is crucial to recovery.
- Employment or having meaningful vocational opportunities.
- The desire of the individual to progress in life and make changes where necessary to achieve his or her goals and dreams.
- A sense of belonging to a group or community and having a valid role to play in that group.
- Spiritual growth and finding an individual philosophy to live by.

Through a range of complex factors, as well as coming to terms with traumatic life events, people are able to change their perceptions about themselves and the world to something more positive and begin to act accordingly.

The experience of growth through adverse experience is something which has always existed in human society, but in many ways has not been allowed to happen for people using mental health services. Psychiatry aims to stop unusual experiences and different behaviour, and does not allow people to grow naturally through learning from them. Mental illness and stigma isolate people further from their communities, making recovery very difficult.

For example, think of some common emotions or experiences: talking with expression, laughing, crying and becoming angry. Most people would agree that these are mentally healthy emotions to express in a safe place. However, how many of us think that mental health services encourage people to express these emotions? Strong expressions of emotions are regarded with fear and are very often interpreted as "symptoms" of an illness rather than understandable human reactions to situations.

Not much thought or research has been given by the psychiatric professions to what recovery is and what it means for people. To often people are offered more of the same, the next new "wonder drug" in the blind hope that it will achieve recovery .

Ownership of experience

The Early Intervention approach has the positive attribution in that there has been an increasing move to look at psychological interventions for people who are hearing voices or experiencing other psychotic phenomena. This is a very positive move, to try to help people to overcome their fear of the voices and look at their own feelings about themselves in relation to the voices. Helping people to live with and understand their experiences, rather than drugging them out of existence, can only be welcomed.

Another approach which has been developed by Ron Coleman and Mike Smith in the UK is for the person to identify a positive voice, or one that is not as hostile as the others, and to try to strike up a rapport with this voice. This has the effect for some people of lessening their fears and anxieties about more derogatory voices and thus allowing them to cope better within their frame of reference. This approach is user led, with the Voice Hearer working through a workbook in partnership with a friend or mental health worker. The Voice Hearer controls the process rather than a therapist, and it does not require professional training to support somebody doing the workbook.

Recovery, therefore, does not necessarily mean that the voices or experiences have disappeared, but rather that the person feels more in control of these, and is able to function well and do the things he or she wants to do in life, rather than being a victim of the voices.

Beliefs underlying the Medical model

Although most of the Early Intervention services have adopted an optimistic approach to recovery from psychosis, the majority of mental health workers still work within the traditional belief system where schizophrenia and manic depression are illnesses which need life-long biological intervention.

There are a number of problems with this approach. Firstly, the medication itself may hinder the individual's ability to emotionally develop and grow if all feelings are suppressed by the drugs. It is not really surprising that people have less relapses on depot medication which strongly suppresses thoughts and emotions. However, in order for individuals to recover in the sense I have described above, they need to be able to work through problems and find ways of coping with the underlying emotions. Crisis situations can be seen as opportunities to learn from experiences and how to cope better in the future. The Chinese word for "crisis" also means transformation—an opportunity to learn from experience.

Secondly, the way in which medication is given can reinforce people's negative beliefs about themselves, that they are victims who are controlled by other people. A big part of recovery is feeling in control and not at the mercy of other people, especially people in authority or those closest to you. For example, threatening to withdraw support or enforce treatment from services for people who are refusing medication, may reinforce previous experiences of rejection or powerlessness. Where families are used to monitor and administer medication, this can also have the same effect.

Many mental health services do not look at each individual's needs closely in regard to prescribing medication. It is generally a standard practice to put everyone who hears voices onto a neuroleptic medication by the services, although the voices might directly relate to traumatic experiences, in which case neuroleptics may actually hinder a person from resolving these issues. Accurate information about medication and side-effects is usually not forthcoming. I have heard neuroleptic medication being offered "to help you get a good night's sleep" on many occasions. This approach I personally find very dishonest and in the long term is not only unhelpful but breaks down trust between users and professionals.

There is also very little help available to stop medication in a supported way with advice about how to cope with feelings and emotions which may have been suppressed by the drugs. While medication may certainly help people at particular times in their lives, the actual role of medication in the recovery process as I have defined it above is a small one. Recovery is a far more fundamental change than simply the removal or suppression of symptoms.

The role of self-help groups

Research in Canada into the significance of self-help groups for service users showed that the people in their study found self-help groups the most helpful service available to them. In the self-help groups they looked at, it is important to emphasise that there were no service providers or clients. For example, in one group service users exchanged phone numbers and addresses in order that they could help each other in crisis situations.

The study also looked at the perception of the helpfulness/harmfulness of various individuals who service users came into contact with. The results are shown in Table 14.1 (Trainor et al., 1997). All groups were found to be helpful.

Table 14.1 Perceptions of helpfulness and/or harmfulness of various individuals

Individual	Mean	Standard deviation
Consumer/survivors	7.9	2.0
Self	7.5	2.5
GP/family physician	6.9	2.6
Friends (non-consumers/survivors)	6.7	2.6
Therapists	6.5	2.7
Family	6.4	2.8
Nurses	6.4	2.7
Social workers	6.3	2.7
Case managers	6.0	2.9
Clergy	6.0	2.8
Psychologists	5.8	3.3
Psychiatrists	5.6	3.1

The results of this survey are summarised below:

- Consumers involved in self-help groups used significantly fewer mental health services after coming into contact with the group.
- They were able to increase their contacts with the wider community.
- They find consumer/survivor organisations the most helpful component of the mental health system.
- They find other consumers/survivors significantly more helpful than any professional group in dealing with their mental health issues.

Early Intervention services, by recognising the importance of peer support and natural support networks to individuals, could improve the quality of mental health services significantly for young people. For example, organising a Voices Group does not require a lot of resources and can prove very beneficial to those who attend. A recent survey of user views in the UK published by the Mental Health Foundation called *Knowing Our Minds* showed the same outcome, that the people perceived as being the most helpful on wards were other patients and the domestics. Those seen as least helpful were the most professionally qualified, psychologists and psychiatrists.

Many people who work in mental health only believe it is possible to manage or control the illness through medication, and the question of recovery is often not even on the agenda. This is most apparent in that there is virtually no "exit strategy" from the services for people, although there are numerous innovative ideas on how to get people into it.

Early Intervention services, as well as looking at how to catch people earlier should also look at early exit strategies from the services by maximising people's use of natural support networks and self-help. Dependency, either financially or emotionally on the Mental Health Service helps in the short term with engagement and compliance, but leads to far greater problems for the individual further down the road.

Trauma and mental health

Another "side-effect" of the Medical model is that even when people present following an obvious traumatic life event, this is often ignored and is seen as a trigger rather than a cause. For example, the incidence of sexual abuse either as adults or children with people using mental health services is very high. Research carried out by Ensink (1992) also showed that approximately 50% of women they interviewed who had incest experiences in their youth were hearing voices related to this experience. However, few people with severe mental illness receive any specific therapy to come to terms with the abuse and how it might be affecting them in the present.

Although socio-economic factors and present relationships are as important as the past for the individual, where there have been obvious life problems there seem to be very few counselling services available to help people resolve these issues. In fact it is considered dangerous by some professionals to try to help people come to terms with trauma, and easier to repress the experiences through medication. The choice of when to deal with the trauma should be made by the individual concerned, but this choice should always be made available.

An example of an assessment in which I was involved a few years ago brought home to me how the medical frame of reference very often means that obvious presenting problems are not looked into more closely.

I went with a CPN to see a young Asian woman who was hearing abusive voices and seeing men in her bedroom almost 24 hours a day. She had been having these experiences for about 19 months. She came to the attention of mental health services after taking an overdose.

On talking to this woman it transpired that her parents had arranged for her to be married when she was 18 to a man who wanted to stay in the UK. He had come over from Pakistan for the wedding. He left the day after the marriage for London, never to be seen again. So here is a young woman whose life has been greatly affected by her parents' decision, which is an accepted tradition. Also, as divorce is frowned upon in the Muslim faith, she would appear trapped in this situation for the indefinite future. She cannot express her feelings about this situation otherwise she may anger her family. Our approach would have been to talk to her more about her feelings about the marriage without her parents being present, so she could express herself more freely. It would then be possible to see more clearly how this event had effected her mental health.

It was interesting that the interview with her almost entirely focused on the benefits of her taking medication, even though she brought up the issue of her absent husband and her feelings towards other men in a number of occasions. In fact her experience that a man she worked with was sending her messages and kept appearing in her bedroom seemed somehow linked to this. However, in the assessment of this woman she presented with classic symptoms of psychosis which the CPN assumed to be biological in origin—and in the discussion about her afterwards the marriage was only mentioned in passing and was not considered a contributing factor to her mental state.

According to research by Romme and Escher (1996), traumatic experiences evoke voice hearing because the event

- is threatening, similar to severe ill-treatment or illness
- is threatening, because it threatens the continuity of one's expectations in the case of losing one's job, a divorce, or death of a dear one
- is threatening, because of an overwhelming emotional confrontation like the death of a father who abused the person or confrontation over sexual identity and "social norms".

One of the differences between "voice hearers" and "patients" in their research were the levels of coping skills and identity they had built up during the lifetime before the trauma happened.

The initial assessment and information gathering about a young person having a first psychotic breakdown is therefore of crucial importance. Asking basic questions about major life events, drug-taking and family problems are important to help to understand the person in the context of his of her life, and to offer support and treatment accordingly. Talking to other people in the person's environment is also important to understand the dynamics which may be effecting that individual. Questions about childhood should be asked once a level of trust between the worker and the person has been built up, as many people will not disclose childhood problems to a stranger.

IMPACT OF DE-INSTITUTIONALISATION

Over the past 10 years with moves towards community care, mental health services have been able to offer service users a much more responsive and flexible service. This change has largely been brought about by the closure of large institutions to a community model of care. There has also been a recognition by many professionals that purely giving medication to people is not an effective strategy for recovery or for engaging young people in therapeutic relationships with the service. The new Trust Strategy for Northern Birmingham places an emphasis on the importance of creating employment and housing opportunities for service users, which will have a far wider impact on their socio-economic lives, and in turn their mental health. Moves to provide services appropriate to the needs of ethnic minority groups will also hopefully achieve higher recovery rates and the role of racism and alienation in the development of mental illness.

Mental health workers, at all levels, through seeing people in their own environment, are able to appreciate the social problems and conflicts which their clients are facing in their everyday lives. However, many still do not link the dynamics of these problems with their clients' mental illness, and therefore consider these issues of low priority in terms of providing support.

A HOLISTIC APPROACH TO INTERVENTIONS FOR YOUNG PEOPLE

In the final section I would like to look at some of the common problems experienced by young people in mental health services. I would like to make a comparison with each of these problems which will highlight the difference between the psychiatric approach and the service User/Survivor perspective. I will look at three areas which are social networks and families; cultural problems, and sustaining relationships.

Social networks and families

Conflicts with families or partners are frequently identified to us as being a major problem by people experiencing mental illness. The person's position within the social network or in relation to his or her family can be characterised in many cases by feelings of helplessness, feeling dominated and unable to be heard or understood. The individual's behaviour in such cases is characterised by angry, unpredictable outbursts of violence, either verbally or physically, against family members and close friends. The other common response is to become completely withdrawn into "victim" mentality. Both are equally devastating and dangerous .

The families or partners involved range from being abusive and controlling to being very protective, tending to do most things for the person. In other words, the family take the role of being the "carer" of an ill person, as would take place with somebody with a terminal illness. In all fairness to the families, in many cases they are told they have to do so by the mental health services, and all hope of recovery is taken away from them as well as the individual experiencing the mental illness. This is obviously not the case in all families, but it does need to be acknowledged as a problem for many service users and carers.

In some cases people become completely isolated from their families as they are unable to resolve the conflicts; and because there is no hope of recovery or information about how to achieve it, many carers "burn out" . Most of the families we meet have problems of their own which have nothing to do with the individual, such as marital problems or serious physical health problems.

Much of the family intervention work that has been developed in psychiatry does not seek to address this feeling of helplessness on the part of the service user, and may in some cases reinforce it. For example, in a situation where the person is feeling powerless within his or her social network, asking the family to supervise medication may increase the power of the family or partner over the individual. The diagnosis of a mental illness also locates the problem within that individual, and does not challenge the social network to change and adapt to help the individual regain a sense of self-respect. While families are part of the problem, they are also part of the solution.

Information where it is available does not address these problems, but rather gives information about symptoms and medication. Psychiatry seems particularly defensive about locating problems with other family members, as opposed to seeing the "illness" within the individual. In the majority of cases family members do not set out intentionally to hurt each other, but, as in all families, in some cases they do.

Rather than having a set family intervention package where information is delivered in a standard form, Early Intervention services need to assess the person, and, in his or her presence, talk to all the relevant people in the person's social network and look at the person's perception of his or her role in relation to the family. Where the service user feels there is an imbalance of power, then,rather than give the family or partner more power, mediation can be used to help the family to resolve the problem.

Cultural and racial problems

The Medical model often allows society a way of not confronting social problems, by labelling people who are distressed because of racial discrimination or cultural conflicts as mentally ill. This is also true of people who have suffered sexual and other forms of discrimination—for example, gay people.

The number of Irish, Asian and African Caribbean people using services in Europe is over-representative of the general population, and many people with mental illness have difficulties in this area. This is apparent, for example, with many young Asian people whose traditional culture is strong in Britain, but they are also educated with Western values.

People who come from minority groups can experience both problems as second-generation immigrants where there is a conflict between traditional and Western culture, and/or racial discrimination. There is also a loss of identity and sense of "roots" which takes place for people who are first- or second-generation immigrants. There are many young Asian people, for example, now becoming involved with the mental health services whose conflicts with their families directly relate to cultural issues.

The Muslim community in Britain has become very insular and protective of their cultural values and beliefs, partly in response to the racial inequalities in the country. One of the great dilemmas of the Asian community is to come to terms with the young people within that community who have both a Western and Asian culture, system of beliefs and values which they have learned as second-generation immigrants. For example, young Asian people would be encouraged by Western youth culture to express their sexuality and by their traditional belief to cover their bodies and not have sexual relationships outside marriage. This undeniably is a social problem which both the Muslim community and other members of the community need to acknowledge as a whole. However, many of the young Asian people entering mental health services are distressed because of these social problems and are being labelled as mentally ill. While they may exhibit symptoms of mental illness, only treating those symptoms does not take into account the person's social environment which is the cause of the problem. This means in some ways that the problem is not acknowledged or confronted, and that those members of the Asian community who are considered to be socially unacceptable for adopting Western values are seen as "ill". I do not wish here to advocate that either system of beliefs is better or worse than the other, only that social problems should not be turned into medical problems and that medicine cannot solve social problems. Also, these problems are not just for Asian people to solve but for everybody in British society to solve together.

Relationships

A common theme which emerges for people experiencing mental health problems is difficulty building and sustaining relationships. Many people have very serious co-dependency issues and become involved with "controlling" or abusive partners, and this is a pattern which has in some cases emerged from their childhood. People involved in such relationships tended to have been either physically, emotionally or sexually abused as children. In many cases, as well as attracting abusive relationships, people with mental illness are often also controlling and emotionally abusive themselves towards those close to them.

Working with young people provides a unique opportunity to help them to break these patterns of destructive behaviour, and to help them to believe that they do not have to remain in abusive relationships or be abusive themselves. Abuse here refers not only to physical abuse, but also to psychological and emotional abuse.

Reasons for entering such relationships have much to do with a strong sense of insecurity within the person and lack of self-esteem. By working positively with young people, building up their confidence and helping them to find a sense of security within themselves, it is possible to help people to build and sustain loving and healthy relationships. This, in the long term, will contribute enormously towards their mental health. There is an old saying that you need to learn to love yourself before you can love others, and this is as true for those with mental illness as it is for others. The journey for those with mental illness is often a difficult one and much support and encouragement is needed. Services which do not aim to achieve the highest possible standards of care reinforce feelings of unworthiness within individuals.

Mental health services should consider working with people on their relationships, with both family members and partners, as a priority. It is the breakdown of relationships, unhealthy relationships and loneliness which will keep people in the mental health services for much longer. Recovery is fundamentally to do with positive relationships and perceptions of the self in relation to other people, and respect for the self and other people.

CONCLUSION

In order to provide a service which is truly meeting the needs of individuals, the mental health services need to play less of a role in people's lives and accept their role as a secondary help to the individual. Everybody needs to take responsibility for the process of recovery, the individual, family members and friends, society and the service.

Where it is absolutely necessary that young people come into the system, either as Outreach clients or inpatients, from the start the aim should be to maximise their support from their own social network. As previously suggested, this could take the form of mediation with the family, community and also helping people with relationship issues. Self-help groups place an emphasis on natural relationships and give people a common experience and purpose to make the journey "home".

Where it is not possible to work with the existing social network, time and effort should be spent encouraging people to find new friends. This could be done by introducing somebody to a self-help group, getting clients to set up a group for themselves and integrating them into mainstream leisure, education and community services. This may take some time and involve accompanying those people and socialising with them before they gain the confidence to go on their own. Education and work, as well as building self-esteem and giving the individuals a valued role, also act as a place where they can meet new friends and start to rebuild their lives.

Dependency on mental health services is very easy to achieve, and while this may seem beneficial in terms of treatment compliance, it can in the long term be damaging to a person's chances of recovery. In fact refusal to be compliant may be a positive sign and independent thinking and actions should be encouraged. Most people are happy to receive help in areas which they find useful and the mental health services should aim to be flexible and work to each person's needs even if this requires supporting them in complementary approaches rather than medication, if this is the person's choice.

Clear boundaries and defining the role of staff needs to take place when a person enters the mental health services. It should be made clear to all patients that the role of workers is support in various areas, but that the choices and decisions about their life will be theirs at the end of the day. In many cases service users will want services to make decisions on their behalf, but this should be avoided unless absolutely necessary. If it is made clear that medication is only a tool to help people rather than a cure, and they are going to have to do some hard work themselves, people have a clear view of what is going to happen.

The use of Crisis Houses rather than inpatient units could also significantly reduce dependency. Where people have to live independently—cooking, cleaning and budgeting for themselves—and have to share the house, a lot of good work in giving people the confidence to live independently can be done. Sharing the house with one or two other people can also provide valuable lessons in building relationships; sharing daily living tasks and having to think about somebody else and their mental health problems. The most significant source of support for our residents is often the other person staying at the house. This is a far more valuable source of support than our own as it is equal and more "normal", one person helping another.

In summary, mental health services for young people need to prioritise social interventions and focus less on compliance with medication. In our service it is very unusual for people not to take medication, because we do not force them to and discuss openly with them the pros and cons of medication. Medication is seen as being a small part of many things people can do to help them cope with mental illness. Social interventions could focus on some of the following topics, but should not be exclusive to these:

- The effects of physical, emotional and sexual abuse on young people.
- Social network interventions and mediations.
- Social networking and making friends.
- Community integration, including leisure, education and employment opportunities.
- Self-help groups and holding high regard for peer support.
- Drug and alcohol abuse and why young people use these to cope, their effects, etc.
- The impact of cultural conflict and racial discrimination on mental health.
- Complementary approaches to healthy living—confidence building, creativity, diet, sleep, lifestyle, aromatherapy, relaxation, stress management, assertiveness.
- Sexuality.
- Communication.

Psychiatry has a way of reinforcing and reinventing its own wisdom and pseudo-science. It is only through trying different approaches such as that employed in our Crisis House that we are able to demonstrate that different approaches can work and do work. The easiest way to change your beliefs about the psychiatric system is to take off your professional hat and listen and talk to service users as yourself.

You will find sensitive, kind, insightful and philosophical people if you can see beyond the symptoms and distress. All madness is understandable if we have time to sit down and "be with" a person. All emotions are valuable—and are also our tutors, including anger and sadness. If we can all try to create our own peaceful oasis in the world and approach people experiencing mental illness without fear, helping somebody else can become beautiful in its simplicity. There is value in just being there. Unless we can change our own perceptions of reality, how can we hope to help others to change theirs?

REFERENCES

Coleman, R. & Smith, M. (1997). *Victim to Victor.* Handsell Publications.

Ensink, B.J. (1992). *Confusing Realities: A Study on Child Sexual Abuse and Psychiatric Symptoms.* Amsterdam: VU University Press.

Harrop, C.E., Trower, P. & Mitchell, I.J. (1996). Does the biology go around the symptoms? A Copernican shift in schizophrenia paradigms. *Clinical Psychology Review,* **16** (7), 641–654.

Martensson, L. (1998) *Deprived of Our Humanity: The Case Against Neuroleptic Drugs.* Voiceless (Mouvement les sans - vois) and Association Ecrivains, Poetes Cie.

Mosher, L. & Burti, L. (1994). *Community Mental Health: A Practical Guide.* London: Norton.

Romme, M.A.J. & Escher, A.D.M. (1989). Hearing voices. *Schizophrenia Bulletin,* **15** (2), 209–216.

Romme, M.A.J. & Escher, A.D.M. (1993). *Accepting Voices.* London: Mind Publications.

Romme, M.A.J. & Escher, A.D.M. (1996). *Understanding Voices.* Rijksuniversiteit Maastricht, Limburg, Holland.

Trainor, J., Shepherd, M., Boydell, K.M., Leff, A. & Crawford, E. (1997). Beyond the service paradigm: the impact and implications of Consumer/Survivor initiatives. *Psychiatric Rehabilitation Journal,* **21** (2) 132–139.

Chapter 15

EARLY INTERVENTION: THE ECONOMIC ISSUES

*Nick Bosanquet**

Mental illness starts as a "clinical" state but it can become for many a way of life which carries people forward, all too often into social and economic limbo. For a short time in the 1950s there was some optimism about improving outcomes with therapeutic communities and the use of drug therapy: but since then there has been little positive to report about results for patients. In fact there is a paradox of historical evidence of the favourable long-term prognosis for schizophrenia and the overwhelmingly negative image of mental illness in current society. The stereotype is of irreversible decline leading to a grim choice between vagrancy and life in an institution. Against such a background of prejudice, even hysteria, it is amazing that the field attracts as many committed and dedicated people as it does to achieve positive results for some patients.

This chapter sets out how such dedication could get even more results and receive recognition as a programme which can give a guarantee of care. Programmes based on early intervention and intensive support could achieve better results for patients. They could also reduce the longer term costs to society from the after-effects of mental illness.

SCHIZOPHRENIA: THE BURDEN OF DISEASE

For most illnesses the disease burden is related to clinical status. The unusual feature of the disease burden for schizophrenia is how much of it continues on long after the actual illness is gone. The costs of schizophrenia

*Imperial College, London.

Early Intervention in Psychosis.
Edited by M. Birchwood, D. Fowler & C. Jackson.
© 2000 John Wiley & Sons Ltd.

are in part those of the illness itself: but they are also after-effects from the way the illness is treated. Current treatment programmes often involve use of older medications which create side-effects; low levels of human contact during long stays in hospital and the loss of contact with outside networks in housing and employment. Rehabilitation is not simply about reducing the long-term effects of the illness itself, but trying to roll back an extreme form of social exclusion. Current treatment leaves people with a social deficit which it is very difficult, indeed virtually impossible, to make up.

The weight of this social deficit is now much better documented. New evidence now makes it possible to calculate the costs of schizophrenia, taking into account continuing and longer term costs as well as immediate treatment costs.

There have been some pioneering efforts in the UK to calculate the costs of schizophrenia. These have used methodology developed in the USA to estimate the direct and indirect costs of schizophrenia. Revised estimates are now possible using data from the special OPCS surveys which provide unique evidence on the effects of mental illness in the UK (OPCS, 1996a, 1996b). These surveys have also produced some preliminary evidence on the psychic costs of long-term mental illness and its impact on quality of life. These effects need to be taken into account along with the economic effects. A full examination of the costs of schizophrenia has to take into account a three-way division of costs between direct, indirect and quality of life costs.

Costing methodology

The main definitions of cost have been set since the late 1950s. Rashi Fein was the first to set out the concepts of direct and indirect costs of illness (Fein, 1958). Direct costs were defined as the actual dollar expenditures on mental illness and indirect costs as the economic loss in dollars (or in work years) that society incurs because some part of society is suffering from mental illness. A full itemisation of all costs would include:

- Treatment costs within the NHS at various stages of illness.
- Costs of lost production as a result of unemployment and inability to work of patients with schizophrenia.
- Costs of lost production as a result of inability of carers and family members to work.

These costing definitions have been in use since the late 1950s and it is worth examining how well they fit to changes in attitudes and service patterns since. There may be changes in perceptions and the range of measures available which mean that they need to be modified or expanded. The measures used in fact reflect the early heavy emphasis in health economics on the measured economic costs of illness. In cost–benefit analysis all benefits are translated into monetary terms and calculations are made of the likely gains in real income from a particular intervention. Since then the emphasis has shifted towards cost-effectiveness analysis with the use of non-monetary methods of calculating the gains to health programmes. There have also been some moves towards cost utility measurement and it is possible to use this approach as well in examining the costs of mental illness. Measurement of social impacts has to take account, therefore, of the wider range of measures now available. We might also be more concerned about changes in costs as care policies change: thus a move to community care may shift costs to families and carers and away from direct health service costs.

UPDATING THE TRADITIONAL ESTIMATES

The most recent UK estimates of direct costs are for 1990–91 (Davies & Drummond, 1994). These estimates give a total annual treatment cost of £396m or 1.6% of the total health care budget. More recent evidence suggests, however, that this may be an underestimate.

- The study carried out by the DoH of the burden of illness estimated that schizophrenia accounted for 9.03% of inpatient expenditure in 1989–90. Even in that period this would have accounted for £750m. In addition it accounted for 1.5% of community health and social care for adults (£74m) but only 0.10% of total expenditure on primary care, pharmacy and outpatient expenditure (£5.7m).
- OPCS survey results on numbers of patients in hospital and their diagnoses also suggest that earlier figures may have underestimated the direct costs of schizophrenia. Within the OPCS sample, some 70% of hospital residents were diagnosed as schizophrenic and there were a particularly high proportion of patients staying one year or more.
- The DoH survey of hospital patients by diagnosis showed that 33,944 patients were treated for schizophrenia in 1990–91, with an average stay of 308 days (DoH, 1994).

The earlier estimates were based on low estimates of service use, particularly in the sensitive area of long-term care. In summary, it is likely that the direct costs of health care are in the range of £900m to 1.1bn, or 3% of total expenditure on health care. The earlier estimates were based on an incidence approach which does not fully reflect the longer term direct costs of support for people with continuing illness.

INDIRECT COSTS

Davies and Drummond (1994) supply some conservative estimates of indirect costs based on the loss of earnings of the patients only. They assumed that 70–80% of people with schizophrenia would be unemployed and that 20% would be unemployed in the absence of the disease. This gave a total of 111,000 people with schizophrenia incurring production losses in the course of the year. Using an annual average wage of £14,912, the annual indirect costs of schizophrenia are in the region of £1.7bn. These estimates are subject to less revision than the estimates for direct costs. The OPCS surveys present some data on economic activity. These confirm earlier estimates that about 80% of people with schizophrenia are outside the workforce; 71% were permanently unable to work and only 12% were currently working (Table 15.1).

The overall estimate of cost is mainly sensitive to the estimates of prevalence — which can range from 130,000 to 180,000. A review by Wing (1994) stressed that the size of the prevalence rate depends largely on the proportion of people who develop the negative syndrome and on the accuracy of case identification and follow up. Figures derived from surveys in Salford and Camberwell in the 1970s were accepted at 2 and 2.8 per 1,000. This would support Davies and Drummond's estimate of 185,400 people in the UK suffering from schizophrenia.

Earlier estimates also need to be adjusted for changes in income levels since 1990–91. Although unemployment in general may have fallen since 1990–91, the OPCS survey results which was carried out after the

Table 15.1 Economic activity by type of institution. Residents with schizophrenia, delusional or schizo-affective disorders

Economic activity	Hospitals clinics and nursing homes (%)	Residential care homes (%)	Group homes (%)	Hostels (%)	Ordinary housing/ recognised lodging (%)	All* (%)
Permanently unable to work	73	71	72	75	63	71
Working	10	12	11	12	14	12
Intending to look, but temporarily sick	3	4	2	4	6	5
Looking for work	1	4	6	–	6	3
Retired	1	1	1	–	2	1
Other	11	8	8	9	9	9

*Includes 19 residents living in another type of residential accommodation.
Source: OPCS.

fall in unemployment, suggests that the change may not have done much to improve the employment prospects of people with severe mental illness.

Thus the estimates of indirect losses can be put at £2.1bn from lost production, uprating the earlier estimate by changes in average income.

A full counting of indirect costs should also include the costs to carers and the costs of early mortality. With the present state of data it is not possible to make reliable estimates for these costs. There are also important costs from lost production because of accelerated mortality: again it is not possible to make a direct estimate of these.

Recent cost estimates are summarised in Table 15.2. Kavanagh et al (1995) at the University of Kent have made detailed assessments of service use which are very helpful in these calculations. Most NHS cost is for hospital services: in addition there are costs to social services and in terms of income support. Total costs of schizophrenia can be estimated at £4.1bn for England in 1996.

THE PSYCHIC COSTS OF MENTAL ILLNESS

New evidence also makes it more possible to summarise the quality-of-life effects of severe illness.

The OPCS surveys bring into focus much more clearly than before the psychological and quality-of-life effects of schizophrenia. They show the very low state of social contact of many people with schizophrenia, particularly those who are living in long-term institutions.

Table 15.2   Costs of Schizophrenia—England 1996

	£(million)
Hospital care	953
Primary care	11
Social services	141
Voluntary services	39
Law and order	56
Social security support	800
Total direct costs	2,000
Indirect costs	2,100
TOTAL	£4.1 billion

The OPCS survey presents the newest material, showing clearly that people with long-term mental illness have a level of independence and choice in society which must rank them as having some of the most deprived status of any group.

- Seventy-five per cent of residents with schizophrenia were men: the recovery rate for women patients to return to a role in society is much better. The average age of patients was in the mid-40s and for the most part they were single with low levels of education.
- One in four residents suffered from physical as well as mental illness. Long-standing physical complaints were most common in affecting the nervous and musculo-skeletal systems. They were also likely to suffer from neurotic disorders. Forty-three per cent of respondents had some neurotic disorder and about a third of residents had significant symptoms of sleep problems, worry and anxiety.
- Forty-three per cent of people with schizophrenia were resident in hospital and, for these, the mean length of stay was 7.2 years. Only 9% of former patients were resident in ordinary housing.
- Under half of all residents with schizophrenia controlled their own finances.
- Most people outside hospital were entirely dependent on social security benefits and disability pensions. Fewer than a third of residents with schizophrenia living in group homes had any additional sources of income.
- At least two-thirds of adults in each type of accommodation reported some difficulty with activities in daily living (ADL). More positively, many were receiving help where they did have problems. The major providers of care were home care workers, staff or owners of homes, landlords and social workers.
- Residents with schizophrenia felt lacking in social support. Fewer than a third perceived no lack of social support, while 43% perceived a severe lack (Table 15.3).
- Social contacts were limited, especially for hospital patients. Forty-five per cent of residents in hospitals felt close to no one in the establishment: however, most still had some family ties. Three-quarters of residents felt close to one or more friends outside the institution. Leisure activities were more positive, as were levels of attendance at day centres for those outside hospital. However, very few attended any educational or training activities (Table 15.4).

The current level of recovery from mental illness is low and there appears to be little evidence on how far this is the result of the long-term effects of medication in terms of negative symptoms. Certainly in any cost-effectiveness framework the quality-of-life losses to people with long-term mental illness need to be taken much more explicitly into account. Some may be

Table 15.3 Perceived social support by type of institution. Residents with schizophrenia, delusional or schizo-affective disorders*

Level of perceived social support	Hospitals clinics and nursing homes (%)	Residential care homes (%)	Group homes (%)	Hospitals (%)	Ordinary housing/ recognised lodging (%)	All[†] (%)
No lack	20	20	26	23	33	23
Moderate lack	24	16	23	31	19	22
Severe lack	41	53	42	34	44	43
Unclassified	16	10	9	13	4	11

*Data available for subject interviews only.
[†]Includes 14 residents living in another type of residential accommodation.
Source: OPCS.

Table 15.4 Attendance at social, training, or educational centres by type of institution. (Residents with schizophrenia, delusional or schizo-affective disorders)

	Hospitals clinics and nursing homes (%)	Residential care homes (%)	Group homes (%)	Hostels (%)	Ordinary housing/ Recognised lodging (%)	All* (%)
Day centre	8	33	36	47	36	24
Club for people with mental health problems	9	21	21	13	27	16
Club for people with physical health problems	1	3	4	–	2	2
Adult education centre	2	2	5	7	2	3
Adult training centre	2	2	7	–	2	2

*Includes 19 residents living in another type of residential accommodation.

unavoidable but we cannot know this until there has been a much more sustained effort to invest in improved care and rehabilitation.

INVESTING IN IMPROVED CARE

Current patterns of service hardly pass a test of providing quality which decision-makers would seek to use for their close relatives. If any of us among the more affluent had to change places with patients, we would be seeking to change services. A pattern of services which the best informed would choose for themselves would include:

- Intensive support and personal contact during the illness phase.
- Use of new atypical antipsychotic drugs to minimise side-effects.
- Intensive rehabilitation.
- Personal choice of programmes to fit individual needs and requirements.
- Voluntary cooperation, even partnership, in treatment.
- Help in maintaining identity and status within society.

The spirit of this "ideal" programme would be much more personal than the official programme, which is usually described in terms of collective groups of patients and bureaucratic entities such as "services". It would also show faster movement than the long-running search for strategy and National Service Framework.

It would also increase voluntary cooperation. In fact the reverse has been happening: the number of patients being treated under Section have been rising, both in absolute numbers and as a proportion of total admissions. Between 1986 and 1997 the number of patients formally admitted to NHS facilities and registered mental nursing homes in England rose from14,780 to 24,191 (Bosanquet, 1999).

Such an "ideal" pattern of services would also make it easier to provide the high level of care required by patients whose behaviour presents continuing risk to themselves or others. At present much time and effort is put into custodial care of patients who have been affected by "social deficit". A more positive approach to treatment and rehabilitation would release funding and staffing for the higher risk group of patients. Such intensive support would also increase the chance of voluntary cooperation with treatment. It is unrealistic to think that there can be success for all patients even with an extremely improved standard of care: but there could be more concentration on the high-risk group. The current pattern of services by creating a large group of lifetime career patients makes it even less possible to concentrate resources and attention on the high-risk group.

For the future we are likely to see some changes in patterns of cost. The pattern of costs in 5–10 years' time may be rather different from today. There is likely to be a continuing reduction in length of stay so that costs of support will shift towards families and carers. Community tolerance for people with a record of mental illness may fall, leading to even greater rejection than in the past. Thus the personal loss and economic costs associated with social exclusion are likely to grow without strong action across society. In the rest of this chapter we set out what this action might be.

Demography in fact creates an unusual opportunity for a fresh approach. Numbers of young people are reducing in the population, and even on the assumption of unchanged incidence there would be a much smaller number of "new" cases of more severe illness. Numbers may well be relatively much higher in inner cities, but this may not continue to be the case. If we can focus on new patients with intensive, effective interventions we can stop the stock of career patients from growing in the future.

Can we develop an effective investment programme which can allow us to grasp this opportunity? The experience of the last 10 years has shown just how difficult it is to fund improvements in care.

Much will depend, however, on developing an active investment programme to improve therapies and care programmes for new patients. Change in demography has created a new opportunity here. This can improve quality of life and social functioning for patients who have been ill long term, which will require a sustained investment programme in social rehabilitation.

Such investment requires a fundamental change in perspective, from short-term cost minimisation to estimates of social gain. Past decisions have been designed to minimise cost for a treatment episode, such as an inpatient stay. The new challenge is to reduce the costs of longer term disability and to increase opportunities for normal living. Mental health services can move from a position where they are seen mainly in negative terms in containing people with problems out of society, to a situation where they are seen as achieving positive gains for many patients using a stronger evidence base than in many other areas of health care.

DEVELOPING AN INVESTMENT PROGRAMME

- UK programme budget data for NHS spending show that for the five-year period 1991/2–1996/7 health service spending in real terms on mental health services rose by 3% to £2.737bn. (Table 15.5).
- Spending on this client group from social services starts from a very low level. Total spending on residential and day care services was £144.1m

Table 15.5 NHS expenditure on mental health (£m)

	1991/2	1996/7	% change
Hospitals	2,397	2,235	−6.8%
Community	252	502	+99%
Total:	2,649	2,737	+3%

Source: Health Committee Public Expenditure on Health and Personal Social Services, HC 959, 1998.

in 1993/4. This contrasts with spending of £738m by social services on clients with learning disabilities.

- Cost per day has been rising steeply within the hospitals. Even so, an audit of acute wards by the Mental Health Act Commission, together with the Sainsbury Centre for Mental Health, showed very poor standards on many wards (Mental Health Commission/Sainsbury Centre, 1997). Some of the most serious problems affected women patients. Only 35% of women patients had access to self-contained women-only facilities. The day-to-day quality of care seemed poor on many wards. On 38% of wards no staff were in contact with patients.
- A King's Fund report on London showed that intensive home-based treatment is not routinely available in most areas, and that the funding gap was widest in inner city areas where needs could be four to five times as great as in other areas (King's Fund, 1997).
- A report by the National Schizophrenia Fellowship (NSF, 1996) showed that there was considerable rationing of new drug therapies.

How can we break through the cycle of low expectations, low support and low social self-esteem? Mental health services are in a poor position to compete for funds because of their image and identity, which is overwhelmingly negative. The first essential step is to establish some positive medium-term aims for these programmes. Health economics has concentrated on defining returns to specific local projects: it has had much less to say about the effectiveness of the service as a whole: yet without such overall aims for the service, there is little incentive to invest in specific projects.

The new care process to deliver these results starts with certain key aims of providing intensive support for patients who have been recently diagnosed with severe mental illness. There is, of course, a continuing need for support for longer-term clients and for resettlement: and there is a successful example of the special "TAPS" programme in North London. Now there needs to be an equal commitment to programmes for patients with recent mental illness.

Of new patients, the 10% with highest severity can have lifetime care costs of £330,000 or more. A programme which can improve recovery can lead to significant savings: and now such programmes are within reach. There is now a potential for effective services, but these have to provide consistent support from initial intervention through to longer term rehabilitation.

In some ways health service culture has shifted so that there is a greater sense of common mission across health services. Health services for patients with cancer or heart disease are concerned about quality of life or depression. There is an awareness that serious illness has many common effects in threatening social and personal stability. There is a new generation of drug therapies which offer much better quality of life and a wider range of options both for new patients and for the treatment-resistant group, yet at present there is severe rationing of these new therapies. There is also a new generation of staff which could be attracted into the work.

There is much positive change in the environment which managers could use. There is also some important change in demography. Outside inner city areas the size of the high-risk group of young people who are particularly likely to have severe mental illness has reduced by 20%, reflecting low birth rates in the late 1970s: yet other changes such as greater use of drugs may have increased care problems for those that do get ill so that the demographic bonus is hard to see. Above all there is clear evidence both from the UK, Australia and the USA that services based on short stay and rehabilitation in the community can work—but they will take substantial investment.

A new generation of managers is now beginning to show how there can be positive local initiative. The task for managers is how to create a sense of confidence in a different future. They have to solve a series of problems about management time, funding, staffing and outside alliances.

Management time

Any diversion of time from short-term operational problems could be seen as dangerous, even frivolous. All the short-term pressures are to concentrate on the crises, enquiries and information requests from above: but unless the chief executive, chairperson and board show their belief in the future then it is unlikely that anyone else will be able to do so.

Funding

Each Trust has to establish how its own funding and that of mental health services in the area have changed. Faced with falling funding and the rising cost of hospital services, many Trusts feel unable to invest in new services and new drug therapies. A realistic assessment of the funding base is an essential first step towards local negotiation about investment.

Defining an investment strategy

This is needed as a focus for developing services and bidding for funding. A full programme would cover inpatient care, intensive home support, rehabilitation, employment schemes and access to housing. Our costing of an investment programme for one Trust in an inner city area showed the spending needed to provide this kind of service for a district with a cohort of 50 patients in the first year and 100 in the second. Such a programme would cost £1.3m or £13,000 per patient (Bosanquet, 1995). The strategy includes some continued use of inpatient beds, but it is realistic to assume that this could be less than under the present system. Any investment strategy has to include greater use of new drug therapies in order to reduce the effects of long-term medication on drugs which have pronounced negative effects, and promote earlier rehabilitation.

Re-skilling of staff

At present there are many unusual aspects about the staffing situation in mental health services. It is an area in which desperate staff shortages are often claimed, but one with little evidence on working patterns or clear aims set for staff. It is an area of social merit but low morale; one in which communication is vital, yet as the Mental Health Commission showed, there was very little contact between patients and staff. It is an area with many training needs but control over training and job structure which is totally fragmented in the interest of mini-professional baronies. There are 80,000 staff working in these services and there may be 1,500–2,500 working for a local Trust: so the investment required is significant.

Yet the manager has some potential resources: first the talent, energy and commitment of staff working in the service at present: then the scope for in-service training using local resources in higher education. Managers cannot afford to wait for a whole new generation of multi-disciplinary training: they have to make it happen using local resources. The Sainsbury report on future staff roles and training (Sainsbury Centre, 1997) has defined the whole agenda in a very useful way: the challenge for local managers is to define and fund what can be done at the local level. They can also broaden out the staff team and ensure that use is made of psychologists and other new skills.

Using new drug therapies

New atypical antipsychotics offer the hope of reduced "secondary" symptoms and speedier recovery. They can reduce long-term costs, as well as lowering the suicide rate among longer-term treatment-resistant patients.

Winning new Allies

At present, attitudes to people with schizophrenia are going backwards with a rising tide of NIMBYism. There has to be a sustained attempt to identify possible allies and to win them over. There are some opinion allies in groups of concerned local citizens. There are also some resource allies in housing and employment. Managers have to win a share of spending on special housing schemes and on employment rehabilitation. Health managers have to use their own health funding effectively: but they can go further in expanding the funding by winning support from others. In fact, as their job is to win for people the chance of a normal life in the community, then it is essential to win allies and to arouse interest among those who are prepared to share the vision of and the challenge of improving opportunities for one of the most deprived groups in society. Family doctors also have an important opinion and resource role. Some evidence suggests that they may, in fact, be more trusted by patients than are psychiatrists (Rogers, Pilgrim & Lacey, 1996).

New partnership with the private sector

In the past the private sector has been used as a branch line for shunting problem patients: the level of suspicion is both mutual and high. Yet there is scope for much more creative partnership. The private sector can offer new advantages in terms of access to capital and speed of innovation. There could also be new relationships with the voluntary sector so that Trusts used options other than direct public employment for providing services.

Support to carers

One positive change in the 1990s has been towards greater involvement of clients and carers in planning services. Any move towards community-based care is likely to mean increased roles for carers compared with the old custodial system. There is likely to be an increase both in time and cost for carers once patients are spending more time outside hospitals.

Strategies for change

Managers face a major task in making progress on this agenda, as well as keeping the existing system going and dealing with day-to-day crises. The task will be greatest in inner city areas which have a combination of increased need with reduced funding. The closure programmes for the hospitals at Friern and elsewhere made some special funding available for patients that were there, but they did not provide for the loss of admission spaces where patients would have been treated. It is also in the inner cities that there are the greatest problems of communication with patients from ethnic minorities and the greatest problems in developing voluntary services that patients will actually seek to use rather than relying so heavily on sectioning of patients.

The development of local management strategy can be helped by networking between Trusts. The Inner City Initiative links 27 mental health and community trusts. In the past two years it has developed a set of agreed performance measures for helping Trusts to improve services. For example Trusts were able to compare their performance in developing care programmes and in filling staff vacancies in very practical ways. The value of benchmarking will increase as Trusts begin to set out more clearly their own local strategies for change.

CONCLUSIONS

The aims of this investment programme would be to ensure that at least 60% of new patients made a full recovery, including a return to employment and normal living. Such an aim would be achievable over a 10-year period and would give a much more positive identity to services. It would encourage investment in order to reduce long-term costs, as well as giving incentives to patients towards voluntary cooperation. Such an approach would create new incentives for funders and for patients. From an overwhelmingly negative area, the mental health service could be a very positive one, identified not just with risk management but with reducing an extreme form of social exclusion.

The "early intervention" strategy needs support from a different and more positive approach to health economics. Assessment of care costs should cover costs in the longer term, as well as those for immediate care. A care programme may seem to have high short-term costs, but may lead to significant savings in longer term support and carer time. The new approach also needs to account for costs in disability to society. Younger people may spend two to three decades out of the workforce and may be pushed into a social and economic limbo with a very low quality of life.

The investment case has to be made over a period of at least five years. It involves comparison of costs of new therapies and care against costs of other treatment, including admissions and days of stay. Outside health services it involves costs of exclusion from the workforce. Early intervention should be seen as a significant means of reducing admissions and support costs.

Above all, early intervention can help make the transition by which spending on mental health services could be seen as a social investment programme. It is a test of new government values for a group which has suffered more from exclusion than almost any other. Currently almost £1bn are spent on adults from 16 to 44 by mental health services. For this age group such spending amounts to 18% of all health spending. Could this be used in ways which promote better outcomes for patients, rather than on revolving-door admissions and custodial care? Early intervention presents a new challenge to past economic reasoning in mental health services.

REFERENCES

Bosanquet, N. (1995). Schizophrenia: developing new strategies for effective care. *British Journal of Medical Economics*, **8**, 51–64.

Bosanquet, N. (1999). Auditing the effectiveness of mental health law. In N. Eastman & J. Peay (Eds), *Law without Enforcement*. Oxford.

Davies, L. & Drummond, M. (1994). Economics and schizophrenia: the real cost. *British Journal of Psychiatry*, **165** (Suppl. 20), 18–21.

DoH (1994). *Hospital Episode Statistics*, Vol. 1. London: HMSO.

Fein, R. (1958). *Economics of Mental Illness*. New York: Basic Books.

Kavanagh, S., Opit, L., Knapp, M. & Beecham, J. (1995). Schizophrenia: shifting the balance of care. Social Psychiatry and Psychiatric Epidemiology, **30**, 206–212.

King's Fund (1997). *London's Mental Health*. King's Fund, London.

Mental Health Commission/Sainsbury Centre (1997). *The National Visit*. Sainsbury Centre for Mental Health.

NSF (1996). *Is cost a factor?* National Schizophrenia Fellowship.

OPCS (1996a). *Economic Activity and Social Functioning of Residents with Psychiatric Disorders*. OPCS Report No. 6. London: HMSO.

OPCS (1996b). *Adults with a Psychiatric Disorder Living in the Community*. OPCS Report No. 8 London: HMSO.

Rogers, A., Pilgrim, D. & Lacey, R. (1996). *Experiencing Psychiatry*. London: Macmillan.

Sainsbury Centre (1997). *Pulling Together*. Sainsbury Centre for Mental Health.

Wing, J.K. (1994). Mental illness. In A Stevens & J Raftery. (Eds), *Health Care Needs Assessment*. Radcliffe Press.

INDEX

The Wiley Series in

CLINICAL PSYCHOLOGY

Ronald Blackburn	The Psychology of Criminal Conduct: Theory, Research and Practice
Ian H. Gotlib and Constance L. Hammen	Psychological Aspects of Depression: Toward a Cognitive-Interpersonal Integration
Max Birchwood and Nicholas Tarrier (Editors)	Innovations in the Psychological Management of Schizophrenia: Assessment, Treatment and Services
Robert J. Edelmann	Anxiety: Theory, Research and Intervention in Clinical and Health Psychology
Alastair Agar (Editor)	Microcomputers and Clinical Psychology: Issues, Applications and Future Developments
Bob Remington (Editor)	The Challenge of Severe Mental Handicap: A Behaviour Analytic Approach
Colin A. Espie	The Psychological Treatment of Insomnia
David Peck and C.M. Shapiro (Editors)	Measuring Human Problems: A Practical Guide
Roger Baker (Editor)	Panic Disorder: Theory, Research and Therapy
Friedrich Fösterling	Attribution Theory in Clinical Psychology
Anthony Lavender and Frank Holloway (Editors)	Community Care in Practice: Services for the Continuing Care Client
John Clements	Severe Learning Disability and Psychological Handicap